Regionalization in a Globalizing World

A Comparative Perspective on Forms, Actors and Processes

Edited by

MICHAEL SCHULZ
FREDRIK SÖDERBAUM
AND JOAKIM ÖJENDAL

D0096222

ZED BOOKS
London and New York

Regionalization in a Globalizing World

Zed Books titles on International Relations

Worlds Apart
The North-South Divide and the International System
NASSAU ADAMS

The Meaning of Environmental Security
Environmental Politics and Policy in the New Security Era
JON BARNETT

The New Imperialism
Crisis and Contradictions in North/South Relations
ROBERT BIEL

Another American Century?
The United States and the World after 2000
NICHOLAS GUYATT

International Political Economy
Understanding Global Disorder
BJORN HETTNE *et al.*

The Age of Transition: Trajectory of the World-System, 1945–2025
TERENCE HOPKINS AND IMMANUEL WALLERSTEIN *et al.*

The World Ahead
Our Future in the Making
FEDERICO MAYOR *in collaboration with* JEROME BINDE

A People Betrayed
The Role of the West in Rwanda's Genocide
LINDA MELVERN

The Global Trap
Globalization and the Assault on Prosperity and Democracy
HANS-PETER MARTIN AND HARALD SCHUMANN

Regionalization in a Globalizing World:
A Comparative Perspective on Forms, Actors and Processes
MICHAEL SCHULZ, FREDRIK SÖDERBAUM AND JOAKIM ÖJENDAL (EDS)

• • •

For full details of this list and Zed's other subject, area studies and general catalogues,
please write to:
The Marketing Department, Zed Books, 7 Cynthia Street, London N1 9JF, UK
or email Sales@zedbooks.demon.co.uk
Visit our website at: http://www.zedbooks.demon.co.uk

Regionalization in a Globalizing World was first published in 2001 by
Zed Books Ltd., 7 Cynthia Street, London N1 9JF, UK and
Room 400, 175 Fifth Avenue, New York, NY10010, USA

Distributed in the USAexclusively by Palgrave, a division of St Martin's Press, LLC,
175 Fifth Avenue, New York, NY10010, USA.

Cover design by Andrew Corbett
Designed and set in 9¹⁄₂/13 pt Palatino
by Long House, Cumbria, UK
Printed and bound in Malaysia

ISBN Hb 1 85649 728 3
Pb 1 85649 729 1

Contents

CONTENTS

CONTENTS

CONTENTS

About the Contributors

Patrik Jotun, Bent D. Jørgensen, Bertil Odén, Fredrik Söderbaum and Åke Widfeldt are colleagues and PhD candidates in the Department of Peace and Development Research, Göteborg University, where Björn Hettne is professor, Michael Schulz is a lecturer and Helena Lindholm Schulz and Joakim Öjendal are researchers. Claes G. Alvstam is Professor of International Economic Geography at the School of Economics and Commercial Law at the same university, while Cyro Banega is a PhD candidate in the Department of Sociology there. Marianne Laanatza is a PhD candidate in the History Department, Uppsala University. Marianne H. Marchand is a researcher at the Research Centre for International Political Economy, Department of Political Science, University of Amsterdam.

Preface

A book project that was initiated back in 1995 – the result of a long-running discussion on regionalization in our university department and elsewhere – has come to an end. If our journey was much longer, and at times more bumpy than we initially expected, it also flushed out many important new insights that enabled us to address the complex and sometimes contradictory trends of regionalization in a globalizing world. The detours, however painful, were in the end rewarding.

The contributors were recruited for this project mainly on the strength of their broad knowledge of the respective regions. We shall see that they addressed the task in different ways, with different perspectives, and reached a variety of results and viewpoints on regionalization. Nevertheless, the chapters do broadly fit into a 'new regionalism' approach, involving analysis from a multitude of angles with a particular emphasis on the views 'from below' and 'from within'. To our own surprise, we must admit, at the end of this process we had a framework for comparing the regions and their various regionalizations.

Yet the contributors diverge on two fundamental issues: the achievability and desirability of regionalization. In a positive (empirical) sense, the degree and scope of regionalization divide not only the authors of this book, but also the research community at large. Should regionalization become general – and we think it will, although not necessarily in any one-dimensional, equitable, final, simple or even global sense – it will indicate a reshuffle of power and attention from the national to the regional scene with far-reaching consequences. In a normative sense, one must ask whether regionalization is desirable, and to have an opinion on this we must try to assess what regionalization actually implies, for whom, and with what results. These are, in our view, mainly issues for empirical inquiry, and our volume contributes to this debate.

Finally, to nobody's surprise, anyone expecting a final and monolithic view on regionalization will be disappointed. Any such outcome would be a distortion, we argue, of what is going on 'out there'.

Acknowledgements

Many persons have been approached and involved in this project. Most of them are colleagues at the Department of Peace and Development Studies (PADRIGU) at Göteborg University, and we wish to thank them for important and enjoyable discussions. Thanks go also to Barry Buzan and Peter de Souza, who in different ways helped us to bring the book to completion. It would have been neither initiated nor finalized, however, without great assistance and support from Björn Hettne. He has been a constant source of inspiration and has contributed intriguing and challenging new perspectives throughout this process. As chairperson of the UNU/WIDER research group he also introduced us to discussions on regionalization and world order that were attracting prominent researchers from various countries, backgrounds and academic disciplines. This helped us into the field and broadened our understanding of the topic. Despite the many analytical and empirical obstacles confronting us, by the early 1990s the WIDER group's insights had convinced us that the study of world regions from a comparative perspective is necessary to an understanding of contemporary global change. Finally, we would like to thank Robert Molteno of Zed Books who, in a both professional and gentle way, has eased this project into its final stage.

Michael Schulz, Fredrik Söderbaum and Joakim Öjendal
PADRIGU, Göteborg

Abbreviations

ACE   Association of Caribbean Economists
ACS   Association of Caribbean States
AEC   African Economic Community
AFL-CIO   American Federation of Labor and Congress of Industrial
            Organizations
AFTA   ASEAN Free Trade Area
AIOC   Azerbaijan International Oil Consortium
AMU   Arab Maghreb Union
ANC   African National Congress
AOF   Fédération de l'Afrique Occidentale Française (French West Africa)
APEC   Asia Pacific Economic Cooperation
APROC   Asia-Pacific Regional Operations Centre
ARF   ASEAN Regional Forum
ART   Alliance for Responsible Trade
ASEAN   Association of Southeast Asian Nations
ASEAP   ASEAN Environmental Programme
BCEAO   Banque Centrale des États de l'Afrique de l'Ouest (Central Bank of
            West African States)
BJP   Bharatya Janata Party
BSECO   Black Sea Economic Cooperation Organization
CACES   Central Asian Common Economic Space
CACM   Central American Common Market
CAEU   Central Asian Economic Union
CAFRA   Caribbean Association for Feminist Research and Action
CANARI   Caribbean Natural Resources Institute (St Lucia)
CARICOM   Caribbean Community
CARIFTA   Caribbean Free Trade Agreement
CARIPEDA   Caribbean People's Development Agency
CARNEID   Caribbean Network of Educational Innovation for Development
CAST   Caribbean Action for Sustainable Tourism

ABBREVIATIONS

CBI	Caribbean Basin Initiative
CCA	Caribbean Conservation Association
CCC	Caribbean Conference of Churches
CCM	Mercosur Trade Commission
CCP	Chinese Communist Party
CDERA	Caribbean Disaster Emergency Response Agency
CDRU	CARICOM Disaster Relief Unit
CEAO	Communauté Économique de l'Afrique de l'Ouest (Economic Community of West Africa)
CEHI	Caribbean Environmental Health Institute
CEO	Chief Executive Officer
CET	Common External Tariff
CFA	Communauté Financière Africaine
CHA	Caribbean Hotel Association
CIS	Commonwealth of Independent States
CMA	Common Monetary Area
CMC	Council of the Common Market
CMEA	Council for Mutual Economic Assistance (also known as COMECON)
CNIRD	Caribbean Network for Integrated Rural Development
COECE	US-Mexican Businessmen's Association; the Coordinadora de Organismos Empresariales de Comercio Exterior
COMESA	Common Market for Eastern and Southern Africa
CPC	Joint Parliamentary Commission for Mercosur
CPDC	Caribbean Policy Development Centre (Barbados)
CSA	Caribbean Studies Association
CSCAP	Council for Security Cooperation in Asia-Pacific
CSCE	Conference on Security and Cooperation in Europe
CSCME	Conference on Security and Cooperation in the Middle East
CSG	Caspian Sea Group
CTC	Citizens' Trade Campaign
CTO	Caribbean Tourism Organization
CUFTA	Canada-US Free Trade Agreement
DEA	Drug Enforcement Administration (USA)
DOM	Départements d'Outre-Mer (French overseas territories)
DPP	Democratic Progressive Party
DRC	Democratic Republic of Congo
EAEC	East Asia Economic Caucus
EAEG	East Asian Economic Group
EAI	Enterprise for the Americas Initiative

EC	European Community
EC$	Eastern Caribbean Dollar
ECA	UN Economic Commission for Africa
ECLA	UN Economic Commission for Latin America
ECLAC	UN Economic Commission for Latin America and the Caribbean
ECO	Economic Cooperation Organization
ECOMOG	ECOWAS Cease-Fire Monitoring Group
ECOWAS	Economic Community of West African States (Communauté Économique des Etats de l'Afrique de l'Ouest – CEEAO)
ECSC	European Coal and Steel Community
EEC	European Economic Community
EFTA	European Free Trade Association
EIU	Economist Intelligence Unit
EMU	Economic and Monetary Union
ENCORE	Environmental and Coastal Resources Project
ETA	Euskadi Ta Askatasuna (Basque Revolutionary and Socialist Organization)
EU	European Union
FCC	Federal Communications Commission (USA)
FDI	Foreign Direct Investment
FCES	Economic and Social Consultative Forum
FEWER	Forum of Early Warning and Early Response
FIFA	Fédération Internationale de Football Association
FLS	Front Line States
FSU	Former Soviet Union
FTAA	Free Trade Area of the Americas
GATT	General Agreement on Tariffs and Trade
GCC	Gulf Cooperative Council
GDP	Gross Domestic Product
GMC	Common Market Group
IGNU	Interim Government of National Unity (Liberia)
IMF	International Monetary Fund
INC	Indian National Congress
IORT	Indian Ocean Rim Treaty
KhJ	Khalqu Jibhassi
KMT	Kuo Min Tang
LAFTA	Latin American Free Trade Agreement
LAIA	Latin American Integration Association
MAI	Multilateral Agreement on Investments
MC	Mekong Committee

ABBREVIATIONS

MENA	Middle East and North Africa
Mercosur	Comisión Sectorial para el Mercado Común del Sur (Southern Common Market)
MRC	Mekong River Commission
MITI	Ministry of International Trade and Industry
NAFTA	North American Free Trade Agreement
NAM	Non-Aligned Movement
NATO	North Atlantic Treaty Organization
NGO	Non-Governmental Organization
NIE	Newly Industrializing Economy
NIS	Newly Independent States
NPFL	National Patriotic Front of Liberia
NRA	New Regionalism Approach
NTB	Non-Tariff Barrier
OAS	Organization of American States
OAU	Organization of African Unity
ODA	Overseas Development Assistance
OECD	Organization for Economic Cooperation and Development
OECS	Organization of Eastern Caribbean States
OPEC	Organization of Petroleum Exporting Countries
OSCE	Organization of Security and Cooperation in Europe
PAFTAD	Pacific Trade and Development Conference
PBEC	Pacific Basin Economic Council
PCS	Prélèvement Communitaire de Solidarité
PECC	Pacific Economic Cooperation Council
PICE	Programme for Economic Integration and Cooperation
PLO	Palestine Liberation Organization
PNG	Papua New Guinea
PRC	People's Republic of China
PTA	Preferential Trade Area for Eastern and Southern African States
RCA	Regional Constituent Assembly (of the Windward Islands)
RENAMO	Mozambique National Resistance
ROC	Republic of China (i.e. Taiwan)
RSS	Regional Security System
SAARC	South Asian Association for Regional Cooperation
SACU	Southern African Customs Union
SADC	Southern African Development Community
SADCC	Southern African Development Coordination Conference
SAFTA	South American Free Trade Area
SAFTA	South Asian Free Trade Area

SAP	Structural Adjustment Programme
SAPTA	South Asian Preferential Trade Agreement
SAR	Special Administrative Region
SEAL	Southeast Asian League
SEATO	Southeast Asian Treaty Organization
SELA	Sistema Economico Latinoamericano
SEZ	Special Economic Zone
SPAT	Small Projects Assistance Team
TCR	Taxe de Coopération Régional (Regional Cooperation Tax)
TNC	Transnational Company
UEMOA	Union Economique et Monétaire Ouest Africaine (West African Economic and Monetary Union)
UMOA	Union Monétaire Ouest Africaine (West African Monetary Union)
UN	United Nations
UNAMSIL	UN Mission in Sierra Leone
UNCED	United Nations Conference on Environment and Development
UNITA	National Union for the Total Independence of Angola
UNSCO	United Nations Special Coordinator in the Occupied Territories
UNU	United Nations University
USAID	US Agency for International Development
USD	US Dollar
USSR	Union of Soviet Socialist Republics
UWI	University of the West Indies
WAND	Women and Development
WANEP	West African Network for Peacebuilding
WCED	World Commission on Environment and Development
WIDER	World Institute for Development Economics Research of the United Nations University (Helsinki, Finland)
WINFA	Windward Islands Farmers Association
WTO	World Trade Organization

Introduction 1

A Framework for Understanding Regionalization

MICHAEL SCHULZ,
FREDRIK SÖDERBAUM
AND JOAKIM ÖJENDAL

Anyone following international events is likely to be struck by the revitalization and proliferation of regionalisms and regionalization, almost as a new 'urge to merge' into regional entities, in the post-Cold War era. The widening and deepening of the European Union (EU) during the last decade is perhaps the best-known example of this trend. Similar processes can be observed in most other world regions as well, made visible through the (re-)emergence, revitalization or expansion of regional projects and organizations, such as the Comisión Sectorial para el Mercado Común del Sur (Southern Common Market, or Mercosur), the Association of Southeast Asian Nations (ASEAN), the North American Free Trade Agreement (NAFTA), the Southern African Development Community (SADC) or the Economic Community of West African States (ECOWAS). One can also note how former enemies or previously excluded members, such as South Africa in Southern Africa and Vietnam in Southeast Asia, have entered the main regional organizations SADC and ASEAN respectively. Even in a conflict-ridden region such as the Middle East, former enemies are meeting for the first time in regional forums, discussing the possibility of future regional cooperation. Furthermore, regional organizations have increasingly become involved, for various reasons, in intrastate and ethnic conflicts, such as those in West Africa (ECOWAS) and in the Balkans (EU).

The 'return' of regionalism is undoubtedly one important trend in contemporary international relations. This wave is often referred to as 'the new regionalism', and is characterized by its increasing scope, diversity, fluidity and non-conformity. Using an interdisciplinary and comparative analytical framework labelled the *new regionalism approach* (NRA) (Hettne and Inotai 1994; Hettne *et al.* 1999), this volume explores in depth the origins, current state, dynamics, significance and future prospects of processes of regionalization as one possible principle of order in a globalizing world. It also seems to us to be important to transcend simple state-centric notions of regionalization and to bring transnational actors into the analysis, taking into account the wide range of heterogeneous linkages and inter-actions amongst market and civil society actors. Ranging over nearly all the important 'world' regions in the global system today – Europe, the Middle East, West Africa, Southern Africa, Caucasia and Central Asia, South Asia, the Caribbean, Southeast Asia, East Asia, North and finally South America – this study emphasizes that regionalization is an unevenly developing, heterogeneous, plural-istic and multidimensional phenomenon, but nevertheless global. The processes are advanced in some areas and embryonic in others, but they all contain important similarities and important differences.

Our point of departure is that the multidimensionality of contemporary region-alization warrants a new type of analysis, which transcends the dominant theories of regional integration, such as neorealism, functionalism, neofunctionalism, institutionalism, market and trade integration, structuralism, development inte-gration and so on. The mainstream theories in the field may still provide valuable and sensible insights, but in our view they are neither designed for nor capable of capturing the multidimensionality, pluralism and comprehensiveness of con-temporary regionalization processes, nor the way in which these are socially con-structed. In contrast to the different versions of mainstream regional integration theory (particularly the 'old' theories), we argue that the analysis should avoid fixed and one-dimensional definition of regions as well as a narrow and simplified focus on instrumental state strategies, regional organizations, security alliances and trading blocs. It is rather a genuine concern with the *processes of regionalization* in various fields of activity that should guide the analysis.

Yet we recognize that emerging regions and processes of regionalization are very much processes in the making and in search of theory. We take the position that lessons have to be relearned, perspectives reassessed; our ambition is that the volume will contribute to further theory building. At this stage, however, there is a need to conduct reflective research and maintain theoretical open-mindedness. Rather than pushing the case for strictly causal theory, we have deliberately agreed on a rather eclectic definition of the NRA, whereby the case studies are to be guided by some key issues within the NRA framework.

In the remainder of this introductory chapter we first try to set the emergence of the new regionalism in a broader context. We then clarify the distinction between regionalism and regionalization. The following section includes an examination of the mainstream theories that have influenced the NRA, as well an elaboration of how we apply this approach. We then outline the main components of NRA and the issues that the case studies are organized around. Finally, we briefly present the empirical cases and the structure of the book.

The New Regionalism

Regionalism is predominantly a post-Second World War phenomenon, although the protectionist trend of the 1930s is sometimes seen as constituting the first wave. During the 1950s and 1960s regionalism was seen as an important strategy for achieving security, peace, development and welfare, particularly but by no means only in Europe. However, economists tended to get obsessed with free trade schemes and customs unions, while most political scientists tried to discover a never-occurring trend towards supranationality beyond the nation-state. The interest and enthusiasm for regional integration died out in the late 1960s and early 1970s because the grandiose projects actually had limited impact or simply never materialized. Furthermore, theorists became more concerned with global rather than regional interdependencies.

The point of departure of this volume is that for more than a decade regionalism has been reasserting its importance in international studies, after a period of almost complete neglect. In order to understand regionalism today it is essential to realize that we are dealing with a qualitatively *new* phenomenon, although studying the renewed trend towards regionalism sometimes involves a feeling of *déjà vu*. The 'new regionalism' refers to a phenomenon, still in the making, that began to emerge in the mid-1980s, starting in Europe with the White Paper and the Single European Act, and gradually turning into a truly worldwide phenomenon.

It is important to underline that the old regionalism must be placed within a particular historical context, dominated by the bipolar Cold War structure, with nation-states as the uncontested primary actors. By the same token, the new wave of regionalism needs to be related to the current transformation of the world. That is, the new regionalism is associated with or caused by a multitude of often inter-related structural changes of and in the global system, the most important being: (1) the move from bipolarity towards a multipolar or perhaps tripolar structure, centred around the EU, NAFTA and the Asia-Pacific, with a new division of power and new division of labour; (2) the relative decline of American hegemony in com-bination with a more permissive attitude on the part of the United States towards regionalism; (3) the restructuring of the nation-state and the growth of interdepen-dence, transnationalization and globalization; (4) recurrent fears over the stability of the multilateral trading order, hand in hand with the growing importance of non-tariff barriers (NTBs) to trade; and (5) the changed attitudes towards (neo-liberal) economic development and political systems in the developing countries as well as in the post-communist countries (Hettne and Inotai 1994; Fawcett and

Hurrell 1995; Gamble and Payne 1996; Hettne, Inotai and Sunkel 1999, 2000a, b and c; de Melo and Panagariya 1993; Stallings 1995).

The content of the new regionalism has also changed. The old regionalism was often imposed, directly or indirectly, from outside and above, in accordance with the bipolar structure of the Cold War and mainly in the interests of the superpowers (hegemonic regionalism). The current trend towards regionalism is a more spontaneous process emerging from below and from within the region itself. Furthermore, the old phenomenon was often specific with regard to objectives and content (free trade areas or security alliances), and sometimes explicitly exclusive in terms of member states. The new regionalism is a heterogeneous, comprehensive, multidimensional phenomenon, which involves state, market and society actors and covers economic, cultural, political, security and environmental aspects. The number, scope, and diversity of regionalisms have also grown significantly during the last decade (Bøås, Marchand and Shaw 1999; Hettne, Inotai and Sunkel 1999; Hettne and Söderbaum 1998; Fawcett and Hurrell 1995; Gamble and Payne 1996; Grugel and Hout 1999; Hook and Kearns 1999).

The new regionalism is taking place in more areas of the world than ever before. Today's regionalism is extroverted rather than introverted, which reflects the deeper interdependence of today's global political economy. The new regionalism is in different ways linked to global structural change, and especially to what is perhaps its dominating feature, globalization. Some would argue that globalization is the more forceful of the two. The new regionalism, therefore, cannot be understood merely from the point of view of the single region in question, but only in a global perspective. In this regard there has been a globalization of regional integration theory and praxis. Here is not the place to take a premature perspective in advance of research on the intriguing relationship between globalism and regionalism. Let us instead underline that it is necessary to recognize that they are mutually constitutive processes existing within the broader context of global structural transformation;[1] and it seems that we are dealing with different and overlapping layers of globalisms/globalizations and regionalisms/regionalizations simultaneously. Globalism and regionalism stand in a symbiotic relationship to one another; sometimes they are mutually reinforcing, at other times contradictory (Hettne, Inotai and Sunkel 1999). The important thing is to avoid dichotomizing them (Pettman 1999).

The contemporary wave of regionalism cannot be understood as a distinct alternative to the national interest and nationalism, but is often better explained as an instrument to supplement, enhance or protect the role of the state and the power of the government in an interdependent world (Axline 1994; Palmer 1991). The states today experience a lack of capacity to handle global challenges to national interests, and increasingly respond by 'pooling sovereignty'. At the same time they give up sovereignty and may ultimately end up as semi-independent parts of larger political communities.

The new regionalism is triggered by forces on the intrastate, subnational level as well. One example is the 'black hole' syndrome, or the disintegration of nation-states due to ethnonational mobilization. Another, less violent form of disintegration of nation-states is the strengthening of microregions. European experience demonstrates that both these forces may be linked with the larger macroregional regionalization process. The so-called growth triangles in Southeast Asia can also be understood from this perspective (Ohmae 1995; Hettne, Inotai and Sunkel 1999; Sum and Perkmann 2000; Keating and Laughlin 1997).

To sum up, the renewed trend of regionalism is a complex process of change occurring as a result of global, regional, national and local interactions, simultaneously involving state as well as non-state, market and society actors. It is not possible to decide which level is dominant, because actors and processes at various levels interact and relative importance differs in time and space.

Regionalism and Regionalization

It is crucial to distinguish regionalism from regionalization. Often the distinction is not made at all or there is excessive emphasis on regionalism, defined as 'a state-led or states-led project designed to reorganize a particular regional space along defined economic and political lines' (Gamble and Payne 1996: 2). In our conceptual toolbox, *regionalism* refers in the first place to the general phenomenon, denoting formal projects as well as processes in the broadest possible sense. In a more narrow and operational sense, regionalism represents the body of ideas, values and concrete objectives that are aimed at creating, maintaining or modifying the provision of security and wealth, peace and development within a region: the urge by any set of actors to reorganize along a particular regional space. *Regionalization* implies an activist element and denotes the (empirical) process which can be defined as a process of change from relative heterogeneity and lack of cooperation towards increased cooperation, integration, convergence, coherence and identity in a variety of fields such as culture, security, economic development and politics, within a given geographical space.[2]

This point requires further elaboration. In spite of the fact that an impressive number of publications are being produced on the 'new regionalism' in most world regions, the great majority of studies maintain a focus on regionalism and/or state-initiated regionalization: regional projects, regional organizations, and instrumental state policies (Fawcett and Hurrel 1995; Hook and Kearns 1999; Gamble and Payne 1996; Grugel and Hout 1999) rather than the processes of regionalization. The focus on state strategies, regional organization and regionalism is perhaps understood by the fact that many studies are carried out by political scientists. It is also interesting to note that most economists are concerned with the impact of regionalist projects and trading schemes and do not really try to understand the regionalization logic amongst market actors in a deeper sense. Many theorists distinguish between regionalism and regionalization but they tend to dichotomize them in the form of regionalism versus regionalization. This is perhaps best illustrated by Wyatt-Walter, who defines economic regionalism as a conscious policy of states or substate regions to coordinate activities and arrangements in a greater region, while regionalization is the outcome of such policies or of 'natural' economic forces (Wyatt-Walter, 1995: 77). However, what is defined as regionalization is analysed primarily in so far as it is the outcome of (states-led) regionalism. These distinctions are biased towards state regionalism and state regionalization, downplaying the importance of non-state actors.

We maintain a more comprehensive (and in our view more logical) conceptual toolbox founded on the recognition that regionalism, the urge to merge, can describe state, market and a wide range of (civil) society actors, and that there exists a corresponding (empirical) process of state, market and civil society regionalization. Such a conceptualization also avoids dichotomization of state and non-state actors, allowing us to trace the multidimensionality and pluralism of the processes taking place.

Needless to say, regional organizations and institutions are important phenomena but they are by themselves not sufficient for understanding the dynamics of regionalization. Given the excessive attention received in the literature, both old and new, it must be emphasized that we conceive *regional organiza - tions* as a second-order phenomenon compared to the *processes of regionalization* in a particular geographical space. We seek also to transcend the tendency in the debate, whereby regionalization is regarded as the outcome of any single deliberative strategy, particularly instrumental state strategies institutionalized into regional organizations.

It deserves to be mentioned that the old regionalism was excessively concerned with measuring the level of regional integration (either in economic or political terms). However, our focus on regionalization allows us to transcend the artificial distinction between cooperation and integration and to accommodate regional cooperation and regional integration as well as regional coherence and regional identity.[3]

Furthermore, regionalism/regionalization has often been seen as something positive and 'good'. For instance, regional cooperation and integration have often been seen as instruments to enhance welfare, stability and the creation of increased understanding and peaceful coexistence within regions as well as in the world more generally. However, we must stress that this is not necessarily the case.

Increased interaction and integration can also give rise to conflict, exploitation, dominance, misallocation of resources and other negative effects. Undoubtedly some actors will lose by regionalization, while others will benefit. Our task is not to defend a particular regional project or ideology, or for that matter regionalization, but to try to understand more about the intriguing and complex dynamics of contemporary regionalization.

Furthermore, the issue at this stage is not whether regionalization will be the ordering concept of the international system, although it does emerge as an interesting possibility in the still-nebulous world order. Current trends suggest that regionalization will continue to influence international relations in the foreseeable future. In our view, it is an empirical (not mainly a theoretical, and certainly not an ideological) question how strong and important this trend is. In order to build systematic knowledge we need to learn more about regionalization, and particularly why it is such a strong a feature in some parts of the world but not in other parts. Nevertheless, we believe that this volume, using its eclectic version of the NRA, will show that regionalization is a more important and comprehensive phenomenon than anticipated in much of the literature.

Mainstream Theorizing

Although the NRA seeks to transcend mainstream theorizing in the field, any attempt to build a new theoretical framework rests at least partly on previous theoretical experiences. This is to take one step back in order later to take two steps forward. What follows is an elaboration of some of the most influential schools of thought in the field, primarily but not only in the form of old regionalism. While the intention is by no means to make a full survey of all mainstream theorizing, it is necessary to have a basic knowledge and overview of the existing theoretical landscape in order to understand what we may demand from a new theoretical construct. We concentrate on various theories grouped in three main sets: neorealism; functionalism and institutionalism; and regional economic integration. The overview is not exhaustive and to some extent it tends to concentrate on the *differences* between the approaches, although of course overlaps do exist.

Neorealism

Neorealism constitutes the most dominant and influential approach for understanding the formation of regions in the field of International Relations. This school of thought looks upon regions from the outside in, and analyses the place of the region in the international system. As a consequence, it argues that regional groupings are primarily formed in response to external challenges. Using a

7

neorealist approach one expects mainly security-related forms of regionalism, and the emergence of regionalism has much in common with the politics of alliance formation. The neorealist approach strongly emphasizes the role of states, state interests, and their motivation in the process of regionalization (and that entry into regionalist projects is subject to relative-gain considerations). States may also enter into regionalist projects from domestic considerations. As Buzan points out:

> A group of weak states forming a security regime because they realized that such an arrangement would strengthen the domestic legitimacy of their regimes, whereas pursuing conflicts among themselves was likely to exacerbate divisions within their fragile domestic structures. (Buzan 1991: 289, with reference to ASEAN)

The state is thus the major player. However, although market and societal forces are downplayed in importance, and subordinated to overall security considerations, there is essentially no difference between economic and political/security regionalism, in the form of either mercantilist bloc formation or security alliances.

The regional security complex theory, which is primarily associated with Barry Buzan, has become a very influential strand of neorealist thought.[4] Barry Buzan (1989: 2) has forcefully pointed out that 'security analysis swings between an over-emphasis on the dominant role of the great powers within the global system, and an over-emphasis on the internal dynamics and perspectives of individual states'. The regional security complex theory is designed to fill the gap between state and system levels, in order to explain why the regional level often comprises the dynamic of security relations among the local states. A security complex 'is defined as a group of states whose primary security concerns link together sufficiently closely that their national security cannot realistically be considered apart from one another' (Buzan 1991: 190). Hence, two aspects are to be considered in this approach – the power balance between the actors, and the character of the patterns of enmity and amity. If a regional security complex exists, the regional level is crucial, it is argued, for understanding the nature of security relations; without it neither the position of the local states in relation to each other, nor the character of relations between the great powers and local states, can be understood properly.

Functionalism and Institutionalism

It is difficult to imagine a regionalist project that does not involve at least some degree of functional cooperation. The functional theory of regional cooperation and integration developed in Europe in response to the devastating experience of the Second World War. Its leading advocate, David Mitrany (1966), argued that collaboration should not place unrealistic demands on national sovereignty or existing power structures within each country. Therefore, cooperation should, at least initially, concentrate on technical and basic functional programmes and projects within clearly defined sectors. This approach is believed to minimize costs, avoid conflicts regarding the distribution of benefits, and generate visible and concrete gains and economies of scale within a given sector such as transport and communications, water, energy, agriculture or education and training.

In the process of building functional links among states, the institutions will normally be decentralized and flexible, corresponding to the needs of the various programmes and projects. The existence of conflict and implementation problems is not denied, but these complications can usually be solved when they appear. As cooperation proceeds, member states' conception and valuation of sovereignty will gradually change, and decision makers will to an increasing extent make decisions in less technical and more controversial areas of activity.

Initially within the paradigm of the European Community (EC), neofunctionalism challenged the functionalist assumption of the separability of politics from economics, and the proposition that functionalist integration would automatically spread, claiming that the technical realm was made technical by a prior political decision (Haas 1958). Neofunctionalists argued that 'the political game must be played' and argued their case with reference to a sector that was politically important, yet could be planned by technocrats (Nye 1987: 51). A second important departure from classic functionalism was the deliberate design of institutions that would lead to further integration. Supranational institutions were seen as the most effective means of solving common problems, beginning with technical and non-controversial issues, but 'spilling over' into the realm of high politics and leading to a redefinition of group identity around the regional unit (Hurrell 1995: 59).[5]

Institutionalism in its various versions, mainly neoliberal institutionalism, has become the contemporary form of functionalism and neofunctionalism. Neoliberal institutionalists base their analysis on a number of core arguments. First, increasing levels of (regional) interdependence generate increased 'demand' for international (regional) cooperation, and therefore for international institutions and regimes. Second, institutions matter because of the benefits that they provide, and because of their impact on the calculations of the players and the ways in which they define their interests. They achieve this through the provision of information, the promotion of transparency and monitoring, the reduction of transaction costs, the development of convergent expectations and the productive use of issue-linkage strategies. Third, neoliberal institutionalism is concerned with ways in which states conceived of as rational egoists can be led to cooperate (in our case regionally). Furthermore, the state will act as negotiator at the intergovernmental level, limited by national political considerations. The actors of regionalization are motivated by procurement of public good, avoidance of negative externalities from interdependence. Hence, regionalism can be accelerated by the creation of institutions and regimes for fostering policy coordination (Grugel and Hout 1999; Keohane 1984).

Regional Economic Integration

In the mindset of most neoclassical economists there has conventionally existed only 'one theory', namely what here is labelled the orthodox theory of regional economic integration (sometimes referred to as trade integration or market integration). The customs union concept constitutes the foundation of this theory. It involves the creation, in linear succession, of increasingly more advanced stages of economic integration: preferential trade area, free trade area, customs union, common market, economic union and political union (Balassa 1962; El-Agraa 1997; Robson 1998). The market forces that are set in play at one stage are anticipated to have a spill-over effect to the next stage, so that its implementation becomes an economic necessity. A related proposition is that because economic integration has its own costs, resources will be misallocated if a more advanced stage is embarked upon before a lower stage is completed.

At the lowest stage there is a preferential trade area whereby member countries charge each other lower tariffs than those applicable to non-members, while preventing the free movement of goods within the area. The second stage is a free trade area in which tariffs and quotas are eliminated among members, but each country retains its own tariffs against imports from non-members. A customs union goes further: in addition to sharing a free trade area, members erect a common external tariff. The common market is a more developed stage of integration. It combines the features of the customs union with the elimination of obstacles for the free movement of labour, capital, services and persons (and entrepreneurship). The next step on the ladder is an economic union, which involves a common currency and / or the harmonization and unification of monetary, fiscal and social policies. Political integration constitutes the ultimate stage of economic integration, and it presupposes the unification of economic and political policies, and that the central supranational authority not only controls economic policy but is also responsible to a common parliament.

The welfare gains of the orthodox theory of regional economic integration can be divided into static and dynamic gains (El-Agraa 1997). Owing to the difficulty in calculating dynamic gains within traditional economic models, it has been conventional to concentrate on the static comparative gains, particularly whether the economic scheme is trade-creating or trade-diverting.[6] Static welfare gains may also arise as a consequence of more efficient allocation of resources, primarily as a result of the free flow of factors of production. Sometimes dynamic gains are also considered, such as economies of scale and positive terms-of-trade effects as a result of increased bargaining power. Other dynamic benefits, such as productivity gains, technological development, harmonization of macroeconomic policies and increased growth effects, are often excluded from the analysis, although they do in fact form part of the theory.

Development integration, an alternative approach which developed in reaction to the Eurocentric orthodox approach described above, explicitly emphasizes the dynamic and development-oriented benefits of regional economic integration, more suited to harsh Third World conditions. It can be understood within the structuralist tradition of economic development, pioneered by Myrdal and Prebisch. Development integrationists claim that the rationale of regional cooperation and integration among less-developed countries is not to be found in marginal change and economic efficiency within the existing structure, particularly not in a comparison between trade creation and trade diversion, but in the fostering of 'structural transformation' and the stimulation of productive capacities, investment and trading opportunities (Haarløv 1988: 23; Robson 1997: 268–95; Axline 1984: 17–18). As Haarløv (1988: 21) points out, it is not left to the market mechanism to define the sectors and scope of cooperation. In order to ensure that the commonly defined plans, such as those for investment and production, are carried out successfully, the creation of supranational institutions may come at an earlier stage than in the orthodox theory.

A balanced and more equitable distribution of costs and benefits has been one of the main arguments for the formulation of the development integration model. The model makes use of two broad sets of distributive instruments: compensatory (transfer tax system, budgetary transfers, preferential tariffs) and corrective mechanisms (planned industrial strategy, regional development banks or funds, common investment code) (Haarløv 1988: 23; Robson 1987: 198–214; Axline 1984: 17–18).[7]

Although certain aspects of development integration thinking are still valid for some economic scholars, most are increasingly elaborating the 'open regionalism' approach. Open regionalism is the new and dominant form of mainstream economic thinking.[8] It is basically an extension of the orthodox theory of regional economic integration, especially the trade integration aspects, adjusted to a globalizing world economy. It is based on neoliberal/neoclassical economics and emphasizes that the integration project should be market-driven and outward-looking; should avoid high levels of protection; and should form part of the ongoing globalization and internationalization process of the world political economy (Anderson and Blackhurst 1993; Bergsten 1994; Cable and Henderson 1994; El-Agraa 1997; de Melo and Panagariya 1993).

According to Cable and Henderson (1994: 8) open regionalism means directing policy towards the elimination of obstacles to trade within a region, while at the same time doing nothing to raise external tariff barriers to the rest of the world, implying that it is compatible with multilateralism. It is open in the sense that it should contribute more to the process of global liberalization than it detracts from it (through discrimination). The major issue is whether the formation of regional economic blocs are 'stumbling blocs' or 'building blocs' towards an open world economy. It is also open because it does not exclude new members (Cable and Henderson 1994: 8). In practice these two aspects are linked, since exclusion matters more if membership has substantial discriminatory effects.

To sum up, open regionalists conceive regionalism mainly as a trade promotion policy, building on regional arrangements, rather than as a multilateral framework. The main justification for open regionalism is that it contributes more to the process of global liberalization and multilateralism than it detracts from it. The normative point of view behind the open regionalism concept is that it at best constitutes a second-best contribution to the task of increasing the amount of world trade and global welfare, and at worst a protectionist threat against the multilateral order. Regionalism can thus be motivated, for a limited time, through the argument that infant industries require protection, or it can be seen as a temporary phase in a wider globalization or multilateralization process.

The New Regionalism Approach

The current development of the global political economy prompts us to reassess and reconstruct. While to some extent building on earlier theoretical experiences, and thereby taking into account their drawbacks, we seek to move towards an open-ended version of the NRA(Hettne, Inotai and Sunkel, 1999; Bøås *et al.* 1999) which is designed to capture the heterogeneous and multidimensional processes of emerging regions and regionalization from a historical and interdisciplinary perspective.[9] Mainstream theories in the field need not be dismissed altogether, and may still be helpful in the analysis of regionalisms and regionalization. However, as Mittelman points out:

> The new regionalism approach (NRA) is an important advance on the different versions of integration theory (trade or market integration, functionalism and neo-functionalism, institutionalism and neoinstitutionalism, and so on).… [A]ll of them are deficient inasmuch as they understate power relations and fail to offer an explanation of structural transformation. In some ways a break with this tradition, the NRA explores contemporary forms of transnational co-operation and cross-border flows through comparative, historical, and multilevel perspectives. (Mittelman 1999: 25–6)

The NRAis connected with the broader theoretical debate within International Relations and International Political Economy. It can be understood within the New International Political Economy tradition and the effort to transcend 'problem-solving theory', state-centric ontologies and rationalist epistomologies. Instead it aims to move towards critical theory and a more comprehensive social science which accommodates state actors as well as market and civil society actors (Murphy and Tooze 1991; Hettne 1995; Cox 1996).[10]

The NRA is founded on the necessity to 'unpack' the state, avoid the state-centrism inherent in mainstream theorizing in the field (neorealism, institutionalism or economic integration theory), and better understand the state–society complexes. We argue that mainstream theories at best provide an incomplete guide to understanding the empirical phenomenon of the new regionalism (Hurrell 1995: 71). The NRA is basically an attempt to understand the challenge eloquently expressed by Andrew Hurrell:

> [I]t might be argued that the early phases of regional cooperation may be the result of the existence of a common enemy or powerful hegemonic power; *but that having been thrown together, different logics begin to develop*: the functionalist or problem-solving logic stressed by institutionalists; or the logic of community highlighted by the constructivists. Thus, neorealists may be right to stress the importance of the geo-political context in the early stages of European unity, and yet wrong in ignoring the degree to which both informal integration and successful institutionalization altered the dynamics of European international relations over the following forty years. (Hurrell 1995: 73, our emphasis)

It has been our aim to avoid rigid theoretical postulates in advance of research. We want to maintain some theoretical open-mindedness. The case studies are therefore guided by issues formulated within an eclectic version of the NRA rather than a strict adherence to causal theory. This is explained by the fact that we want to open up a broad and deep interdisciplinary and holistic understanding of what characterizes regionalization processes in various parts of the world. We also seek to account for the pluralism and multidimensionality of current processes of regionalization and the involvement of non-state actors in a historical, global, multilevel and constructivist perspective. Who the driving actors are, the extent of convergence in various sectors, the extent of commonalities in terms of identity, the way political ambitions are formed, and so on, mean that differently initiated take-offs create different logics of regionalization. Furthermore, the globalization effects on regionalization foster manifold outcomes too. The NRA approach is designed to accommodate such aspects.

The authors emphasize different aspects of regionalization because of empirical differences in the regions under investigation, but also because of some differences in theoretical perspective. However, all the authors agree on certain common denominators and theoretical points of departure that constitute the main thrust of the NRA. For instance, we all agree that regions and regionalization must be understood in a global perspective, as well as that the interrelated global-regional-national-local levels cannot easily be analytically separated in advance of research.

We all agree that regionalization is to be seen as a comprehensive and multidimensional process, which implies increased regional cooperation, integration and complementarity with respect to a number of dimensions such as culture, politics, security, economics and diplomacy. This implies that there is a pluralism of regionalisms and regionalizations, which are most likely overlapping, heterogeneous and often contradictory. Moreover, a historical analysis is crucial to a full understanding of regionalization.

Furthermore, we underline the socially constructed character of regionalization, which also implies that regionalization can be deconstructed. In a broad sense, social constructivism places emphasis both on material forces and on its tenet 'that international reality is a social construction driven by collective understandings, including norms, that emerge from social interaction' (Adler and Barnett 1998: 10). Social constructivists claim that understanding intersubjective structures allows us to trace the ways in which interests and identities change over time and new forms of cooperation and community can emerge.[11] Furthermore, constructivist theories focus on regional awareness and regional identity, on 'cognitive interdependence' and the shared sense of belonging to a particular regional community, and on what has been called 'cognitive regionalism'.

The problem of defining regions attracted a significant deal of attention during the first wave of regionalism, but the results yielded few clear conclusions. In this context it is worth repeating that the *problematique* of the NRA is not the delineation of regions *per se*, but the processes and consequences of regionalization in various fields of activity and at various levels. There are no 'natural' or 'given' regions, but these are constructed, deconstructed and reconstructed – intentionally or non-intentionally – in the process of global transformation, by collective human action and identity formation. It should therefore be very clear that we do not by any means suggest that regions will be unitary or homogeneous units. Regions are overlapping and come in the plural. A focus on regions and processes of regionalization (rather than regional organizations) does imply, however, that the most commonly used units of analysis until now, *states*, are not isolated entities or discrete categories. States cannot be understood without reference to the neighbouring environment, the region, in which the country has developed. By the same token, regions are not discrete categories and must be understood in a global perspective. Neglect of the global / external factor was often an error of old theories of regional integration. The NRA is based on the fact that, while each region has its own internal dynamics, at the same time there exists pressing evidence that regions must be understood in a global perspective.

For these reasons, we maintain an eclectic and flexible definition of regions. Regions necessarily involve a geographical dimension, and the main task of identifying regions implies judgements about the degree to which a particular area in various respects constitutes a distinct entity. This distinct entity should be distinguished as a territorial subsystem (in contrast with non-territorial subsystems) from the rest of the international system. This implies that there are many varieties of regional subsystems with different degrees of 'regionness', or the degree to which a particular region in various respects constitutes a coherent unit (Hettne 1993, 1999; Hettne and Söderbaum 1998).[12]

Many theorists agree with the minimum definition of a region set out by Nye: 'a limited number of states linked together by a geographical relationship and by a degree of mutual interdependence' (Nye 1965: vii). In an effort to transcend state-centrism, however, the NRA does not perceive regions as simple aggregations of states. The regional frontier may very well cut through a particular state's geographical area, positioning some parts of the state within the region and others outside. For instance, it could be argued that some parts of China, mainly the coastal areas, form part of an East Asian regionalization process while mainland China does not. A less dramatic example is the well-consolidated nation-state of Sweden where, nevertheless, the eastern part increasingly inclines to the Baltic, the west to the Atlantic and the south to Europe. Similar processes can be found in Spain and Italy, for instance. Furthermore, what is referred to as a region with regard to economic relations may not always be seen as such from a political or a cultural perspective. However, there is reason to believe that the diverse ideas and processes tend to converge as the regionalization process intensifies.

Furthermore, in many regions it is possible to discern a group of countries constituting the core of the region, while one or several other countries or subnational areas constitute a semi-periphery or periphery of the region in question – as exemplified by the EU member states and the former Eastern Bloc countries, and by the case of Mercosur and the Andean countries. Although this peripheral status should not be defined in terms of geography, the two often coincide.

Since regions are social constructions, there are no given regions, and no given regionalist interests either, but the interests and identities are shaped in the process of interaction and intersubjective understanding. The relevance of 'hard structuralism' is limited in such a situation. We agree with Wendt that 'structure has no existence or causal power apart from process' (Wendt, 1992: 395). Structuralism thus has to be transcended and in order to understand structural change we must move from structure to *agency*, *actors* and *strategies*. In accordance with social constructivism more generally, the NRA seeks to address the fact that agency, and particularly the role of often previously excluded transnational actors, is an under-researched field in the study of regionalism and regionalization.

To a large extent, regionalism can be seen as a political phenomenon, shaped by political actors (state and non-state) who may use regionalism for a variety of not necessarily compatible purposes. Thus, by looking at regionalization from a political perspective, the issue raised is formulated in the question: what kind of actors are driving the project, with what means, and for what purposes?

As indicated above, we emphasize that regionalization may occur either through 'formal', top-down, state-driven or through 'real', bottom-up, market- and society-induced processes of regionalization (Hettne 1999; Hurrell 1995; Oman 1994). Contrary to the overemphasis in the debate on top-down regionalist projects, particularly concerning regional organizations and regional trading arrangements, both processes must be given equal attention in the theoretical framework. The main actors and driving forces of top-down regionalization are states (governments) and 'authorities' at various levels. 'Market and society regionalization' refers to the growth of the often undirected processes of societal and economic (private business) interaction and interdependence (Hurrell 1995: 39). The actors are from markets, business networks, firms, transnational corporations, peoples, NGOs and other types of social networks and social movements contributing to the formation of a ('real') transnational regional economy and civil society. For obvious reasons, this type of regionalization may be affected by inter-governmental regional cooperation and integration (state regionalization), but it is crucial to separate the processes analytically. Often this distinction is not made.

Transcending top-down, state-driven notions of regionalization is particularly important in order to understand the spontaneous processes of regionalization, the making of regional civil societies as well as cross-border regions where the structures of nation-states are weakened as a result of globalization and regional-ization processes. In the latter case the reaction of the governments is sometimes to cling firmly to whatever state power they have left, and therefore to be hostile to changes, including what is perceived as giving away national sovereignty.

In this context it must once again be pointed out that the NRA is compatible with an interdependent world economy (although it remains cautious with regard to free trade, or 'dogmatic globalism'). The NRA assumes the 'return of the political in a globalized world', in contrast with the concept of open regionalism, based on the notion that it is market forces that are shaping underlying processes. The NRA views globalization as a strong and in some of its dimensions irreversible force, but one that will (or should) be significantly modified by regional forma-tions in defence of social order and attempts at political control over the market. In this view, if globalization is the challenge, the new regionalism can be a response; an attempt to bring globalization processes and transnational transactions under some political-territorial control. This can be regarded as revisiting Karl Polanyi at a regional level; a second 'great transformation' (Hettne 1999; Polanyi 1957).

Rather than a premature causal theory and set of variables, which are unlikely to capture the complex heterogeneity and multidimensional dynamics of regional-ization, we have outlined a set of *issues*, extracted from the above exploration, that concern all the regions under investigation as feasible case studies. This focus makes it possible to recognize the specific peculiarities and contexts of various regions. Therefore, the questions put forward to the authors are related to the 'hardcore' issues of regionalization and the NRA.

The first set of questions is related to the region and the regional level of analysis. What constitutes the region in focus? Which criteria can be used in order to differentiate macroregions from microregions, as well as to assess the territorial, historical, political, economic and cultural aspects of regions?

How are the regionalization processes formed and how do they relate to the various agencies? What are the motives for regionalism and regionalization? Why is there an 'urge to merge'? Furthermore, how and in what way are the main actors – states as well as actors from the market and civil society – involved in, contributing to or opposing the regionalization process? Who are the drivers and what are the relative strengths of the various types of actors?

Finally, the answers to the questions above enables trend identification. What are the future prospects for regionalization? Before moving to the authors' own analysis we will introduce the case studies in which the authors were asked to raise and explore the issues guiding this book.

Structure of the Book

The 'tour of the world' starts in *Europe*, where the old as well as the new regionalism began. Björn Hettne shows that the current integration within the EU, in the context of open conflicts in Europe and particularly in the Balkans, presents both a paradigm and a paradox.

The *Middle East*, the home of three world religions, has a long history of conflicts with an impact on the options for regional cooperation at least as damaging as those in any other region. Moreover, Marianne Laanatza, Helena Lindholm Schulz and Michael Schulz show that there are processes of subregionalization in play. Above all, the peace process and regional cooperation need each other in a dialectical relationship. To put this in other words, if the Palestinian–Israeli conflict could find a solution, regionalization could gain momentum.

Africa provides again, as it did in the 1960s, intriguing examples of the dynamics of regionalization. In *West Africa*, Fredrik Söderbaum sees both possibilities and constraints. Nigeria is a regional giant, with a similar role to that of India and South Africa in their respective regions, and is viewed with similar suspicion by its neighbours. The pattern of regional peacekeeping interventions in Liberia and Sierra Leone has made West Africa the pet of regionalist advocates: regional stabilization and conflict resolution taken care of by the regional actors themselves. However, the stability of the conflict resolution could be questioned.

Whose security, and what security? As far as the regional organizations are concerned, these are largely failures, and to a large extent they can be explained as contributing to the process of neopatrimonialism. There is a strong pattern of informal market and society regionalization in West Africa. Important aspects of these processes are not separated, however, from the neopatrimonial logic and trans-state regionalization.

Southern Africa, with South Africa as the first among equals, is entering a process of regional cooperation strikingly different from the regional war of the 1980s. However, South Africa is a regional hegemon for good and for bad. High hopes are pinned on its role, but Bertil Odén asks, *inter alia*, whether South Africa will in the long run benefit or exploit Southern Africa? The answer is slightly disappointing.

The next region we investigate is *Central Asia and Caucasia*. This is a rather embryonic, heterogeneous and diverse regional formation, which is in the midst of a state- and nation-building process constituted by open conflicts, warfare, and ethnonationalism. However, as Patrik Jotun claims, it also reveals some interesting trends towards regional economic cooperation. It is not an easy task to assess in which direction this ethnically fragmented region is heading.

Meanwhile *South Asia* is, in Bent Jørgensen's analysis, experiencing a turbulent time characterized by a complex mix of conflict resolution, religious extremism, Indian hegemonism, ethnic revitalization, nation-state decay, and a certain degree of regional cooperation. It seems, however, in spite of all the difficulties, that India can neither dominate the region as it has in the past, nor maintain a semi-conflictive equilibrium. A regional dialogue is likely to be deepened. The alternative is frightening.

Joakim Öjendal concentrates on *Southeast Asia*. Southeast Asian regionalism, epitomized in the ASEAN, is perhaps known as the most successful regional cooperation project in the so-called Third World. Although its formal intention of increasing economic cooperation was not successful, ASEAN contributed to stimulating and building political cooperation between the states in the region, providing valuable political stability. After the Cold War, political cooperation is more complex and new priorities have been introduced. Neither the extension of the association nor the creation of a free trade zone will suffice to induce a much-needed revitalization of regionalism. ASEAN member countries have nevertheless laid a solid foundation from which they can continue to build a more substantial community.

Claes G. Alvstam takes a critical view of the nature of regionalization in *East Asia*. Employing a deep historical perspective he shows that the foundations of genuine regionalization are rather meagre. Conflicts and deep-seated differences will continue to dominate the regional system. In spite of this there are also signs of increasing regional contacts and institution building. It remains to be seen whether these will turn out to be more than facades and charades.

North America, Marianne Marchand shows, is a case of neoliberal, market-oriented regionalization process. NAFTA is very much an elite project, simultaneously triggering many oppositional reactions from various state actors, but even more from actors in civil society. The lack of political structures casts doubt on the viability of the project.

The Caribbean is an unusual case of regionalization since the size of the region is very small compared to all the other regions studied in this volume. Given the low viability of individual nation-state projects, Åke Widfeldt assesses what options the microstates in the region have in terms of future cooperation. In particular the region's relation with the US and the NAFTA defines the potential for future regionalization. The author explains that the regional economic strategies of sustainability must be considered in any future cooperation.

Finally, in a joint endeavour, Cyro Banega, Björn Hettne and Fredrik Söderbaum discuss the genuine, if unfinished, case of regional cooperation in *South America*. Given a strong history of regional cooperation and integration, political convergence has paved the way for deepened regionalization through Mercosur. The process has shown some success in recent years, but much continues to depend on the willingness of the regional giants, Brazil and Argentina, to overcome their historical rivalry.

NOTES

1 Global structural transformation is the aggregation of the various processes of change that together transform the international system. Beyond the notoriously ambiguous label of 'globalization' this also includes other transformation processes with systemic influences, such as regionalization, (unfinished) nation-state projects and, not least, 'localization' and fragmentation from within.

2 By the same token, *globalism* refers to the ideology promoting worldwide organization and the corresponding vision of a borderless world. *Globalization* refers to the empirical trend that inspires or bears out this belief. Basically, globalization is the process of compression of the world driven by market expansion, a global production pattern, cultural homogenization as well as fragmentation, and functional logic. It represents the ultimate manifestation of the post-Westphalian logic, in which territory, in a classical nation-state sense, has lost its meaning ('the end of geography').

3 *Regional cooperation* can be defined as an open-ended process whereby individual states or other actors within a given geographical area act together for mutual benefit in certain fields (such as infrastructure, water or energy) and in order to solve common tasks, in spite of conflicting interests in other fields of activity. It may be formal and involve a high degree of institutionalization, but may also be based on a much looser structure. It constitutes one component of all regionalization processes analysed in this book.

In its conventional usage *regional integration* refers to a deeper process than regional cooperation. Basically, 'integration' means forming parts into a whole. As Nye (1987: 26) points out, the concept can be broken down into economic integration (formation of a transnational economy, often reductionistically referred to as negative integration), political integration (formation of a transnational political system, often referring to a minimum degree of transfer of sovereignty or functions to supranational organs), and social integration (formation of a transnational society). Regional cooperation may (or may not) form part of the process of regional integration, but always forms part of the broader processes of regionalization.

Regional convergence and coherence is also a necessary concept in understanding the process of regionalization in the world today. There are of course different paths to regional convergence and coherence. Besides occurring at the regional level – through regional interaction and cooperation – it may take place either as a consequence of structural transformation at the systemic level, or by way of separate processes of convergence, homogenization and elimination of extremes in terms of structure and behaviour at the domestic level (Hurrell 1995).

Regional identity is a contested concept. It must not be ignored, however, and plays a much more significant role in the new regionalism than in the old. It is thus evident that many parts of the world have seen a marked increase in regional awareness and regional identity. This shared perception of belonging to a particular community can be explained by internal (domestic and regional) as well as external (global) factors, in response to the 'Other'. To a certain extent, all regions are 'imagined', subjectively defined and cognitive constructions. There is also an inherent 'sameness' in many regions shaped by pre-Westphalian empires and civilizations. In order to be successful in the long run, it seems that sustainable regionalization necessitates a certain degree of compatibility of culture, identity and fundamental values. We do not know how strong these enlarged 'imagined communities' and cognitive regions are, or how much internal crisis and resurgent nationalism they can withstand. It could also be the case, however, that regional identity can mutually reinforce national/ethnic identities.

4 Because regional security complex theory also takes into account the patterns of enmity and amity, it transcends, to some extent, the neorealist school of thought and moves towards the liberal camp.

5 Although the neofunctionalists tend to emphasize involvement leading towards a more highly institutional end, rather than the classical functionalist piecemeal solution of problems, the two approaches share certain fundamentals. First, they both stress welfare creation and functional needs to build peace and security. Second, both tend to downgrade the role of symbols and identity, and to emphasize utilitarian factors in community and nation-state formation. Third, both tend to rely on pluralistic societies in which individuals and groups are free to shift their activities and loyalties. Fourth, both tend to emphasize the role of the technocrat, though the neofunctionalist technocrat is politically aware and is expected to have close links with the centres of power (Nye 1987: 53). Last, both affirm an insularity in the regionalization process, paying little regard to extraregional powers (in contrast to federalists who may overstress them).

6 Trade creation and trade diversion both result from the removal of trade barriers between members, and both increase trade within the union. However, the terms refer to gain and loss effects respectively. Trade creation refers to a replacement of high-cost domestic production by low-cost products from another member, while trade diversion represents a union-induced shift in the source of imports from lower-cost external sources to higher-cost partner sources.

7 The distribution of costs and benefits is one of the most crucial issues confronting regional economic integration efforts, especially among the less-developed countries. In contrast to the development integration model, the orthodox theory of regional integration is founded upon the notion that each member will simply gain on the basis of comparative advantage – all members will be better off with the union than without it, if the union is trade-creative (the so-called second-best) – and the inherent equalization of factor prices will at least not hurt the low-income countries.

8 Adjustment-adapted market integration is another version of neoliberal/neoclassical economic integration theory (Haarløv 1997). This approach, which is very compatible with open regionalism, strives to align regional integration with the basic principles of the structural adjustment programmes. It amounts to synchronizing economic integration in the areas of trade and industry with open regionalism. Institutionally, the approach emphasizes flexibility and

selectivity. The new approach envisages that the first step in renewed regionalization efforts would be to implement what has already been agreed upon in existing organizations (including 'multi-speedism' and 'variable geometry').

9 Conventional economic analysis often treats political, social and cultural aspects as exogenous variables, while political scientists often neglect socio-economic variables and realities. The NRA, as presented in this study, is a much more comprehensive and interdisciplinary venture. The theoretical and methodological implications of these innovations cannot be over-emphasized.

10 The work of Robert Cox is one important example of the structural transformation tradition (Cox 1996); it has had great influence on the new and critical IPE theorizing.

11 Social constructivists share with neoliberal institutionalists the idea that norms and beliefs may shape behaviour. Contrary to the rationalist/neo-utilitarian approach of the latter, however, actors' interests, motives, ideas and identities are perceived not as exogenously given but as socially constructed by reflective actors, capable of adapting to challenges imposed by the actions of others and changing contexts. According to the social constructivist approach, conflicts cannot be resolved unless people learn to create mutual interests through inquiry and debate, tools with the power to change positions, volitions and ultimately identities.

12 The level of regionness can both increase and decrease. The regionness concept ranges from regional area, regional complex, regional society and regional community to region-state (Hettne and Söderbaum 1998).

2 Europe: Paradigm and Paradox

BJÖRN HETTNE

We are living in an age of regionalism, a new wave of regional integration with roots in the mid-1980s. In this wave as well as in its predecessor, which came in the 1950s and 1960s, Europe has been in the lead. As the prototype of the Westphalian state system, she is now showing the way beyond Westphalia. Europe thus represents the most advanced supranational regional arrangement the world has seen so far, and it may consequently serve as a paradigm for the new regionalism, in the sense that the conceptualization of this phenomenon conventionally draws on empirical observations of the European process. There are, in spite of the perhaps conspicuous Eurocentrism involved, some good reasons for this view. The EU is undoubtedly a concrete model, often referred to as an example to follow by other regional organizations such as ASEAN, the South Asian Association for Regional Cooperation (SAARC) and Southern Africa's SADC. In more negative terms, the integration process, and the introverted attitude this gave rise to in Europe, has been seen as a threat (the so-called Fortress Europe) to the global trading system, and therefore a pretext for organizing competing regional trade systems such as NAFTA, Mercosur or the East Asian Economic Caucus (EAEC, the so far unrealized Asianized variety of regionalization in Asia Pacific).

Thus, the emphasis in this chapter on the new regionalism as a process 'from within' does not mean that it is purely indigenous to each respective region. Even if the initiatives are taken within the region, the factors which make these initiatives necessary are global. It is the process of globalization and the many challenges implied that makes regionalization necessary, even if there are more autonomous internal forces at work as well. These forces differ from one region to another.

In this chapter I shall try to pinpoint the historical basis for European region-ness or Europeanness by looking at the Westphalian system in terms of convergences in economic policies, political regimes and security arrangements. The last-mentioned dimension is expanded into a discussion of emerging conflict structures in the new Europe, focusing in particular on the Balkans. Thus Europe is seen as larger than the EU, but where the actual boundaries are situated is an open question. Finally some future trends in the Europeanization process, particularly as regards identity and conflict, are discussed.

The Formation of a European Region

The concept of Europe is by no means unambiguous. From a geographical perspective Europe constitutes the westernmost part of the large Eurasian land mass. In the small European part of this huge area there are many different religions, languages and peoples, creating an enormous diversity which only can be understood against the background of historical popular movements in a disintegrating empire, creating Europe as a social system and subsequently as a civilization. The era of intra-European migration may not be over. Neither, of course, is the possibility of further interregional population movement. This source of demographic and social change has continued in modern times, making Europe an extremely heterogeneous region (Madood and Werbner 1997).

In geopolitical terms Europe took shape after the division of the Roman Empire, when it constituted what was left outside the more organized and powerful Byzantine and Arab worlds. During the period of high medievalism, it became a consolidated cultural area based on Latin Christendom, but expanding in all directions through trade, missionary activities and the crusades (Bartlett 1993). By 1300 Europe existed as a distinct cultural identity (*ibid.*: 291). Peoples in Europe shared a number of cultural practices and (their elites) a common experience of higher education, received from universities in Paris, Bologna and Oxford, which by that time had attained their classic form. Europe had become Europeanized, a certain level of regionness had been achieved.

The process of state formation, starting at the end of the medieval period, implied a fragmentation of the European identity as the new territorial states became introverted (mercantilism) and later were trapped in nationalism, which developed in earnest after the French Revolution. With a Braudelian distinction between events, cyclical movements, and long-term qualitative change, it can be said that the Peace of Westphalia was the first in a series of events contributing to the formation of a specific European international order. This order went through cyclical movements, from repeated attempts at continental unification to reassertion of a decentralized state system, with the latter always predominant (Watson 1997).

The starting point for understanding the origin of regionness must be the historical and cultural preconditions for regional identity, without which there is no base for a process of regionalization. The meaning of Europe is not merely an academic but a deeply political question. For a long time what is now the EU had a near monopoly on the concept, but today the situation is more complex. Many countries are applicants for future membership in the EU, which again raises the issue of what it means to be European (Michalski and Wallace 1992).

Europe can mean quite different entities, depending on the context. With the break-up of the Soviet system, Europe is moving further to the east, but how far? As a paradigmatic world culture Europe extends far beyond its geographical area, being present in most Third World regions (through the modern elites with Western education), and dominant in the Americas, Australia and New Zealand. The expansion of Europe, controlling 84 per cent of the land surface of the world in 1914, can even be identified with the 'expansion of international society' (Bull and Watson 1985; Watson 1992).

Europe thus represents a paradox in terms of unity and diversity. The heterogeneity of Europe exceeds that of most other regions, but at the same time there is an unmistakable 'Europeanness' from north to south and west to east. It is argued that the elements of unity have been on the increase, a process which will be referred to as 'Europeanization' (which is one variety of the process of regionalization). However, this process is not free from conflicts and setbacks. On the contrary, the process of integration is accompanied by interstate rivalries and the emergence of neonationalism as well as processes of national disintegration, for instance in the form of ethnonationalism, low-intensity civil wars and microregionalism. A future positive balance between processes of integration and disintegration cannot be taken for granted. The new regionalism is not a predetermined project. There may be more than one post-Westphalian scenario.

The Westphalian System

The starting point for analysing the particular European experience in political organization is the emergence of nation-states and the international system they formed, and in which they became constituent parts. The dominant approach to international relations – to consider the international system as a form of anarchy – took shape during the 'modern' phase in European history, which roughly started with the Peace of Westphalia in 1648. This marked the beginning of the 'Westphalian era', which now, according to some analysts, is about to end. A Westphalian system is an interstate system constituted by sovereign states and the particular political logic that characterizes each single state. Inside the state are the citizens with obligations and rights defined by citizenship and allegiance to the nation-state. This is the Westphalian rationality. The outside world is conceived as anarchy, with neither rights nor obligations. The pre-Westphalian order was characterized by a diffuse, multilevel structure of authority. A post-Westphalian rationality, on the other hand, would assert that the nation-state in certain respects has lost its functional usefulness, and that solutions to problems of security and welfare therefore must be found increasingly in different forms of transnational structures, multilateral or, as this chapter argues, regional.

To stress state formation and nation building as a historical process is also to say that it is difficult to tell at what particular date a state was born. The concept itself is not crystal-clear. A state has been defined by Tilly as 'an organization employing specialized personnel, which controls a consolidated territory and is recognized as autonomous and integral by the agents of other states' (Tilly 1975: 70). These criteria should, according to the same author, be considered in a relativistic per-spective, so as to make it possible to speak of a process of gradual increase in 'stateness', with reference to a particular political unit (*ibid.*: 34). The relativistic view of stateness also implies the possibility of decreasing stateness – the disinte-gration of a state and the exhaustion of nation-building funds. This concept has served as the main inspiration for analysing the process of regionalization in terms of increasing (or decreasing) regionness. The political logic in the latter process is somewhat different, however. Homogenization within a region cannot imply cultural standardization in accordance with one specific ethnic model, but rather compatibility between differences within a pluralist culture. This would necessi-tate some sort of regional civil society.

In Europe, the sixteenth century was a time of rising stateness, culminating in the later seventeenth century, the era of absolutism. The rather drawn-out state-building process in Europe was a violent one; people gradually learned to conceive of their own state as a protector and the rest of the world as ruled by anarchy and therefore a threat to their security. In the postcolonial era, state building became a global process, and the state a universal political phenomenon.

Once the 'first industrial nation' (Mathias 1969) had been born – Britain – it provided the model to imitate for the rest of Europe (as well as its North American replica). Not to imitate would mean permanent dependence on the 'workshop of the world' and danger to the other nation-state projects. This basic dilemma was to be repeated more generally in the relation between the West and the decolonized world. In order to develop it was deemed necessary for the 'new nations' to imitate the Western model – it was a 'modernization imperative'. For this reason it is possible to speak of a 'Westphalian' political logic even outside Europe.

It is important to realize that the traditions of state formation and nation building are completely different in the European East and in the European West. In the West, the typical political structure was the consolidated nation-state, in which the cultural differences among different sections of the population

25

gradually, but in varying degrees, disappeared through a process of more or less forced assimilation. In the East, it was rather the empire, encompassing a great number of ethnic nations and minorities, who normally enjoyed a certain degree of autonomy within the imperial polity. This political order follows what we could call a 'pre-Westphalian' order. Some of these cultural and linguistic minority groups, but far from all, carried their own nation-state projects. Thus, different political logics can coexist in time and space.

The European West

In the West one can further distinguish between 'state-nations', nation-states and the small democracies ranging from ethnically homogeneous to culturally hetero-geneous entities with inbuilt guarantees, the so-called 'consociational democra-cies'. The state-nations were the early state formations in which the state created the nation, sometimes using coercive methods, and with some conflictive cleavages built into the state structure. Spain, England and France are examples. The nation-states, such as Italy and Germany, were products of nationalist movements: the nations created their own states.

The more homogeneous states are the Nordic group, which even as a group (the Nordic security community) is very homogeneous. Denmark and Sweden are old state-nations, albeit of a homogeneous kind. Norway and Finland are more recent creations of national movements. Consociational democracy characterizes some of the small West European democracies such as Belgium and Switzerland. Consocia-tional democracy contradicts the principles of one-nation-one-state and majority rule, and guarantees certain rights to minority groups. This is done under the assumption that ethnically divided states have to live with ethnic cleavages rather than wish them away. Some basic principles of the consociational model are ethnic autonomy in the form of some federal arrangement, proportionality in the alloca-tion of certain opportunities and offices, consultation with all groups before important decisions, the right of vetoing certain types of decisions, and the estab-lishment of a 'grand coalition' of ethnic groups (or rather the elites within these groups). The point of all this is of course to avoid the destructive effects of majority rule in multiethnic societies, where there can be no change of power as long as voting takes place along ethnic lines.

The European East

Europe lacks an obvious frontier towards 'the East', which is as much an ideologi-cal concept as it is a geographical term. Rather, this area has historically been a moving zone of tension between the Europa paradigm and what in the European intellectual tradition has been known as 'oriental despotism', the negative 'Other', concretized in the Russian and the Ottoman empires. Thus, the historical frontiers of Europe separate it from Islam and the Orthodox Church. Both frontiers play their role in the current Balkan crisis as well as in the tensions of the post-Soviet region. Both frontiers, and boundaries, have to be transcended in the new Europe.

In the East there are three distinct subregions that have inherited traditions from three empires: the post-Soviet secession states, Central Europe, and the Balkans. Each of these subregions contains a more or less explosive set of ethnic tensions. This is particularly true in the Balkans – the Bosnian, Albanian and Macedonian questions – but the European post-Soviet secession states (not to speak of their non-European counterparts) are also problematic. Russia contains many frustrated minorities, the Baltic countries many frustrated Russians, and Ukraine, Belarus and Moldova lack experience as sovereign states. Not even Central Europe, now in comparatively successful transition, is free from the ethnic question: the division of former Czechoslovakia, the Hungarian diaspora, the Germans in Silesia, for instance.

The Soviet empire contained 'European' as well as 'non-European' areas. The Soviet 'hegemony' did not assume the Gramscian quality of acquiescence (Cox 1996). The situation was therefore more akin to an older type of imperial dominance, and in fact there was a striking continuity between the Tsarist empire and the now dissolved socialist state. The major factor cementing the latter's successor, the Commonwealth of Independent States (CIS), is, precisely, the very serious conflict pattern characterizing the region (Rubin and Snyder 1998).

Homo Sovieticus is, thus, extinct. Instead there are many 'black holes' which can be seen as emerging nations only in a rather optimistic scenario. In order to avoid economic fragmentation and political tensions, they will have to sort out their relations within some kind of regional framework. The level of regionness is low. Some countries of the external ex-Soviet empire will 'escape' the region by 'de-easternization', and consequently 'join Europe', but for most of them this option is not open. Economic nationalism on the level of the previous republics does not make sense. The urge for self-determination defies economic logic. Inmates of the 'prison of nations' are nevertheless beginning to fight each other. Russia is demographically dominant, and there are even 25 million Russians outside Russia, lacking a clear citizenship status.

The only CIS country that to some extent can match Russia is Ukraine, and the tension between the two powers is clearly visible behind the handshakes. Caucasus will go its own way, which means many different national paths and many conflicts in the coming decade. This will have an enormous impact on southern Russia, an area already becoming unsafe for Russians. The Central Asian republics may also want to build a future of their own, if they can. There are many external interests involved, but under all conceivable circumstances it will become a non-European area.

Even with all these separatist tendencies, old Russia remains a giant and a geopolitical challenge for Europe as well as the other blocs when (perhaps even before) the era of economic austerity is over. The crucial issue is whether Russia will become 'European' or not. If Russia follows its anti-Europe tradition, as urged by the conservatives, with their deep-rooted scepticism about the West, as well as the current communist–fascist alliance, the situation in the Europeanized regions with Russian populations will become problematic. If this problem can be solved through enlightened minority policies in the countries concerned, Russia, separated from Europe by Belarus and Ukraine, would perhaps rather look towards the Pacific. For Russia, the Western model of modernization has always been painful, a sort of surrender.

Eastward Enlargement and Transformation

Since the breakdown of the communist system in 1989, the European border as defined by the West has been moving eastward. The Central European countries sharing the European core values are getting ready to join the EU as formal members, but the process of regionalization or Europeanization, to be discussed in more detail below, is actually occurring in a much larger part of Europe. This may serve the purpose of illustrating the difference between the *formal* region, defined by organizational membership of states, and the more spontaneously emerging *real* region, defined by convergences in the economic, political and security fields. The formal process may be slowed down by resistance from hesitant members with different stakes in keeping the regional organization closed. It may also, on the contrary, be premature, in view of the actual degree of convergence so far. Thus, security concerns may overrule the principle of convergence, since there are problematic states that may be more easily handled within the organization. Outside Europe, whatever her ultimate external borders may be, lies what has been called an 'arc of instability' (*Economist*, 7–13 November 1998: 40). This zone of war is conventionally seen to lean towards the east.

It is important not to exaggerate the continuity of this divide, but rather to look for the specific problems at each occasion (Burgess 1997). The current Western approach is to include or at least consider membership for those countries that make the 'transition' into 'democratic market economies'. The burden of adaptation will lie on the potential candidates themselves. It is ironic that the core countries constituting the model to copy are themselves still moving towards the orthodox market systems laid down in the Economic and Monetary Union (EMU) settlement. Demands on others are stricter than practices at home (Kearns 1996). 'Europe' is a moving target. This makes the so-called transition very precarious and painful, and the risk of failure great, as clearly shown in the problems of German unification and subsequent integration. Those who fail to adapt (demonized Serbs, unruly Slovaks or repressive Romanians) will be defined as 'different', as part of 'non-Europe'. Most of the post-Soviet area will belong here.

The Europeanization of Europe

During the Cold War era, Europe was merely an arena for the global bipolar conflict, but gradually, and with surprisingly few manifest conflicts, it was transformed from object to subject, in the sense that through increasing regionness it became an actor in its own right. The situation seemed to ripen in the mid-1980s and the process culminated around 1990. This can be symbolized by the Maastrich Treaty (1991). More important, though, was the Soviet Union's withdrawal from enforced hegemony in the east, which dramatically reinforced the break-up of Eastern Europe. The countries were free to leave the bloc to the extent that they were welcome into 'Europe'. There is undoubtedly a European regionalism 'from below', even if assessments as to its strength and future significance vary, particularly after 'the Maastricht hangover' and the subsequent demobilization of Europeanness up to the failed Amsterdam summit in 1997. Against this it must be said that the Helsinki summit in late 1999 provided a welcome breakthrough on a number of issues, particularly those connected with security. Integration and disintegration seem to go together, creating the 'European paradox' (Hettne 1997b).

As far as the global level is concerned, it can nevertheless be assumed that hegemonic decline and multipolarity in the post-Cold War period will further emphasize the development of a more autonomous and homogeneous Greater Europe, a process often referred to as the 'Europeanization' of Europe. The essential meaning of this concept is increasing economic and political homogeneity and the elimination of extremes, for instance fascism and communism. Europe is nevertheless compatible with a high degree of pluralism. Pluralism within a democratic framework may even constitute the region's very meaning.

Economic Policies

The economic regionalization of Europe from the intensification of the internal market project in the mid-1980s and onwards (the '1992' project) has been fully consistent with economic globalization; indeed, both processes have been founded on the same neoliberal paradigm. So far European integration has promoted globalization rather than responding to it (Ross 1998). The economic convergences contributing to increasing regionness happened in a context of liberalization, deregulation and orthodox anti-inflationary policies which were built into the constitutional future of Europe, as spelled out in the Maastricht Treaty. In subsequent years the EMU became the main route, and what the Treaty had to say about other political areas was soon forgotten. The Amsterdam summit confirmed this priority, finally realized in January 1999 with the Euro in place and eleven of the members constituting a single currency zone. The convergence criteria of the EMU illustrate a process of regionalization directed from above and in accordance with a strict schedule, occasionally and selectively generous in its application. Obviously it is hard to distinguish the politics from the economics of monetary integration.

The process of economic homogenization, so far associated with globalization, has led to a state of liberal hegemony in Europe. Democracy and the market (but increasingly also protection against the market) will therefore provide the basis for future integration. The homogenization of the political framework in Europe is, and will be, expressed in the enlargement of the EU, unless the 15 present members take an exclusivist attitude to the rest of Europe, which would be an untenable position as it would imply different degrees of European citizenship.

The '1992 project', a vision rooted in the internationalized segment of European capital, had a mobilizing impact which made the EU magnetic. Attitudes among the present 15 members on the question of whether to deepen or enlarge the Union are, however, very mixed, while an increasing number of countries are queuing up. As the new millennium opens, a Union of 25 members is in sight. Beyond that, the EU will more or less coincide with Europe as a whole, becoming the definition of the region. As specified in the Copenhagen summit (June 1993), conditions for membership include: stable democracy, the rule of law, a market economy, and acceptable minority rights (*Economist*, 26 June 1993).

The transformation going on in the post-communist countries can be interpreted as forming part of the general homogenization process, the Europeanization of Europe. If we take the ex-communist countries in Eastern Europe as our main case in point, we can identify at least three important aspects of the transformation: the creation of a more pluralist political system, the retreat of the state from the economy and the deeper integration of the country in question in the world economy. This package is usually seen as the credibility test of the fledgling market democracies in the east, but the three dimensions are not unproblematic or free from internal contradictions.

Regime Convergence

Homogenization here implies the reduction of differences within a political space, in this case an emerging region. The recent process of homogenization in Europe has gone through three phases: in the South, the disappearance of fascist regimes in the mid-1970s; in the West, the self-assertion of the Atlantic partners in Europe in the early 1980s; and in the East, the fall of the communist regimes in the late 1980s. Regime convergence must be distinguished from fluctuating political trends, which may be more or less coordinated (with time, rather more than less).

Fascism and communism (some countries have tried both) can be seen as nationalist 'catching up' ideologies in a historical context of Western technological superiority over Eastern and Southern Europe. The elimination of the Mediterranean dictatorships removed some anomalies from the European scene and put the continent on the road towards political homogeneity, a basic precondition for substantial economic integration. As far as Eastern Europe is concerned, the system simply had exhausted its potential, not least as a model of development. Political homogenization also implies an increased similarity as far as economic and even social policies are concerned. With the introduction of the Euro from January 1999, the course toward economic union and a common financial structure is now firmly set.

In the early 1980s the great peace demonstrations in Northern Europe had undermined the Atlantic bridge, and in the late 1980s there were further signs of a more fundamental European autonomy *vis-à-vis* the US. The Gulf War and after that the Yugoslavian civil war temporarily reversed this tendency of eroding US influence, but in 1999 the Helsinki summit removed any doubts about the new Europe's intention to deal with its own crises, even if legitimate doubts remain about its capacity to do so.

Thus, the EU increasingly appears to act as a single actor in world politics, albeit gradually and not without birth-pangs. The EU is outgrowing the original integrative framework and this makes it necessarily more concerned with 'domestic' issues. There are actors which want to make Europe a global power, but these forces are countered by other interests and movements favouring a non-hegemonic world system. There are thus several 'Europes' – or social projects in Europe – and, consequently, several possible future scenarios, regarding both internal developments and external policies.

There is also a trend towards heterogeneity in Europe, because of the new 'springtime of nations' and the wave of nationalist separatism. This disintegrative process may in fact be seen as forming part of the Europeanization process, since it implies a denial of certain identities (Soviet, British, Spanish) without necessarily contradicting an identity with Europe.

Post-Maastricht Europe has lost speed, as far as purposeful regional integration is concerned. At the same time various problems, which need to be managed jointly, continue to accumulate: security, environment, refugee migration and economic recession. The fundamental problem is that the EU institutions originally were designed in a different age and with a different purpose – in a context of Cold War and a transatlantic alliance, and to create a coherent and homogeneous capitalist core out of the competing great powers of Europe. Now the Cold War is over and thereby its unifying force. Furthermore, the specific alliance within Europe which gave such a solid base for the integration process, the French–German axis, is loosening. Instead there will be changing alliances on specific issues, further sharpening the unpredictability of the integration process in Europe.

The increasing gap between growing challenges and insufficient capabilities means repeated crises for planned integration, but not necessarily therefore the end of Europeanization. Regionalization is, furthermore, not necessarily planned. However, the processes of integration and disintegration will go on, and one or the other will predominate at any particular point in time.

Security Convergence

In modern times, Europe became fragmented, mainly through the emergence of a large number of nation-states. Peace in the established (Westphalian) interstate system was maintained through – or, rather, was the result of – a balance-of-power mechanism, which functioned reasonably well throughout the nineteenth century. Before that 'long peace' a balance was created only through a long period of wars. This balance was disturbed towards the end of the nineteenth century when Great Britain's role as the workshop of the world (which from the point of view of the other states constituted a modernization imperative) was challenged by countries trying to 'catch up', for instance France and Germany.

The long peace broke down and, after two great wars of hegemonic succession, was replaced with the Cold War order. The two post-war military blocs, albeit with a group of neutrals in between, manifestly expressed Europe's political subordination to the superpowers. The 'regional integration' was imposed from above and from outside. It was an era of hegemonic regionalism.

From the viewpoint of economic organization, the security imperative imposed a more or less corresponding cleavage pattern. Since economics is commonly seen as belonging to the area of 'low politics', there tends to be more change and flexibility in the economic field. In periods of detente, it became evident that economic contacts tended to follow a logic of their own. In periods of high tension, economic relations have had to adapt to the political imperatives built into the security arrangement.

The first economic regional institutions in post-war Western Europe were the European Coal and Steel Community (ECSC) (1951) and the European Community (EC) (1957). Behind the European Free Trade Association (EFTA) (1959) there was first of all the traditional British national interest of avoiding involvement in any supranational European scheme, and, second, diverse national security interests of minor states expressed in different forms of neutrality.

In the East the context for regionalization was completely different. In the case of the Council for Mutual Economic Assistance (CMEA) (1949) the national interests involved seem to have been 'the less integration, the better'. In fact, most cooperation within the bloc was simply bilateral and the CMEA was a hindrance rather than an instrument of regional integration. A more relaxed security situation signalled its dissolution. Much the same can be said of EFTA, which, as neutrality disappeared from the security agenda, gradually became a 'waiting room' for the EU membership candidates. All this underlines the predominance of the security factor.

Thus, during the Cold War, the overall pattern of integration in Europe, whatever the underlying rationale of the process, was fundamentally shaped by the security imperative. It was essentially political – and far from the ideal world of Adam Smith, where the size of the market determines the degree of economic efficiency. In the emerging security order, beyond the Cold War, the pattern of relations will be shaped by a European civil society for which not even the EU is an adequate organization. Security, however, is still to be the main concern. The difference is that the security threats will be seen as increasingly internal, integration and disintegration being two sides of the same coin.

This paradox explains much of the current turbulence in Europe. At the same time as 15 countries are building a single market, and at least as many are on the waiting list, there are several civil wars at the borders of Europe and one recently concluded within Europe. One state has split up peacefully and further divisions are possible in a number of states, and not only in the East. Militant separatist movements can be found in half a dozen countries. Almost everywhere nationalism is rampant, a type of nationalism redolent of 'pre-war times' in the past.

To make sense of this it is necessary to realize that the benefits of integration are unevenly distributed along new types of class lines, making a pattern in which a transnational class can take advantage of structural changes associated with the process of integration, whereas classes rooted in national and local economies conceive the continent-wide market more as a threat. The protection of these interests has become institutionalized in the nation-state, which for a long time has been the guarantor of security and stability in Europe.

There is already a certain competition between existing institutions regarding their respective roles in the emerging security order. This political creation will take place in the context of crisis rather than through orderly planning. The Gulf War was one type of such crisis. Another was the breakdown of the Yugoslav federation and the subsequent Bosnia and Kosovo wars. A third was the disintegration of the Soviet internal empire. Thus, due to the element of surprise and the pressing time factor, the actual organizational solutions may be suboptimal.

It is in this perspective that the recent vitalization of the North Atlantic Treaty Organization (NATO) should be seen. In the longer run NATO will be fundamentally transformed, and the EU will sooner or later take upon itself a stronger political and military role, possibly as the European, increasingly more independent leg of NATO. The internal divisions surfacing in connection with the Gulf War revealed the problems involved in creating a new security order for Europe, but also the need for a common European political (and consequently military) front. However, security orders are not really created on the negotiating table, they emerge from responses to real challenges (of which there have been quite a few in Europe), and therefore they cannot be predicted.

European Conflict Structures

We now turn to the crucial issue of regional conflict resolution. Europe has always been a battlefield, and the question arises whether the process of Europeanization has also led to an increased capacity for conflict resolution at the regional level. Will Europe slide back into its ugly tradition of wars, as indicated by the civil wars in former Yugoslavia, or will she be transformed into a security community?

Manifest and latent conflict structures are of different types:

- Security crises of the more or less classical type have not disappeared. There are still great power rivalries in Europe. The axis between France and Germany seems to have become less reliable, and in the East, Germany and Russia will face each other again. Great Britain has not abandoned the Atlantic project.

- There is also the 'grass fire' type of conflict in the Balkans, linking Bosnia to Kosovo and Macedonia, and further to Greece and Turkey. This is characteristic of primitive security complexes.

- A third area of conflict is the intrastate arena where we can make a distinction between microregionalism, ethnonationalism, and low-intensity civil wars.

The third area of conflict deserves further comment. *Microregionalism* is related to macroregionalism in the way that the larger regionalization process creates possibilities for smaller economically dynamic regions to get direct access to the larger system, bypassing the nation-state. Within each state there will be winners and losers from regionalization, and the state is less and less likely to be able to control the situation. Multiethnic states with little integration between their various parts will show a particular vulnerability to microregionalism. Microregionalism is frequently proactive, given the emerging economic possibilities for subnational regions to reach macroregional and global markets and networks in a more direct way. Microregions thus often link up economically with macroregions, disregarding the national centres; therefore, macroregionalism and microregionalism form part of the same larger process. The rationality behind the process is typically post-Westphalian, although in many cases it may lead to Westphalian responses from the challenged state. Such conflicts rarely result in violence, however.

Ethnonationalism is an expression among subnational groups of the search for new political identities and claims for increased autonomy or even separation, as the role of nation-states erodes. Ethnonational movements question the legitimacy of established nation-states in a fundamental way: the creation of a new state is seen as a solution to current problems for the aspiring nation. It is thus basically a Westphalian and reactive phenomenon, and normally involves violence.

The distinction between microregionalism and ethnonationalism is not always clear. The former Czechoslovakian federation broke up when the Czech part seized on the opportunity for a quick divorce in order to make the transition and join the EU. The disintegration of the Yugoslavian federation was partly caused by Croatia's and Slovenia's drive towards the West. Belgium is in the risk zone. Catalonia in Spain and Scotland in Great Britain are bypassing Madrid and London, not to speak of a number of less dramatic cases of disloyalty of sub-national regions to previous national rulers.

The third type of intrastate conflict, also often related to crises of identity, is the non-territorial law-and-order problems associated with anti-state or anti-society subgroup formation, what Enzensberger has called 'low-intensity civil wars' (Enzensberger 1994). This is the organized violence of social deprivation, exclusion and frustration. The types of groups covered by this concept are many: neo-nazi skinheads, motorbike gangs and white militia. Many of these groups are extreme rightists, but also former revolutionaries. A case in point is the Basque Euskedi Ta Askatasuna (ETA). These latter conflicts, to elaborate further on the terminology introduced above, have a pre-Westphalian (warlord/mafia) quality: the 'state' regresses to primitive structures, such as providers of protection against immediate payment (Tilly 1985). Violence has become second nature to these groups, which is one of the reasons why they cannot become reabsorbed into organized society. The importance of the regional dimension here lies in the need for supranational coordination of police activities against these forms of crimes.

The Balkan Crisis: Multiple Conflicts

A region in which most of the above-mentioned conflicts can be found is the Balkans, geographically known as Southeastern Europe. It is a subregion which in many respects forms part of Europe, but in others constitutes non-Europe, which to some extent explains the ambivalent attitude of organized Europe. 'Balkaniza-tion' is often understood as the opposite of regionalization as here defined. The connotations are a senseless and seemingly uncontrollable fragmentation, as well as brutal forms of violent identity politics and local particularism. To discuss the prospects of regional cooperation in this region may therefore sound paradoxical.

However, the Balkan crisis, triggered by the dissolution of Yugoslavia, immediately underlined the power vacuum in a Europe still searching for a viable security order. The ethnic mosaic in this region is enormous. The major conflict is between the Serbs and the Croats who happened to live in areas claimed by the state of 'the

Other'. The Slovenians, geopolitically in a safer position than the Croats, in a rather homogeneous (ethnically 'clean') area, and further away from Serbia and closer to Italy and Austria, were the first to withdraw. Other groups claiming their independence from a Serbianized Yugoslavia were the Albanians of Kosovo (as well as those living in Macedonia and Montenegro), and the Macedonians who, apart from being the dominant community in Macedonia, are minorities in Bulgaria and Greece. The so-called 'Macedonian question' illustrates how closely related the Balkan conflicts are with history and the interpretation of history. The fledgling nation is surrounded by neighbours equally eager to cut it into pieces.

Without doubt, successful regional conflict resolution is the ultimate test for an autonomous regional security system. Bosnia provided the first test in Europe, and few observers would consider this an unqualified success. The hasty steps taken at Maastricht have a lot to do with the Bosnian crisis. It was feared that an uncontrolled and violent dissolution of the Yugoslavia federation would have far-reaching consequences for the whole of the Balkans, the most turbulent of the European subregions.

Europe was unprepared for such a challenge, as was again seen in the case of Kosovo. It was never evident which of the security organizations existing in Europe was to take charge. The EU troika of foreign ministers, rather than NATO or the Conference on Security and Cooperation in Europe (CSCE), first took the initiative, which was consistent with the status of an emerging new Europe. The need to intervene was due to the 'grass fire' risk, but increasingly also to massive violations of human rights. The intervention process did not proceed without differences between participating countries, however. Austria and Germany were more understanding toward the secessionist republics, whereas other countries, among them France, were more anxious to retain the Yugoslavia federation. Great Britain was very hesitant to intervene. Opinions also differed with regard to a possible military intervention, if and when mediation failed. This is the reason why the EU (at the time still an economic organization) was and is inefficient. The regional approach thus did not succeed. Kosovo, unfortunately, repeated the mistakes of Bosnia.

The Balkans is a 'non-region', or a region which can be defined only negatively as an explosive regional security complex. There is no regional cooperation, and there has hardly ever been any, since it always has been divided between competing empires and nation-states. 'Balkanization', as was noted above, has entered the political vocabulary as another word for disintegration. But then, the concept 'Balkanization' is typically applied to other regions as a warning, a negative example. Applied to the Balkans itself, 'Balkanization' should mean increased regionness, just as we speak of the Europeanization of Europe. But could there be any 'Balkanization' of the Balkans in that positive sense of the word, basing itself on whatever real region exists, beyond the overt conflicts?

What forms could a regionalization take? There are, if we exclude the cata-strophic options of isolation and further disintegration or the establishment of external rule, three future routes:

1 Formal cooperation by governments anxious to increase the level of regionness (positive Balkanization).

2 Informal cooperation, made possible by increasing homogeneity through con-vergences in terms of partly externally imposed political regimes, economic policies and security arrangements.

3 Passive integration through participation in European structures.

Cooperation between governments will take place on a bilateral basis, of course, and, as has happened in other regions, bilateralism may turn into trilateral-ism and regionalism. More likely, there will be hostile alliances, perhaps along religious or other historical lines, hindering overall regional integration in the sub-region. Passive integration is not an ideal form, of course, since the conditions will be decided and imposed entirely by external actors. It will be almost like a colonial situation, or, to put it less bluntly, the situation of a protectorate.

This leaves informal cooperation through more or less spontaneous conver-gences in various policy areas as the most viable road. Convergence in these policy areas will not, of course, be wholly spontaneous. It will depend on a number of externally imposed conditionalities associated with participation in European structures: democracy, human rights, clean government, market economy, and of course non-aggression. The prospect of full-scale integration is bleak and will remain so for a long time, particularly for Yugoslavia. On the other hand, no permanent borders and boundaries must be allowed to establish themselves between 'Europe' and 'non-Europe' in the Balkans. The urge to be part of Europe seems to be a common goal for all Balkan countries, and this seems to be the first time that all the countries in the subregion are sharing the same goal. To secure that goal certain standards must be met, and here we find the convergences that consti-tute Balkan regionalization, positive Balkanization, today.

Future Prospects

The current world order was to a large extent shaped by worldwide reactions against the old Europe-dominated world. The project of re-establishing a hege-monic world order centred on Europe may therefore be seen as a nostalgic dream inherent in the Europa paradigm. It is essential that this particular dimension of the paradigm is transcended and replaced with a vision of pluralism and intercul-tural dialogue. The new Europa paradigm should, ideally, be one of empathetic participation in symmetrical interregional relations, for which role Europe's colonial experience, ugly as it may be, has uniquely qualified her. A return to the old tradition of dominance would spell disaster.

The Idea of Europe

The question 'what is Europe?' can only be answered by the political process of self-recognition. It is a social construct. The content of 'European' can be defined normatively by a strong role for civil society, reflected in various institutionalized forms such as parliamentary decision making, and a democratic culture stressing above all individualism and human rights inherent in the individual human being. Western societies are described as unsafe and anarchic by critics from other civilizations. This is not without foundation. Western freedom has become 'messy', and the post-communist condition is perhaps the best proof. In positive terms and from a Western perspective, however, this is a 'de-easternization' of former Eastern Europe – or, as spokesmen for civil society in those countries called it, 'a return to Europe'.

The wars in Yugoslavia were wars against European values as here defined, even if Europe herself did little to defend them. It is therefore important that the new Europe is defined in terms of civil society rather than national citizenship, and that the progressive conception of citizenship as embodying rights and obligations is delinked from ethnic nationalism. The idea of the new Europe must be pluralist, anti-racist and associated with a post-national citizenship (Delanty 1995). It must also be social, even if the recent region building has been based on a neoliberal paradigm. The social market concept is increasingly important in the formation of a new world order, in which there will be a competition between different kinds of capitalism. 'Sustainable capitalism' has to be both ecological and social, and here, too, Europe could show the way.

However, ideas come in waves. The pioneers dreamed about a security community, the implementers could only think of the internal market, but current political changes suggest a new wave of (albeit modest) regulation in the interest of social welfare, security and political stability. The strong resistance to that kind of European ideal confirms that, more than any other region in the making, there exists in Europe an 'imagined' or 'invented' European society. Otherwise there would have been no need for Euroscepticism. However, the degree of imagination and social construction, as contradistinguished from essentialism and primordialism, is much more evident than in the case of national and ethnical identities.

Hegemonic Europe?

In both political and cultural terms Europe will remain heterogeneous. Centralism on a continental level is compatible with neither the Westphalian spirit nor the European civil society tradition. Therefore the idea of a unified Europe ruled from Brussels is as unrealistic as ever. In the new European landscape several subregions, which transcend the old Cold War division, are emerging. Some of them reflect very old historical formations: the Swedish Baltic Empire; the Habsburg Empire; and the group of Balkan countries once under the Ottoman Empire.

One interpretation of this new trend is that we witness a return to the classic balance-of-power politics in a new subregional form, where sources of power are more economic than military. The objective need for it is obviously the emergence of unified Germany as the regional political and economic power, also representing a centralist tradition. This threat of regional hegemonism is an evident factor behind the attempts to form subregional groupings. The perspective of German regional hegemony is particularly obvious in Central Europe, 'Mitteleuropa' from the German point of view. Eighty per cent of former Czechoslovakia's foreign investment came from Germany; 2.5 million Sudeten Germans want their property in Bohemia back. The division of Czechoslovakia makes it more easily absorbable.

On the other hand, the new Germany, with its strong federal traditions, may itself form part of various subregional formations through the 16 *Länder*. Hamburg/Bremen, for instance, cultivates a 'Hanseatic' project to revive the old medieval trading system in Northern Europe and give it a modern shape. The purpose is evidently to provide a challenge to the southern German growth pole centred on Munich, which, together with Milan and Barcelona, is one corner of Southern Europe's strong economic triangle. At the same time Germany will be 'embedded' in Greater Europe. Germany will become European, rather than Europe becoming German.

The Baltic countries are swiftly building up economic relations with the Nordic countries. At the same time they will provide a gateway for trade with the republics of the former Soviet Union, and with Russia in particular, provided that the nationalistic urge to turn away completely from the east can be modified. Since Europe is an idea rather than a territory, there should be no clear-cut borders and boundaries. Europe has become a 'supranational community of cultures, subcultures and transcultures inserted differently into radically different political and cultural traditions (Modood and Werbner 1997: vii). The 'Europe of Nations' belongs to history and, despite resurgent nostalgia, it can never come back, since even the nations are becoming increasingly heterogeneous. The optimal political structure to accommodate diversity is a post-Westphalian region-state, a pluralist state more similar to a loose empire than the culturally standardized nation-state of Westphalia.

Future Patterns of Conflict

Globalization basically implies the growth of a functional world market, increasingly penetrating and dominating the so-called 'national' economies, which in the process are bound to lose much of their 'nationness'. Economy is being delinked from both culture and politics, both of which are becoming intrinsically mixed in 'the politics of identity'. The states are becoming the spokesmen of global economic forces, rather than protecting their own populations and their cultures against these demanding and unexplainable changes. This implies that the state is becoming alienated from civil society, defined as inclusive institutions that facilitate a societal dialogue over various social and cultural borders, and, furthermore, that identities and loyalties are transferred from civil society to primary groups, competing with each other for territorial control, resources and security. This is a morbid replay of the nineteenth-century Westphalian logic. The contradictions involved may end up in a collapse of organized society.

To what extent do the Bosnian and Kosovan conflicts represent a more violent future for Europe? There are, as Mary Kaldor (1999) points out, 'old' and 'new' wars. The 'new' are related to identity politics and the social cleavages associated with globalization. They correspond to the internal conflicts that were above termed ethnonationalism, low-intensity civil wars, and the new terrorism. The processes associated with microregionalism and internal exile are less violent but nevertheless conflict-generating.

Europe as a political structure will have to grow, and as it grows it will necessarily turn further inwards. New levels of economic and political action will appear: microregions, transnational growth zones, and ethnonationalism. The latter will possibly be less destructive in the new 'organized' Europe. Nationalist movements creating tensions in the context of present state structures will partly achieve their purpose in a Europe without clear-cut borders: the Hungarians, the Tyroleans, the Basques, the Macedonians and other minorities living in several states, but not permitted to create a nation-state of their own. Regionalism erodes the position of the states, but subregionalism may cut across the states. The political landscape of Europe is being transformed fundamentally. Sooner rather than later another expansion of the EU will define 'Europe', change the character of the community, and force a restructuring of institutions. This will be the end of the old European Community and the start of a new project: perhaps the United States of Europe? Or perhaps a sliding back to the 'Europe of the Nations'?

To many people 'more Europe' is still the answer. But what is the question? The single market is a fact, and the EMU is now the privileged project. A joint defence identity no longer appears to be a distant dream. The second pillar (interior affairs) is slowly beginning to be erected. The process of regional integration goes on but at the same time is slowing down, and neonationalism is rising.

As has been the case before, deeper regional integration will come only because it becomes necessary, and this is also the case with enlargement. There can be no rational choice between the two, as is often assumed. Both processes are linked to various kinds of political crises, from social crises of exclusion to security crises of sedition and civil wars, crises that have to be managed by transnational cooperation – the more institutionalized the better.

3 Regionalization in the Middle East?

MARIANNE LAANATZA,
HELENA LINDHOLM SCHULZ
AND MICHAEL SCHULZ

[T]he Middle East remains a peculiar exception to the overall trend of regionalism. Among various regions, the Middle East is not only the least integrated into the world economy but is also characterized by the lowest degree of regional economic cooperation. (Çarkoglu *et al*. 1998: 31)

Although the Middle East is often regarded as a 'peculiar exception' to global trends and norms when it comes to regionalization, discussions on prospects for a process of increased regional cooperation in the Middle East flourished in the 1990s (Nonneman 1992; Guazzone 1997; Roberson 1998; Çarkoglu *et al*. 1998). These discussions are to a large extent connected to the peace process, initiated with much jubilation at the Madrid conference in October 1991. The real turning point in Arab–Israeli relations, however, was the agreement between Israelis and Palestinians in the Declaration of Principles of September 1993. Since then a troubled process of building confidence has ensued.

This chapter deals with previous as well as contemporary attempts to build regional cooperation in the Middle East.[1] We will examine these attempts through a division between ideologically induced and more practical motivations for regional cooperation, between macroregional and subregional cooperation schemes, and between cooperation in the sphere of economy/development, on the one hand, and security/peace on the other. It is important to underline from the outset that what is at stake is 'regional cooperation' rather than 'regionalization', as that term is defined throughout this book. However, increased regional cooperation might serve as a first step in a more profound process of regionalization.

Arabism versus Oil as Integrating Factors

Until the 1990s, most attempts at regional cooperation were produced on the basis of ideological pan-Arabism,[2] rather than pragmatic politico-economic interest or visions of trade as peace-promoting.

Ideologically Inspired Regional Cooperation: the Role of Pan-Arabism

The very ideological foundation of pan-Arabism is to merge the 'artificially divided' Arab states, seen as sharing a common Arab identity based on the Arabic language. The first concrete organization aiming at realizing the ideas of Arab nationalism was the Arab League, founded in Alexandria in 1945. The ultimate goal of the Arab League was to liberate Palestine. The contradictions between state building in the postwar era and regional nationalism in the form of Arabism were soon felt, however. Serious divisions emerged between the Arab states on what kind of unitary state would be the goal (Kerr 1967). The most concrete confederate state to be established was the United Arab Republic, consisting of Egypt and Syria, declared in 1958 and brought to an abrupt end in 1961.

Under the umbrella of the Arab League, several institutions and organizations have been formed and several cooperation agreements have been signed. In the economic sphere, the Arab League decided in the mid-1960s to create an Arab Common Market. Little progress has been made in this regard, however (Shtayyeh 1998). A collective security pact was signed in the 1950s, aiming at establishing a mutual defence system and common security. Jordan and Iraq, however, refused to sign. In 1955 Iraq entered the Western-oriented Baghdad Pact.

Despite the multitude of regional organizations, most of the cooperation within the Arab League has taken the form of bilateral or multilateral cooperation schemes. The Arab League has thus in reality been based firmly on the state system and interstate relations rather than on pan-Arab ideology (Salamé 1988; Nonneman 1992b: 37). It might be argued, however, that the Arab region at this time exhibited a form of regional consciousness. Many times, at least in the Israeli–Arab conflicts, the League behaved as one actor. Under the surface of pan-Arabism, however, there was always deep-rooted mistrust and a serious ideological polarization between the so-called progressive leadership in the Arab republics and the conservative Arab monarchies. The 1970s saw not progress along the lines of pan-Arabism, nor the formation of a regionally integrated entity, but the gradual consolidation of the state system (Luciani 1990; Owen 1992). State interests and state nationalism took a *de facto* lead over pan-Arabism, although Arabism continued to play an ideological role. One contributing factor was the decline of pan-Arabism as a source of political identity in the aftermath of the 1967 war and the death of Egypt's President, Jamal Abdel Nasser, in 1970.

Economic Processes and Pragmatic Integration

As '*Thawra* (Revolution) was retreating in the face of [the] rising *Tharwa* (Wealth) – of the oil states' (Korany 1997: 147), it was shown that economic processes were perhaps more favourable to regional cooperation and integration than ideological visions.

When it comes to economic exchange, however, intraregional trade is extremely low, which is one important factor that has hindered deeper integration. The bulk of Arab trade is with the European Union. From the point of view of global trade, the Middle East is, despite the oil factor, a rather marginal region. The extent of Middle Eastern trade is 4 per cent of the total world trade (Çarkoglu *et al*. 1998: 86). In 1995, Arab exports of commodities to other Arab countries were a mere 4.2 per cent and intra-Arab imports stood at 5.9 per cent (*MEED*, 4 July 1997). The main exceptions to this pattern are Jordan, Lebanon, Syria, Oman and Bahrain, whose intra-Arab trade is larger (Çarkoglu *et al*. 1998: 82). What is more, the intra-Arab trade pattern largely consists of agriculture and raw materials, implying a lack of complementarity. Trade has thus not served as an integrating factor.

The oil boom established one form of *de facto* economic integration and more pragmatic relationships between the Arab states (Owen 1992; Richards and Waterbury 1996). The Organization of Oil Producing and Exporting Countries (OPEC), and Saudi Arabia especially, played a considerable role through the massive transfer of resources to the poorer Arab states. 'Capital flows have been the major integrating factor in the Middle East' (Çarkoglu *et al*. 1998; Padoan 1997: 192; Fischer 1993). At the same time, however, international aid flows have exceeded intra-Arab aid flows by far. In addition, intra-Arab capital flows are declining and are likely to continue doing so, partly due (until the Spring of 1999) to the more than ten-year long recession of the oil economies (Fischer 1993: 438).

Labour flows have been considerable. Labour migration has implied another form of integration, demonstrating how people and population flows need to be taken into account when assessing integration prospects (Fischer 1993; Choucri, 1997: 96; Çarkoglu *et al*. 1998). Egypt, Jordan, then North Yemen and the Palestinians sent labour *en masse* to the smaller oil states. For the sending countries, remittances were an extremely important source of foreign exchange until the Gulf War in the early 1990s. For receiving countries, the import of labour was crucial in the modernization process resulting from the oil boom.

This pattern has been changing. The recession of the oil economies after the 1980s led to a reduction of the number of Arab guestworkers in favour of Asian labour. This trend was reinforced when the Gulf States expelled Palestinian, Jordanian and Yemenite guestworkers as a punishment for the positions taken by the Palestine Liberation Organization (PLO) and the other two countries in the

Gulf War. Thus, migration patterns are to an increasing extent globalized rather than regional, and one important prerequisite for regional integration appears to have reached a limit.

The persistence of state-led economic structures and protectionism is often cited as a factor which has hindered regional cooperation (Fischer 1993: 431 ff.; Çarkoglu *et al*. 1998). In addition, the economic performance of the region as a whole has been rather dim during the last decades and since the oil boom reached its peak at the end of the 1980s. Average annual growth over the last decade is largely negative. However, this crisis has resulted in a process of economic liberalization (Harik and Sullivan 1992; Abdel-Fadil 1997). Gradually, Arab states have abandoned economic nationalism and import substitution strategies for liberalization and privatization. In several cases, the International Monetary Fund (IMF) is the author of structural adjustment programmes, as for example in the cases of Egypt and Jordan.[3] Arab economies, however, are still heavily protected. In addition, the levels at which Arab countries have undertaken gradual liberalization strategies and integration into the world market vary considerably from country to country. A gradual opening up of economies might nevertheless serve as a factor leading to increased cooperation.

To summarize, most macro-Arab regional schemes have been based on Arab nationalism, which has resulted in little real integration, although bilateral and multilateral cooperation have existed. As far as economic processes are concerned, trade has not acted in favour of regional cooperation/integration. Instead, the oil boom served as one form of regional cooperation/integration, with its resulting massive capital and labour transfers. However, this pattern appears to have reached a limit, while the restructuring of economies might point towards more favourable conditions when it comes to possibilities of economic exchange.

Another form of regional cooperation is that which has emerged in the shape of organizations connected to the subregions of the Arab world, which is the focus of the next section.

Subregional Cooperation in the Arab World: the GCC

The establishment of the Gulf Cooperative Council (GCC) in 1981 could be seen as 'integration as a response to crisis' (Starkey 1996: 145). The Iranian Revolution of 1978–9 served as a catalyst for Bahrain, Kuwait, Oman, Qatar, Saudi Arabia and the United Arab Emirates to form the GCC, which so far has served mainly as a security regime. The Iran–Iraq War of 1980–8 and the Gulf War of 1990–1 have forced the GCC members to continual crisis response.

In one way, the GCC is perhaps the organization which has been most success-ful in formulating a functioning framework for regional cooperation (Nonneman

1992c). This outcome is due to a number of factors. All states are sheikhdoms with politics based on family projects, all have small populations that are difficult to mobilize, and all are based on enormous oil wealth. Also, the GCC countries by and large share an ideological outlook based on a conservative Arab–Islamic foundation combined with a traditional regional identification and loyalties to a large extent directed toward the tribal structure. In addition, the perceptions of common enemies in Iran and Iraq have further fostered a shared identity.

From about 1989 some of the GCC members began to adopt a more conciliatory position *vis-à-vis* Iran. This rapprochement has continued since the Gulf War; it took a historic turn with the visit of Iran's President Khatami to Saudi Arabia in May 1999. The United Arab Emirates have also called for a reconciliation with Iraq – another area of contention in the GCC. There is a split within the Council over the sanctions against Iraq, and US bombing raids against Iraq in the Autumn of 1998 met with outright condemnation from Arab countries formerly allied with the US. Nevertheless, the Gulf War has implied increased Gulf links with Europe and the US.

Despite common experiences and shared concerns, 'common security' has failed to materialize into joint defence (Nonneman 1992c: 57; Joffé 1998: 54). Instead, the Gulf region is still heavily dependent on international partners for its security, a condition augmented by the Gulf War. The failure of the Gulf Plus Two organization[4] (the Gulf States plus Egypt and Syria), formed after the war, further pushed the Gulf States towards the West for military protection. The US now has a permanent station in the Gulf. US weapons sales to the Gulf have also reinforced US economic interests in the region (Merr 1998: 94). Intra-Gulf disputes over the preferred security regime (to continue to depend on the US or to opt for regional security through a pact with Iran) have added to regional tensions.

Although continued integration in the Gulf States is made more difficult by internal conflicts (Schofield 1992), such as the territorial dispute between Bahrain and Qatar over islands, reefs and territorial waters, the GCC has been able to serve as a forum for handling disputes and crisis.

Despite the emphasis on security, one of the aims of the GCC is to create a free trade area. One of the challenges for the GCC is the relationship to the European Union, since a large part of GCC exports is made up of oil and petrochemical products to the Union. The EU represents about 25 per cent of Gulf trade. Japan is also a major trading partner, representing 18 per cent of total Gulf trade (Aliboni 1997: 218; Salamé 1998: 36). In late 1997, the GCC decided to form a tariffs union.

The GCC countries suffered a slump in their economies as a result of the declining oil prices and to various degrees initiated programmes to save public spending. The spring of 1999, however, witnessed a 60 per cent increase in the oil price (*MEED*, 7 May 1999), giving rise to new optimism in the oil economies.

Subregional Cooperation and the Arab Maghreb Union

The Arab Maghreb Union (AMU) was established in 1989 with the aim of creating a customs union along the same lines as the (then) European Community. The West Sahara conflict was left outside the framework and member states were to respect each other's territorial integrity (Zartman 1997: 216). The AMU was meant to be an area with open borders for free movement of goods, services, capital and persons, as well as cultural cooperation. The AMU attempts to stimulate trade between the member states, to increase non-traditional exports and to reduce imports. All AMU members – Algeria, Libya, Mauritania, Morocco and Tunisia – trade with Western Europe, which absorbs about 65 per cent of their trade (Aliboni 1997: 218). Intra-Maghreb trade in 1990 was 2.3 per cent (Abdel-Fadil 1997: 132). The AMU area, meanwhile, is worth about 1.5 per cent of the total trade of the EU (Aliboni 1997: 218).

In 1994, Egypt joined the AMU. This Egyptian move is interesting and might indicate a reorientation of Egypt's regional and foreign policy, related to its declining role as mediator and broker in the Middle East (Joffé 1998: 49). The North African states, including Egypt, are members of Arab, Islamic as well as African regional organizations.[5]

Difficulties in the project have concerned controversies over the Western Sahara (Zartman 1997: 216–17) as well as differences in economic structure between the countries. Whereas Morocco and Tunisia have by and large successfully completed their IMF-sponsored structural adjustment programmes, Algeria still declines an IMF programme. Morocco and Tunisia have also diversified their production structures.

AMU relations with the EU are today tightly linked to the Euro-Mediterranean Partnership Initiative (see below). There are also Southern European anxieties concerning competition with North African agricultural products on the European market (Salamé 1998: 38). Morocco and Tunisia have already suffered from the full integration of Spain and Portugal into the EU, which has meant a reduction of agricultural exports from Morocco and Tunisia to the EU (Joffé 1998: 64; Merr 1998: 95). Relations with Europe also include the migration from the North African states to Europe. This is one of the reasons for the scepticism towards cooperation with the AMU in some European countries. In terms of security, there is a risk that the interests of North African countries will be subsumed under European security interests (Joffé 1992: 210).

To summarize, all kinds of integration schemes in the Arab world have remained low-level. In terms of regional organization, little has been achieved. Most projects have not reached beyond bilateral or multilateral cooperation. Fundamental political conflicts and colliding power ambitions have impeded Arab regionalization, as has heavy state control over economies. Also, the ideological tensions between radicalist one-party regimes and conservative monarchies, as well as disputes related to the unequal distribution of resources, have served as constraints against deeper forms of integration (Aarts 1997: 10).

Mashreq and the Palestinian–Israeli Conflict

The core of Middle Eastern politics is usually seen as the Arab–Israeli and the Palestinian–Israeli conflicts, resulting in five wars of different scales. Those conflicts have defined the Mashreq subregion since the end of the Ottoman Empire, and of course their result is that mutual hostility has made regional cooperation impossible. The Arab boycott of Israel has hindered any trade between Israel and the Arab states, although exports from the West Bank to Jordan continued on a relatively large scale until 1988, when King Hussein cut administrative ties between the West Bank and Jordan. Israel's trade relations are also directed outside of the region. For Israel, the US and the North American Free Trade Agreement region are important trading partners, while the East Asian economies have also grown in importance (Padoan 1997: 187).

Despite conflicts, wars and disasters, there have also been proposals aiming at greater cooperation, including calls for a confederation to include a Palestinian state and Israel, a Palestinian state and Jordan, or all three entities. A confederation between a future Palestine and Jordan is perhaps a more realistic option than one including Israel and a Palestinian state, although such proposals have been presented. A Jordan–Palestine confederation was most explicitly elaborated in the Amman Accord between Jordan and the PLO in 1985 and is still high on the agenda.

The decline of the Arab–Israeli conflicts is therefore a necessary condition for regional cooperation. As Çarkoglu *et al.* (1998) argue, however, this necessary condition might not be sufficient: too much focus has been placed on state actors and too little on what they call 'Level II-actors', the business sector and civil society. Suspicions at the level of civil society and domestic constraints might be a serious impediment to regional cooperation. Peace agreements between state actors are therefore not enough, and increased focus on civil society and the potential for cross-border activities among populations are necessary ingredients in regional cooperation schemes.

The Peace Process and the 'New Middle East'

During its first years, the peace process gave rise to calls for a 'New Middle East', a region characterized by open borders, economic liberalism and a climate of cooperation. The concrete, but perhaps truistic relations between peace and regional economic cooperation were underlined as discussions and plans increasingly focused on the potential economic benefits of peace and the 'peace dividend', as well as prospects for increased foreign capital investment as a result of a more stable political structure (Fischer, Rodrik and Tuma 1993; Çarkoglu *et al*. 1998).

The different regionalist discourses related to the peace process all include Israel as a partner to the Arab states, as opposed to previous exclusively Arab definitions of the region. Through the Declaration of Principles in 1993 and their mutual recognition, the long-standing refusal by the Arab states to negotiate with Israel was broken. Israel on the other hand had accepted negotiation with the PLO as the representative of the Palestinian people, and hence recognized that they too had national rights. Several of the Arab states gradually began to change their attitudes towards Israel. The first step in that direction was taken with the Camp David Accords of 1978–9. Egypt's and Israel's peace has, however, always been called a 'cold peace'. In addition, the relations between, on the one hand, King Hussein of Jordan and the Israeli leadership, and, on the other, between Israel and King Hassan II of Morocco were always special (Sachar 1996). So far, there is nothing to indicate that the recent death of both kings will seriously alter those relationships.

In the years immediately following the Declaration of Principles, Israel's diplomatic standing in the world increased considerably: relations were opened between Israel and a number of countries such as China and India, and important Muslim countries outside of the Arab world. In the Arab world, too, Israel's position improved substantially. Apart from the peace treaty with Jordan (1994), Israel has established relations with a number of Arab countries, in the form of representative offices in Morocco and Tunisia and contacts with Qatar and Bahrain. The Gulf States have supported the abolition of the secondary and tertiary boycott of Israeli products.

One of the regional projects very much connected to the peace process was born out of the multilateral working groups initiated at the Madrid conference in 1991. In addition to the bilateral negotiations[6] set up under the Madrid formula, five multilateral working groups were set up in which issues of a regional character were discussed: environmental issues, water, arms control, refugees, and regional development (for details see Peters 1996). Participants in the working groups are Egypt, Jordan, Israel, the Palestinians, the Gulf States and the Maghreb countries minus Libya. The US and Russia are co-sponsors of the peace process; the EU and Japan are observers. Syria and Lebanon are invited but have not as yet participated; Syria's position is that there should first be a comprehensive peace, and Lebanon follows the Syrian line.

Linked to this is the US-sponsored Middle East and North Africa (MENA) concept. This project has also given rise to the idea of 'Middle Easternism'. From the perspective of Israelis (and Arabs) advocating this project, the 'New Middle East' represents a vision of a region characterized by mutually beneficial cooperation in order to foster peace and development. Behind this concept lies a firm belief in interdependence theory, as well as the idea of pooling resources in order to achieve economies of scale beyond the nation-state borders. 'Briefly it is the importing of a "Jean Monnet approach" (the founding concept of the European integration process) to the Middle East region to reorient it from an economy of strife to an economy of peace' (Korany 1997: 137).

The MENA project is controversial. In the Arab world, discussions abound over various regional scenarios (Abdel-Fadil 1997; Korany 1997). The heart of the matter is whether Israel will/should become a fully integrated member of the Middle East or not. In Arab critiques, the MENA idea is seen as an US-sponsored project aiming to consolidate Israel's position in the Middle East from an economic point of view. Israel would become part of the Middle East, and that, according to Arab critiques, would grant it a hegemonic position. From this point of view, the peace process represents not integration but rather fragmentation of the Arab world.[7] According to this perspective, normalization of relations should be a result of the peace process and not precede final peace agreements.[8] Apart from the purely political text of this discourse there are also different economic motives and interests. For many Arab parties, the incentive would be to attract foreign capital and investments rather than to promote a free trade area in the Middle East (Abdel-Fadil 1997: 130). Sceptics on the Israeli side argue that there is much less for Israel to benefit from in the regional integration paradigm than conventionally argued. Typically, Israeli sceptics argue that Egyptian–Israeli trade has remained marginal, despite the peace treaty and despite verbal commitments to deeper regional cooperation (Korany 1997: 138). Thus many opposing 'actors perceive each other as either intending to dominate the region or as not having the economic potential to benefit the other side' (Çarkoglu et al. 1998: 128).

Peres's The New Middle East in a way augments such worries since it is ripe with notions of Israel's technological advantage and willingness to share it with its less fortunate Arab neighbours (Peres 1993).

> This scenario, furthermore, projects a perfect division of labour among the regional participants. Israel would become the provider of high technology, research and services for the Middle East, while Palestine and the remainder of the region would provide both cheap labour and capital. (Vandewalle 1994–5: 21–2)

Macroregionalism and Multilateralism

The multilateral working group on economic development is the one that has resulted in the most visible attention. Until the Spring of 1996, the monitoring committee of the working group promoted a great many activities: the Middle East Development Bank, decided upon in practice but yet to be realized; the Middle East–Mediterranean Travel and Tourist Association; and the establishment of transport, energy and other projects. Since 1996 and the gradual deterioration of Israeli–Palestinian relations, the work of the committee has become more difficult (Shtayyeh 1998: 29).

One ingredient of the regime emerging in relation to the multilateral negotiations is the MENAsummit process.[9] This has the purpose of encouraging regional efforts led by the private sector to institutionalize cooperation and integrate Israel into the Middle Eastern region (*ibid.*). The first such conference, in Casablanca in November 1994, was held in an atmosphere of enthusiasm and optimism. Sixty-one countries were represented and 1,114 businessmen from different parts of the globe participated. A joint declaration was produced, acknowledging the links between peace and economics and underlining 'the new partnership between governments and the business community' (Casablanca Declaration, 1994).

The meeting in Casablanca was followed by the Amman summit in October 1995. Here, agreement was reached over the Middle East Development Bank. There were also extended discussions on cooperation in tourism, transport and communications. The EU pledged to make a strong contribution to the funding of regional projects such as the development of the Dead Sea region, the creation of a tourist region north of the Red Sea and the construction of a promenade between El-Arish and Ashkelon.

The third MENA summit in Cairo in November 1996 clearly took place in a different context: increasing political tensions within the region, and in particular the halting Palestinian–Israeli peace process, marked the atmosphere before and during the meeting.[10] Calls for increased Arab–Arab cooperation, not just on government and policy levels, but with the Arab business community taking its own initiatives, were expressed. At the same time, however, Egyptian and Israeli business communities established a joint business council (*Middle East Journal*, 1997: 263).

The fourth regional meeting in Doha in 1997 was a far cry from the jubilant gathering in Casablanca. Israeli politics under Benyamin Netanyahu had revived a climate of animosity and enmity, and most Arab countries decided to stay away from Doha, despite American pressure. In the end, the event was downgraded from a summit to a conference, implying that governments would participate through official representatives rather than ministers. A large number of private companies nevertheless attended the conference.

In addition, as we have seen, economic integration currently exhibits a number of problems apart from political constraints. Most Middle Eastern economies trade primarily with countries outside of the region. Apotential complementarity pattern between Israel and the Arab world would consist of value-added agricultural and capital-intensive light manufacturing products as well as technology from Israel, while the Arab side would concentrate on food products, oil, and labour-intensive manufacturing goods. There is thus a low level of complementarity between the Arab countries (Fischer, Rodrik and Tuma 1993; Çarkoglu *et al.* 1998: 128), and, when Israel is brought into the equation, the differences in technology and economy are so vast that there is a risk that they create structures of dominance rather than mutual benefit.

Political and Security Cooperation

Under the umbrella of multilateralism, some progress has also been made in changing perceptions in terms of security. In 1995, the multilateral working group on arms control decided to establish a regional security centre in Amman. There has also been a change in perceived security threats in the region, most noticeably in the Gulf War, when an Arab–Arab conflict superseded the Arab–Israeli one. However, the years between 1996 and 1999 implied a step back towards more familiar Middle Eastern politics. Up to now, the talks on arms control have not reached the same degree of implementation of cooperative schemes as those on economic development, which is to be seen as no surprise.

The bilateral agreements have underlined the need for macroregional security regimes. The Israeli–Jordanian Peace Treaty acknowledges the necessity of regional cooperation in security-related matters:

> the Parties recognise the achievements of the European Community and European Union in the development of the Conference on Security and Cooperation in Europe (CSCE) and commit themselves to the creation in the Middle East, of a Conference on Security and Cooperation in the Middle East (CSCME). (Article 4. Security, in the Treaty of Peace between the State of Israel and the Hashemite Kingdom of Jordan, 26 October 1994)

Despite the setbacks between 1996 and 2000, such a wording implies a regional change in security perspectives unthinkable only a few years earlier. The Conference on Security and Cooperation in Europe is seen as the model to inspire a similar structure in the Middle East.

Reaction: Revival of Arabism

The impasse of the peace process between 1996 and 2000 has led to a crisis of the embryonic Middle Eastern cooperation. At the Arab League meeting in Cairo in 1997, member states decided to freeze the process of normalization with Israel. At the same time, the primary boycott was reinforced and all multilateral negotiations were suspended (Shtayyeh 1998: 28). This crisis has in turn led to a renewal of the discourse on pan-Arabism, which is now formulated as a counterstructure to the Middle East vision: 'I also believe that so-called Middle Easternism has died. We need to focus on Arab interests' (Essam Rifaat, *al-Ahram Weekly*, 30 October–5 November 1997).

According to this view, it is uncertain if Israel is seriously committed to the peace process. Therefore, Arab integration should be fostered as an alternative to Middle Easternism or the MENA concept.[11] The Arab Economic Unity Council and the Arab League Economic and Social Council have declared the goal of establishing an Arab Common Market within ten years starting from 1998 (Zarrouk 1998: 4). The prime mover in these talks has been Egypt, underlining that country's ambition to play a significant role in different integration schemes (Guazzone 1997: 249). If from what we know of Arab integration in historical perspective there appear to be few prospects for such a regime in the near future, one favourable factor might be the process of economic liberalization occurring in the Arab world.

Europe and the Middle East

Two significant regional cooperation schemes are the Euro-Mediterranean Partnership Initiative[12] and the Barcelona process,[13] created to transform relations between Europe and the Middle East/North Africa and to integrate the Mediterranean countries into a European framework. One of the reasons for the EU initiative was the need to balance its eastward expansion (Joffé 1998: 60). The Barcelona Declaration, signed in 1995, called for the establishment of a common area of peace and stability, and for economic and financial partnership as well as partnership in social, cultural and human affairs. A Euro-Mediterranean free trade area is to be established by the year of 2010,[14] and between 1995 and 1999 US $6 billion is to be injected as EU development aid. Free trade will be implemented through a network of bilateral agreements. Such agreements have been signed between the EU, on the one hand, and Tunisia, Israel, Morocco, Jordan and the PLO on the other. The last-mentioned is an interim agreement in force since July 1997 (Joffé 1998).

Although the visions of the project boil down to economic prosperity, the real consequences may not all be rosy. According to some observers, the consequences of the Euro-Mediterranean free trade concept might in fact imply an elimination of one third of the local companies in the Arab countries concerned, as local industries will suffer from the consequences of competition. Extensive foreign direct investment is needed to counteract such a prospect – and this capital inflow has not yet begun. This scenario has made Egypt reluctant to sign a free trade agreement. The same goes for Lebanon, although its special relationship with Syria is another reason for not signing.

A new conference was held in Malta in April 1997 and another in Stuttgart in April 1999. In Malta, voices were heard from the southern Mediterranean countries that European commitment might not be wholehearted, given EU barriers to agri-cultural imports, immigration restrictions and reluctance to involve itself in the peace process (*MEED*, 11 April 1997). One of the reasons for EU involvement, however, is precisely its interest in keeping migration from the southern Mediter-ranean region at bay. In this sense, the Partnership Initiative is directly contra-dicted by the Schengen Agreements, the Trevi Accords and the Dublin Agreement, severely restricting the free movement of non-EU citizens. In other respects, too (such as terrorism and drugs), the Middle East is frequently seen as a threat from a EU perspective (Salamé 1998: 38).

The Peace Process and Subregionalism: Israel–Palestine–Jordan

The peace process has also highlighted prospects for subregional cooperation through establishing a 'peace quartet', consisting of Israel, Egypt, Jordan and the Palestinians. Those four parties met in Taba in 1995 and decided to promote regional cooperation between them. It was also decided that once Syria and Lebanon were involved in the peace process,[15] they would be welcome to participate. Although Egypt may well play a crucial role in this potential regime, we focus here on Israel, the Palestinian areas and Jordan.

Israel, Jordan and the West Bank and Gaza are in fact linked together in a number of ways (Diwan and Walton 1994: 22; Vandewalle 1994–5; Jarbawi 1995). Shimon Samir, Israel's first Ambassador to Amman, said: 'There's a certain intimacy between Israelis, Palestinians and Jordanians. We share the same landscape' (*Jerusalem Post*, 24 March 1995). Or, as Israel's Foreign Minister between 1966 and 1974, Abba Eban, expressed it: 'Israeli, Jordanian and Palestinian leaders are tied together inextricably. Geography, history and mutual interest give them no escape.' It needs to be underlined, however, that from a Gaza perspective, there are no historically close links to Jordan. Rather, Egypt is the natural outlook due to geographical proximity, family ties, education and business activities.

Economic Development

One perpetual issue is the future relationship between Israel on the one hand and the West Bank and Gaza on the other; 'integration' versus 'separation' have been key principles in this discussion. After the terror attacks (in the form of bus bombs) carried out by Hamas and Islamic Jihad in 1994 and 1995, Israeli politics (especially in the form of Prime Minister Yitzhak Rabin's way of thinking) began to direct itself towards political and physical separation between 'Arabs' and 'Jews'. This issue has been hotly debated and, from a Palestinian point of view, it has been argued that political 'separation' might in any event allow for economic 'integration'.

Since the Israeli occupation of the West Bank and Gaza was initiated in 1967, Palestinian trade has been subjugated totally to Israeli dominance. The Palestinian economy has been drawn into a complete and destructive dependency, with its labour force being forced into low-paid menial jobs in the agricultural and construction sectors in Israel, and its market subject to Israeli economic policies (Roy 1995). A West Bank/Gaza asymmetrical integration into the Israeli economy is thus a historical fact. The dependency which this has created implies that the Palestinian economy would need some form of continued economic integration with Israel. The problem is how to transform the skewed relations that do exist.

The Paris Agreement of 1994 regulates economic relations between the two parties (Elmusa and el-Ja'afari 1994; Diwan and Walton 1994; Owen 1994; Roy 1994; 1999). In theory, the agreement allows, for the first time, the free flow of Palestinian agricultural produce to Israel, although there are exceptions and regulations regarding quality of produce related to health and sanitary issues. The movement of industrial goods is also to be free under the agreement. Concerning imports, the Palestinian Authority is allowed to make its own decisions on specific aspects of the import regime and in relation to specific goods. By and large, however, the Palestinian areas apply the Israeli import regime in terms of rates of customs, purchase taxes, levies, franchises, etcetera. This means, in effect, that the Paris Agreement is an agreement on a customs union.

In reality, the effect of Israeli closures[16] has far outweighed the Paris Agreement and any verbal commitments towards free trade and movement. Estimated unemployment in the West Bank and Gaza in 1998 was 30.6 per cent compared to 18.0 per cent in 1993 (*MEED*, 12 June 1998). Since the initiation of the peace process, real GNP has declined, private investment has declined, and poverty has increased. The West Bank and Gaza have become further separated from each other since the initiation of the peace process, and the Israeli and Palestinian economies have become less integrated than prior to the signing of the agreements. The Palestinian economy partially recovered during 1998, largely because there were fewer comprehensive closures of the West Bank and Gaza. Growth rates increased as did trade flows (*UNSCO Quarterly Report*, 30 April 1999). Job creation both by the Palestinian Authority and through private investment also rose. However, rising population figures implied a decline in growth of GDP per capita (*MEED*, 16 July 1999). In the Summer of 1999, unemployment was 14 per cent, its lowest since 1995 (*ibid.*).

The West Bank is also tightly knit to the Jordanian economy, through banking, currency, and business ties between influential families residing on both sides of the river Jordan, as well as by the export of food products to the Gulf States via Jordan, although Israeli protection has reduced Jordanian exports to the West Bank and the Arab boycott has restricted Palestinian exports to the Arab world. More than half the Jordanian population is Palestinian. Jordan and the PLO have signed a treaty on economic cooperation (Jordan–PLO Economic Agreement, 7 January 1994) regulating banking, currency, trade and other macroeconomic issues. This agreement followed upon an Israeli–Jordanian agreement to reopen Jordanian banks in the West Bank (active between 1948 and 1967). In 1995, a bilateral trade agreement was concluded. Although Jordan has an interest in market opportunities in the West Bank and Gaza, as well as a degree of control over the holding of Jordanian dinars by West Bankers, the Jordanian economy is historically a very closed one, and a rapid opening up might prove devastating to Jordanian industry (Diwan and Walton 1994: 34).

Trade relations between Israel and Jordan prior to the peace agreement were close to non-existent, especially if Palestinian agricultural exports to Jordan are not included as part of Israeli–Jordanian trade. Since the Jordanian–Israeli peace agreement, a number of agreements have been signed between the two countries. The potential for trade between Israel and Jordan, however, remains rather low, since Israeli demand for Jordanian produce is limited because of competition with local products, and because the Jordanian market is small (Padoan 1997: 198).

Jordan is involved in a far-reaching liberalization process as part of its IMF-sponsored structural adjustment programme (renewed in May 1999), designed to bring Jordan out of the deep economic crises that hit the country hard at the end of the 1980s. In 1998, it was clear that ten years of reform had not substantially altered the Jordanian economy. The 1992–4 boom resulting from the (mainly) Palestinian returnees from the Gulf economies during the Gulf War had now ebbed out. Unemployment figures are estimated at 15–20 per cent and wage levels have declined by approximately 20 per cent since 1989 (*MEED*, 13 November 1998). Although Jordan has managed to reduce its international debt in terms of percentage of GDP, the country still suffers from macroeconomic imbalances. The decline of trade with Iraq has hit the Jordanian economy seriously, and alternative trade partners have not been secured. Jordan has thus not benefited to any considerable degree from the peace agreements and the new economic relations with Israel. Neither has the peace process resulted in greater export potentials in the Palestinian areas (*MEED*, 30 April 1999; *MEED*, 13 August 1999).

Israel, on the other hand, recovered from a severe economic and financial crisis during the latter half of the 1980s. Between 1996 and 1999, however, Israel has again experienced a severe slump in its economic performance. Growth rates have been slow and in the first half of 1999 GDP grew only 0.2 per cent (*MEED*, 27 August 1999). Economic stagnation is partly due to the ebbing out of the positive effects of the immigration from the former Soviet Union, but is also a result of the Asian crisis. The poor economic performance under the Likud-led government was an important factor in its failure to secure victory in the elections of 1999.

Although there is potential for increased trade among the three entities, especially in the form of border trade, most estimates provide rather low figures when it comes to value (Awartani and Kleiman 1997).

Security

Security cooperation, too, has found expression in concrete action on the sub-regional and particularly the bilateral levels. The Gaza–Jericho Agreement of 4 May 1994 divided security responsibilities between Palestinians and Israelis, but also established a Joint Coordination and Cooperation Committee to recommend security policy guidelines, deal with security issues raised by either side, and provide channels for exchange of information. There were also District Offices, responsible for directing joint patrols and joint mobile units. The sight of joint Israeli and Palestinian security patrols was surely a new phenomenon in the Middle East. There was a definite change in discourse at the leadership level, with Palestinian Authority ministers and former PLO revolutionaries recognizing the security needs of their former arch-enemy and even devoting themselves to resolving Israeli security predicaments. Security has always been one of Israel's main concerns, and following the withdrawal of the Israeli Defence Forces from Palestinian population centres and the many terror attacks in the form of suicide bombing of buses and other public places in Israel between 1994 and 1997, security remained the most important issue for Israel.

Security cooperation was, needless to say, severely wounded during 1996–9, reducing the parties to continuous crisis response rather than constructive long-term cooperation. Nevertheless, security cooperation did continue, and reportedly a number of terror attacks were prevented due to security collaboration. In October 1998 the Wye River Memorandum was signed, committing the Palestinian Authority to additional security arrangements (Aruri 1999: 17–28).

The peace agreement between Israel and Jordan also involved complementary security arrangements. Israel and Jordan share an interest in a common security arrangement around the border. From Israel's perspective, Jordanian cooperation is needed to prevent guerrilla attacks across the border. Jordan, for its part, prefers Israeli to Palestinian control of the western side of the Jordan river (Lesch 1995: 123).

Conclusions

[I]t seems quite unreasonable to expect a natural tendency among the region's countries to cooperate and trade with one another. (Çarkoglu *et al.* 1998: 128)

There is a broad consensus on the bleak perspectives for regional cooperation. This study has underlined the difficulties and obstacles that exist when it comes to regional cooperation. These obstacles are both political and economic. What is sometimes suggested in the literature is a 'functional approach' (Fischer 1993; Çarkoglu *et al.* 1998), implying that cooperation should be sought in some vital sectors, such as water management/sharing and energy (Çarkoglu *et al.* 1998: 129).

If we speak of *regionalism* or *regionalization*, therefore, we are forced to concur with previous pessimistic outlooks. Middle Eastern regionalism/regionalization does not really exist. Yet the last few years have witnessed processes of change towards increased regional cooperation. Contemporary rhetorics and arguments for cooperation indicate a different conceptualization than was common during the era of Arab nationalism, Israeli–Arab antagonism and the bipolar world structure, in that definitions of Middle Eastern regional schemes all include Israel. Simultaneously, however, and to complicate the picture further, there is a contemporary revival of Arabism. Ideological pan-Arabism in its earlier forms has not led to any 'real' regionalization process, however, and this may not be a realistic option in the foreseeable future.

What was initiated during a few years at the beginning of the 1990s was abruptly interrupted by Benyamin Netanyahu's politics between 1996 and 1999. The cooperative climate that had emerged appeared to have evaporated completely. The Netanyahu stance brought the Arab states closer together, at least for a short time. With the election victory of Ehud Barak in Israel's prime ministerial elections in May 1999, there were initially expectations for renewed rapprochment, but since the outbreak of violent clashes in 2000 these hopes have once again been reduced. As has also been argued, however, the real benefits of regionalization/ regional cooperation differ between the parties and are not self-evident.

In addition, the regional schemes discussed in this chapter are not designed only by the regional actors themselves; strong external interests and motives lie behind them. The MENA project is favoured by the United States, the Barcelona process by the EU. One important factor is therefore the relationship between external and internal forces, between global and regional processes, and the extent to which regional cooperation might be a response to globalization or indeed a feature of it. This relationship has not been our focus, but we nevertheless think it is of crucial importance, and wish to conclude with a few words about the fears that arise from these external projects.

One of the unmistakable problems with both the Middle Eastern integration concept and the Euro–Mediterranean cooperation project is the extent to which both can be interpreted as neocolonialist.

> It might even backfire, reminding the majority of the population of 'projects', 'doctrines' and 'plans' devised by others and imposed on the region from outside. (Korany 1997: 146)

To many in the Middle East, however, such issues smack of neo-imperialist or neo-colonialist political interference which, on occasion, becomes intervention against state sovereign immunity or cultural intrusion. (Joffé 1998: 52)

The regional initiatives outlined in relation to the peace process may well spur economic growth and 'development'. At the same time, there is an obvious risk of Middle East subordination to European economic interests and US security hegemony, which reinforces hesitation, suspicion and ambivalence in large parts of the region.

Also, these projects may well augment already tense socioeconomic polarizations between city hubs and the *nouveaux riches*, on the one hand, and city slums, rural areas and the new poor on the other. The bulk of Middle Eastern populations might well continue to be marginalized from modern economic sectors and the spread of business cultures. Also in this sense, the regional initiatives outlined here might be not so much a sign of 'new regionalism' as a sign of neoliberal globalization. That is, regional initiatives in the 1990s are originating not so much in common interests and collective bargaining from within the region, but are linked to Western projects of economics and security.

Nevertheless, and despite these gloomy calculations, we would like to end this discussion with Fischer's more optimistic prediction of 'large potential gains from increased integration and cooperation that are unlikely to be reaped until the region becomes more peaceful and less torn by conflict' (Fischer 1993: 444). The conclusions thus remain as ambivalent as the process itself.

NOTES

1 The Middle East is here defined as the Arab states (i.e., members of the Arab League), Israel, Turkey and Iran. The Arab world is often divided into three subregions: the Maghreb, or Western countries (Morocco, Algeria, Tunisia and to some extent Libya); the Mashreq, or Eastern countries (Jordan, Iraq, Syria, Lebanon, the West Bank/Gaza); and the Gulf countries (Saudi Arabia, Kuwait, Bahrain, Qatar, United Arab Emirates, Oman, Yemen). Egypt is because of its strategic geopolitical position a link between all three subregions. In this chapter, we deal primarily with the Mashreq region minus Iraq and including Israel and Egypt, but also with the Gulf countries (excluding Yemen) and the North African Maghreb countries (excluding Libya). Although both Turkey and Iran have acquired new regional significance in the post-Gulf War era, for reasons of space they are not discussed here. It should be noted, however, that Turkey is an important trading partner of the Arab Middle East (Çarkoglu *et al*. 1998: 84). Turkey and Israel have also engaged in a new security cooperation, to the dismay of the Arab world.
2 Both politically and academically, Arab nationalism is a hotly debated issue. For recent analyses see Tibi 1997; Kramer 1996. For a constructivist rethinking of Arab nationalism, Gershoni and Kankowski (1997) is highly useful.
3 The oil-producing Gulf States have so far not been subject to IMF programmes, although restructuring has been initiated in some cases.
4 On the Damascus Declaration forming the Gulf Plus Two security pact, see Hollis 1995.
5 Morocco, however, left the Organization of African Union in 1984, when Polisario/SADR became a member.

6 Four negotiations were established, between Israel and (respectively) Jordan, the Palestinians, Syria and Lebanon. Initially, the Jordanians and Palestinians formed a common negotiation team.

7 On the fragmentation of the Middle East, see Guazzone,1997b and Joffé 1998.

8 'Normalization' is something of a dreaded word in much contemporary Arab intellectual discussion; the pros and cons of 'normalization' prior to settled peace agreements with all parties concerned are hotly debated, particularly in Palestinian, Egyptian and Jordanian circles.

9 The large-scale conferences held in Casablanca (1994), Amman (1995), Cairo (1996) and Doha (1997).

10 In September 1996, there was an outbreak of violent clashes between the Israeli Defence Forces and Palestinian protesters and police. The outbreak of large-scale violence occurred in relation to the decision by Israel's Prime Minister Netanyahu to open another entrance to the Hasmoean tunnel in Jerusalem's Old City.

11 Arab integration could also be seen as a stepwise approach to regional cooperation on a wider basis, i.e., Arab integration first, then a broader Middle Eastern approach (Abdel-Fadil 1997; Korany 1997).

12 The Euro-Mediterranean Partnership Initiative is built upon an older idea, a proposal put forward by Spain and Italy in 1990 called the Conference on Security and Cooperation in the Mediterranean, which would include all the countries bordering the Mediterranean (Joffé 1998: 57).

13 The Barcelona process was initiated in 1995 when the European Union met together with 12 Middle Eastern/North African partners. The Barcelona process is independent of the peace process, but nevertheless related in both timing and objectives.

14 Agricultural products will be excluded from agreements until 2005 because of internal European differences on the Agricultural Policy of the EU (Joffé 1998: 60).

15 Prospects of which seemed to increase with the victory in the Israeli prime ministerial elections of Ehud Barak in May 1999.

16 The Israeli policy of general closure was initiated in March 1993, in response to a deteriorating security situation. Since then, there has been a permanent closure of the West Bank and Gaza by Israel, implying overall restrictions on the movement of labour, goods and factors of production. In order to enter Israel from the West Bank or Gaza (or the West Bank from Gaza and vice versa), any individual needs a permit, which is difficult to obtain. In addition to this general closure, there is a new concept of 'total closure', referring to absolute banning of any movement. This type of closure is imposed in relation to security threats against Israel or as a response to attacks against Israel. A third type of closure is 'internal closure', implying restriction of movement between localities within the West Bank (Roy 1999). The closure policy has hit the Palestinian economy hard. The direct losses suffered by the Palestinian economy between 1994 and 1996 amounted to US$2,800 million, to be compared to the donor funds disbursed during the same time, of US$1,490 million (*MEED*, 16 July 1999).

Turbulent Regionalization in West Africa

4

FREDRIK SÖDERBAUM

The mosaic of countries collectively known as West Africa is shaped by a complex mixture of partly reinforcing and partly contradictory processes of structural change, such as globalization, regionalization, structural adjustment, marginalization, nation building, civil war, state decay and fragmentation from within (Keller and Rothchild 1996; Lavergne 1997; Shaw and Okolo 1994; Zartman 1994). The heterogeneity, diversity and close relationship between the various processes makes it difficult to conceive what is 'regional' in this process of turbulent change.

Many observers claim that there are great potential benefits to be had from future regionalism and regionalization in West Africa, but that, in general, most of the large number of regionalist projects are 'failures,' and that there is a low degree of regional economic cooperation and integration (Asante 1997; Nyang'o 1990; Okolo and Wright 1990; Onwuka and Sesay 1985). This chapter provides a radically different picture compared to this much too simplified and Eurocentric analysis, which overstresses the role of regional organizations, trading schemes and instrumental state strategies. Drawing on the new regionalism approach (NRA), as outlined in the introduction to this volume, the analysis reveals that regionalization constitutes a vital component of the current turbulence and complex dynamics of contemporary West Africa. It should be clear from the outset, however, that attempts at regionalization are carried out by actors and serve their interests, and that this is by no means necessarily a harmonious or benign process. Although a particular regionalization dynamics exists in most fields of activity, this chapter concentrates on actors and regionalization processes in what are perhaps the two most important spheres: security and political economy.

The analysis is structured as follows. As a common point of departure, an attempt is made to outline what characterizes West Africa as a region and what marks the transition from old to new regionalism. The second section focuses on security regionalization, with the emphasis on, first, the particular logic of what is labelled neopatrimonial quasi-state regionalization, and, next, the regionalization of civil war and the Nigerian-dominated attempts made at regional conflict resolution in Liberia and Sierra Leone. The third section focuses on three different forms of regionalization in the field of political economy: state, market and (civil) society regionalization; and finally on the hybrid and most clandestine form, so-called trans-state regionalization. The threads are brought together in the concluding section of the chapter, where the future of regionalization in West Africa is also discussed.

The West African Region[1]

West Africa is commonly referred to as a world region grouped by the following 16 countries: Benin, Burkina Faso, Cape Verde, Côte d'Ivoire, The Gambia, Ghana, Guinea, Guinea-Bissau, Liberia, Mali, Mauritania, Niger, Nigeria, Senegal, Sierra Leone and Togo. These countries form a possibly fairly compact regional subsystem linked together through history, culture, ethnicity, socio-economic mobility and migration, commerce, trade and business, monetary and credit systems as well as state-to-state relationships and a significant number of regional organizations (Hopkins 1973; Lavergne 1997; Okolo and Wright 1990; Shaw and Okolo 1994; Zeleza 1993).

The fact that West Africa has manifested itself as a rather distinct region by no means implies that it constitutes a homogeneous entity. On the contrary, it may also be defined in terms of its great heterogeneity and complex diversity. West Africa is a grandiose melting pot of various religious, linguistic, ethnic, cultural and socio-economic traditions and political-economic regimes. There are, for instance, some 500 ethnic groups and a fascinating mixture of Muslim, Christian and other identities, which are scattered all across the region with little regard to political frontiers. The West African people are the most mobile in Africa, and population movements, labour flows, family ties, ethnic business and trade networks link the region together in many interesting ways. Although there exists a diverse heterogeneity of cultures and ways of life, these also express a certain complementarity as well as commonality (Adotevi 1997) – a certain degree of 'West Africanness'. Furthermore, the West African countries are extremely diverse in terms of size and power, and, at least historically, the region has grouped countries with very divergent political ideologies and economic strategies, including African Marxist, Muslim and military as well as pro-Western development capitalism regimes. There is also a special relationship between the landlocked and the coastal states, some of which can be defined as entrepot economies.

The patterns of regionalization created through history should not be ignored. The precolonial kingdoms, empires and cultures of West Africa were relatively well integrated. To some extent, present-day movements of people, goods and trade follow the links created during the time of the precolonial empires, kingdoms and various political formations. Some analysts even claim that today's quest for regional unity represents a search for common West African cultural roots (Adotevi 1997). The colonial legacy has had, and continues to have, a deep impact on contemporary regional relations. The division into various colonial empires and the artificial borders drawn up at the Berlin Conference in 1884–5 cut across ethnic lines and often tore apart viable economic and socio-cultural units (Hopkins 1973; Zeleza 1993). More than half the number of the present-day countries in the region used to be French colonies, and as such they were, with the exception of Togo, ruled and administered through the Fédération de l'Afrique Occidentale Française (AOF, or French West Africa). The French empire was centralized. But in contrast to the British policy of indirect rule, which tried much more to build on what existed and emphasized the separate development of the various satellites, the French system and its assimilation policy allowed and promoted a considerable degree of horizontal integration among the various colonies. Although to some extent the British territories, too, were jointly administered, this system provided less room for horizontal interaction. The Portuguese policy did not allow or promote any horizontal integration whatsoever.[2]

Colonialism integrated the West African countries into the international economy, but first and foremost as primary export producers. Dependence on the global economy, especially on the former colonial powers, has also shaped regional relations in the postcolonial era. France has maintained close ties to its former colonies, particularly through the Franc Zone, French investments and trade links as well as the strong presence of French military personnel. The special relationship between France and the Francophone West African countries has worked both ways. On the one hand, it has sustained French imperial dreams, and, on the other hand, the former colonies have used France as a counterweight against the hegemonic aspirations of Nigeria.

When trying to understand the dynamics of West Africa, the role of Nigeria can neither be ignored nor underplayed. Nigeria is, by far, the most populous country in Africa: with almost a hundred million inhabitants, it dwarfs every other country in the region in demographic size. Apart from the fact that almost every second West African lives within the borders of Nigeria, a considerable number of Nigerians are living in other West African countries, especially in the main urban centres. Nigeria's economic potential goes hand in hand with its demographic weight. For instance, its GDP of roughly US$30 billion is equivalent to more than half the GDP of the region as a whole. Its industrial sector is by far the largest and most diversified; its agricultural sector is central to the food security of many countries; its labour force is both the largest and among the most skilled in the region; its banking and financial system is the largest and among the most sophisticated; its school and education system is by far the most developed; and its infrastructural base is the most extensive in the area. Nigeria has often tried to shape the region in order to suit its own interests, but has also been counteracted by the Francophone bloc.

Regionalism has been on the political agenda in West Africa ever since colonialism. The old regionalism had at least two main influences: the dreams of pan-Africanism and collective-self-reliance, and the European experience. Regardless of what particular regional idea has dominated, West African attempts at regional cooperation and integration have emphasized large-scale, state-led initiatives from above, which has resulted in the creation (and demise) of a large number of intergovernmental regional organizations and economic integration schemes, especially during the 1960s and 1970s. Rooted in discussions dating back to the mid-1960s, the Economic Community of West African States (ECOWAS) was created in 1975 as the first West African organization which managed to bridge the Francophone–Anglophone gap. Yet many of the problems associated with the organization relate to what has been perceived, especially by the Francophone countries, as a Nigerian-led strategy to enforce hegemonism. This has led the French West African countries to strengthen further their ties with France and amongst themselves: one result is the Union Économique et Monétaire Ouest Africaine (UEMOA, or West African Economic and Monetary Union).

There was a renewed trend towards regionalism and regionalization in West Africa, as in most other parts of the world, in the 1990s. It was connected with the comprehensive structural changes occurring after the end of the Cold War, such as the worldwide trend and example of regionalism, the restructuring of the nation-state and the end of 'Third Worldism'. Particularly important in this regard is that whereas the ideologized climate and bipolar pattern of the Cold War tended to be recreated at the regional level in most parts of the world, including West Africa, the current situation, with an obvious lack of interest in Africa on the part of the major economic and political powers and institutions in the international system, creates a power vacuum and room to manoeuvre for intensified regionalisms and regionalization.

There is emerging a complex and heterogeneous mix of 'old' and 'new' versions of regionalisms and regionalization in West Africa, with clandestine as well as more positive outcomes. Many 'old' forms of regional cooperation and integration are still in existence, but both main organizations referred to above, UEMOA[3] and

ECOWAS,[4] have undergone some major restructuring, at least in terms of objectives. New forms of state regionalization are emerging with a more liberal as well as more comprehensive and holistic approach in terms of community building (Lavergne 1997). At the same time there is a novel logic developing in the form of non-formalized market and civil society regionalization as well as the more destructive trans-state regionalization. During the last decade a particular and turbulent regional security dynamics has also erupted, to which we now turn.

Security Regionalization

Conflict, instability and insecurity are tragic characteristics of independent Africa in general and West Africa in particular. Controversies have frequently arisen between the states, occasionally escalating into armed conflicts or the expulsion of nationals. Other conflicts have taken the form of border disputes, often related to the control of natural resources. Nevertheless, although West Africa has been, and to some extent continues to be determined by international conflicts and competing national interests, the root of the problem lies primarily within the states themselves. Differently expressed, insecurity in West Africa is primarily not caused by large-scale, inter-state conflict, but is mainly a consequence of conflicts and regime breakdown within those arbitrarily delineated territories labelled 'nation-states'. This does not mean, however, that there is an absence of regionalization. On the contrary, there exists an intriguing and turbulent regionalization dynamic in West Africa in the field of security. This section draws attention to two main aspects of this sphere: first, the particular logic of neopatrimonial, quasi-state regionalization and military regime networking; and, second, the regionalization of civil war, including a focus on *whose* security is actually promoted by attempts made at regional intervention and conflict resolution (the main focus is on the conflicts in Liberia and Sierra Leone).

Neopatrimonial, Quasi-state Regionalization

In order to understand the particular logic of security regionalization at work in West Africa, we need to understand the nature of the West African state. The term 'quasi-state', coined by Robert Jackson (1990), is widely recognized as a label which fits most West African states. This term is used as a description of states which enjoy international recognition but lack substantial and credible statehood by the criteria of international law. In their international relations, quasi-states place the main emphasis on formal and absolute sovereignty – maintenance of existing borders and the principle of non-intervention in domestic affairs – because it enhances the power of the governing political elite and its ability to stay in power (Clapham 1996).

To this picture can be added more about the domestic political situation. The postcolonial state in West Africa is to an overwhelming extent ruled by personal leaders, military regimes and/or warlords (would-be leaders), who are often portrayed as embodying the idea of the state. These personal rulers often use the coercive instruments of the state to monopolize power and further their own interests, and to deny or restrict the political rights and opportunities of other groups (Bøås 1997: 361–2; Médard 1982). Such 'privatization of the public' has at least two important consequences: (1) political power becomes personal power; and (2) politics becomes mainly a matter of self-enrichment (Bøås 1997: 363). In line with this thinking, it is often held that most West African states are also neo-patrimonial (states in which patrimonialism and bureaucratic norms coexist). The argument raised here is that the bulk of the West African states, therefore, can be understood as neopatrimonial quasi-states, and that this label also explains a great deal about the turbulent regionalization dynamics at work in the region.

The official rhetoric of regional cooperation often follows conventional language: it emphasizes securing national stability from internal and external threat. This is the Westphalian security logic and the principle of absolute sovereignty, which personal leaders and military regimes can use to further their own interests (Clapham 1996). In essence, the rulers can pay lip service to established norms but create organizations and security alliances to serve neopatrimonial elite interests. The basic motivation for regional cooperation of such states, whether ruled by personal rulers or by military regimes, is first and foremost not national security and welfare but a desire for regime stability, self-enrichment and the well-being of one's own group (the neopatrimonial elite). It should be clear that regional cooperation among neopatrimonial quasi-states will not suddenly take on enlightened forms and serve either national or human security, although it may, by coincidence, sometimes do so.

It is also evident that neopatrimonial quasi-states are typically more concerned with trying to ensure absolute sovereignty, and to maintain control and regime stability at the national level, than with sharing sovereignty and decision-making power with other states through genuine and 'deep' regional cooperation and integration. Regional defence pacts and alliances become very unstable and their functioning depends often on personal friendship among military and personal rulers.

There has been a considerable degree of informal military regime networking in West Africa, whereby personal rulers and military regimes have been able to pool power and sovereignty and seek informal alliances – often with extra-regional powers (mainly France or the superpowers) – in order to stabilize their weak regimes, mainly against internal opposition and rebels. There was 'relative stability' from the 1960s to the end of the Cold War, in the sense that so-called domestic conflicts and coups did not escalate into brutal civil wars and did not become regionalized. The conflicts in (West) Africa were 'solved', or at least 'stabi-lized' according to the Cold War logic, by the strong presence of the French military and/or the protection of the military regime in Nigeria.

In the post-Cold War era the superpower overlay has disappeared and there is a political and military power vacuum, to a large extent filled by Nigerian hegemonic aspirations, partly frustrated by French links with its former colonies. Further-more, and perhaps more importantly, in the post-Cold War era the West African neopatrimonial quasi-states face severe financial difficulties. The state has been privatized through structural adjustment programmes, which means that there is not much left to plunder in state budgets and government resources. This has led instead to a militarization of the weakest neopatrimonial quasi-states, and conse-quently to the eruption of civil wars in cases such as Liberia and Sierra Leone, and to an explosive situation in most other states in the region as well. Analysis reveals that the privatization of the state results in its militarization, and consequently in the privatization of violence, with devastating consequences for people living in this part of the world.

The Regionalization of Civil Wars: 'Whose Security'?

The aim here is to provide an account of some main aspects of the regional dynamics at work in the West African 'war zone', including in whose interest this logic works, and not to try to explain the civil wars as such. There is a zone of war and destruction ranging from Senegal down to Liberia, into which rebel leaders and most West African states are sucked for a host of complex reasons. The series of crises began in Liberia in 1990, when the corrupt dictatorship of Master-Sergeant Samuel Doe was challenged by several warlords, amongst them the current President Charles Taylor. The conflict in Liberia was an organized effort by a number of leaders exiled in other countries to overthrow Doe's corrupt regime. The extremely brutal Liberian civil war was 'regionalized' quickly, and in August 1990 the ECOWAS Ceasefire Monitoring Group (ECOMOG) was sent to Liberia to try to bring about a ceasefire between the rival factions, to restore order and to establish an interim government until elections could be held (Vogt 1992). For a long time the ECOMOG mission was unsuccessful, but after several years of tur-bulence, of peace agreements made and broken by most of the warlords, and of failed attempts at dismantling the rebels, the conflict finally ended in 1997 when Charles Taylor was elected President in relatively free and 'fair' elections.

A similar civil war erupted in neighbouring Sierra Leone in March 1991. Just as in Liberia, the conflict in Sierra Leone arose within the context of a neopatrimonial state with little legitimacy left and in severe economic crisis. The original political objective of the Revolutionary United Front (RUF) was to overthrow Momoh's one-party rule and restore multiparty democracy in Sierra Leone, but gradually the conflict spiralled out of control into unimaginable anarchy. There was a close relationship between the civil wars in Liberia and Sierra Leone. For instance, the RUF entered eastern Sierra Leone in March 1991 from Liberian territory controlled by Charles Taylor. The rebels were supplied by Taylor and supported by mercenaries from Liberia and Burkina Faso, as well as from Sierra Leone itself (they had fought previously in Liberia) (Bøås 1997). After several turns and new military rulers the ECOMOG force helped to oust the latest military ruler, Major Johnny Koroma, and to restore the democratically elected President Achmed Tejan Kabbah, who had been ousted in a coup in May 1997. Yet by late 1999 most rebels had not surrendered their arms, while ECOMOG was working in parallel with the UN mission in Sierra Leone (UNAMSIL).

The coup attempt in Guinea-Bissau in 1998 represents yet another, albeit somewhat different, example of the intriguing regional conflict dynamics in West Africa. The ruling regime of President Vieira (who himself gained power through a coup in 1980) was challenged by rebels. The ruling regime was so weak that its survival was doubtful without immediate external military support, which in this case arrived from Senegal and Guinea. Once again, it is a case of domestic unrest being regionalized more or less immediately. One main reason for the quick involvement by Senegal was that this country was itself facing domestic upheaval: Casamance separatists have been fighting for independence since 1982 in a part of Senegal which is culturally integrated with Guinea-Bissau. It is believed that the rebel leader in Guinea-Bissau, Military Commander Ansumane Mané, is involved in smuggling weapons to Casamance separatists in eastern Senegal.

At the time of writing, in late 1999, there is relative peace in the war zone. However, this peace is very controversial. To establish it, perhaps the most brutal warlord, Charles Taylor, has become an elected President, while in Sierra Leone another warlord, the RUF leader Foday Sankoh, ironically enough became head of the national minerals commission with the rank of vice-president. Moreover, former junta leader Koroma was appointed chairman of the national commission for consolidating peace. Furthermore, while the Nigerian-led ECOMOG interventions in Liberia and Sierra Leone, which are unique in African history, are generally viewed as high-profile success stories, the question has to be asked whether there is more to these two cases than meets the eye. Have the ECOMOG interventions enhanced security, at what cost, and with what consequences? In particular, *whose* security interests have been promoted by these settlements?

There are several explanations, some paradoxical, for the ECOMOG intervention in Liberia and Sierra Leone. As indicated above, the international interest in Africa has decreased significantly in the post-Cold War era. A power vacuum was created in West Africa after the Cold War: in the wake of the Gulf War, the major powers and relevant institutions, including the United Nations (UN) and the

Organization of African Unity (OAU), simply stood by and watched the emergence of another so-called 'black hole'. As then ECOWAS Secretary-General Abbas Bundu put it, the decision to intervene in Liberia was made because of the 'realization that there was a problem from which everyone was running' (*West Africa*, 2–8 March 1992: 385). The ECOMOG interventions were legitimized in terms of the threat to international peace and the need to save human lives by ending the bloodshed. The shared view in the region was that 'the ECOWAS States cannot stand idly by and watch a member State slide into anarchy' (*West Africa*, 1–7 July 1991: 945).

It is clear that ECOMOG played a very important role in the settlement of the conflicts. However, the argument put forward here is that the intervention can also be explained by more myopic motives on the part of the neighbouring countries, especially those of the regional giant, Nigeria. Most of the West African governments, and especially Nigeria, were frightened by the spectre of a civilian insurgency overthrowing a military government. The Nigerian president at the time, Babangida, spelled it out at the ECOWAS summit: '[T]oday it is Liberia, tomorrow it could be any one of you' (Ellis 1998: 3). The Nigerian military regime was also worried about the presence of Libyan-supported revolutionaries in the National Patriotic Front of Liberia (NPFL). The fear was that if the NPFL seized power in Liberia, this country could become a base for other Libyan-supported rebels in the region. It was therefore necessary to intervene in Liberia in order to enhance regime stability and survival in the region (not to protect human lives).

It is important to understand that the role of Nigeria in the interventions cannot be overestimated. In spite of the fact that ECOMOG intervened under the ECOWAS flag, the interventions in both Liberia and Sierra Leone were essentially Nigeria-dominated operations. Without Nigeria there would simply be no ECOMOG. For instance, although its contribution fluctuated over time, Nigeria provided three-quarters of a total of 15,000 troops and 80 per cent of the material and financial requirements of the Liberian intervention force (Mortimer 1996). There was roughly the same Nigerian dominance in the intervention force in Sierra Leone, although it phased out over time.

If Nigeria has been significant for the initiation and maintenance of ECOMOG, it has also been the cause of many of its problems. In the eyes of the NPFL in Liberia, ECOMOG was an instrument of Nigerian self-interest and regional hegemony, and its intervention ultimately prolonged the agony. According to Mortimer (1996: 153), in effect ECOMOG's 'practical role became to protect Liberia's Interim Government of National Unity (IGNU) under Amos Sawyer, which was itself the production of an ECOWAS-sponsored conference'. There is little doubt that the military rulers in Nigeria used the ECOMOG mission for their own interests and in order to consolidate despotic rule in their own country. Adibe claims that 'ECOWAS violated the cornerstone of every successful peacekeeping mission – strict adherence to the principle of impartiality' (Adibe 1997: 482).

This raises another important question about the legitimacy of ECOMOG-style regional interventions. According to Ofuatey-Kodjoe (quoted in Adibe 1997: 485),

> the notion that a group of states headed by military dictatorships have the right to intervene in another state in order to establish a democratic regime is grotesque. And the notion that these states can in fact achieve that objective by the application of outside force may be only an exercise in wishful thinking.

This situation was not improved by the unscrupulous behaviour of large sections of the ECOMOG troops, who actively took part in the crimes committed against civilians and got heavily involved in the political economy of warlordism. The various factions in the warlord political economy, including ECOMOG, fought not only for control over Liberia and Sierra Leone, but also over the abundant natural resources – such as diamonds, gold, hardwood, palm oil, marijuana, rubber and looted goods – as well as for access to networks of commerce, smuggling and political affiliation over a wide area (Bøås 2000). There was a lucrative trade for middlemen who could buy looted goods, diamonds and other natural resources; the warlords could get weaponry and ammunition in return. According to Bøås (2000), several ECOMOG officers made fortunes from the warlord economy as the ECOMOG forces seized control of Liberia's main ports and trading networks. The very questionable role of the ECOMOG force is perhaps best illustrated by its Liberian *nom de guerre*: 'Every Commodity and Movable Object Gone'.

There existed a diffuse and complex set of personal relationships, friendships, loyalties and alliances among the key principal actors, that maintained conflicts and made them escalate and spread the way they did. On the one hand, there was what can be labelled 'rebel networking', primarily amongst NPFL and RUF leaders, but also involving the regimes in Burkina Faso and, initially, Côte d'Ivoire. On the opposing side, there was the Nigerian-led ECOMOG intervention force, which also involved (mainly) Guinea, Ghana and The Gambia. Initially the more moderate Francophone states, such as Senegal and Togo, were sceptical towards the whole ECOMOG operation. Gradually, however, the countries in the region managed to come closer to a common position on the problem, partly because Ghana and some of the more influential Francophone states, especially Côte d'Ivoire and Senegal, got more actively involved in the process, while Nigeria slightly downplayed its own role, at least offically (Mortimer 1996). The peacekeeping force was also made into an all-African force through participation from Botswana, Egypt and Zimbabwe. There were also parallel UN operations both in Liberia and, subsequently, in Sierra Leone. In addition, other actors, such as the OAU and the US, also assisted in the efforts to bring about peace.

Perhaps the single most important explanation of the settlement of the Liberian crisis, however, is that at the time Nigeria's need to be considered an international peacemaker and promoter of democracy had never been greater. Its international reputation was at its nadir as a consequence of the Ngoni affair, culminating in the hanging of Ken Saro-Wiwa and seven other Ngoni activists. In essence, the Nigerian-dominated ECOMOG force started out trying to prevent Charles Taylor from seizing power – in the name of humanity, democracy and political stability – but seven years later the interests of the Nigerian regime and Charles Taylor had converged to produce a ceasefire agreement. The main difference seems to be six years of war, mass rapes, mutilations, warlordism, a few hundred thousand victims and a few million refugees (Bøås 2000; Magyar and Conteh-Morgan 1998; Vogt 1996).

But the Nigerian-led ECOMOG intervention force was generally viewed as a success story around the world and in the international media, and the Nigerian leader Abacha was able to seize the opportunity to emerge once again as the defender of democracy and human rights by ordering ECOMOG troops into neighbouring Sierra Leone in order to restore to power the democratically elected government of President Achmed Tejan Kabbah (Bøås 2000). The notion that it was better to keep the Nigerian ECOMOG soldiers outside the country also played a role in the discussion. Kabbah's government was as corrupt and neopatrimonial as any other, but as in the case of Liberia a former rebel leader had been given legitimate status in order to stop the fighting. The alternative might be frightening, but it illustrates once again that both neopatrimonial quasi-states and warlords are the winners. The losers are the rape victims, the child and youth soldiers, the citizenry, the mutilated, the dead and the several million refugees.

The Political Economy of Regionalization

In order to understand the turbulent and often contradictory dynamics of the political economy of regionalization in West Africa, there is a need to transcend regional organizations and intergovernmental state strategies, and to include in one's focus a heterogeneous set of market and civil society actors. Although the dividing lines between the various actors is blurred, an attempt is made here to analyse, first, state regionalization, then market and civil society regionalization, and finally the hybrid form, trans-state regionalization.

State Regionalization

Formal regionalism has been on the political agenda in West Africa ever since independence (actually it started, formally, during the colonial era). In the 1960s and 1970s regionalism was seen as a key strategy to overcome dependence and sustain development on the African continent. The West African governments participate in a vast number of continental, regional, subregional and bilateral organizations and agreements, many of which were created during the old regionalism. It is quite safe to say that West Africa has experienced the creation and demise of more intergovernmental regional organizations than any other part of Africa. There is a very complex web of membership within which regional organizations have emerged, been dissolved and then re-emerged with a slightly different membership and purpose. Depending on definition, there are between 40 and 70 intergovernmental regional organizations currently in existence in West Africa (Söderbaum 1996). There is, however, a striking discrepancy between rhetoric and implementation: the results of state regionalization in West Africa are modest, with a few exceptions among the Francophone countries particularly and in certain concrete sectors such as transport and communications, river basin development, medicine and health, provision of technical services, and research, education and training.

The two dominant organizations in West Africa, UEMOA and ECOWAS, were formulated and developed against the backdrop of the old regionalism, but are now being reformulated and given a new content (see notes 5 and 6). It remains to be seen how forceful these re-makes will be, and to what extent they will contribute to development. In order to understand the dynamics, the dominant actors and the road ahead it may be useful to summarize how UEMOA and ECOWAS have worked so far, not least since these two organizations have received a considerable degree of attention in the debate. Although both organizations, especially ECOWAS, have a comprehensive and multisectoral mandate – including sectoral cooperation in transport and communications, resources, social and cultural affairs, and so on – both place extra emphasis on trade integration, and in the case of UEMOA also on monetary and capital integration.

Most of the trade barriers for raw materials and lightly processed goods have been significantly reduced or eliminated within both UEMOA and ECOWAS. The overall results of this trade liberalization are not very comprehensive (Okolo and Wright 1990). With regard to trade with manufactured goods, the Communauté Economique de l'Afrique de l'Ouest (CEAO, or Economic Community of West Africa) and UEMOA member states have agreed on a number of trade-promoting measures, such as the preferential treatment (Prélèvement Communautaire de Solidarité, or PCS) and the Taxe de Coopération Régional (TCR, or Regional Cooperation Tax), which was introduced in 1976. The more ambitious objective – to erect a common external tariff, originally intended to be operational by 1985 – has not been achieved. Although relatively high by African standards, recorded intra-UEMOA trade seemed to reach a 'stable point' at about 10–12 per cent of the total recorded trade of the Union's members in the 1980s (Shaw and Okolo 1994). The low figure is partly explained by the application of preferences to specified products and countries only, resulting in inefficiencies and market segmentation. Quite a number of integrative decisions have been agreed on by the ECOWAS member countries, but implementation has been poor, and tariffs and non-tariff barriers remain high among member countries.[5] Apart from some progress during the initial years, intra-ECOWAS trade as a proportion of total trade by ECOWAS members has not increased significantly. Official intraregional trade currently stands below 6 per cent of the total trade of regional countries, much of which is conducted by the most developed countries – Nigeria and Côte d'Ivoire, and to a lesser extent Ghana and Senegal – which have been able to further exploit their monopolistic/oligopolistic positions (*ibid.*). However, as will be discussed below, the inclusion of unrecorded trade raises the figure significantly. In addition, the analyses below on trans-state regionalization will reveal that policy makers have deliberately prevented formal trade liberalization.

UEMOA is one of two currency areas within the Communauté Financière Africaine (CFA) Franc Zone, and the member countries share a central bank, the Banque Centrale des États de l'Afrique de l'Ouest (BCEAO, or the Central Bank of West African States). There is thus a high degree of monetary integration within the Zone, and the parity towards the French franc remained fixed from 1948 until 1994, when the common currency was devalued by 50 per cent. Monetary policies are determined in collaboration with the French central bank, and credit policies, banking regulations and some fiscal policies are harmonized throughout the Zone.

Although the effects of monetary unions are complicated to evaluate, it is more or less generally agreed that the CFA system has contributed to growth and development among the member countries from independence and at least until the early 1970s (Devarajan and de Melo 1987; Guillamont, Guillamont and Plane 1988; Robson, 1983; 1998). After 1973 a variety of events at the international, regional and national levels have disrupted the system, such as the breakdown of the Bretton Woods system, the oil price shocks, the debt crisis, the falling terms of trade, and the fluctuations of the French franc. Moreover, too 'soft' credit policies within the region led to the collapse of the banking systems of many countries during the 1980s. Since then the picture has been more complex, and some analysts argue that too much emphasis has been placed on stability and the control of inflation instead of concentrating on creating productive capacity (Olukoshi 1995).

It should be evident from the discussion above that there have been considerable problems with state regionalization in West Africa in the past. Although it might have had some limited positive impact on economic development in certain sectors, especially amongst Francophone members, most analysts claim that state regionalization has failed. One problem is that this form of regionalization has been plagued by the rhetoric of unity and unrealizably high ambitions. One cannot simply wish regional integration into existence. As Lavergne points out, 'the approach is one whereby the heads of state assemble on a regular basis and pronounce ambitious declarations of what they are going to do, as a prelude to actually doing very little' (Lavergne 1997: 4). Furthermore, most regional organizations have largely lived lives of their own, as political elite projects separated from market demands and civil society. The regional programmes have seldom been integrated into national development plans, and vice versa.

The distribution of the gains and costs of the integration process is undoubtedly one of the critical issues for the functioning of state regionalization. This has been perceived as a failure within ECOWAS, partly as a consequence of the indulgent safeguard and escape clauses and shortages of funds, including those experienced by the ECOWAS Fund itself. The compensation mechanism has worked slightly better in UEMOA, and it has generated some commitment to the integration process on the part of the less-developed member states – Burkina Faso, Mali, Mauritania and Niger (Robson 1983; Asante 1985). However, the real contribution of the compensation mechanism to increased regional trade and long-term development is actually dubious, and many times the projects have been implemented in the most- and not the least-developed member countries.

Almost every intergovernmental regional organization in West Africa is faced with chronic shortages of funds and arrears in contributions. Apart from the TCR/PCS system within UEMOA, there is no automatic system in the contributions to regional organizations, and in the present situation of crisis, members do not seem to prioritize their obligations to regional organizations. This can be related to the excessive number of regional organizations operating in the region. There is an astonishing degree of overlap and duplication of activities of various organizations (Söderbaum 1996). It is not even clear how many of them are operational or what it is that they do. Just as serious, many organizations have tackled the same or similar problems simultaneously, without any consultation or coordination of instruments, and with different solutions to the same problems.

The problems of regional organizations in West Africa are closely connected to what is rather vaguely termed a lack of political will. This seems to be related to the weakness of these states, as well as to what was referred to above as quasi-statehood, and a corresponding obsession with absolute sovereignty which makes it difficult for regional cooperation and integration to emerge. Another explanation is that regional organizations are also involved in the game of neopatrimonialism and state corruption. In fact, there is no evidence suggesting that regional organizations are isolated from the funtioning of the states more generally; they would therefore also tend to reinforce patronage networks.

Market and Civil Society Regionalization

Although it is clear that the colonial legacy and the polarized structure of the Cold War increased the political differences in the region, these cleavages have often been exaggerated in the debate. To some or perhaps even to a large extent these remain surface phenomena, often existing only at the political level and among the elite groups in the major cities. Too little attention has been awarded to the multitude of vibrant, multidimensional and dynamic processes of *de facto*, 'soft', market and (civil) society regionalization in West Africa. Examples include the mostly informal cross-border traders and financiers, the Nigerian, Senegalese and Lebanese business networks operating all over the region, and the wide range of society-induced and cultural integration processes driven by migrants, NGOs, social movements, family ties, students, and ethnic, religious or social networks whose identities and activities do not by any means correspond to the artificially constructed national frontiers.

It should be recognized that there are a growing number of important and influential civil society organizations, networks, and non-governmental organizations (NGOs) in West Africa (Clapham 1996, Chapter 10). These processes of grassroots / bottom-up regionalization (albeit sometimes driven by non-state elites) arise for many different reasons, such as the post-Cold War transformations, the shift in development ideology and structural adjustment, the rise of information technology, the history and culture of regional relations, or the small size of the national civil societies and their consequent need to transcend the structures and boundaries of individual nation-states. It is not that the national space and national civil societies are disappearing, but rather that they are becoming intertwined with emerging regional civil society. There are important trends towards increased cooperation, networking, knowledge- and information-sharing, joint pooling of resources and problem-solving amongst a great variety of civil society actors: NGOs, think-tanks, and social movements in issue areas such as economic justice and debt, the environment, health and HIV/Aids, human rights and, not least, vibrant regional research and education networks. In this context it should be recognized that non-African NGOs and solidarity organizations, as well as the aid agencies, are participating in these processes, enhancing regional networking and coordinating activities amongst partners in several countries and thus facilitating regional communication and dialogue. Some of these activities and relationships have a long history, while others, especially the NGO-induced processes of regionalization, are recent phenomena.

The network idea is fruitful for understanding the dynamics at work in civil society. The West African Network for Peacebuilding (WANEP) is an interesting example of this trend. Established in 1997, it could be called the NGO equivalent of ECOWAS.

WANEP enables groups and organizations involved in peace building to exchange experiences and information on issues such as human rights, conflict resolution/ transformation, social, religious, and political reconciliation, and peace building. WANEP's activities seek to forge personal and professional relationships, allow for cross-fertilization of ideas and expertise, exchange research programmes, and intervention in social, religious and political conflicts in West Africa. (Conflict Prevention Newsletter, October 1999/3: 8)

Many of the networks being erected in Africa are interlinked, networks of networks. WANEP is a member of the Forum of Early Warning and Early Response (FEWER). Twenty-two international NGOs, lobbyists, academics and governments joined forces with UN agencies to set up FEWER, which aims to complement existing early warning systems and processes, and to make research more relevant to policy and useful to local actors.

Market regionalization has been a particularly fertile source of informal regional networks. It was mentioned above that regional trading schemes have had little effect upon trade, investment and production patterns in West Africa. Official intraregional trade remains low, or concentrated in clusters. It must be recognized, however, that a more comprehensive economic integration is actually taking place through informal channels and networks that avoids taxation and existing trade barriers. These informal cross-border activities may be survival strategies, well-organized business strategies, criminal strategies, forms of popular resistance, or a form of opting out of conventional economies as a consequence of the effects of globalization and the adverse effects of structural adjustment and the privatization of the state. They are mainly built upon the differences in trade and financial structures between countries in the region and are generally more effective than the more formal activities (Bach 1997; Meagher 1997).

Riley (1999: 73–4) points out that The Gambia, Ghana, Nigeria and Sierra Leone are all centres of extensive informal trading systems. For instance, The Gambia forms the base of a huge smuggling economy extending to many parts of West Africa. This can be explained by its location, a strong currency (in spite of not being part of the CFA Franc Zone) and very liberal import policies. Ghana is another often-cited example. Especially in the mid- and late 1970s, a large parallel economy developed in response to the overvaluation of the Ghanaian cedi, whereby mainly cocoa and unprocessed minerals were unofficially exported into several of the CFA Franc Zone countries in exchange for consumer goods and vehicles. This type of trade has continued in spite of the liberalization of the economy since the 1980s. Nigeria is yet another centre for informal trading activities. High official trade barriers in Nigeria caused an inflow of consumer goods such as alcohol, cigarettes and electronic equipment, while subsidized petrol, fertilizer and agricultural products were exported. The exports secure funding in the CFA franc, which is then used to finance the smuggled imports. The importance of these informal activities must not be underestimated. Customs statistics from neighbouring countries suggest that the illicit trade involves several billions of CFAfrancs (Riley 1999).

Sometimes the informal economies are idealized and described in positive terms as survival strategies that provide people with living options, in a situation of severe economic crisis and state decay. Other analysts point to the disruptive effects of activities built upon rent seeking and arbitrage, which have no positive influence on productivity, development and agriculture. Several of these analysts also argue that the informal activities are often intertwined with state activities, thus representing a hybrid which can be labelled trans-state regionalization (Bach 1997; Meagher 1997; Lavergne 1997).

Trans-state Regionalization[6]

The regionalist schemes in West Africa have failed to involve the private sector and civil forces in the process, often as a result of political decisions. The concept of trans-state regionalization shows that there may exist a quite controversial reason for the failure of more formal types of state regionalization/regionalism. Trans-state regionalization is not linked to any institutionalized and formal process, although it depends on state policies and the inclusion of state agents. In fact, trans-state regional networks do not seek the implementation or rationalization of regional economic integration schemes and tariff liberalization, but rather depend on the exploitation of boundary disparities or political and economic differences on a rent-seeking basis, even demanding their preservation in order to prosper (Lavergne 1997: 8).

The state dimension is also related to the fact that politicians and government officials are actively involved in these types of activities. For instance, the parallel economy in Sierra Leone, which exceeded the offical economy in size, expanded as a consequence of the systematic corruption, theft of state revenues and personalist rule of President Siaka Stevens between 1965 and 1985 (Riley 1999). This type of state was later referred to as the 'shadow state', one in which corrupt politicians are sheltered by the formal facade of political power based upon informal markets (Reno 1995).

The viability of trans-state regionalization is dependent on the lack of transparency of the state, as well as the flexibility and adaptability of the trans-state activities. It is clandestine because it stimulates neopatrimonalism and undermines the regulatory capacity of the state. In fact, the expansion of trans-state regionalization is tied to state decay and states' declining financial capacities and territorial control. The decline of the state is further magnified by its privatization. Trans-state regional networks emerge as strategies for surviving or for accumulation. The changes made by liberalization and structural adjustment ensure that trans-state regionalization stems no longer only from the exploitation of existing (West) African border disparities. Rather, it has expanded to new trades in illicit drugs, including heroin and cocaine, and light weapons and other merchandise of war, which means that the networks expand also to Europe, Asia and America (Bach 1997).

The profits involved in the more conventional as well as the new types of trans-state regionalization are considerable. These survival and accumulation strategies have become vital for large groups of the population and sometimes for the state apparatus itself. According to Bach and Hveem (1998), managing boundary disparities through trans-state regionalization is a vital component of the policy orientations of Benin, Togo, The Gambia, Niger and, to a lesser extent, Chad. The discussion above on the political economy of warlordism suggests that it is possible to add Liberia and Sierra Leone to this list. One could also argue that large segments of the populations of Nigeria and Ghana are sucked into this type of cross-border regionalization in various ways.

Attempts to restrict trans-state flows have been unsuccessful and have met with destabilizing boomerang effects (Bach and Hveem 1998). One solution to clandestine trans-state regionalization is the coordination of economic policies to eliminate the rationale for these activities, for instance through regional coordinated structural adjustment programmes. There is a risk, however, that this only pushes these 'entrepreneurs' further into criminal activities mainly associated with drugs and weaponry smuggling.

The Future of Regionalisms and Regionalization in West Africa

West Africa is undergoing a deep process of structural change whereby the role of the regional factor has become stronger in several important respects during the last decade and more, albeit by no means only in a positive sense. Although there is a certain degree of continuity of post-independence regionalisms and regionalizations in West Africa, especially among the Francophone countries, it seems that something new and often quite turbulent is in the making.

The new dimensions of security regionalism are demonstrated well by events taking place in the 'war zone'. The myopic motives behind Nigeria's ECOMOG interventions in Liberia and Sierra Leone cannot be overlooked. Charles Taylor and other rebel leaders created the politics of warlordism, setting up modern West African equivalents of the Mafia. Sadly enough, the ECOMOG intervention force got involved in this dirty business, and rather than becoming known as an enlightened peacekeeping force it won the *nom de guerre* mentioned earlier. Although the ECOMOG intervention force initially was part of the problem, however, the countries in the region gradually managed to agree on a common position and strive for a solution to the crisis in support of UN forces and the OAU. Whatever the final analysis of the ECOMOG interventions in Liberia and Sierra Leone, the regionalization of civil war and the quite remarkable attempts at regional conflict resolution reflect the increased role of the regional factor, with both positive and negative effects. That is, there is a much greater role for action and mediation at the regional level in the post-Cold War era, and the West African experience reveals that the affected neighbouring countries have more legitimacy, both in the international community and within the affected states themselves, for peace enforcement, peacekeeping and peace making than before, even if these states are themselves dictatorships.

The record of state regionalization in West Africa is modest, with a few exceptions such as the CFA/UEMOA and some regional organizations with clearly defined mandates to deal with specific matters. Yet, despite many negative effects, the gradual emergence of market-oriented economies and multiparty political systems as part of structural adjustment programmes has harmonized political and economic systems, in turn improving the conditions for state-led initiatives of regional cooperation and integration.

The future dynamics of regionalization in West Africa will be determined in the relationship between state regionalization and market and civil society regionalization, and will be influenced especially by the extent to which they are mutually reinforcing rather than competitive or parallel, as tends to be the case today.

The crux of the matter is the politics of West African regionalisms and regionalization. State regionalization in West Africa has been over-politicized, which has tended to create suspicion in the national centres of decision making. The political leaders and their representatives have acted according to an anachronistic Westphalian, quasi-state rationality in their obsession with absolute sovereignty. Although this behaviour may seem rational from the perspective of individual state elites in order to maintain quasi-statehood or neopatrimonialism, it is clear that – collectively – the decision makers have failed to adjust to the realities and challenges of a post-Westphalian, interdependent world order.

Since the (often) repressive and neopatrimonial states in West Africa to a considerable extent form part of the problems of both development and security, their gradual relaxation, democratization and restructuring must also be part of the solution. During the last decade important moves towards democracy have occurred, but to some extent these remain surface phenomena. Multiparty elections do not by themselves create democracy, and as long as many of the political regimes remain authoritarian, neopatrimonial, centralist, exclusivist and often corrupt, the state-driven regional cooperation projects will continue to serve such interests, rather than democratic and developmental ones. To put it differently, it can be argued that ECOWAS and the other regional cooperation schemes legitimate authoritarian regimes in the name of democracy, stability and development, despite the negative record of these regimes on issues such as gender relations, social change, the rural poor and other marginalised groups in society, population growth, the environment and competition for scarce natural resources, mass migration, food shortage, drugs, disease and AIDS, crime and the proliferation of guns and weaponry, and the role of the armed forces. There is little doubt that unless all stakeholders, from the state and particularly from the market and civil society, are more closely involved in the quest for peace, development and reconstruction in West Africa, the root causes of conflict and underdevelopment in the region will remain unidentified and unsolved. By the same token, there is certainly a risk that if the neopatrimonial quasi-states and governments remain exclusive, the intergovernmental regional organizations will continue to remain illegitimate – just another instrument of state repression – in the eyes of civil society and the broader stratas of the population.

Thus there needs to be a change of attitude on the part of politicians and the national bureaucracy towards regionalization and the role of neighbouring countries. The bureaucracies tend to be excessively nationally oriented and seem to work against, and not hand in hand with, market and civil society actors. A cooperation culture and a vision of a common destiny need to be encouraged among institutions, bureaucracies and national administrations. Political leaders and policy makers ought to be less concerned with the implementation and execution of regional development projects and the top-down measures associated with contemporary regional organizations, which are neither integrated into national development plans nor in touch with the realities on the ground.

Even if this cooperation culture could be fostered it is clear that all-embracing West African regionalization among 16 structurally very different countries will be extremely difficult. Whatever the future holds, too much effort has been expended on grandiose projects and the top-down visions of pan-Africanism. Considerable doubts also arise about the future viability of ECOWAS, although it is possible, or perhaps even likely, that the ECOMOG adventures will have a positive effect on economic cooperation, which was the original mandate of the organization. Nigeria's new democratic regime may very well try to be more constructive than its predecessors. As far as policy discussions are concerned, the Anglophone–Francophone divide needs to be bridged, which raises the question of whether the Francophone countries will continue to drag their feet within ECOWAS. On the other hand, according to a much more optimistic scenario, UEMOAmay serve as a catalyst for broader West African regionalization. If UEMOA member countries were able to coordinate policies with Nigeria and Ghana, this would be a great step forward.

NOTES

1 This section draws on arguments raised in Söderbaum (2000).
2 AOF included present-day Benin, Burkina Faso, Côte d'Ivoire, Guinea, Mali, Mauritania, Niger and Senegal. Togo was under German rule until 1919, when it became part of the French empire, albeit not of AOF. The Gambia, Ghana, Nigeria and Sierra Leone were British territories, while Cape Verde and Guinea-Bissau used to be Portuguese colonies. Liberia was founded in 1822 by freed American slaves and was never under colonial rule.
3 In 1994 the Francophone countries (with the exception of Guinea) – Benin, Burkina Faso, Côte d'Ivoire, Mali, Niger, Senegal and Togo – agreed to deepen and widen economic cooperation and integration through the amalgamation of CEAO and the Union Monétaire Ouest Africaine (UMOA, or West African Monetary Union) into UEMOA. In 1997 the former Portuguese colony Guinea-Bissau also joined this previously exclusive Francophone grouping. Togo was a member of UMOAbut not of CEAO (primarily because it remained hesitant to join an economic grouping excluding Nigeria), and became a member of UEMOA, while Mauritania, which had been a member of CEAO only, resigned.
4 In 1993 the ECOWAS member countries agreed on a new and high-profile ECOWAS treaty, the Abuja Treaty, largely modelled on the EU. In addition to the objectives contained in its founding text, the Treaty of Lagos, which aimed mainly at trade integration, the Abuja Treaty provides *inter alia* for the establishment of a common market and a single currency in the economic field, while in the political sphere the aims are to increase political cooperation in order to ensure democracy and good governance, a common foreign policy, a regional conflict resolution mechanism, a West African parliament, an Economic and Social Council and a supranational Court of Justice.
5 Only products set up on the Common List and made by specified enterprises are actually eligible for trading preferences – by 1995 only slightly over 200 products were on the Common List – and the implementation of the rather complex Trade Liberalization Scheme did not begin until 1990 (Rwegasira 1997).
6 This section draws heavily on the work of Daniel Bach (1997; 1999).

5 Regionalization in Southern Africa

The Role of the Dominant

BERTIL ODÉN

Southern Africa as a region is characterized by the following main factors:

1 For historical reasons the level of integration is high in a number of areas, on a pattern once decided by the mining and agricultural interests and the colonial powers.

2 During an intermediate period, starting in the mid-1970s, regionalization efforts were used as instruments in the conflict between apartheid South Africa and the rest of the region. With the fall of the apartheid system in the early 1990s more normal conditions for regionalization returned.

3 The region is highly asymmetrical in economic terms. South Africa as a country and South African companies and institutions dominate in many fields, such as mining, agriculture, manufacturing, trade, transport and communications or financial services.

4 The region is rich in natural resources such as water, energy, minerals and good soils. Their use and exploration contain potential benefits of cooperation as well as conflict and competition. The benefits of cooperation and the risks of non-cooperation are evident also in other issue areas, such as health, environment, migration, and the struggle against organized crime.

5 Southern Africa can be regarded as a regional security complex, meaning that the security concerns of one state cannot be considered apart from the security concerns of neighbouring states (Buzan 1991: 90).

6 A number of regional organizations have been established. The oldest, with the highest level of integration, is the Southern African Customs Union (SACU),

originally formed in 1910, with South Africa, Botswana, Lesotho, Namibia and Swaziland as present members. With the exception of Botswana, these countries form the Common Monetary Area (CMA). Both ventures are totally dominated by South Africa. The five SACU member states, together with Angola, the Democratic Republic of Congo (DRC), Malawi, Mauritius, Mozambique, Seychelles, Tanzania, Zambia and Zimbabwe, are also members of the Southern African Development Community (SADC), previously the Southern African Development Coordination Conference (SADCC).[1] A fourth organization is the Common Market of Eastern and Southern Africa (COMESA), in which most SADC countries are members, together with a number of countries in East and Central Africa.

Guided by the set of questions outlined in the introduction of this book, the chapter is designed as follows. First there is a section on various ways to define Southern Africa as a region and a brief historical exposé of regionalization processes in the region, focusing on the integrating and disintegrating forces. Thereafter, the three main regional organizations, SACU, COMESAand SADC, are discussed. This is followed by an analysis of the political economy of regionalization in Southern Africa and South African dominance in the region. Then, the security perspective is considered. Finally, some concluding comments are offered on possible future scenarios of the region, and Southern Africa's role in the global political economy.

A History of Southern African Regionalization

Since the beginning of the 1980s the most common definition of Southern Africa has been South Africa plus the SADCC (from 1992, SADC) member states. When South Africa became a member in 1994, Southern Africa and SADC could be used synonymously.

This definition is, however, of recent origin. Historically, Southern Africa has been used to cover various countries in the southern part of Africa. The minimalist definition included South Africa and the neighbouring areas, then called Bechuanaland (Botswana), Basutoland (Lesotho), Swaziland and South West Africa (Namibia) – the present SACU member states – while geographically the Zambezi river was sometimes used as the border line, which meant the inclusion of Zimbabwe and the southern part of Mozambique as well. Angola and Tanzania can trace their belonging to the region to their roles as Front Line States (FLS)[2] and as SADCC/SADC members. Previously Tanzania clearly formed part of East Africa and Angola of West or Central Africa. The main historical and regional economic links of the most recent members, Mauritius, the DRC and the Seychelles, have been with East and Central Africa and the Indian Ocean Rim rather than Southern Africa.

The colonial history of the Southern African states is rather heterogeneous. Angola and Mozambique were Portuguese colonies until 1975. Apartheid South Africa and present Namibia, illegally occupied by South Africa until its independence in 1990, were special cases, as was Southern Rhodesia (Zimbabwe) after its unilateral declaration of independence in 1965. Malawi and Zambia (formerly Nyasaland and Northern Rhodesia) were British colonies up to their independence in the first half of the 1960s, while Tanganyika came under League of Nations/UN trusteeship, administered by Great Britain. Present Botswana, Lesotho and Swaziland were British protectorates, and became independent in the second half of the 1960s. The colonial history of Mauritius, the DRC and the Seychelles also differ from the others. The colonial legacy continues to be an important practical obstacle to increased regionalization, for instance with regard to the language barrier and different (colonial) traditions of public administration.

In the 1970s the main line of division in the region ran between independent countries and a bloc constituted by the Portuguese colonies and the white minority-led countries. During the decolonization and struggle against apartheid South Africa, the FLS cooperation also became a vehicle for a redefinition of the region. This was further enforced when SADCC was formed in 1980. One of the main objectives of SADCC was to reduce economic dependence on South Africa (Amin, Chitala and Mandaza 1987). This was a difficult task because South Africa dominated so many sectors and the apartheid regime used its dominance in order to defend the apartheid system.

It is crucial to understand that the level of integration in Southern Africa is high in a number of areas, particularly transport, migrant labour, mining and trade. In these and other areas South African actors are dominant and therefore the region can be analysed along centre–periphery lines. This structural pattern of South African dominance developed mainly during the colonial period, which coincided with and partly was an effect of the emerging exploitation of minerals, especially gold and diamonds in the Witwatersrand area of South Africa. During the first half of the twentieth century the successful mineral companies developed into large conglomerates with interests in a number of economic sectors. Later in the century some of them developed into full-fledged transnational companies (Odén 1998).

Cecil Rhodes is perhaps the best-known ideologue and exponent of northward economic penetration from South Africa, followed by political imperialism in the region. Such plans contradicted the interests of the colonial powers (Great Britain and Portugal), however, and never materialized. Subsequent South African governments unsuccessfully tried to persuade Great Britain that current Botswana, Lesotho and Swaziland should form part of South Africa.

For many hundreds of years the history of Southern Africa has been one of migration: from the Bantu people moving southwards towards the South African coast in the thirteenth and fourteenth centuries to the Great Trek of the Boers and the *mfekane* turbulence setting groups of Zulus, Ndebeles and others on the move northwards in the nineteenth century.

Labour migration, which has a history of more than a hundred years, is to a large extent a consequence of the mining expansion and of colonial and commercial agricultural production. Migrants – mainly from Mozambique and Lesotho, during some periods also from Malawi, Botswana and Zimbabwe – were recruited for the South African mines, and to a lesser extent as farm and domestic workers. During the colonial period people from Mozambique and Malawi also worked in the two Rhodesias in mines and on farms and plantations.

The pattern of the regional transport network is primarily based on the needs of the colonial administrations, mining and export agriculture, as it developed during the early twentieth century. The railways and harbours have played an important role in the transit traffic to and from the landlocked countries in the region. After the 1920s a regional trade pattern with a strong South African dominance evolved, whereby present Botswana, Lesotho, Namibia and Swaziland virtually became economic provinces of South Africa. The regionalization process during the colonial and early postcolonial periods was thus driven not by a free market, but by first international and then national capital's manipulation of human and natural resources in the region.

Although the attempts to use SADCC as an instrument to reduce the member countries' dependence on South Africa during the period 1980–92 were not very successful, some important achievements resulted and at least economic dependence did not grow. For instance, many transport links were rehabilitated and communication systems were developed. Regional cooperation emerged in the fields of energy, soil conservation, agriculture and other areas. SADCC mobilized significant flows of aid to the region and improved the general climate of regionalization in the member states. Borrowing an expression from SADCC's former executive secretary, Simba Makoni, the national political and economic elites began to 'think SADCC'. It was at this elite level that a certain feeling of 'regionness' emerged.

Over time three main categories of external forces have shaped the regional political economy and the regionalization process in Southern Africa: before independence, the colonial powers; after independence and during the Cold War, the superpowers[3] and to a certain extent the former colonial states; and from the early 1980s onwards, the Bretton Woods institutions and bilateral aid donors. In the post-Cold War, post-apartheid era the regionalization process is increasingly determined by intraregional relations, while the role of external forces is reduced.

There is now a potential for SADCC's successor SADC, with South Africa as a member, to be used for constructive purposes in the new era, thus creating a more enabling regional climate in terms of security interaction, political relations and economic development cooperation. Much depends on the political will of the member states to develop the organization. Another factor that improves the potential for regionalization in Southern Africa is the ongoing convergence of macroeconomic policies, investment and currency regimes in the region via the structural adjustment programmes. This makes regional cooperation and integration easier compared to when SADCC was launched in 1980.[4]

In this context it is important to note that apart from state-driven regionalization efforts within the framework of SADC and other regional organizations, such as SACU and COMESA, spontaneous cross-border trade, migration, investments and other activities are carried out by individuals, groups and other parts of the civil society. Some of these have traditions making postcolonial borders irrelevant, others are based on price and institutional differences between countries with common borders.

Regional Organizations

All the three main regional organizations in Southern Africa, SACU, COMESA and SADC, are presently undergoing transformation (Haarløv 1997; Odén 1996; Øster-gaard 1993). A new agreement was signed in 1969 following the independence of the three territories Basutoland (Lesotho), Bechuanaland (Botswana) and Swaziland. Namibia was for all practical purposes part of the customs union during its occupation by South Africa and became a member of SACU after achieving independence in 1990. SACU has been quite unique in the sense that it has had no institutions of its own. All activities have been carried out by South African authorities. The discussion on SACU has mainly focused on the problems associated with trade integration between unequal partners. In the 1969 agreement a compensation clause was included whereby the smaller countries were allocated a larger than proportional share of the total customs union revenue pool as compensation for delayed payments and the lack of influence over the trade and industry regime, which was unilaterally decided by South Africa.

Since 1969 there has been an intense discussion on whether the revenue compensation to the smaller countries is sufficient. In 1976 the agreement was amended with a stabilization factor in the revenue-sharing formula. Despite its drawbacks the smaller members have remained within the union, and the SACU revenue constitutes a major part of the total government revenue in all the countries – although the relative importance of the SACU revenue in Botswana has been reduced by the rise in revenue from diamond production.[5] A number of practical matters, such as the efforts to create an effective national customs system, also reduced the inclination of the smaller countries to leave the organization.

Negotiations on a new SACU agreement have been going on since 1994 and are supposed to result in significant changes, such as the formation of common institutions, more equal decision making and reform of the system of sharing the customs revenue. The negotiations have dragged on longer than expected amid uncertainty over the signing of a European Union–South Africa free trade agreement, initiated in 1995 and finally concluded in early 1999, in combination with discussions on the SADC Trade Protocol. What type of regional trade regime will come out of these complex, interrelated trade negotiations is difficult to envisage.

The predecessor to COMESA, the Preferential Trade Area for Eastern and Southern African States (PTA) was to a large extent the creation of the UN Economic Commission for Africa (ECA), forming one subregion that eventually should be merged with others into the African Economic Community (AEC) in line with the Lagos Plan of Action and the Abuja Treaty. The PTA was formally inaugurated in 1982 in accordance with the trade integration concept. COMESA was officially launched in 1994, when 12 of the then 22 member countries ratified the agreement.[6] COMESA continues the PTA trade integration project, striving towards a common market. At the same time the agreement is broader, including cooperation in almost all economic fields.

The original goal of the PTA was to implement a free trade area by 1990. Initially, however, the gradual reduction of tariffs was restricted to a limited list of products and several members of the organization got waivers from the decided tariff reduction scheme. Implementation soon lagged behind the timetable, which subsequently was rescheduled to make the year 2000 the new goal. By 1996 a few countries were reported to have reached the set goal of tariff reduction, while the rest were significantly behind schedule. In addition to the tariff reductions some practical improvements in cross-border transport and customs procedures – which in the real world often are more important for increased intraregional trade than the former – have been made. The share of intra-COMESA trade has not increased, however, and remains around 5 per cent of the total trade of COMESA members.

SADC, finally, is being transformed from a project cooperation and aid mobilization scheme to a much more ambitious development integration project. The aim of the former SADCC was to reduce economic dependence on South Africa. Its approach was different from the trade and market integration model, and the responsibility for project coordination was divided between the individual member states along sectors. SADCC became popular among some of the aid agencies, both because it did not build up a large bureaucracy and because the donors could pick and choose between a wide range of projects on the SADCC list. Aid to

SADCC projects was also presented, at the time, as part of an anti-apartheid policy. The majority of the implemented SADCC projects are in the transport and communications sector. A number of the transport corridors have been modernized and intraregional communications have improved significantly.

With the apartheid system being dismantled in South Africa and with South Africa potentially joining in the near future, SADCC decided to transform itself into SADC in 1992, becoming a legal entity and not simply a project coordination conference. The level of integration aimed for in the SADC Treaty and the Windhoek Declaration is very ambitious: it is 'deep' as well as 'broad', and covers both security and foreign policy.

In 1996 President Mandela of South Africa succeeded President Masire of Botswana as chairperson of SADC for a three-year period. Since then, efforts to implement the Sector Protocol on Trade, aiming at a SADC free trade area and later a common market, have been strengthened. The main focus of the SADC regionalization discussion has moved from infrastructural cooperation to market and trade integration. In 1998 SADC had been under organizational restructuring for six years, but this process and the capacity of the organization are still weak in relation to its objectives. Nine sector protocols that are supposed to guide the future regionalization had been signed in late 1998, but ratification by the national parliaments is lagging behind.[7]

With the new SADC and COMESA treaties, competition between the two organizations has become more evident than before. South Africa and Botswana remained the only SADC non-members of COMESA until 1997, when Lesotho and Mozambique decided to leave the organization. Several years of effort to avoid overlap and find a clear division of labour between the organizations have been unsuccessful. SADC has decided that its member states should form a PTA-South, and the non-SADC members should form a PTA-North – but this proposal has not been accepted by COMESA. How the two organizations will coexist or merge must be settled in order to improve the framework for intergovernmental cooperation in the region.

SADC's position relative to that of COMESA has improved during recent years, for various reasons: South Africa is a member of SADC, but not of COMESA; COMESA has had managerial problems; and civil war or other armed conflicts have occurred in a number of the member countries such as Somalia, Eritrea, Ethiopia, Sudan, Burundi, Rwanda and the DRC.

The Political Economy of Regionalization and South African Dominance

The end of the Cold War is important for understanding the changes in Southern Africa. Today, the region no longer constitutes a scene of superpower conflict. The remaining superpower's interest is focusing on access to strategic minerals and defence against perceived threats to the interests of US companies. In President Clinton's new Africa policy, presented in 1997, increased access to African markets was emphasized. In the field of security, the US has an interest to promote South Africa's role as 'local police' in the region, in order to improve political stability.

The economic and resource dominance of South Africa is crucial for understanding the political economy of Southern Africa. The GDP of South Africa is almost four times that of the other SADC countries taken together. Its industrial production is five times larger, and its capacity in sectors such as energy and financial services, as well as its military strength, dwarfs the rest of the region. It is important to recognize that in several respects this dominance has increased since 1990.

Transport and communication is one important field. South African interests dominated this sector during the apartheid era, and with the help of destabilization the landlocked neighbouring countries were kept dependent on South Africa for transit transport. With the fall of apartheid, commercial competition replaced destabilization, and in just a few years South African shipping, port management, railways, road transporters, forwarding agents and air companies have further strengthened their dominant position. If this development means that state-owned enterprises in the neighbouring countries, taken over or managed by South African companies or parastatals, become more efficient, the region as a whole may benefit. If the benefits go only to South African interests, however, it will result in increased South African dominance.

Since the end of the nineteenth century South Africa's mining and farm labour has partly consisted of migrant workers. In the mid-1970s neighbouring countries provided two-thirds of the workers in the South African mines. Since then the share of migrant workers has diminished, along with a reduction of the total number of mine workers due to the closing of a number of gold mines. The number of registered migrant mine workers has almost halved from around 300,000 in the mid-1970s. Since the late 1970s Lesotho has been the main source of migrant mine workers, with Mozambique second.

A large number of Mozambicans have also been working on South African farms since the 1970s. During recent years the flow of illegal immigrants to South Africa has increased. They do not come only from neighbouring countries, but also, for instance, from Nigeria, DRC, Rwanda and Burundi. The existence of an estimated 2–3 million illegal immigrants is a major problem for the new South African government.[8] The war in the DRC has generated new migrant flows in the region, and the continued war in Angola also generates new refugees moving to Namibia and Zambia. A tradition of many centuries thus continues. If not controlled, this situation may produce political and social instability.

With regard to regional trade, the four smaller SACU member countries, Botswana, Lesotho, Namibia and Swaziland, are thoroughly integrated into the South African economy and take between 80 and 90 per cent of their imports from South Africa. Of the other SADC countries, Mozambique takes more than half, and Malawi, Zambia and Zimbabwe about a third of their total imports from South Africa (EIU 1998). These shares have increased since 1990, and for instance the SACU (almost entirely South African) exports to the rest of the SADC increased by 25 per cent between 1993 and 1994, almost 50 per cent in 1995 and around 20 per cent in 1996. Meanwhile, intraregional trade between the SADC countries, excluding South Africa, has also increased slightly but still remains, on average, less than 5 per cent of the total trade of these countries.

The region constitutes an important market for South Africa's manufacturing industry, which with a few exceptions is not competitive in the OECD markets. One of the reasons for South Africa's dominance in this field is higher protection of the South African market compared to many neighbouring countries, which have reduced their import protection as part of the implementation of SAPs. South Africa's level of trade protection will be reduced gradually over a period of 5–12 years, however, as a result of the agreement between the World Trade Organization (WTO) and South Africa.[9] The argument is that better access to South African markets through lowered South African protection, and particularly a free trade area agreement, may stimulate production in neighbouring countries.

The rapid increase of foreign trade between South Africa and neighbouring countries, which has taken place without trade regime changes, is thus one important sign of South African dominance. Another is the significantly increased investment by South Africa-based companies in neighbouring countries in the 1990s (in parallel with investment in South Africa by overseas companies), although initial hopes of a host of immediate opportunities have not been met. The complex infrastructural and bureaucratic reality in war-damaged and/or parastatal-dominated neighbouring countries has also become clearer to these actors. The list of reported South African investments in other SADC countries since 1994 is impressive and contains significant ventures in tourism, retail trade, the food industry and selected manufacturing.[10] A number of mining and metal industry projects have been contracted or are under negotiation, such as Mozal, Pande gas and Moatize coal in Mozambique, gold in Zimbabwe and Tanzania, platinum in Zimbabwe, copper in Zambia, diamonds and Kudu gas in Namibia. All of them may not be implemented, but those that are will have a significant impact on the regional economic structure.

Developments since 1990 show clearly that market players in the region, especially if they are South Africa-based, are quicker to adjust to the new regional and global dispensation than are the governments. The increasing economic superiority of South African economic operators contributes to a further strengthening of the existing centre–periphery structure. Investment by South African companies, and particularly large-scale resource-based investment, makes political and economic actors in the host country more dependent. But it also creates a counter-effect, as both the involved South African company and the South African government become more dependent on political stability and economic development in the host country. South African investment in neighbouring countries thus creates an interdependence, rather than straightforward South African dominance. When South African companies invest in neighbouring countries to gain lower unit costs in production, mainly for the South African market, they compensate for part of the trade imbalance through the capital account. Increasing exports from the neighbouring country to South Africa also reduce the South African trade surplus with that country. Migrant labour generates capital flows to the labour source country. A complex interdependence results from these and other effects.

This counter-trend is enforced by another factor. In a few important domains, South Africa's superior position is eroded and an increased South African dependency on resources from the rest of the region is developing. Obvious examples are water and hydropower energy. Due to their conflict potential, other issues also need to be treated at a regional level. The government of South Africa has a strong interest in increasing cooperation in order to control organized crime involved in drugs, cars and arms. Other examples are the already mentioned areas of migration, environmental issues, AIDS and other diseases, where the interdependence between South Africa and its neighbours is not as unbalanced as elsewhere. A number of these interdependence issues, as well as the economic asymmetry, may be dealt with under various SADC sector units or outside the SADC framework, in specific cooperation projects, programmes or institutions which do not necessarily have to be intergovernmental. They may also include only those directly affected, on the principle of 'variable geography'.

A fairly recent phenomenon in Southern Africa is the development of micro-regional development zones, exemplified by the Maputo Development Corridor,[11] the attempts to develop the Beira and Nacala corridors in a similar manner, and specific 'Spatial Development Initiatives' in South Africa. The mixture of private and public efforts to create rapid economic growth in a limited geographic space, ignoring national borders, is reminiscent of the unbalanced growth development strategies launched in the 1960s.

Monitoring or compensatory measures of some kind have to be applied in order to avoid aggravating economic and social imbalances in the region. Such measures normally have to be state-driven and based on intergovernmental agreements and institutions. These are easier to implement in issue areas with public sector ownership and where the interdependence is less asymmetric. A number of so-called 'regional goods' fall into this category, such as transport, communications, electric power and water resources.

The South African government has stated in various policy documents its commitment to further regionalization and its awareness of the risks of polarization. When it comes to implementation, the picture is more ambiguous. The record of the South African government's positions in and attitude towards bilateral negotiations with other SADC countries does not give the impression of a strong will to improve regional imbalances. Complaints are also voiced from the other SADC and SACU countries on the South African positions in the renegotiation of the SACU agreement and of the SADC trade protocol. This is a normal part of negotiation strategy but also contains the perception that there is a gap between the South African official standpoint and its actual behaviour. One explanation is certainly differing interests in South Africa and a gap between the government's official position and the perceptions of some of the negotiators from the 'old regime'.

South African domination is regarded with strong reservations by most other SADC member governments, and particularly, it seems, by various interests in Zimbabwe, including the government. In the poorer countries the position seems to be more ambiguous. On the one hand there is hope for investment and employment as a result of increased links with South Africa, since there are expectations that South Africa will take the lead and improve the situation of the whole region. On the other hand, there is a reluctant attitude towards the penetration of South African companies with superior economic power and sometimes also with records of collaboration with the previous apartheid government.

Regional Security

For decades the regional security situation was dominated by the conflict between apartheid South Africa and regional opposition to this system (Ohlson and Stedman 1994). The legacy of South African destabilization in the rest of the region is particularly serious in Angola and Mozambique. Since 1994 there have been few signs of enmity between the states in the region, [12] although some suspicion of the South African military forces remains in the neighbouring countries for historical reasons.

Most open or potential conflicts in the region are domestic. The notorious Government–UNITA conflict in Angola continues to threaten regional stability, although from August 1998 it has been overshadowed by the war between Kabila's regime and the rebels in the DRC, both parties supported militarily by a number of governments in neighbouring countries, of which Angola, Namibia and Zimbabwe are SADC members. Parallel to this, other SADC countries, notably South Africa and Zambia, are trying to find ways to negotiate a resolution of the conflict. The changes of political leadership by military means in the DRC and Congo-Brazzaville in 1997 emphasized that political stability cannot be taken for granted.

The Government–RENAMO antagonism in Mozambique and the African National Congress (ANC)–Inkatha conflict in South Africa's KwaZulu/Natal province have cooled down significantly, although they continue to be obstacles to the nation-building processes in the two countries. In South Africa as a whole the violence is still at an unacceptably high level, although it is mainly criminal rather than political. In Mozambique there is a movement towards normalization among the previously warring parties, but many abnormalities remain. It should be mentioned that even the resolution of violent conflicts, as for instance between the Mozambican government and RENAMO, can have negative regional spill-over effects in the form of a thriving cross-border trade in arms.

Conflicts may develop in other countries as well, not necessarily becoming violent but still problematic because they erode political and social stability. Examples are domestic political developments in Zambia, where high expectations of the Chiluba government have turned to frustration, and Zimbabwe, where criticism of the Mugabe regime is met by increasing arrogance and repression of opposing individuals or groups, and where the state of public finances, already parlous by 1998, has deteriorated further, partly due to the military intervention in the DRC. The antagonism between traditionalists and modernists in Swaziland, and the increasing subregional power conflicts between the politicians/parties/regions in Malawi, are other cases in point. All these manifest and latent conflicts affect regional stability. Regional conflict prevention measures may, however, inhibit their development into open conflicts. The SADC military intervention by troops from Botswana and South Africa in Lesotho in September 1998 in order to avoid a potential military coup can be regarded as an example of preventive regional peacekeeping, although better planning probably would had reduced the fatalities and the physical destruction.

There are potential conflicts in other countries that may develop into armed violence, but on the whole the basis for political stability and economic development has improved significantly. For a number of years all countries in Southern Africa, with the exception of Swaziland, have had multiparty political systems and in most countries respect for human rights and a plurality of opinions has increased. Nevertheless, there is a risk of backtracking both on human rights issues and towards *de facto* one-party systems in a number of countries. The familiar signs of power, arrogance and the suppression of critical groups, organizations and individuals are evident, for instance, in Zambia, Zimbabwe, Namibia and Malawi.

With the primary security threat removed from the region, the question of promoting economic development rapidly ascended the list of priorities. There are hopes for peace in both Angola and Mozambique, which would make infrastruc-

93

tural rehabilitation and agricultural reorganization possible, and improve the situation substantially for many people. This in turn may improve political stability and the security situation, reducing the risk of sliding back into war. Regional security cooperation could also improve stability and help to identify and forestall conflicts of interest between countries in the region; another aim would be to contain internal conflicts in individual countries to prevent them from spilling over into other countries.

The military interventions in Lesotho and the DRC in 1998 came after earlier successful non-military interventions to block undemocratic behaviour a few years earlier in two SADC countries. One was the rescinding of the non-constitutional dispersion of the parliament and government of Lesotho in 1995 by King Letsie III, through successful pressure from the heads of state of South Africa, Botswana and Zimbabwe. The other was the strong pressure exerted by a number of SADC governments on the RENAMO leader Dlakhama when he threatened to withdraw from the elections in Mozambique in 1994.

This promising trend has been turned into a much more ominous one, however, by the war between the rebels and the Kabila regime in the DRC, and the support for the two sides in the conflict from very odd alliances, involving at least eight governments and a number of opposition or marginalized groups in at least five countries besides the DRC itself. In fact, the military interventions in the DRC and Lesotho in 1998 may move security thinking in the region back into the military modes of realist power politics. This would be a significant setback, as the region needs a broader and wider security concept, one that links security and developmental issues.

There are several issues that contain a regional security dimension, such as uncontrolled migration, water supply, environmental degradation, and the proliferation of AIDS and other diseases. These issues know no national borders and have a strong conflict potential, and therefore ought to be handled at the regional level. One example is the SADC sector protocol on *Shared Watercourse Systems*, which may be the forum in which regional water resource management can be implemented. This is one of the areas in which South African dependence on its neighbours will increase. It is therefore not surprising that the South African government has made strenuous efforts to develop cooperation in this field. This was also the first SADC sector protocol, agreed upon in 1994.

The SADC Organ on Politics, Defence and Security, which was formed in early 1996, would ideally be an instrument for handling security issues in a broad sense, including peacekeeping and military interventions should these be deemed necessary. Opinions are still divided, however, on the mandate and formal status of the SADC Organ, especially between President Mandela as chairman of the SADC Summit and President Mugabe as chairman of the Organ (Cawthra 1997; Malan and Cilliers 1997).

The Future

A high economic growth scenario is a necessary but not sufficient condition for positive regional development. The results of high economic growth have to become available to the majority of the people; unemployment has to be reduced; and health, education and skills have to be improved. The alternative is increasing polarization between the elite and the majority of the population. Such a development may impose on the region a permanent structure similar to that of Brazil. A colonial pattern may emerge, with typical enclaves of growth and wealth consisting of a number of urban centres and certain rural areas where production based on valuable natural resources is concentrated, linked together in a pattern rendering national borders unimportant. These enclaves would form an archipelago of wealth in a sea of poverty, consisting of rural areas where the majority of the population would live. Southern Africa would continue to be a typical example of the centre–periphery model.

Such asymmetric and unbalanced development is not intended – if we are to believe the rhetoric – by the present ANC government in South Africa, which stresses that South Africa's future is linked intrinsically to the future of the region as a whole. It may emerge by default, however, if strong policies to avoid such development are lacking. It would be a historical irony if what the apartheid state failed to achieve through its political and military designs from 1974 to 1990 were to be accomplished economically through the structural power of South Africa's finance, industrial and merchant capital in the post-apartheid era (Ahwireng-Obeng and McGowan 1998). It is therefore imperative that analysts and policy makers should begin to identify strategies to domesticate South Africa's capital and make it realize how much its fate is tied to that of the region as a whole. This might contain its exploitative tendencies and increase its acceptance in the region.

It is not easy to find strong interests in the region that support a more balanced regionalization. Some political leaders have an awareness of interdependence in strategic areas, but they often continue to prioritize national interests. Large sectors of both the public administration and the business community are not interested and are sometimes even hostile to actions needed to create a more balanced regional development.

Interestingly, though, regional civil society networks are emerging. Trade unions in both South Africa and other countries are very aware of regional issues, seeking to avoid the erosion – by competition for investment between individual countries – of employment and wage levels enjoyed by their own members, and of national labour legislation. Balancing these issues in a sustainable regionalization process is difficult. Some intellectuals and politicians discuss this issue, but the general interest is often modestly represented, and the national perspective tends to dominate.

It is easier, however, to pinpoint the threats to a high-growth scenario in the region, all of which illustrate the close interrelation between economy, politics and security.

1   An increased militarization of the region as an effect of the military interventions in Lesotho and the DRC. This would imply more public resources channelled to the military sector and less for development purposes. It may also imply that security issues increasingly are defined in the context of realist power analysis, de-emphasizing the broader security agenda which is so important in the Southern African context.

2   Conflicts regarding the use of regional water resources that may create local political destabilization and reduce regional cooperation in other areas.

3   Conflicts related to regional migration flows.

4   The combined effects of brain drain southward in the region and AIDS, reducing the supply of highly skilled staff in the other SADC countries to a critically low level, threatening already weak public administration, education, health, and commercial activities.

5   Prolonged drought periods, affecting agriculture and livestock production and consumption, and further reducing water and hydroelectric supply.

6   Weak political support for regional organizations and measures to balance the increased asymmetry between South Africa and the other Southern African states.

7   Breakdown of the economy and democratization process in any of the countries, with Zimbabwe as the most likely candidate.

The complex interrelations between the economic, political and security spheres will determine regional development. South Africa's dominant position in the region should preferably be utilized in a constructive way along the lines of a 'benevolent hegemon', taking long-term regional perspectives rather than short-sighted national interests into consideration. The other countries in the region would have to accept such a benign hegemony and put sufficient effort into the regionalization activities in order to increase their own influence. As is shown above, however, the preconditions for such a scenario do not seem to be in place.

In order to avoid misunderstanding, it should be pointed out, finally, that regional balance is not simply a regionalization issue. Imbalances in Southern Africa occur also as a result of globalization and national development, and to believe that they will be cured by regionalization only is to oversimplify. Regionalism is no panacea for a more balanced Southern Africa, but it is important to understand that it might contribute to such a development under certain circumstances.

What Role for Southern Africa in the Global Political Economy?

In the post-Cold War, post-apartheid future the external political and economic interests in Southern Africa will probably be modest. Demand for some of its minerals will continue to exist, however, and therefore also an interest in obtaining guaranteed access to them. Southern Africa as a market is minor in a global perspective, although some branches constitute important markets for international producers, notably of mining equipment and technology. The main South African mining conglomerates are also important players on the world market.

South Africa's share of global production and foreign trade diminished from the late 1970s to the early 1990s.[13] Since then it has been stabilized as a result of the economic growth taking place in the region. From a global perspective, there is little difference between South Africa as an individual country and Southern Africa as a region. The total GDP of Southern Africa (including South Africa) is just a third bigger than South Africa's, and the latter's exports to the rest of the world amount to twice those of the other SADC member countries taken together.

Economically, the perspective is different from the point of view of South Africa, compared to that of the other SADC countries. The latter could have significantly stronger leverage if they acted together with South Africa, but South Africa would not gain as much from the arrangement. Regional groupings provide perhaps the only viable vehicle whereby developing country governments can exert bargaining influence in multilateral organizations and in their relations with developed countries and transnational corporations. The collective bargaining position of Southern African governments, including South Africa, could be increased with respect to at least three major policy issues: the role of foreign direct investment; influence within multilateral organizations; and bargaining against donors on development policy.

It is often claimed that unilateral trade liberalization is superior to regional integration arrangements. The World Bank perspective on regionalization as a second-best solution is clearly expressed in the following quotation:

> as regionalism emerges as an integral part of the world trading environment, it should not be allowed to divert attention from the fact that the first-best policy remains most-favoured-nation liberalization and the ultimate goal multilateral free trade. Regional arrangements should be implemented in a manner that harnesses them securely to the long-run goal of multilateral liberalization. (World Bank 1995: 21)

In line with World Bank thinking, de Melo, Panagariya and Rodrick (1993) argue that countries can benefit more from a regional free trade area than from unilateral trade liberalization only if one of the countries is willing to accept a suboptimal position for whatever reasons. They claim also that unilateral trade liberalization is less attractive for the countries outside the bloc if the world gets divided into inward-looking blocs. The outside countries will then be better off, either seeking access to one of the blocs and adopting its trade policy, or liberalizing trade among themselves. Leaving aside its free trade argument, the problem with this perspective is that it is too narrow; it leaves a number of other important regionalization issues aside, such as the political, security, environmental, cultural and other aspects. If a broader regionalization paradigm could be employed, in line with the argument of this book, the Southern African region should be able to improve its position and play a role in the global political economy. As this chapter has made evident, however, the structure and balance of forces in the region are not very conducive to such a development. More likely is a scenario in which the centre–periphery structure of the region continues, while the marginalization of the region in the global context may be checked, but hardly reversed.

NOTES

1 The original nine members of SADCC were Angola, Botswana, Lesotho, Malawi, Mozambique, Swaziland, Tanzania, Zambia and Zimbabwe. After its independence in 1990, Namibia joined the organization. South Africa became a (SADC) member in 1994, Mauritius in 1995 and the DRC and the Seychelles in 1997.

2 The FLS was a group of countries supporting the liberation struggle in Zimbabwe, Namibia and South Africa. It originally consisted of Angola, Botswana, Mozambique, Tanzania and Zambia. After its independence in 1980, Zimbabwe joined the group.

3 The Cold War mainly affected military, security and foreign policy structures in the individual countries. Legacies also include heavy debt burdens to Russia in the cases of Angola and Mozambique, and the organization and thinking in the military and security sectors, which now are under restructuring.

4 Non-coordinated trade liberalization as part of the nationally oriented SAPs may, however, result in selective de-industrialization in other countries in the region, as the textile industry sector showed in Zambia and Zimbabwe in 1995, which may be destructive for the regionalization process.

5 For Botswana the SACU revenue constitutes 15–20 per cent of the total government revenue, for Lesotho the share is 45–55 per cent, for Swaziland 40–45 per cent and for Namibia 20–25 per cent.

6 The 22 member countries at that time were: Angola, Burundi, Comores, Djibouti, Eritrea, Ethiopia, Kenya, Lesotho, Madagascar, Malawi, Mauritius, Mozambique, Namibia, Rwanda, Seychelles, Somalia, Sudan, Swaziland, Tanzania, Uganda, Zambia and Zimbabwe. Zaire became the 23rd member in 1994. In 1997 Lesotho and Mozambique announced their intention to leave the organization. Tanzania followed suit in 2000. Egypt was admitted the same year.

7 After the SADC Summit Meeting in September 1998, nine protocols have been signed: *Shared Watercourse Systems; Energy; Combat of Illicit Drug Trafficking; Trade; Transport, Communications and Meterology; Education and Training; Mining; Tourism;* and *Immunities and Privileges.* An important decision was also taken at an extraordinary SADC Summit Meeting in 1996 to establish an SADC Organ on Politics, Defence and Security. At the 1998 Summit the protocol for the SADC Tribunal was also signed.

8 According to some estimates, quoted in South African media, they may be as many as eight million. No information is available, however, on how this very high figure is calculated. The aggregate figures used do not seem to distinguish between migrants arriving during recent

years and those who have been resident in South Africa for many years. In 1996 a new law was introduced, according to which immigrants who have lived more than five years in South Africa were entitled to apply for South African citizenship.

9 In 1997 the South African Department of Trade and Industry argued, after carrying out a study, that South Africa did not have the highest average tariff level. Although this may be correct, it is clear that South African trade protection is very high in those branches where manufacturing industry in the neighbouring countries is most competitive.

10 Some of the most active South African companies have been Illovo Sugar, which have bought sugar estates and factories in Mozambique, Tanzania, Malawi, Mauritius and Swaziland; South African Breweries, which has bought whole or parts of breweries in Angola, Botswana, Lesotho, Mozambique, Tanzania and Zimbabwe; Afrox with investments in Malawi, Namibia and Zambia; Protea Hotels, which has taken over hotels in Botswana, Malawi, Mozambique and Tanzania; and South African retail chains such as McCarthy Retail, PicknPay, PepStores and Shoprite Checkers, which have also invested in the neighbouring countries.

11 The implementation of this project started in 1997 and 90 per cent of the financing is planned to come from the private sector, with a new toll road from Witbank to Maputo and the upgrading of Maputo harbour as the main infrastructural projects, linked to a programme of economic development in the manufacturing, mining, tourism and agricultural sectors (Harrison and Todes 1996).

12 Minor exceptions are the disputes between Botswana and Namibia over the ownership of islands in the Chobe River. One of these disputes (Sedudu/Kasikili) has been taken to the International Court of Justice in the Hague.

13 Between 1981 and 1992 Southern Africa's share of global production declined from around 0.9 per cent to around 0.6 per cent and its share of global exports from around 1.4 per cent to around 1.0 per cent (rough calculation, based on World Development Reports).

6 Regionalization in Caucasia and Central Asia

PATRIK JOTUN

In most parts of the world a tendency toward regionalization has been visible during the last few decades. In the former Soviet sphere, disintegration of first the Soviet bloc, and later the Soviet Union itself, transformed this part of the world in a few years from a very coherent region into sovereign states with very different political and economic systems. This disintegration is something of an illusion. Despite the replacement of one political and economic system with another, most parts of the disintegrated region have engaged since the abolition of the Soviet Union in a process of reintegration.

This chapter deals with Caucasia and the former Soviet part of Central Asia. Caucasia and Central Asia will be treated and analysed as one region and it will be considered in relation to its neighbouring regions. This will be accomplished by relating the regionalization process to changes in the role of the nation-state, with special attention to security, economic development and ethno-national identities in the region. Since the suspension of the *Pax Sovietica* the region has been plagued by a number of ethnic conflicts. Attention will be given therefore to the insecurity produced by these conflicts and the role that the regional actors play in conflict resolution and securing safety. Because in Central Asia and Caucasia regional relations do not work properly – there are no working mechanisms for conflict management – this region tends to be tormented by conflicts.

Due to the threats related to security and major economic problems, the important question in Caucasia and Central Asia today is not regionalization or isolation. It may instead be summarized as *what kind* of regionalization is preferred, and what will the actual outcome be? In what sense is it one region and to what extent do Caucasia and Central Asia form part of a range of different regions, corresponding to various delimitations, contents and actors (one pan-Turkic region, one region including Russia, one including Turkey and Iran, one excluding the non-Turkic nationalities, etc.)?

This chapter begins by briefly considering the regional delimitation issue. An analysis follows of the various actors' roles in the process of regionalization, particularly in terms of security and economic development. Finally, the prospects of regionalization in Caucasia and Central Asia will be discussed.

Caucasia and Central Asia as a Region

When discussing Caucasia[1] and Central Asia[2] as a region,[3] I make no claim that this is a 'natural' region of any sort. The treatment of Caucasia and Central Asia as one region will only be used as a point of reference in discussing several other regional possibilities: thus several regional delimitations centring on Caucasia and Central Asia will be analysed. That Caucasia and Central Asia are both one region and several different regions demonstrates the pluralism of the new regionalism.

A region can also be defined either as an area with peaceful contacts and coop-eration, or it may include conflicts and be defined as a *regional security complex* on the grounds of interaction, peaceful or not. Caucasia and Central Asia, where there are several conflicts, exemplifies the latter case (Buzan 1991: 186–229). Taking different criteria into consideration, researchers and politicians make several different regional delimitations involving Caucasia and Central Asia.

There are three main reasons for selecting Caucasia and Central Asia as the broad focus of this chapter:

1 Caucasia and Central Asia have many common denominators and patterns of regional interaction. The Turkic language is a major language and Russian is a lingua franca. They have a common history, being parts of the Silk Road in historic times. Several nationalities living in one of the two main divisions have great diasporas in the other. The primary reason for analysing them as one region instead of two, however, is their common past as parts of the Soviet Union for 70 years. The Soviet Union gave the two areas a common infra-structure and political culture, and its legacy permeates economics, social life and culture. This chapter will examine the patterns of interaction that – to a great extent – are rooted in the Soviet period. In the post-Soviet era some parts have turned towards the West; Russia has tried to form a region around itself; and Caucasia and Central Asia to some extent have formed a region of their own.

2 The names Caucasia and Central Asia are of recent and European origin. As in other parts of the world, water has not always divided peoples. On the contrary, rivers, lakes and even seas are relatively easy to travel across and they facilitate

the transportation of commodities, people and ideas. Mountains and large forests are much more difficult to cross. Consequently water ties people together, instead of dividing them. As this is also true about the Caspian Sea, its eastern and western shores are a lot closer to each other than, for example, the northern and southern parts of Caucasia. This is manifested in the fact that Azerbaijani (west of the Caspian Sea) and Turkmen (east of the Caspian Sea) are mutually comprehensible languages, whereas the Turkic idioms in Central Asia are divided into no less than three linguistic subgroups. In our age of satellite photos and maps, rivers and lakes seem to be perfect dividers between regions, but this is true only in regard to maps, not economic, political, cultural and social ties.

3   The states in Caucasia and Central Asia are largely treated in the same manner in international politics. From a Russian point of view, they are the southern 'Near Abroad'. For Turkey and Iran they are the northern Muslim belt and the central link of the Silk Road. By most other countries – including the West – they are commonly treated as the poor southern part of the Former Soviet Union (FSU), which Russia continues to be able to control if it chooses to do so. Hence the world basically acts as if Caucasia and Central Asia are one region, regardless of the many differences existing within this region.

Caucasia and Central Asia have had different experiences in terms of change and political climate during the break-up of the Soviet Union. Central Asia experienced a fairly calm transition from the Soviet Union. Former communists are still in power in all five states and the old structures have changed gradually, except in Tajikistan,[4] which has been tormented by an extended civil war. In Caucasia, by contrast, the former communists have not been able to cling to power and profound political and economic changes have taken place. In Caucasia, too, there are dozens of minority nationalities claiming territorial rights and thereby challenging the state elite. In Central Asia, on the other hand, one finds five larger nations and several geographically distanced minorities which nowhere constitute anything approaching a majority, and which do not demand any kind of autonomy.[5] And while historically Central Asia has been a region of its own, with several important centres for trade, culture and politics, Caucasia, by contrast, has never been a region of its own, but rather a peripheral zone of several other regions and empires.

Types of Regionalization in Caucasia and Central Asia

It was, of course, the end of the Cold War followed by the collapse of the Soviet Union that opened up the possibility of regionalization comprising Caucasia and

Central Asia. As the process of regionalization has just started, it is difficult to delimit the region and to identify the content of the process. Several different kinds of actors are involved.

The governments situated in Caucasia and Central Asia and those of the countries adjoining the region have been quite active in the process of regionalization. A number of regional organizations have been established which include all, or several of the states of Caucasia and Central Asia. These regional organizations form the basis of sometimes competing and sometimes complementary regional compositions. Several of them include one or several neighbouring countries. The most flirtatious neighbours are Russia, Turkey, Iran and (during the last few years) China. In addition to the governments and their organizations, various forms of non-governmental organizations (NGOs) have also become regional actors.

The collapse of the Soviet Union is often described as an example of the victory of oppressed nations over an outmoded empire, celebrated by the creation of new nation-states. Since independence, however, the 15 newly independent states (NIS) have been plagued by the very problems that face other nation-states: subnational regions, defined on ethnic or economic grounds, which do not accept the sovereignty of the central state. The situation becomes especially critical when the central state is unable to provide even the minimum requirements of security and welfare to the citizens. The break-up of the Soviet Union is rather the result of the collapse of a specific political system than a process of actual deregionalization. The NIS have proved weak and unable to provide welfare and security to their populations. People have turned to other organizations and ideas to protect themselves from poverty and aggression. Ethnic and national identities have proved attractive to people whose entire surroundings – in terms of economic, political and cultural structures as well as ideas – have fallen apart. In the current chaos of ethnically based movements, increasing influence of international economic actors and interstate migration, most states in Caucasia and Central Asia have begun out of necessity to cooperate in different forms.

In and around Caucasia and Central Asia, there are several cultural, political and economic systems, though they cannot be said to knit together the entire Caucasia and Central Asia region. These social systems include religious, ethnic, linguistic and other kinds of cultural and social ties, but also trade and a certain division of labour. The political systems are basically the remains of the old Soviet framework. There is a widespread consensus on the basic political culture, and between the various state leaderships, both in purely political bodies and the executive administrations (police forces, ministries etc.). Cooperation, assistance, meetings and other forms of informal contact between politicians and administrators in various parts of the region constitute the political interaction between the states. A common political language, knowledge and way of thinking encompass all of Caucasia and Central Asia, including the countries where political systems have changed profoundly. A common past as parts of the Soviet Union is immensely important to political as well as economic ties in Caucasia and Central Asia and cannot be overemphasized. Various forms of a common social system thus primarily link Caucasia and Central Asia with Russia, while new social systems of various kinds are taking shape or being recreated which link the region with Turkey and Iran.

Security Regionalism

As mentioned above, political structures developed differently in Caucasia as compared to Central Asia after *glasnost* and the end of Soviet rule. All three states in southern Caucasia have suffered violent conflicts and the uprooting of the old political system, even though ex-communists have regained power in two of them (Azerbaijan and Georgia). In Armenia the nationalist opposition took control of the republic as early as 1990. The change of political power took place with relatively little violence, even though the military conflict between Armenians and Azerbaijanis over Nagorno-Karabakh has kept Armenia on a war footing. Armenia's relations with Moscow have traditionally been very good and a high level of cooperation has continued due to mutual national interests.

In Georgia there were some violent clashes between the opposition and the communists in 1989, but the actual change of power occurred without violence in 1990. After that, however, there has been a very destructive civil war, both between various non-communist groups, as well as between Georgians and ethnic minorities in Georgia. Russia has exploited the chaotic situation and pressured President Shevardnadze to accept Georgian membership in the CIS and the presence of Russia's military bases in Georgia.

In Azerbaijan political developments have been just as turbulent as in Georgia. At the end of the 1980s Khalqu Jibhassi (KhJ or the Azerbaijani Popular Front) grew strong during the conflict over Nagorno-Karabakh. In early 1990 the conflict between Armenia and Azerbaijan turned from riots between nationalist groups into a real war with tanks and helicopters. The newly elected General Secretary of the Azerbaijani Communist Party, Ayas Niyas Mutalibov, cracked down hard on the KhJ to restore order. After a few years of coups and political as well as military turbulence, Gaidar Aliyev[6] emerged as the strong leader of post-Soviet Azerbaijan. Since then Aliyev has gradually strengthened his grip on power by controlling the media firmly and putting several opposition leaders in prison (Jotun 1997: 6–12).

Northern Caucasia (southern Russia) has also experienced various degrees of political turmoil. Adygei, Karachaevo-Cherkessia and Kabardino-Balkaria have remained fairly stable and peaceful, with non-violent ethnonational organizations trying to gain support from the public for a unification of the Adygei, Cherkess and Kabardin groups into one nationality (a kind of pan-Cherkess or Circassian movement). The split into three different nationalities is blamed on the Russians, who allegedly did this to split their nation. North Ossetia and Ingushetia have also had fairly stable passages of internal political development, but have experienced serious ethnic confrontation between them over *Prigorodni raion*. The very violent conflict in Chechnya is well known through the mass media, and its regional consequences will be examined below. Dagestan is – despite the war in Chechnya – probably the most chaotic republic in Northern Caucasia owing to a very low standard of living in combination with an extremely diverse ethnic and religious composition.

In Central Asia, however, the old guard has continued to cling to political power. Only Tajikistan has experienced civil war and the violent removal of the old regime. After intervention, mainly by Russia and Uzbekistan, the old administrative order has been reinstalled and Tajikistan today can hardly be described as a sovereign state. In practice Russia controls the political leadership. Even though all communist leaders and parties in Central Asia have made cosmetic and rhetorical changes, the political systems and structures of the Soviet period basically remain intact. In Kyrgyzstan, Askar Akayev is president and has made some changes, but parliament is still controlled by the old official order and the opposition parties do not have equal access to mass media and other resources.

In Kazakstan the former First Secretary of the Communist Party of Kazakstan – Nursultan Nazerbayev – is President. There are constant allegations of political repression from various groups in Kazakstan, even though it is also said to be one of the more open and democratic of the Central Asian states. In Uzbekistan, too, the former First Secretary – Islam Karimov – remains in power. The leaders of the opposition parties – primarily Erk, Birlik and the Islamic Renaissance Party – have frequently been arrested, even though a positive change has been noted since 1996 due to pressure from Western countries. In Turkmenistan we find Central Asia's most repressive political system. The former First Secretary – Saparmurad Niyazov – has increased his dictatorial powers and leaders of the very weak opposition – the party Agzybirlik and the underground paper *Dayansh* – are imprisoned, beaten, sent to psychiatric clinics and in some cases even murdered. Personnel from Amnesty International have also been arrested and harassed.

In Central Asia the same persons and structures remain in power as before the collapse of the Soviet Union. Democracy is hardly implemented and the opposition is ruthlessly persecuted. The secret police forces have changed their names from KGB to various Turkic and Farsi[7] names, but the structures and connections to the old system remain the same. This must not be confused with economic politics, which has been changed drastically, together with several political policies and emerging foreign policies.

One reason for states to cooperate in regions is that cooperation can increase security, especially if there are transnational conflicts within the region. In a process of regionalization there may be at least three different kinds of conflicts or tensions:

- Subnational conflicts (often expressed as separatism);

- Tensions between states within the region;

- Tensions with states on the periphery or outside the region.

Caucasia and Central Asia have experienced all three kinds of security threats during the 1990s. Subnational conflicts in the region – mostly of an ethno-nationalist character – are considered first. These conflicts all affect regionalization in various ways. In this chapter limitations of space restrict the subnational conflicts considered to the cases of Tajikistan and Chechnya, even though several other subnational conflicts have affected regionalization (primarily the Abkhazian and South Ossetian conflicts in Georgia). Second, tensions between different states in Caucasia and Central Asia will be analysed. The major conflict in this category in Caucasia and Central Asia is the Nagorno-Karabakh conflict between Armenians and Azerbaijanis, but some tensions among the other states will be illuminated as well. Third, the security implications of states on the periphery of Caucasia and Central Asia (principally Russia) will be examined. This section thus deals with security in its narrow sense, and does not include threats to the environment, health and other areas.

Subnational Conflicts within Caucasia and Central Asia

Subnational conflicts often take the forms of ethnonationalism and/or economic microregionalism. Subnational separatism has until quite recently not been seen as a real problem to the world order in general. Instead it has been viewed as a malady that can be taken care of by the state that is 'infected'; other states should not interfere in any way, unless asked to do so by the infected state. During the past decade, subnational separatism has begun to pose a serious threat to a great number of states, and several nation-state projects that previously were seen as successful have failed completely. Most of the NIS have been plagued by such challenges since their independence in 1992.

All the successful subnational movements have diminished the power of the nation-state as such. The sacrosanct borders and sovereignty of states have become less important, and human rights and other issues have become reasons for other states to disregard the formerly inviolable rights of states. In this context the regions have often acquired a new important role as moderator between nation-states and ethnonational movements. In some cases the region can also act as a counterpart to a state. The CIS has had this role in several conflicts in Caucasia and Central Asia: Abkhazia, South Ossetia and Tajikistan. Chechnya represents a case where this has not worked at all. In both Abkhazia and South Ossetia, CIS peace-keeping forces have been deployed to separate the conflicting parties and – even though not without friction – have been quite successful. A less successful case for the CIS peacekeepers is the civil war in Tajikistan. The other states in the region – primarily Russia, Uzbekistan and Kazakstan – have sided with the current government and thereby created enmity between the region and the Tajik opposition.[8]

The root of the Tajik conflict is partly different ideologies, partly various (sub-national) regional identities and (subnational) regional clan structures in Tajik-istan. The old guard in Dushanbe consisted mostly of people from Kulyab,[9] Khodjent and central Garm who supported the old communist order. It was mainly people from Kurgan-Tyube and eastern Garm who opposed the old regime and endorsed ideologies based on Islam and/or Western nationalism and democracy. Nationalists from the autonomous region Gorno-Badakhshan, who formed an ethnically based opposition, also joined the latter. Fellow Tajiks from northwestern Afghanistan moved into Tajikistan and supported the Islamists when the communist regime fell.

In the spring of 1992 the opposition demonstrated in Dushanbe against the rule of President Nabiev. The demonstrations escalated in April and May, becoming armed clashes between pro- and anti-government forces. In May President Nabiev accepted several members of the opposition into his government. This did not help and the conflicts spread to the southern provinces of Kulyab and Kurgan-Tyube. In September 1992 Nabiev had to resign and the opposition took over government. After the Russian troops decided to help the old guard, the new government had to resign in November. The old guard formed yet another government in December under Imamoli Rakhmanov as President, with the support of Russia, Uzbekistan, Kazakstan and Kyrgyzstan.

The new government began a ruthless campaign of reprisals against the opposi-tion. Thousands of people were reported killed in southern Tajikistan during early 1993. More than 60,000 people fled to Afghanistan, and hundreds or thousands died on the way. The Kurgan-Tyube region was administratively abolished and merged with the Kulyab region (the new region was named Khatlon, but is in reality run as a greater Kulyab), so as to completely prevent the Kurgan-Tyube clans from mounting any effective resistance. During the spring of 1993 a CIS peacekeeping force was deployed in Tajikistan, with the Russian 201st motorised rifle division as its main force. The CIS force had as its objective to support the Russian border guards in preventing the opposition fighters from entering Tajiki-stan from Afghanistan. A Tajik army has been set up to control insurgents, but the attempt has not been a success. In September 1995, for example, the 1st and 11th Tajik Brigades started to fight each other and it took the government one week to separate them. Since then, there have been several mutinies and other problems.

Even though the forces in Tajikistan are officially CIS forces, the intervention in reality is a regional initiative, and the region in this case is made up of Central Asia and Russia. The Russian soldiers in the 201st division are recruited regionally in Central Asia. The Tajik conflict can also be described as regional because of the underlying forces. As the opposition in Tajikistan consists of an ethnic minority and Islamists, whereas the government basically is the old order, the threat in Tajikistan is a threat to all leaderships in the Central Asian states and indirectly also to the Russian leadership. The same kind of opposition and tensions are present in all of Caucasia and Central Asia, but in the other Central Asian states the tensions have not (yet) led to open conflict. In Caucasia similar (but in no way identical) tensions have led to changes of power. It is therefore easy to understand that the leaderships in all Central Asian states perceive the Tajik conflict as a regional threat to all Central Asia and thus try to crush the opposition in Tajikistan before it can spread to other parts of the region. It is also worth noticing that other powerful states such as Iran have played a surprisingly small – virtually non-existent – part in the Tajik civil war, so as not to anger Russia.

The sovereignty of Tajikistan was increasingly undermined by the government's reliance on Russian and Uzbek support. Tajikistan can no longer even be considered a state in its own right, but rather as a protectorate of Russia. The region has not (or no more than officially) acted as a mediator, but clearly supported one side of the conflict. Conflict resolution has therefore failed, if viewed from the perspective of peace, but been a success if seen from the perspective of the governments whose goal is to keep the Islamists from gaining a foothold in Central Asia.

The situation in Chechnya, the unfortunate events which led to the war and its regional implications, are impossible to understand without taking the Chechen identity and the social structure of the area into consideration. This identity and structure are by no means unique to Chechnya, but are rather one example of a situation that prevails in all of Caucasia and Central Asia. Since 1990 Chechnya has experienced the social effects of increasing ethnic tension, corruption and illegal trade. Much of the social and economic life of Chechnya came to be organized in a handful of *tukhums* or 'companies'. Among other things, they organized their local communities, helped each other, took care of the old and sick, traded with various sorts of goods (legal as well as illegal), etc. A Soviet Air Force general, Dzokhar Dudayev, was named President of an 'independent' Chechnya in October 1991. Dudayev had plenty of contacts with Russian officers and was used by the Russians to support the Abkhaz rebels with military training against Georgia.

Dudayev was aiding the Abkhaz as a favour to Russia. Simultaneously, Dudayev contributed to the partly successful attempt to organize the Confederation of North Caucasian Mountain Peoples. Since Moscow decided to attack Chechnya in November 1994, the Chechen side has put a great effort into regionalizing the conflict, to achieve support from other (primarily Muslim) peoples.

Russia also had a regional aim. Bombers and massive artillery supported the army invasion. The objective was not solely to get rid of Dudayev, but rather to demonstrate to other nationalities within Russia as well as Caucasia and Central Asia that they should not try to follow the Chechnian example. The images from Grozny of dead people and destroyed buildings spread via television to most places around the world, including Caucasia and Central Asia and the other national minorities in Russia. Everyone could dislike or hate Russia, but no one wanted to get the same treatment as the Chechens. The war in Chechnya thus taught two important lessons to the Caucasia and Central Asia region. First, it was obvious that the Russian army was not as effective as it had been during the Soviet era. Second, it became clear that Russia was prepared to use its army if it needed to, and that Russia was still the major power in the region.

At the same time Dudayev used the Russian bombing of Grozny as a symbol of a small nation's struggle for freedom when appealing to his Muslim brothers in other parts of Caucasia, Central Asia and the wider Muslim world. He described the Russian aggression as an attack by a vicious barbarian European aggressor on a Muslim people. Apart from strengthening the Chechen identity, the war has also led to a strengthening of the identity of the Caucasian Mountain peoples and – not less important – of the Muslim identity. It has also increased dislike of the Russians in all of Caucasia and Central Asia.

Tensions between States within Caucasia and Central Asia

The relation between security and regionalism has changed quite profoundly during recent decades. The term *regional security complex* is often used as an analytical instrument to group conflicting or opposing states into regions. Within regional security complexes changes in the structure may be described by two components: the pattern of amity and enmity, and the distribution of power among the states. Since the end of the Soviet era, the pattern of amity and enmity between various parts of Caucasia and Central Asia has changed profoundly with the growth of nationalism. A pattern of enmity that had not existed – or at least had not been visible – during the Soviet time, became apparent. Apart from the conflict between Armenians and Azerbaijanis concerning Nagorno-Karabakh (Artsakh), tensions have appeared between Kyrgyzstan and Uzbekistan (even in 1990), and most recently between Uzbekistan and Tajikistan.

In the Fall of 1998 a rebellion started in the northern Tajik province of Leninabad. The rebels quickly took control of this rich part of the country, but within a few days government troops managed to fight back and the rebels dispersed. The Tajik government immediately blamed Uzbekistan for training and supporting the rebels. Since this incident the Uzbek peacekeeping battalion has been withdrawn from Tajikistan and Uzbek–Tajik relations have been very strained.

The conflict around Nagorno-Karabakh is the bloodiest in the region and has initiated several regional attempts at conflict resolution. Russia and Kazakstan made one serious attempt in 1992 and Iran has made another. Both attempts failed, however, and the Organization of Security and Cooperation in Europe (OSCE) (with strong influence from Russia) has been the most successful mediator.

Relations with States on the Periphery of Caucasia and Central Asia

Russia is involved in regionalization through both the CIS and bilateral treaties. The bilateral treaties between Russia and the separate states of Caucasia and Central Asia primarily concern security policy and military cooperation. Many states in Caucasia and Central Asia (most notably Armenia, Kazakstan, Kyrgyzstan, Tajikistan and Turkmenistan) have bilateral security treaties with Russia that go far beyond the CIS treaties. These bilateral treaties tend to tie the states of Caucasia and Central Asia closer together and thus support the regionalization of the CIS area. The primary reason why Russia uses bilateral agreements instead of deepening the CIS agreements is that the Ukraine, Moldova and Azerbaijan refuse military integration of any kind, and much of the political integration too.

Relationships between Russia and the separate states in Caucasia and Central Asia are fairly good, with the exception of Azerbaijan and, to some extent, Georgia. Azerbaijani–Russian relations are quite complicated. The Azerbaijanis have traditionally been very loyal to Russia, but after the Nagorno-Karabakh war broke out, many Azerbaijanis were disappointed at the lack of Russian support. After this, relations deteriorated drastically because of disagreements over the oil off the Azerbaijani Caspian Sea coast. After severe internal conflicts in both Azerbaijan and Georgia, Russia has managed to force them to join the CIS. Azerbaijan is nowadays strong enough to resist having Russian forces on Azerbaijani soil, but Georgia is not. Russia has used the Abkhazian and South Ossetian conflicts to pressure Georgia to accept several Russian military bases, even though the Border Guards were to be removed by 1 July 2000.

Right after the collapse of the Soviet Union, when Russia was at its weakest, many researchers began to talk about the re-emergence of 'the Great Game'. This term was used to describe the competition between the United Kingdom, Tsarist Russia, China and (to a lesser extent) France for influence in Central Asia and the Middle East around 1900. In the 'new Great Game' of the 1990s there had been a change of players, but the logic was the same. The players in the 1990s were Russia, Turkey, Iran, China and, to a limited extent, the Western powers. This time, however, the Great Game had not even started (at least not in the sphere of security) when Russia emerged as the one and only security power in Caucasia and Central Asia. In the economic field, however, the situation is different.

Even though Turkey and Iran were very active in the early 1990s, they have now yielded to Russian military supremacy. Instead they compete with Russia in the economic sphere. Iran also often shares strategic positions with Russia and has over the past few years often behaved as Russia's ally.

Thus security has influenced and continues to influence the process of regionalization in Caucasia and Central Asia. After a period of weakness around 1992, Russia is once again the unchallenged number one force in Caucasia and Central Asia in terms of military influence. All regionalization in the sphere of security thus excludes Turkey and Iran, at least for now. Security regionalization in Caucasia and Central Asia is instead including Russia in every way.

Economic Regionalization

The Soviet Legacy

The present economies of Caucasia and Central Asia are the results of 70 years of planned economy. Since the collapse of the Soviet Union several changes have begun to take effect. Most of them, however, are very slow processes, partly because of the mechanics of the planned economy. Different areas of the Soviet Union were specialized in different commodities: tyres were produced in one republic, engines in another, car seats in a third and the assembly of the car was undertaken in a fourth. This has led to some major problems concerning independence after the collapse of the Soviet Union. The NIS are more or less forced to continue their economic relations with each other, and when one of them decides to export a commodity to countries outside the FSU, this creates serious problems for the other republics. Azerbaijan and some states in Central Asia have begun to sell their oil to the West. This has caused a shortage of oil in those parts of the FSU that used to get oil from this area.

The planned economy of the FSU was very sensitive and when this complex system was disturbed almost all of it collapsed. When one product was lost within the planned Soviet economic system it immediately affected production in other republics; most of the industrial production in the FSU, therefore, was greatly damaged when some republics sold their products outside the Soviet economic system. During 1992 and 1993 most countries in Caucasia and Central Asia tried to solve this problem by trading with the West, Southeast Asia and other regions outside the FSU. This approach largely failed, and instead they began trying at least partly to reintegrate the old economic ties. This time the transactions are not part of a planned command economy, nor has it been possible to use a completely free price system in hard currency. The commodities have been sold, but at artificially low prices that have been set in bilateral negotiations to ensure the continuation of the complex trade patterns. Simultaneously, however, the free market trade with countries outside the FSU has been growing steadily, if still slowly. Turkey, Iran, China and Southeast Asia have slowly emerged as new trading partners for Caucasia and Central Asia, basically by providing manufactured goods. Together with the establishment of new trade patterns, a manufacturing industry has begun to emerge. It is clear that the economic interaction between the states in Caucasia and Central Asia has proved very important. The number of regional economic organizations was increasing rapidly in the early 1990s to ensure the continuation of trade between the republics, and their activities have since then increased and matured.

During the first half of the 1990s the economies in Caucasia and Central Asia deteriorated to a fraction of their capacities in the 1980s. This economic collapse has of course affected everything from social life to conflicts in all parts of Caucasia and Central Asia.

Table 6.1 GDP per capita in Caucasia and Central Asia

	1990	1995	1997
Armenia	4084	2127	2407
Azerbaijan	2804	988	1088
Georgia	3919	1012	1313
Kazakstan	4477	2426	2606
Kyrgyzstan	2706	1339	1540
Russia	5904	4220	4305
Tajikistan	1920	694	685
Turkmenistan	2903	1517	1115
Uzbekistan	2312	1956	2013

Source: EIU Country reports, 3rd quarter 1998. Numbers are in ppp (purchasing power parities) and US dollars. Russia has been included as comparison.

Against the background of strong economic ties from the Soviet past and the 'illusion of disintegration' it is clear that Caucasia and Central Asia to some extent constitute an economic region. However, the nature of this economic region is currently being changed. There are two basic changes taking place. One is the reorientation of economic ties from the FSU to the other neighbouring states: Turkey, Iran and China. The other is the transformation from a planned economic system towards a market-oriented one. These changes have led to two important economic developments in relation to regionalization: (1) the development of the oil and natural gas industry; and (2) the attempt to recreate the Silk Road in a new version. Russia, China and several Western countries are involved in the first project and the surrounding states (except Russia) are involved in the second project.

Oil, Natural Gas and Regionalization

Azerbaijan, Kazakstan, Turkmenistan and Uzbekistan have quite large resources of oil and natural gas. Since the collapse of the Soviet Union the known reserves of oil as well as natural gas have increased significantly.

Table 6.2 Reserves of Oil and Natural Gas in Caucasia and Central Asia

	Oil (billion barrels)	Gas (trillion cubic feet)
Azerbaijan	1.2	19
Kazakstan	3.3	15
Turkmenistan	1.4	189
Uzbekistan	0.3	88

Source: John Roberts, *Caspian Pipelines*, 1996: 4.

There are basically two problems facing the states of Caucasia and Central Asia in the area of oil and gas production. The first problem is to acquire technology, skills and capital to take care of their potential wealth. The second and more serious problem is how to transport the oil and gas to the customers. Both these problems have increased economic regionalization. Turkey, Iran and Russia have provided technology and skills which integrate the industries of the region. Dozens of agreements (both between companies as well as bi- and multilateral agreements between governments) have been signed during the past seven years.

Both oil and natural gas are found in and around the Caspian Sea. To get the oil to a port with ocean access, regional cooperation is necessary. Pipelines must cross several countries, hence enabling all to benefit from the oil. The transportation of oil and gas from Caucasia and Central Asia to the markets in the West is literally tying Caucasia and Central Asia together as a region. Azerbaijan, Kazakstan, Turkmenistan and Uzbekistan are all planning to link their pipeline systems. In addition there is one oil pipeline which will carry Azerbaijani oil through Northern Caucasia to the Russian Black Sea port of Novorossiisk. Oil from Kazakstan will also be transported via a pipeline from the Tengiz oil field to Novorossiisk. Another pipeline will take Azerbaijani oil through Georgia to the Black Sea and possibly further, through Turkey.

There are plans to build pipelines from the Caucasia and Central Asia pipeline system across Afghanistan and Pakistan to ports in the Indian Ocean. Other plans are to build pipelines from Kazakstan to China, to get direct access to the increasing demand for oil around the Pacific Ocean (in addition to China, also Japan and Southeast Asia). The pipeline system is thus integrating the economies of Caucasia and Central Asia. The pipelines and oil wealth also generate security issues, which further integrate the states of Caucasia and Central Asia. One example of this is the pipeline from Azerbaijan to Novorossiisk. This pipeline crosses Chechnya. Since the ceasefire in the summer of 1996, the Chechen leadership has been very eager to cooperate with Russia on oil transport and to guarantee the safe passage of oil through Chechnya. It is not an overstatement to say that oil transport has been an important factor for peace in Chechnya.

Gas has a fundamentally different role to oil. It is difficult to ship gas and it therefore has more of a regional than a global function. Gas will primarily be both produced and consumed within the region. Gas pipelines will distribute gas within the region, including Turkey and Iran.

Competition over the 'black gold' has also led, however, to tensions and security problems. This rivalry has for several years more or less paralysed the CSG (Caspian Sea Group), with a negative effect on Russia's relations with Azerbaijan and – to some extent – Georgia. Azerbaijan has signed several agreements of oil exploitation with Western corporations, in spite of intense Russian opposition. After a failed *coup d'état* in 1994, Azerbaijan's President Aliyev accused Russia of supporting the attempted coup. Russia still has a share in the Azerbaijani-led consortium – Azerbaijan International Oil Consortium (AIOC) – exploiting the oilfields of Shirag, Azeri and Guneshli off the Azerbaijani coast of the Caspian Sea, but Western influence is becoming dominant. Russia has since 1994 been split on this question between security considerations (Foreign Ministry, Defence Ministry etc.) and economic considerations (Lukoil, Rosneft and parts of the government), with the latter getting stronger during the last few years. This situation – when positions taken on different issues are not determined by clear-cut national interest but by other cleavages inside the different states, creating coalitions across the national boundaries within the region – is in fact an important step towards regionalization (Jotun 1997: 12–18).

The Silk Road and Regional Organizations

The Silk Road is an idea to restore the role of Caucasia and Central Asia as a trading link between its neighbouring regions: East Asia, Southeast Asia, the Middle East and Europe. The idea has the support of the states of Caucasia and Central Asia as well as the Economic Cooperation Organization (ECO) and several other regional organizations. It includes the Iron Silk Road (railroads across Central Asia), highways, linking airways, seaways with port facilities and other types of communications. Every state acts according to its own national interests, however, only cooperating in so far as it gains influence, security and wealth. The political systems of the neighbouring states (Turkey, Iran, Pakistan and China) are so different that regionalization which leads to an 'own actor' capacity for the regional entity seem very far away. As a result there is a multitude of regional organizations and cases where some actors have shut out other actors. Small countries also use the key actors to gain advantages, but often refrain from themselves engaging in regional organizations, where they would be controlled by the more powerful states.

Turkey has emerged as a very active and relatively potent player in the Caucasia and Central Asia economic regionalization game. At the same time as Turkey is trying to become a member of the EU (European Union), it also wants to play a leading role in the regionalization of Caucasia and Central Asia. Turkey's role in the EU is very dependent upon domestic politics, but its role towards Caucasia and Central Asia has wide political support and is therefore less dependent on the impermanent political leadership in Ankara.

Turkey uses its ethnic and linguistic bonds with Caucasia and Central Asia,[10] but plays the role of an important outside big brother, rather than becoming part of the Caucasia and Central Asia region itself. After a short period of 'pan-Turkic' euphoria around 1992, Turkey has clearly taken a position of 'active outsider'. Turkey has hosted a number of 'Turkic summits' for the states in Caucasia and Central Asia with Turkic official languages. The Turkic summits promote multilateral cooperation in the areas of trade, finance, labour, and culture. The third Turkic summit in Bishkek in August 1995 resulted in a 21-article Bishkek Declaration. It included, however, more rhetoric than substance – the substantial part being to set up conferences on security, cooperation and confidence building (*OMRI Daily Digest*, 950829).

Perhaps the most important regional organization is the Economic Cooperation Organization (ECO).[11] This organization comprises the states of Central Asia, Azerbaijan, Turkey, Iran, Pakistan and Afghanistan. It was originally created in 1964,[12] but had been dormant for many years until it was revitalized following the break-up of the Soviet Union. The ECO contains around 325 million people and covers almost eight million square kilometres.

The ECO will take on both strength and weakness by including Turkey, Pakistan and Iran: strength, since three of the major non-FSU powers close to the region are involved; and weakness, because they do not trust each other and have very different political systems. The ECO is basically a multilateral economic organization. It deals with trade, creation of trade routes (the Silk Road project, harbours, railroads, airports, highways, etc.), finance and aid.

The original ECO strategy (from 1991) was to achieve preferential tariff reductions and the establishment of common institutions. The three original members agreed to tariff reductions of 10 per cent on selected commodities in May 1991. After the meetings in 1992, when the Muslim states of the FSU and Afghanistan were incorporated, there have been two strategically important meetings: they produced the Quetta Plan of Action in February 1993 and the Istanbul Declaration in July 1993. An Outline Plan was adopted in Almaty in October 1993 on transport and communications development (Pomfret 1997: 659)

The ECO Committee of Preferential Tariffs met twice in 1993 and once in 1995. The preferential tariff reductions did not work out well, in spite of very modest goals. It has been a very difficult task for the original members to implement the tariff reductions, whereas the NIS have had the opposite problem: the setting up of new customs and administrative organs (Pomfret 1997).

The common institutions in the ECO are even at the planning stage restricted to: (1) a trade and development bank, (2) an insurance company, (3) a shipping company, and (4) an airline. The bank will be based in Istanbul, the insurance company in Pakistan and the secretariat of ECO is in Tehran. The negotiations have reflected intense state rivalry and the difficulties states have in accepting anything that is not directly beneficial to themselves (Pomfret 1997: 659). The ECO's Transit Trade Agreement and Agreement on the Simplification of Visa Procedures for Businessmen were, however, signed at the 1995 summit. These agreements will play a vital role in promoting regional trade.

One major obstacle to trade within the ECO is the poor transport network. This is an area where several agreements have been signed and things actually do advance. For instance, the railroad between Iran (Meshed) and Turkmenistan (Tejen) in May 1996, and between Kazakstan and China before that, were both important steps in the Silk Road project. Since seven of ECO's members do not have ocean access, the transport agreements are of vital importance, holding the possibility of reducing their dependence on Russia.

Another obstacle to intra-ECO trade is that the economies of the constituent countries are fairly similar: all have poorly developed industries based on raw material production, agriculture and textiles. This problem will not be solved until manufacturing and processing industries are developed. Turkey is the most advanced member in this respect. Turkmenistan and Iran depend heavily on their exports of oil and gas. Azerbaijan and Kazakstan plan to use the export of oil as their main economic engine. Uzbekistan, Kyrgyzstan and Tajikistan can only hope to export minerals. Cooperation in the oil and gas industry is therefore of great importance to regional economic development (Pomfret 1997: 663–4).

One further obstacle to regional trade is that trade (especially in the NIS) is poorly monitored and statistics are very unreliable in the few areas where they exist at all. It is estimated that 85–90 per cent of the republics' external trade in the Soviet Union was intra-union trade. The republics in Central Asia traded much more with Russia and Ukraine than with each other, since all of them basically produced raw materials and agricultural products. Azerbaijan is the only NIS in the ECO that has been able to change the pattern of trade completely. According to Economist Intelligence Unit trade figures, Azerbaijan's total trade (imports and exports) was in 1995 directed towards (in descending order): Iran (20 per cent), Russia (15 per cent), Turkey (14 per cent), United Arab Emirates (6 per cent), Turkmenistan (5 per cent), and Georgia (5 per cent). The shift away from Russia towards Iran and other regional states is increasing every year (*EIU* Country Report, 3rd Quarter 1995: Armenia, Azerbaijan and Georgia).

According to the Iranian leader Rafsanjani, OPEC and ASEAN are examples of how the ECO should develop: that is, the ECO should present itself as one actor towards the rest of the world in specific cases. Turkey and the states in Central Asia, however, want to keep it as a purely economic organization, without any security implications. The Uzbek President, Islam Karimov, openly criticized Iran in 1996 for politicizing the ECO and using it to condemn the US and Israel (*OMRI Daily Digest*, 960516).

Another regional organization created at the initiative of Turkey is the Black Sea Economic Cooperation Organization (BSECO), which includes the countries around the Black Sea and all of Caucasia. This organization was quite active in the early 1990s, but has become increasingly inactive owing to disagreement between the states, primarily Russia and Turkey. During 1995 and 1996, however, there were intense discussions on turning the BSECO into a free economic zone. These plans have not yet yielded any results.

The Caspian Sea Group (CSG) is another regional organization, comprising Russia, Azerbaijan, Kazakstan and Turkmenistan. The CSG is meant to take care of various aspects of the geopolitical situation in and around the Caspian Sea, such as trade, shipping, fishing, environmental protection and natural resources. During the past few years the CSG has been quite paralysed by the dispute about rights to oil and gas in the Caspian Sea.

In contrast to Iranian foreign policy during the 1980s, the Iranian stand towards Caucasia and Central Asia during the 1990s has been surprisingly economic in character. In the 1980s Iran's foreign policy was basically guided by religious considerations, but since the early 1990s economic goals seem to guide Iran's actions, at least in its relations to Caucasia and Central Asia.

In addition to the regionalization involving the neighbours of Caucasia and Central Asia, an inner core of Central Asian states – the Central Asian Economic Union (CAEU) – has been formed by Kazakstan, Kyrgyzstan and Uzbekistan. CAEU has fairly far-reaching agreements on trade, political integration and travelling. The tripartite agreements to establish a customs union[13] (though aiming to go further) date from 1994 (Pomfret 1997: 665). Further agreements signed after 1994

aim at 'greater institutional substance': to form an interstate council for coordination of the governments in the economic sphere, and to found a Central Asian
Bank. 'The task is to draw up, by 1996, a six-year integration plan, taking into
account the potential of Kyrgyzstan, Uzbekistan and Kazakstan,' said Kazak
President Nursultan Naserbayev in early 1995 (*OMRI Daily Digest*, 950213). During
their 1996 meeting, the three countries made a five-year integration plan and
stressed the need to create a 'mutually beneficial division of labour' (*OMRI Daily
Digest*, 960510). The deepening of the integration seems to have gone smoothly so
far,[14] and in several areas they have begun to become a common market
(Sharipzhan 1997).

Kazakstan and Kyrgyzstan have embarked on a cooperation with Belarus and
Russia which was also originally a kind of customs union. An agreement was
signed between Russia, Belarus and Kazakstan in 1995. On 29 March 1996 this
agreement was extended to (eventually) cover free movement of capital, labour,
services and goods. Simultaneously Kyrgyzstan was admitted. This agreement is
also known as the Treaty of Four (Fossato 1997).

The difference between these attempts at regionalization and other attempts
elsewhere in the world is the common Soviet past. The implementation of agreements is not as difficult to set up as in other regions. On the contrary, it has often
been rather more problematic for the governments to implement the new customs
which were supposed to be set up after the fall of the Soviet Union. The borders
between the states were often only lines on maps; no one had cared about them in
reality. There have been notable disagreements, however, between Russia and
Kazakstan concerning the abolition of border controls between the two states. In
early 1996, Russia decided to lift all customs controls.

The Treaty of Four also has far-reaching agreements in such areas as finance and
information systems. The quadripartite agreements also included the establishment of an Integration Committee, an Intergovernmental Council of presidents
and an Inter-Parliamentary Committee. The goal of the treaty is to achieve a
payments union, a power union, a transport union and an inter-bank union,
possibly even including a single currency (Kangas 1996).

The various governmental organizations include different sets of states and
therefore promote different delimitations of regions comprising Caucasia and
Central Asia. Even though the governmental organizations primarily deal with
trade, infrastructure and to some extent security, they pave the way for regionalization in very different fields by facilitating cooperation by NGOs across state
borders and by directing attention to cooperation within the region in the media,
the universities, and other opinion-forming circles. Many of the measures taken by
the governmental organizations are meant to promote enterprises and social and
cultural exchange throughout the region. They thereby influence regionalization

both directly and indirectly, advancing delimitation as well as homogeneity, but determining actual content to a lesser extent.

Transnational corporations in the oil and gas industries represent the influential capital-strong market actors. Small and medium-sized companies – primarily from Turkey – are also of great importance to the process of regionalization. Various political, religious and cultural organizations in the area and from Turkey also play an active role. In the early 1990s various pan-Turkic and pan-Islamic organizations played an important role in the political and cultural awakening, but for the past three or four years the pan-Turkic euphoria has decreased considerably in Caucasia and Central Asia as well as in Turkey.[15]

Apart from the organizations mentioned above, several states in the region have also signed bi-and trilateral agreements. Azerbaijan, Georgia and Turkmenistan are particularly hesitant to strengthen the regional organizations and prefer bilateral trade agreements. Turkmenistan is afraid of being dominated by its larger neighbours, in particular Uzbekistan. Due to its high dependency on natural gas, Turkmenistan runs the risk of being a gas supplier in any regional organization. Therefore, it has signed several far-reaching bilateral agreements with Russia and Iran. Turkmenistan tries to play off the larger countries against each other, thereby gaining more than it ever could in multilateral agreements. This is why it does not participate in the Central Asian Common Economic Space (CACES) or the inner core of the CIS. Apart from letting CACES, Russia and Iran compete for influence, Turkmenistan has also increased its cooperation with Turkey and Armenia significantly. For instance, Turkmenistan accounted for 21 per cent of Armenia's foreign trade in 1995 (*EIU* Country Report, 3rd Quarter 1995: Armenia, Azerbaijan and Georgia). This is a very high proportion, especially considering the war between Armenia and Azerbaijan.

Environmental Issues, Migration, Corruption and Regionalization

In addition to the economic profits, there are unfortunately also environmental problems connected with oil bonanzas. These problems have just surfaced, but are very likely to increase within the near future. Pollution and other kinds of environmental problems are also closely associated with economic development.

In Caucasia and Central Asia the environmental movement has been fairly active during the 1990s. At the top of their agenda are issues such as water resources, oil pollution, nuclear power and tests, and uranium extraction. All these issues demand regional responses. Environmental issues arising in a Caspian Sea context are of particular concern to the CSG.

In Central Asia water is the number one environmental problem. The two major rivers – Amu Darya and Sur Darya – lead water from western Tibet to the Aral Sea. Since the late 1950s much water has been used for irrigation, in particular to grow cotton. This has caused the Aral Sea to diminish to one third of its size in 1960, and it is still diminishing. For the Karakalpaks – who traditionally have been fishermen around southern Aral – this has been a catastrophe. Several fishing villages now lie in the desert, dozens of kilometres from the Aral Sea. In this way the scarce water resources have caused enmity between several groups along the rivers and become a regional matter, where the people downstream accuse those upstream of stealing their water. In April 1993 the World Bank, the UN Environmental Programme, the UN Development Programme and the governments of Kazakstan, Uzbekistan, Turkmenistan and Tajikistan launched the Aral Sea Environmental Assistance Programme, aimed at stabilizing and in future reversing the crisis (Gharabaghi 1994: 148–9).

The economic collapse in Caucasia and Central Asia in combination with environmental problems and conflicts has led to a considerable migration both within and away from the region. At first glance migration within the region may seem to increase regionalization, but a more thorough analysis shows that this is not the case. The migration actually counteracts regionalization, since it is mostly a form of ethnic cleansing. The major migrations within and from Caucasia and Central Asia during the 1990s were:

1   Russians moving from southern Central Asia to northern Kazakstan and Russia;

2   Meskhetian Turks moving from Central Asia (primarily Uzbekistan) to northern Caucasia and Azerbaijan;[16]

3   Armenians from Azerbaijan and Central Asia to Armenia;

4   Azerbaijanis from Armenia, Nagorno-Karabakh and the surrounding areas to parts of Azerbaijan not controlled by Armenians (around 850,000 people);

5   Georgians from Abkhazia (and to some extent from South Ossetia) to Georgia proper.

The extensive emigration of Russians has important economic repercussions in Caucasia and Central Asia. Since a very large share of technicians and other highly qualified personnel at companies and in the bureaucracies were Russians, this has caused serious industrial and administrative problems.

In Caucasia and Central Asia – as in most other parts of the FSU – the parlous state of the economy is very visible (see Table 6.1). The standard of living has declined throughout the region and the social security nets provided by the states are virtually non-existent. Begging in the streets is common in most major cities of the region. Even though the governments – especially in Central Asia – have not yet privatized much of industry, the parts of the economy that are under government control have practically collapsed. The functioning part of today's economy is therefore to a large extent out of government control. In several parts of Caucasia and Central Asia much of the economy, politics and society has been taken over by more-or-less criminal, Mafia-like organizations. In some parts of the region the political leaders are enmeshed in corruption, which makes the problem even worse. The corruption of officials is embarrassingly open and – to many people – an accepted part of the present system. The political and economic spheres are already very integrated with each other, and to quite some extent with the societal sphere. Many people in Caucasia and Central Asia are today forced to become part of the corruption to survive, and thus do not want any crackdowns on the corrupted organizations.

Corruption affects the process of regionalization in several ways. First, it subdues the market mechanisms which tend to increase regionalization. Second, it weakens the state structures and instead strengthens subnational organizations and movements – regional, clan-like, ethnic or of any other kind. Most of the corruption channels are carried over from the communist system (especially in Central Asia, where they are virtually unchanged). In many parts of Caucasia and Central Asia the traditional structures basically remain the same as in the early 1900s, before the communist takeover. Many of these structures changed only nominally during the communist period and have now changed names and symbols once again. The major difference during the last few years is an increase in unofficial transactions and financial corruption that siphons ever more privileges to a few; spells poverty and powerlessness to most people; and incapacitates the economical and political systems.

Prospects

There are several processes of regionalization going on in Caucasia and Central Asia, but they have not gone very far yet and are still to some extent counteracted by the dissolution of the Soviet structures. The processes are, further, not going in the direction of one clearly delimited region, but are rather the result of regional cooperation in several different fields involving different state and non-state actors. The 'real region' consists of several different 'formal regions'. Several social systems are forming across the states within the region, but they have not yet reached very far in regionalization.

In the area of security, Russia plays a very dominant role. After a brief period of weakness in 1992, Russia has again become the unquestioned guarantor of regional security. Russian dominance, together with the many conflicts within Caucasia and Central Asia, makes it accurate to view this as a regional security complex. Tajikistan has practically lost its independence, since its government is completely dependent upon Russia to withstand the forces of its opponents. This is, however,

121

not a sign of regionalization, but rather of the traditional dominance of militarily stronger states over weaker. Russia has pressured Georgia into several security agreements and Azerbaijan is openly opposing Russian dominance. Armenia, Turkmenistan, and Tajikistan welcome Russian dominance in the security sphere, whereas Uzbekistan and Kazakstan try to cooperate and compete with Russia at a more equal level. The other surrounding powers have accepted Russian dominance, which is of course facilitated by the Soviet past. All those in the present power structures can communicate in Russian, have the same security and administrative traditions and share the same perspectives on power, security and conflict management.

Even though the economies of the former Soviet republics were intimately intertwined until less than a decade ago, there has been a profound structural change in economic and financial systems as well as patterns of trade. Turkey, Iran, China and several other countries have entered the stage as important trading partners and several economic cooperation organizations have emerged. New communications links have been built and old ones have been destroyed by wars. The importance of oil and natural gas increased in the early and mid-1990s, then dipped again (and was rising sharply once more as this book was going to press).

The several cooperation organizations strengthen the bonds between Caucasia and Central Asia and various bordering states such as Russia, Turkey, Iran and China. The economic and security interests of these surrounding states prevent the states of Caucasia and Central Asia forming a single region. Instead they have cooperation with each other and other countries in a range of different delimitations. There are many different regional organizations striving in different directions, built on different ideas, with contradictory goals. The reason for this is that the leaderships in the various states would lose too much on regionalization. The states are therefore competing with each other, trying to increase their own power instead of reaching agreements that will benefit all.

The conclusion is therefore that there is not one region forming, but rather a range of different regions corresponding to various contents and different kinds of actors. Cooperation in the fields of trade, finance, culture, security, education, etcetera, in combination with the very strong bonds from the Soviet period, has led to a kind of region – even though it has neither a fixed delimitation, nor anything approaching an 'own actor' capacity (and will most probably not gain any such capacity in the foreseeable future). It is also important to notice that the processes of regionalization, such as it is, take place concurrently with globalization, nation building and state building after the collapse of the Soviet Union, and fragmentation within the post-imperium states in the form of ethnic conflicts. It is by no means clear that regionalization is stronger than these other processes in Caucasia and Central Asia.

CAUCASIA AND CENTRAL ASIA

This combination of changed economic policies, newly emerged foreign policies and a continued control of internal politics has led to some interesting features in regard to regionalization. The market economy is saluted as the saviour and the states in Southeast Asia and China are viewed as models to follow. The attempts at economic regionalization with neighbours to the south (via the ECO) have been only partly successful. The preferential tariff reductions and common institutions have been disappointments. All members of the ECO have made substantial liberalization measures during the last years, and aim at market-based economies on the East and Southeast Asian model. The future therefore seems to lean towards several quite weak regional organizations, with most power remaining with the somewhat liberalized states.

NOTES

1 The Caucasus mountain range lies between the Black Sea and the Caspian Sea. The area to the south of this range is called South Caucasia (or Transcaucasia) and the areas on both sides of the range are called Caucasia. South Caucasia is made up of three states: Armenia/Haiastan (Armenian name of Armenia), Azerbaijan and Georgia/Sakhartvelo (Georgian name of Georgia). In the south, Caucasia borders Turkey and Iran. Northern Caucasia is part of southern Russia. It includes seven autonomous areas; Adygey, Karachaevo-Cherkessia, Kabardino-Balkaria, North Ossetia, Ingushetia, Chechnya and Dagestan.
2 East of the Caspian Sea there are five states – Kazakstan, Kyrgyzstan, Tajikistan, Turkmenistan and Uzbekistan – which all were part of the former Soviet Union (FSU). These five states are included in the definition of Central Asia in this chapter. In traditional Russian terminology Central Asia – actually *Srednii Azii* (Middle Asia) – is defined as these states excluding Kazakstan. Other definitions incorporate parts of eastern China and/or parts of Iran and Afghanistan.
3 The Caucasia and Central Asia region covers a territory of 4.3 million square kilometres and has a population of more than 65 million people.
4 The former communists were for a short period of time ousted (in September 1992), but regained power after a few months (December 1992). For further details see, e.g., *Det nya Cen-tralasien* by Bo Petersson and Ingvar Svanberg, eds.
5 The only exceptions to this are the Karakalpaks in northern Uzbekistan and the Pamir peoples in the Gorno-Badakhshan area of eastern Tajikistan.
6 Aliyev was a communist hardliner in the Soviet politbureau even before Gorbachev's time as General Secretary. However, he was sacked and sent to Nakhichevan by Gorbachev.
7 Farsi is an Iranian language – also known as Persian – which is spoken by Persians and Tajiks.
8 The analysis of the civil war in Tajikistan and its regional consequences is based on a vast number of sources. Some of the most informative are: Michael Orr, 1996, 'The Russian Army and the War in Tajikistan', CSRC; Bo Peterson, 1996, 'Tadjikistan', in Petersson and Svanberg (eds) *Det nya Centralasien.*
9 Kulyab, Garm and Kurgan-Tyube were provinces (*oblasti*) within Tajikistan.
10 Azerbaijanis, Turkmen, Uzbeks, Kazaks, Kyrgyz and many smaller groups in Caucasia and Central Asia speak Turkic language. Central Asia is often (even in Turkey) considered the original homeland of the Turkic culture and way of life.
11 Most arguments about the ECO are taken from the articles written by De Cordier 1996 and Pomfret 1997, supported by *Daily Digests* from OMRI.
12 It was created under the name Regional Cooperation for Development, as a civilian counterpart to CENTO, comprising Turkey, Iran and Pakistan. It thus was an organization for pro-Western

Muslim countries in Southwest Asia. Its original purpose was to coordinate economic cooperation in an attempt to increase regional integration of transports and telecommunications (De Cordier, 1996: 47–8).

13 Economists speak of five different levels of economic integration: preferential trading club, free-trade area, customs union, common market and economic union (Chacholiades 1990). A preferential trading club consists of two or more countries that reduce their duties on imports of all goods from each other. A free-trade area/association means the complete abolition of duties on imports from each other, but the countries in the association may have different duties on imports from other countries. A customs union is a free-trade area with a common external tariff on all goods imported from the rest of the world. A common market is a customs union that allows free movement of all factors of production (goods, services, labour and capital) between the member countries. An economic union, finally, is a common market where the member countries have unified their fiscal, monetary, and socio-economic policies.

14 In April 1995 the CAEU decided to give priority to 'cooperative production of small electrical engines, gas meters, medicines, and fertilisers derived from Aral Sea deposits'. A common position on the Tajik conflict was also emerging (*OMRI Daily Digest*, 950425).

15 In the early 1990s many pan-Turkists believed that all the Turks would unite in some form of federation or at least confederation; and that all Turks would act together, helping each other. Many people travelled between Turkey and the Turkic republics in Caucasia and Central Asia. Cultural exchange associations were set up. Even within Turkey's (normally very Europe-directed) Foreign Ministry pan-Turkic euphoria was clearly visible. Turkey would educate the new diplomats of Caucasia and Central Asia, and in the meantime Turkey would represent these states. The ties with the long-lost brothers would finally be restored. Several associations in Turkey began to describe Central Asia as the true, ancient home of all Turks and the place where the true Turkic culture had been preserved. However, when it became clear that the Turks of Central Asia had been a lot more Sovietized than expected, the euphoria soon cooled down.

16 In an attempt to reach Meskhetia in Georgia. However, they are not allowed to settle in Georgia, so they are temporarily living in Azerbaijan and southern Russia.

South Asia: An Anxious Journey towards Regionalization?

BENT D. JØRGENSEN

Until recently, South Asia has been a rather well-knit and easy-to-define region, or so it seemed. However, the effects of the post-Cold War era have questioned the definition, shape and rationale of the region. The traditional antagonists, India and Pakistan, who in the past kept each other at loggerheads in a close security relation, are now directing their foreign policies beyond the confines of the South Asian region. The end of the Cold War has meant a totally different international environment, which has forced the South Asian people, markets, and states more closely into competitive economic relations with the rest of the world. The ambitions of India and Pakistan to participate in other regional organizations like the Association of Southeast Asian Nations (ASEAN) and the Indian Ocean Rim Treaty (IORT), have led to a seemingly paradoxical situation; there are tremendous political and economic efforts to promote regionalization in different forms, but not necessarily with the aim of strengthening the South Asian region (Muni 2000).

National and regional centrifugal forces have within the last decade increased to such an extent that there is a fear that the South Asian region will cease to have any significant role to play as a region in the future. As we shall see, this is not necessarily because of increased interstate conflict. The centrifugal forces have more to do with the fact that the countries and their differences have been over-shadowed by other more significant subnational political and global economic concerns. Thus, judging from South Asia, even if the states still play the key role in international relations, their decision-making capacity has decreased in favour of the global economy, neighbouring regions, and subnational forces.

Five different processes, and their prime actors, are identified in this chapter as crucial in relation to regionalism in South Asia. Why these particular processes have been chosen becomes clearer as the chapter unfolds. The *first process* is the attempt at promoting peace and internationalism, also called Third Worldism. Regionalism in South Asia has to be understood in the light of this particular form of internationalism, which is, or at least was, a strong tradition in some South Asian states. The *second process* is the formation of the regional security complex in the Cold War era. This was a period in which security concerns came to dominate all intraregional relations between people and states. The *third process* is the ethnic or subnational challenge, not only to the nation-state, but also to regional and international peace. In recent decades, the cross-border activities of ethnic movements have placed intraregional relations under strain. Ethnic conflicts in border areas seem to be one of the main security issues in the region and also a main threat to development and stability in these areas. The *fourth process* is the formal regionalization that became a salient political force during the 1980s and 1990s. The South Asian Association for Regional Cooperation (SAARC) has played the main role in attempting to integrate the region, but it has met many obstacles and difficulties due to intraregional tensions and disputes. The *fifth process* is the rise of interregional relations in which the economy has come to dominate international relations in the South Asian region.

Before we discuss these processes it is worth defining the region, as such a discussion will cast some light on the essence of 'regionness' in South Asia.

Defining South Asia

As with all world regions, it is possible to define the South Asian region according to a variety of principles.[1] Before we enter into a discussion of various principles of regional definition, we can reveal that most state-centric principles of demarcation lead to the same seven states: India, Pakistan, the Maldives, Sri Lanka, Bangladesh, Nepal and Bhutan. To trace the territorial borders of a region is basically a matter of identifying those states which relate to each other in economic, cultural or political ways, and share some similarities. As we shall see, there are several factors binding the South Asian region together. Iran, Afghanistan, China, and Burma are all bordering states, but for various reasons, depending on defining principles, they will possess relatively more intense relations and share higher concerns with other countries, constituting regions in their own right. If we consider non-state relations, it is evident that the region is not as easy to define. Non-state relations have become more salient and they are crucial aspects of regionalism.

Natural Boundaries and Ecology

The South Asian region can rightfully be defined as the territory confined by the Himalayas, 'the Roof of the World', to the north and the Indian Ocean to the south.

This definition is at first sight almost self-evident as it clearly separates South Asia from China, Tibet and Central Asia. On the other hand, a 'natural boundary' between states or regions never exists independently of a political power which constantly nurtures its existence. The Himalayas do not meet the Indian Ocean anywhere, and therefore the Indian subcontinent is geographically open to Southeast Asia towards the east, and to the pastoral plateau of Central Asia to the west. Especially the latter has been the entrance through which invaders have brought major changes to the subcontinent throughout the ages. This trend was only interrupted with the British conquest and the establishment of Afghanistan as a buffer state/zone between Central Asia and India. Today this buffer of Afghanistan, in disarray, constitutes a major security issue in both Pakistan and India. Hence, so-called natural boundaries like the Himalayas have to be reconstructed constantly by states sufficiently strong to impose the significance of the boundaries in international affairs. It should be remembered though, that these natural boundaries are of great concern to those in power in the subcontinent. For this reason they are crucial to our understanding of security concerns and the geographical shape of individual polities and the region as a whole (Muni 1993: 15).

Natural and human geography is a factor that certainly has importance in the definition of the South Asian region – as a means not so much to define the boundaries, as to define its cores of population. The river valleys of the Ganga, the Brahmaputra, and the Indus have for millennia been among the most densely populated agricultural land in the world, and sustained large populations with rice. This area has strongly influenced those surrounding it: the coastal land and the high plateau or the Deccan, which are areas with comparatively lower agricultural production. Towards the east, the dense malarial forests of present-day northeast India and Burma have been populated by highland people with different agricultural methods, and the area has constituted an ecological frontier towards Southeast Asia.

Natural boundaries have certainly been barriers for people and commodities. They have also been gateways, however, or enticingly fertile land for people entering and leaving the territory which today we consider to be South Asia. In order to understand the utility of these natural preconditions, we need to add the human factor to the picture.

Political History

For a historical definition of South Asia, we could pick any moment in time and look at the 'political map' illustrating polities and their relations in the southern part of the Asian continent. This would be to commit the common nationalist anachronistic fallacy of utilizing historical polities as models for the construction of modern political entities: states, provinces, or, for that matter, regions. The freedom struggle of the Indian National Congress is an illuminating example of a political movement which strove, not only to wrench power from the British, but also to construct a state with reference to historical polities which were assumed to have covered the entire subcontinent – but in fact never did so.[2] The Moghul Empire,[3] hitherto the largest polity on the Indian subcontinent, was never clearly bounded as are present-day modern states, and the extent of its political control was shifting and disputed. Even if such empires or ancient states are important for our understanding of the present political culture, we should be aware that when it comes to present territorial claims, these historical entities are primarily a source of political rhetoric.

In search of a historical definition of South Asia, we ought to look for the period in which the modern state apparatus and modern nation building took shape. We look, in other words, for the juro-political and ideological foundation of the polities in the region, and not least their present relations. The region of South Asia might then be defined as the group of states formerly included in the British Empire on the subcontinent.[4] Despite the preceding period of Moghul rule, it was during the late colonial era that this region came under common rule for the first time in history, and that modern political and economic institutions were created. Furthermore, it was towards the end of British rule that national elites were formed and organized in, for instance, the Indian National Congress and the Muslim League. The colonial institutional set-up and ideological foundation was utilized, further developed and transformed to fill the needs of the new states.

Historical polities offer an infinite number of possible states, regions or other possible political constructions, whose accentuations are determined more by contemporary concerns than by history itself.[5] Historical definitions of the region like the one presented here, however, are relevant because historical processes, and particularly the political relations that are created in their wake, interact with the institutional and cultural fabric of specific locations.

Sociocultural Factors

The Brahminical or Sanskritic social order and its close links to the South Asian political culture have deep historical roots in the region. For several scholars this is the prime integrative factor in South Asia, distinguishing it from neighbouring regions.

> Broadly stated, the unifying factor of such order was its hierarchically structured social system along with a moral code explicating mutual obligations and at the same time preserving plural identities therein. In due course, such pluralities did acquire their specificities and distinctness in various regions but without subverting the core of the social system. (Phadnis 1989: 31; Srinivas 1989)

The caste system, with which this Sanskritic social order is commonly associated, has political implications for the region. It is obvious that caste is linked to the Hindu tradition and mythology and hence is also an inseparable part of sister religions like Sikhism, Buddhism and Jainism. Even though India and Nepal are the only countries with a Hindu majority, however, the concept of hierarchical caste or strata is so prevalent that it pervades all religious communities in the region. Most Muslims will disclaim the caste system and so does the Christian community, but, as Urmilla Phadnis indicates in the quotation above, the Sanskritic order has been able to sustain its hold on people despite various alien civilizations penetrating the subcontinent. Efforts by the British or the modern state to alter the Sanskritic social order by juridical measures have largely failed. On the contrary, the social order, and particularly the caste divides, have gained new political salience in the modern society (Kothari 1988).

Yet, in terms of cohesion, sociocultural factors have a double-edged impact. Politicized culture, and more specifically religion, is simultaneously the most potent integrating and disintegrating factor in the region. The rifts between belief systems are of political importance in all the major countries in the region, and they play the double role of being strong integrative forces in nation-building efforts,[6] and, partly because of that, at the same time challenging every effort to cooperate in the region.

The most decisive cultural factor integrating the region, however, is the common colonial background of the modern elite. This elite was initially created in a colonial discourse and fostered for more than a century, which laid the ground for a rather homogeneous and all-South Asian elite, sometimes referred to as 'the veneer'. Despite the fact that leaders of states in the region are bound by mutual conflicts, it is remarkable to what extent they express their grievances in the same terms and with the same rhetoric.[7] Talking about common culture, there is, however, always a risk of reification. Furthermore, the modern history of South Asia, and especially the era of the nation-states, has loaded the regional relations not only with cultural and historical similarities, but also with severe and deep-rooted conflicts and discontinuities. These relations have been 'translated' into the modern attempt to create bounded territorial and homogeneous nations and, possibly, a 'region'.

Economy

We will deal with the changed role and nature of the economic forces as a separate process below, but here we touch briefly upon contemporary economic relations in the South Asian region. Economy is an apparent integrative factor in formal regional corporations like NAFTA and EU. If we look at the seven South Asian countries in SAARC, we find that economic ties are relatively strong between India and the landlocked mountain kingdoms of Nepal and Bhutan. Of the external trade of the smaller states, 70 per cent is with India. Due to the extreme size of India, however, the trade among the SAARC countries is less than 3.2 per cent of their total external trade (Indunil Thenuara, *The Hindu,* 'Business News', Sunday 24 March 1996).

The economic ties between India and Pakistan are particularly weak. The deep-rooted conflict between the two countries has effectively hampered mutual trade, which is about 1 per cent of their total external trade. Both countries have more formal trade[8] with Germany, for example, than with each other. Mutual investments are insignificant and the economic infrastructure linking the economies is poor. As we see below, there are contemporary and powerful attempts to create strong regional economic integration in South Asia, but so far the economy is not a strong integrative factor.

To sum up, the economy, and the ecological, historical, and cultural definitions of the region briefly described above, all point to a few important observations. First, South Asian society has a lot in common in terms of culture and shared history. Second, it seems extremely difficult to trace the boundaries of the region more specifically than to the territory and people south of the Himalayas, and even with such a vague delineation one should be cautious. Third, history in South Asia has loaded international relations not only with cultural and historical similarities, but also with severe and deep-rooted conflicts between states and between religious and ethnic communities. With this in mind, we will make an attempt to understand the dynamics of the South Asian region by highlighting the five crucial processes.

Aiming at Peace and ThirdWorldism through 'the Large Region'

Ever since independence, countries in the region have endeavoured to associate themselves with various countries and regions not congruous with those seven countries commonly perceived as the South Asian region. Before and after independence, India was struggling with colonial ties and attempted to tighten relations with other former colonies in Asia and Africa. Jawaharlal Nehru firmly believed in Asian regional cooperation in which India and China would play significant roles, not only as major powers but also as peace makers.[9] Consequently, Sino-Indian relations were friendly after 1947–8 and Nehru had great expectations of warm Sino-Indian relations up to the mid-1950s. In a speech in the Lok Sabha (House of Commons) in September 1954 he gave expression to the common view that the enemy of India was to be found elsewhere than in China. The West and the subnational disintegrative forces were considered as more fundamental security concerns than China: 'Countries like China and India, once they get rid of foreign domination and internal disunity, inevitably become strong; there is nothing to stop them' (Nehru 1961: 305). India adopted and gained acceptance from China for her policy of *Panchsheel,* or five principles of peaceful coexistence.[10] This policy of Asianism would be challenged, however, and Nehru's admiration of China would wane towards the end of the 1950s. China took a tighter grip on Tibet from 1950 onwards, and in 1959 Chinese troops finally occupied the entire Tibetan territory.

It was implicitly understood that China and India accused each other of claiming territories that did not rightfully belong to them. But more significant for Third Worldism, the content and political potency of the concept of imperialism was swept away by intra-Asian conflicts. From now on the Cold War had swept away the path of mutual understanding on which Nehru had put India. Second, the region could not play the significant role in world politics that India, at least, had wanted. The superpowers were preoccupied with conflicts elsewhere and South Asia was somehow left in a 'geographical vacuum' between the oil in the Middle East and the communists in East and Southeast Asia. In other words, the regional aspirations of Nehru and other Asian leaders of the late 1940s were contradicted by both intra-Asian conflicts and the global Cold War.

The interstate relations, especially the economic ties, within the South Asian region became weaker rather than stronger after independence. India's dominance prompted the smaller states, otherwise keen to eradicate colonial dependency, to strengthen their relations with the former European colonial powers and other Western, and later Asian, states. The rationale became a matter of sovereignty within a region dominated by one regional great power. In other words, this regional imbalance gave new South Asian meanings to the concepts of independence, imperialism and sovereignty, at least from the point of view of the smaller states.

Events to which we will soon return inclined the South Asian countries to a relatively more realist stand in international affairs from the end of the 1950s. This is not to say that India and to some extent Sri Lanka, the most democratic countries, abandoned their attempt to unite the former colonies in the South around the mutual experience of economic and political exploitation by the North. The two countries played an active role in the Non-Aligned Movement (NAM) from 1961 onwards and Group 77 from 1964. The aims have been economic cooperation and development in the South, to minimize dependency on the North, and, politically, to stay clear of the superpower military alliances. It could be said that Asianism turned to globalism. Later, as we will see below, the South Asian region began to take shape and we got, at least on a rhetorical level, a new South Asianism.

During the last three decades it has become evident that the Third World has come to occupy a very diverse political and economic position, and it has become increasingly difficult to assert a united front against the North. Today, grassroots movements in the South are again attempting to establish a front not against Northern exploitation as much as against Western culture. Gandhi's sarcasm is heard again. When he was asked about Western civilization, he replied: 'It would have been a good idea!'

The Creation of a South Asian Security Complex

Security is a relational term, which binds people and states together in relations of enmity or amity. Thus the concept of regional security complex is an attempt to model a system of relations of amity and enmity based on mutual security concerns (Buzan 1986: 5–6).

The pattern of amity and enmity in South Asia is clearly dominated by two circumstances, namely the persistent India–Pakistan rivalry, and the dominance of India in relation to her six neighbours. The security concerns of these seven states link them together to such an extent that we can describe South Asia as a regional security complex (Buzan 1983). The concept of regional security complex is, however, intended not only to define the region, but also to illuminate the political dynamics in the region historically, at present, and in the future. Initially, we will search for the origin of the *regional* pattern of amity and enmity.

The Indian National Congress (INC), representing a variety of ethno-religious groups, was the obvious successor of the British in the colonial empire. It was under its large umbrella that people of diverse origin, religion, and mother tongue had fought first for legal and human rights and, from 1885 onwards, for independence. Its initial base was an Anglicized elite with little popular support. Bearing the Sanskritic society in mind, it is not difficult to imagine this elite forming a rather introverted 'caste' detached from the great masses of people.

The change came in the 1920s when leaders within and outside the INC in different ways began to mobilize the masses against British colonialism.[11] M. K. Gandhi, not himself a Brahmin, probably had the greatest appeal to the masses. His language was partly modern, partly rooted in the subcontinental religious symbols and values. This local religious foundation paired with two modern factors, namely the British advocacy of divide and rule policies[12] and Western parliamentarism, had a disintegrative effect on the Indian leadership and consequently the people (Kothari 1970: 62ff). The Muslim leaders, primarily belonging to the middle class, soon either felt discriminated against or saw the opportunity to gain political and economic strength by adopting the means and methods of the INC in general and Gandhi in particular. The Muslim League started to formulate a nation-building project of its own, mobilizing the Muslim masses especially in the areas of Muslim majority: present-day Pakistan, Bangladesh and the Indian state of Kashmir. INC counteractions and a vicious circle of violence accelerated up to and after independence, when India was split into two states, India and Pakistan.

The creation of Pakistan has often been described as an outcome (almost natural) of the Hindu–Muslim divide. This is certainly a disputable interpretation. It is probably more appropriate to describe the emerging India–Pakistan conflict as the development of contending elitist social projects, one secular and one theo-cratic, receiving ideological influences from the universal nation-state ideologies of liberalism and nationalism respectively. The Muslim leadership invented the 'two nation theory' in 1940, claiming that the Muslims in fact were a nation, which according to the predominant nation-state logic entitled them to a sovereign state; sovereign over a Muslim territory and a Muslim people. As this was an integral part of the European nation-state model, as was the secular and liberal ideology of the INC, the British had few arguments available with which to restrain the antag-onists. There was no moral, no logic to adhere to, and in that situation, the nation-alist stand often gets the upper hand: India became divided. Only after India gained independence could further separatism be avoided by leaning on a more realist ideological foundation.

The ideological divide in South Asia paved the way for severe and persistent bilateral agony. Those who demanded the creation of Pakistan all claimed to belong to a group constituted by a single formative principle: religion. This was done not *for* Islam but *against* the Hindu majority. The INC, on the other hand, which came to constitute the new state-bearing elite in independent India, was not formed *for* Hinduism but *against* British colonialism. While the multiethnic and multireligious INC had to emphasize secularity and avoid classification with any single group identity, the latter was necessarily the very foundation of the new nation-state of Pakistan (Buzan 1983: 78; Rizvi 1986: 96). Among the Indian leaders, Pakistan was perceived as a temporary sociopolitical problem for which India would find a solution sooner or later (Muni 2000). The major military build-up in the region has taken place between India and Pakistan. And three wars have been fought between the two countries; two over the partition of Kashmir (1947, 1965) and one over the partition of East and West Pakistan and the subsequent creation of Bangladesh (1971).

The India–Pakistan rivalry has other elements. India is a huge regional great power in terms of its economy, population and military forces. Despite US military support to Pakistan during the Cold War and India's larger territory requiring cor-respondingly greater defence, Indian superiority is unquestionable. Keeping the irreconcilable positions in mind, it is not surprising that Pakistan perceives India as a threat. This is even more true of the smaller states within the complex. Their even smaller military, demographic and economic size has caused unequal relations of dependency with India. India seems to have had difficulty in accepting the full independence of its small neighbours, including Pakistan. This could be due to a profound big-brother complex and to the awareness of India's objective strength. The result has been that Indian leaders from time to time have taken the security concerns of India to be those of the region. Since 1947 India has attempted to establish a security consensus and at the same time dictate security policies in the region, especially towards the superpowers and China. Her main strategy has been to maintain a high level of stability and avoid major conflicts which might legitimize interference by extraregional forces.[13]

The Indian attempt to treat the region as a state with security concerns formulated in New Delhi has constantly created tension in the region and defined the central security concerns of the smaller states. Every attempt to take an independent stance towards India, or to create extraregional alliances with the superpowers, has met with diplomatic, economic, and even military responses from India. Nepal's endeavour to establish closer links with China in 1962 and 1989–90 (Muni 1993: 27) and Sri Lanka's invitation to the US to establish a naval base in Trincomalee on the Sri Lankan east coast in the early 1980s have been greeted with harsh disapproval or even threats by India. These experiences left the smaller states with no other objective than to strive for better bilateral relations with India, or try the regional option.

The predominant bipolar pattern of hostility in South Asia has provided the principal opening for external interference in the subcontinental security complex. The regional conflicts have, at least during the Cold War, fitted into the bipolarity between the superpowers on the global level, and between China and the Soviet Union/Russia on the superregional level. India tried, as mentioned above, to take a neutral stance towards the superpower rivalry in order to preserve its managerial role in the region. It was the inconvenient lesson learned in the disastrous Sino–Indian war in 1962 that forced India to establish a more formal alliance with Moscow; it was also the new hostility between China and the Soviet Union which made this alliance possible (Ayoob 1989: 110). After the Sino–Indian war, India's military budget doubled. The aim was to be prepared to meet Chinese aggression on the northeastern and northwestern flanks and to hamper Chinese assistance and military training to secessionist ethnic movements.

From independence until the end of the Cold War, the South Asian region has been defined and locked up in conflictual security relations. India has been the regional great power, the hub, which has held the region together and also determined what was allowed to figure on the regional agenda. It was in this environment and with the decline of global bipolarity that SAARC emerged. Before we enter into a discussion of this attempt to bind the region together, we need to understand probably the single most severe security threat posed to the South Asian states: the ethnonational challenge.

Interconnecting Regional Security and Ethnonational Conflicts

Anyone who opens a South Asian newspaper realizes that ethnic clashes are common all over the region. At present, almost every state in South Asia is haunted by serious ethnic conflicts. Escalating conflicts between Hindus and Muslims are seriously affecting the political climate all over India and occasionally even in Bangladesh. Several ethnic conflicts are confined to particular Indian states such as Punjab, Assam and Nagaland. In Pakistan, Bangladesh and Sri Lanka the ruling majorities are seriously challenged, and even attacked, by ethnic minority movements. In the long run, Pakistan might not be able to keep the state together, and Sri Lanka has been under persistent pressure from the Tamil Tigers since 1983. From another perspective it is evident that in all these conflicts we find severe violations of human rights and threats to civilian lives.

The fragility of the South Asian states has strongly contributed to the internationalization of ethnic conflicts. Patterns of amity and enmity among nation-states in a regional setting have a close resemblance to traditional perceptions of ethnic relations (for example, Jews–Arabs in the Middle East, Vietnamese–Khmer in Southeast Asia, Muslims–Hindus in South Asia). From an outsider's perspective, these conflicts might appear to be international, as for instance between India and Pakistan, but for the natives they are also, and perhaps to a larger extent, ethnic. Because ethnic and national boundaries never fully correspond, patterns of amity and enmity cut across regional interstate relations.[14] Hence, several major ethnic groups extend over international borders. It is not a coincidence that most of these groups are involved in severe ethnic conflicts with states and other ethnic groups in the region. The phenomenon of refugees, which has been the cumulative negative result of decades of ethnic conflict, has further complicated the regional scene and put constraints on the safety and security of states and people. One of the more unfortunate consequences of ethnic conflicts is people fleeing their homes and states. Depending on methods of measurement, it can be argued that South Asia 'would clearly be one of the most persistently and seriously affected' concerning refugees (Muni and Baral 1996: 6).

The risk of secession and internationalization of ethnic conflicts makes the border provinces highly sensitive security concerns. The military forces deployed in these areas are meant to defend the country not only from outsiders, but certainly also from insiders. The hill states in the northeastern corner of India, especially Nagaland, and the northwestern states of Kashmir and Punjab are all important strongholds for the Indian army, which attempts to preserve internal stability. These are also the states which the Indian government has tried to homogenize by means such as migration, education, the mass media, government funds, or simply repression. Very often, such steps fuel ethnic tensions further, as has been evident in both Kashmir and Nagaland. In other words, the security of the nation is pursued by means of direct or indirect violence against the people residing along the boundaries.[15]

The linkage between internal or subnational conflicts and international and regional conflicts is a complex phenomenon, and these conflicts can only be understood in relation to each other. The Indian attempt to create stability in the region is sometimes countered by the attempt to preserve internal stability. The Tamil uprising in Sri Lanka, the ethnic tension in Bhutan, Nepal and Bangladesh have all become direct security concerns for the Indian government via the local elites in border states within the Indian union (Muni 1993: 25). Often through state governments or parties, local elites have put pressure on the central government to take action against India's neighbours in order to protect those perceived as fellows (Hindus in Pakistan, Tamils in Sri Lanka, Biharis in Bangladesh, Nepalese in Bhutan) across India's international border. In this way Indian 'centre-state' relations elevate to the regional level and thereby become international security issues.

The situation in Chittagong Hills in Bangladesh, for instance, illuminates this point. This is an area of severe conflict between the state and the dominant Bengali nation and the Chakma highland minority. Fleeing severe violations of human rights in the Chittagong Hill Tracts, Chakmas are today to be found in great numbers in India and particularly in northeast India where they are among culturally and linguistically similar groups. Initially, organizations in India impelled the Indian government to take action against the violence committed against the Chakmas in Bangladesh. Nevertheless, the supportive attitudes have changed gradually. Within the last decade, refugees in former havens such as Arunachal Pradesh have been harassed or forcefully expelled from their camps. The northeastern states now demand that the flow of people across the border should be terminated. What started off as an ethnic conflict in Bangladesh has turned into an international issue between India and Bangladesh and now into internal tension between the Indian central government and the northeastern states.

Another issue is Kashmir and the resulting India–Pakistan conflicts. It was already on the international agenda in 1947 during the partition of India and Pakistan. For the two national leaderships, the question was whether the strategically important state of Jammu and Kashmir[16] should belong to either India or Pakistan. Internally in Kashmir, the question was whether Kashmir should join the Indian union, Pakistan, or gain independence. The irreconcilable positions of the Muslim and Hindu elites on the national level led to a war between India and Pakistan from October 1947 to the end of 1948, in which Pakistan gained control of one third of the territory (Azad 1989; Blinkenberg 1972). Since then, India and Pakistan have fought two major wars in 1965 and 1971 and hundreds of military encounters in Kashmir.

On the national level, Kashmir posed a serious problem for the Indian leadership after independence. Kashmir is regarded as strategically important and therefore the ethnic insurgence is treated as a threat to Indian security, and the Kashmiri Muslims as a fifth column exploited by Pakistan. The Kashmiri Muslims seem to have mixed feeling concerning the interference from outside. One indication of this is that the attempt by Pakistan to utilize the Kashmiri Muslims as a fifth column in the 1965 war was not very successful. Furthermore, since 1953 Kashmiri groups have frequently demanded independence from both India and Pakistan (Rizvi 1986: 100).

In 1989, the Kashmir issue made the headlines again. This time, the spark came from within Kashmir. Among other things, Muslims were disappointed with the amount of resources allocated for development in the state compared to other states, and that the accord signed with the centre in the mid-1980s was a mere a piece of paper (Puri 1989). In this tense situation, the demand for an independent Kashmir was asserted, with support soon coming from across the border in Pakistan. The Kashmir issue is not the only example of an internationalized ethnic conflict in India–Pakistan relations. During the 1980s Pakistan built and supported training camps for militant Sikhs on Pakistani soil. Similarly, Indian intelligence has supported ethnic organizations in Sind and Baluchistan demanding autonomy and secession from Pakistan.

We find that ethnic conflicts not only prevail on the national level, but also that by and large they constitute major security concerns and shape the security complex of South Asia. The Tamils in Sri Lanka and India are a major security issue in the relationship between the two countries. Sikhs and Kashmiris, or even the whole Muslim Indian minority, play a similar role in India–Pakistan relations. International relations in the South Asian region, in other words, present not only rational or realist strands for analysis, but emotionally embedded issues which complicate any assessment, not to mention solution, of international conflict. In fact, ethnic conflicts have been among the fiercest issues in the region, so intense that they have been a major stumbling block to any attempt at regional co-operation, which is the next process considered here. No issue concerning ethnopolitics has ever reached the agenda of the South Asian regional organization, SAARC.

The Balancing of Political Regionalism and Interdependence

The initiative to cover South Asia with a formal regional organization did not come from India, but from the smaller states. Due to her size and geographical links[17] to her neighbours, India has a preference for bilateral relations. Her hegemony made the smaller states opt for a regional organization and hence, a change from bilateralism to regionalism, or from a skewed to a more balanced regionalism in which the smaller states together would be able to counter Indian dominance (Baral 1988). This stand was reaffirmed during the inter-summit meeting of SAARC in March 1999, where India refused to lift India–Pakistan relations to the regional agenda (India News Network, 19 March 1999).

The impetus for formal regional cooperation also came from outside the region itself. The experience of the Vietnam War, the success of the ASEAN in Southeast Asia (see Chapter 8), and the Soviet intervention in Afghanistan in 1979 paved the way for the Carter Doctrine (Muni, 2000), encouraging the formation or strengthening of non-US regional organizations in non-communist parts of Asia. The Cold War was still on, but it had lost much of its momentum in the sense that the US had become increasingly wary of any direct military involvement in anti-communist struggles. The Soviet Union, for its part, became increasingly locked into the Afghanistan war, internal grievances and reforms during the 1980s.

The creation of SAARC in 1985 should therefore be seen as an initiative taken by the smaller states in order to balance the power of India, as well as an initiative encouraged and made possible by the larger global context, which constituted an environment in which the USA and the Soviet Union left more room for manoeuvre to South Asia. The initiative to form SAARC came from Bangladesh's President Zia-ur-Rahman in May 1980. Sri Lanka especially, but also Nepal, Bhutan and the Maldives, supported the proposal, while India and Pakistan were less enthusiastic. President Rahman's reference to 'peace, stability and security' (Palmer 1991: 80) as goals for regional cooperation was met with suspicion by India. So was the general incentive – the Carter Doctrine – as India distrusted the US foreign policy in general and its involvement in the region in particular.

The removal from its programme of 'bilateral and contentious issues', however, and security issues in particular, made the organization attractive even to the two antagonists in the region (Hettne 1990: 120; Muni 2000). The five principles of *Panchsheel* (see note 10) were included in the programme, which also safeguarded the organization from 'contentious issues', which of course included the principal security issues between India and Pakistan. In its final shape in the Dacca Declaration of December 1985, SAARC came to cover a vast array of issues such as trade, shipping, natural resource management, energy, river waters, food policy, joint development programmes, technology transfer, people-to-people contacts, and tourism (Muni 2000). Several of these issues were, of course, 'contentious issues' which initially were played down within the SAARC framework, but which in the course of time found their way into discussions, mainly in the informal talks parallel to the official summits and meetings.

India's initial cautious stand towards multilateral cooperation has gradually changed since 1985. Whereas the smaller states considered, or hoped to see,

SAARC as a joint force to meet the Indian dominance, India on the other hand came to conceive of SAARC as the tool through which it could strengthen its position in the region. It is understandable, therefore, that Pakistan has been more reluctant to participate in scale with the others and to hand over the necessary powers to the organization (Muni 2000).

Scaled down by internal cleavages, the achievements of SAARC have not been impressive. Until recently the scope of action has been limited to the cultural and educational fields and yearly meetings with presidents and prime ministers. If we consider the obstacles, however, it is obvious that, compared to other regions, the scope for comprehensive regionalization in South Asia has been rather limited. SAARC is unique in its constitution. Unlike other regional organizations emerging during the Cold War, SAARC incorporated the global bipolar conflict within the confines of the region instead of constituting one side only, as was the case in Europe and Southeast Asia, for instance. Considering the India–Pakistan rivalry and the weak economic ties in the region, it is rather surprising that the seven states have been able to cooperate at all. A plausible explanation is that bilateral and security issues in particular have been excluded from the SAARC agenda and that neither of the superpowers had any genuine interest in promoting the India–Pakistan rivalry.

After the Cold War, SAARC has gained strength – driven not primarily by political motives, as during the initial phase, but by economic concerns. SAARC has become a potential tool for economic cooperation. The states seem to follow market rules rather than being guided by ideological or even high-priority security concerns. The closer and warmer relations between India and China are but one example, illuminating how economic and political elites attempt to maximize international trade. The South Asian Preferential Trade Agreement (SAPTA) is a concrete example, in which India and Pakistan are starting to bury the hatchet and work towards an increase in trade and the development of cooperative financial institutions. By the year 2000 (and no later than 2005) the South Asian Free Trade Area (SAFTA) should be a reality. It is not that the security issues are resolved or have become obsolete. On the contrary, the Sino-Indian and India–Pakistan borders are as indeterminable as ever (illustrated by the fighting during Spring/Summer 1999). It is just that at present the states in South Asia, China and elsewhere in Asia are chiefly concerned with other matters than territorial border disputes.

The national leaders, at least in India, seem to realize that they have to take new steps to tackle a new world order. One of the strategies adopted has been to test different 'regionalization projects', though these are different in kind from the original SAARC project and are driven by different motives than during the Cold War. The new regionalism, to which we will return below, is closely connected with the context in which the states and the region are developing. Most significant are the dominance of the world market and the corresponding weakness of governmental politics.

From Security Regionalism to Economic Regionalism

Even if Sri Lanka was the first country in the region to advocate the 'Open Door Policy' in 1977, the breakthrough for a liberal political economy first came in 1991 when India gave up the old policy of import substitution and opened its economy to the world market. India pulled the entire region into a new development strategy to produce for the world market, using the vast and inexpensive labour force of South Asia. It was the fall of the Soviet Union and the communist bloc which forced India to seek new economic opportunities, and it was the markets and economic models of East and Southeast Asia that attracted the growing middle class in the region. In other words, there were both push and pull forces behind the turn of development strategy when Narasimha Rao took office as Prime Minister of India in 1991. All of a sudden, the Minister of Finance, Manmohan Singh, came to play the key role in Indian politics. Singh turned India inside out, decreasing taxes and tariffs and inviting foreign capital and skilled manpower to India – and indirectly to the entire region.

Indian reforms, however, could also be viewed from a different angle. The Indian middle class has entered the economically strong international middle class and detached itself from the great masses. The economic concerns of the Indian state have come to overshadow the national political ideologies and priorities, particularly since 1991. Considering the prospects for regionalization and regional co-operation, particularly through SAARC, this development is interesting. As the new Prime Minister, Inder K. Gujral, stated in 1996:

> I am a strong believer in regional cooperation. I believe that *the concept of region must expand*. I feel that SAARC must have Burma, Afghanistan and the induction of Central Asian countries. Only then will you have a vast market and resources available to build a huge economy in this region. With the Indian economy being the largest in the region, I am willing to have asymmetrical relationships. I am willing to give more than I take.... I believe that larger nations must have larger hearts also. (Interview with I. K. Gujral in *India Today*, 30 June 1996, New Delhi, my emphasis)

There are several interesting conclusions that can be drawn from this statement, which fits into the so-called 'Gujral Doctrine'. First, it is interesting to note that, as already mentioned, economic concerns preside over conventional security concerns. India is supposed to be the hub around which the region should centre, not because of political, but economic strength. Second, India is prepared to contribute economically to find new markets in an expanded region. Gujral is even prepared to cooperate more closely with Pakistan. 'One model to follow is the Indo-China one in which, although we have some contentious issues to be settled, it does not prevent us from having relations on anything else' (*ibid.*). To illustrate the somewhat warmer relations, India sent observers to watch the Pakistan national election in January 1997 (India News Network, 22 January 1997). Another political improvement was several rounds of peace talks between the two countries during 1996 and 1997. Pakistan, however, has been reluctant to increase its economic cooperation with India, mainly because some parts of the Pakistani business community fear competition, especially from India's textile industry. As the South Asian countries, by and large, hope to sell the same commodity on the world market, cheap labour, it is not surprising that the prospects for competition are higher than for cooperation. Yet, India and Pakistan have both agreed to form SAFTA by the year 2000, and no later than 2005.

The elite, however, is divided between the market-oriented, vast and growing middle class, and the political elite for whom the nation-states, and the old antagonisms between them, are still crucial as sources of legitimacy. The India–Pakistan conflict, which has overshadowed regional relations and hampered the move towards regional cooperation since independence, could now be downgraded because political security has given way to economic concerns. The vested economic interests that drag India and the other South Asian countries into this new development strategy, however, do not possess any particular commitment to regional cooperation. For these interests, regionalism might as well be an economic tool that has no particular geographic or geopolitical meaning, but should presumably be assessed according to its economic output. The economic forces, in Sri Lanka during the 1970s, and during the 1980s in India, Pakistan, and to some extent Bangladesh, have gained more and more influence in the formulation of domestic as well as foreign policies. The new foreign policy could as well be termed transregionalism or multiregionalism.[18] In fact, India is involved in a row of regional projects and organizations ranging from membership of the Indian Ocean Rim Treaty[19] to affiliation with ASEAN (Muni 2000). In the former, Pakistan is also participating.

The actual outcome of multiregionalism is difficult to assess. A growing ethnic challenge in the shape of a strengthened *micro*regionalism, for instance, might change the geographical landscape of the region considerably. In Europe macroregionalism and microregionalism have gone hand in hand (Hettne in this volume), and there are some indications that South Asia and India will choose the same path. Since the shift to the Open Door policy in India in 1991, a few microregions have become able to act more independently. Among others, the states of West Bengal, Karnataka and the economically dynamic Maharashtra are making efforts to attract investors from abroad by promoting their own region. Yet, the region is in this sense no longer a bounded territory in accordance with the old nation-state discourse. The region is rather a centre with a periphery, which might extend over contemporary state and international borders. Mumbai, Poona, Bangalore and Calcutta are emerging centres. Calcutta is interesting in this respect owing to its proximity to the India–Bangladesh border. The Calcutta elite, with Chief Minister Basu in the forefront, is trying hard to attract foreign capital and to link the city to the international world market and the global information networks. If SAFTA materializes in the near future, there are reasons to believe that parts of Bangladesh will become more crucial in economic, and perhaps even sociocultural, terms than remote parts of present-day West Bengal. In a not-so-remote future, the territorial border will be less significant. Gujral seemed to have similar thoughts although he, probably for diplomatic reasons, sees Dhaka as the future hub of Bengal:

> Seven Northeastern Indian states flank Bangladesh. 'These are natural markets for Bangladesh. Dhaka could well become the Hong Kong of the region,' Mr Gujral said …. '[S]imilarly, the southern Indian states could provide markets for Sri Lanka and the Maldives…. We think in terms of reviving the type of economic cooperation units which used to exist in pre-partition days.'[20]

Gujral seemed to be wishing himself back to the colonial 'economic cooperation units'.[21] The backlash against multiregionalism might come from at least two different sources. First, in northeastern India the state and particularly its territorial border is, and in a foreseeable future will be perceived quite differently from the way it was in the mind of Gujral. Since the end of the 1970s strong local movements have fought to seal off the border with Bangladesh. The reason has been the movement of people from Bangladesh into northeastern India. Tripura has a majority of Bengalis, who are looked upon as foreigners by the Tripuri 'sons of the soil'. The attempt to strengthen the territorial borders is one expression of a strong politicization of ethnic identities in the region. In other words, the nation-state discourse is strong in the peripheral areas, whereas it seems to get weaker in the regional centres and cores.

Second, the weaker elite groups might simply realize that they have been let down by the microregional establishment in West Bengal, for instance, and use democratic strength as well as non-democratic means to change the course of events. Ethnonationalism, and in India casteism, is always at hand. The revival of fundamentalism and postcolonialism, which is often non-Western, is evident all over the world and not least in India and South Asia. This was the fear of many observers when the Hindu nationalist Bharatya Janata Party (BJP) seized power in February 1998. BJP turned out to be more pragmatic than fundamentalist, although its power by and large rests on fundamentalist groups and organizations.

Paradoxically, the nuclear test bombing in May 1998 brought India and Pakistan into a situation of mutual interest. They were both subjected to sanctions from the West, and in this situation they saw a common enemy. India, with greater power, has been more vocal in its critique of the West. On the one hand, this stand fits in well with the ideology of Hindu fundamentalism; on the other hand, it fits into the broader concept of 'Asian values'. The latter is a concept that so far has been a manifestation of anti-West sentiments in the neighbouring Southeast Asian region, with which India has gained closer contacts during the last decade. Similar influences from the Middle East have been felt in Pakistan.

Hindu nationalism could have been a tool to recapture the dominant position of politics over economy and borders and boundaries over networks and multi-regionalism. As it appears today, however, nationalism seems to be in the hands, not of religious fanatics, but of pragmatic centralists attempting simply to keep the nation-states intact, especially in India and Pakistan. The question, of course, is if the centrifugal forces of both subnational ethnopolitics and economic microregion-alism will challenge the national control of the central elites in the future.

Conclusions

The region as a concept is certainly contested and broad, and the weakening of the nation-state further widens it. As long as nation-states were naturalized, the borders and the rationales of regions were quite obvious. Now other projects, carrying new discourses and new political platforms, are challenging the hegemony of the nation-state. As a result, new constellations of regionalization appear. Regionalization is still an attempt to cooperate at the international level in order to meet various challenges, but the challenges have become more intense and diversified and hence the regionalization projects have become more disparate and varied, too. The government of India seems to be experimenting with all possible (and presumably some impossible) regional constructs in order to keep managerial power in the hands of the state. In that way, the state itself redefines the nation-state discourse. The Hindu nationalist attempt to create an Indian nation can be seen as one such experiment.

The state is commonly perceived as the active agent in international relations and also in the processes of intended regionalization. To understand such processes as regionalization, however, we would gain by examining ideological or discursive attempts to construct and reconstruct the state in relation to challenges, whether these derive from inside or outside the state itself. The state is too often taken for granted in world politics, neglecting the fact that states, particularly in South Asia, are constantly struggling to recreate the image and 'body' of the state and its sovereignty over a certain territory. Regionalization and the end of the Cold

War have not changed or altered these attempts and motives. Rather, we can expect regionalization, in its various shapes, to be an attempt to find new solutions to the 'national question' in countries like Sri Lanka, Pakistan, and India. These solutions are not meant to supersede the state as a sovereign, but rather to strengthen its sovereignty over a given territory and not least its diverse population. Yet it is not a matter of course that the states will succeed in these endeavours, and, even if they do, they might in the long run, through a successful regionalization, create a vehicle for the exact opposite: a body with suprastate authorities.

The current challenges from outside (the world market) and inside (ethnonational movements) have put the South Asian states in a dilemma over the regional security complex discussed above. The global economy compels the nation-states to cooperate in one or another way. The difficulty is to cooperate and at the same time maintain national identities that depends on constructing the neighbouring states and peoples as enemies. Every government in South Asia attempts to strike a balance between too much hostility, which could lead to less cooperation or even war, and too much cooperation, which could mean lost popular support in each of the states. A good example is the Pakistani fear of 'being soft on India'. It is still an open question if the Pakistani state would survive the loss of India as an enemy. It should also be remembered that in the construction of the nation, a lot of people are sacrificed. The production of national identity is in fact a violent endeavour. The process of regionalization, on the other hand, at least offers the possibility of more peaceful and mutual cooperation.

Turning to the economic dimension of the present development in the region, it is important to note that globalization and regionalization appear to be immediate sources of peace and stability. India, not least among regional nation-states, is pushed into closer ties with its neighbours by strong and influential Indian firms looking for investments and markets for their products. The wave of democratization within the last decade has had the same effect. These changes are, however, no guarantee of a sustainable development in which the broader masses of people are peacefully included slowly and without friction. The ethnonational centrifugal forces are not appeased by economic reforms, which at best exclude and at worst worsen the situation of the majority of people. The long-term crisis of legitimacy of states is of importance in this respect.

To sum up, the South Asian region is experiencing a period of major changes from the end of the Cold War, to geographically bound regionalization, and to a new era of multiregionalization. This development is led by a growing internationalized elite, attached to the larger international community and living on the international opportunities provided by the world market. This elite is by and large detached from the vast South Asian masses of people. The latter have, of course, their own political structure and leaders grounded in a given territorial context. However, whereas this structure was very rigid about a decade ago, it is now becoming more flexible, leaving room for social mobility. This mix is bound to create social tension and violence in the long run.

Whether regionalization in any form will ease this tension it is still too early to say. Regionalization offers solutions more than it provides ready-made concrete recipes for action. Ethnic tension could be eased once a regional political arena is established under the umbrella of SAARC. Ethnopolitical movements could be coped with in a more cooperative manner if states were keen to cooperate on this issue. The economic ties between semi-autonomous regions in South Asia would pave the way for more equal partners like West Bengal, Northeast India and Bangladesh. Yet the question remains whether the South Asian countries will choose this option, which was formulated in the Gujral Doctrine, or choose the nationalist stand. The latter will not only continue the tense relations in the region, but will also pave the way for new tension due to the overall processes of globalization in which the nation-states are under pressure from economic forces as well as ethnopolitical movements.

NOTES

1 See Björn Hettne's 'four ways of conceiving a *world region*' (Hettne 1989: 54).
2 It can be argued persuasively that the Indian central state (and other states in the region for that matter) is still engaged in continuous efforts to construct its polity in congruence with a particular bounded territory (Krishna 1996).
3 The empire expanded and consolidated itself over an area covering most of the Indian peninsula from the sixteenth century, deteriorated from the mid-eighteenth century, and was formally dissolved in 1859 when the British Crown took over the possessions of the British East India Company.
4 Burma, also a part of the British Empire, was formally separated from India in 1937 and was thereafter not meant, either by the Indian or by the Burmese leadership, to be included in the new Indian state (Bhargava 1986: 68–88).
5 For a comprehensive discussion of history in relation to nation building and nationalism, see Eriksen, 1993: Chapter 5.
6 India, using a secular constitution, is here an exception, although the Hindu nationalist attempt to turn India into a Hindu nation is such a strong contemporary force that it can be neglected neither by the observer nor by those political leaders in India who attempt to uphold the secular Indian state.
7 The best-known example in recent years was the dialogue between Rajiv Gandhi and Benazir Bhutto, two very modern politicians.
8 A considerable part of India–Pakistan trade passes through third countries or is illegally smuggled between the two countries.
9 Nehru opened the Asian relations conference in New Delhi, 23 March 1947, with these words:

We welcome you, delegates and representatives from China, that great country to which Asia owes so much and from which so much is expected.... During the past two hundred years we have seen the growth of Western imperialism.... It is fitting that India should play her part in Asian development ... she is the natural center and focal point of the many forces at work in Asia.... We have no designs against anybody; ours is the design of promoting peace and progress all over the world.... We, therefore, support the United Nations structure.... But in order to have One World, we must also, in Asia, think of the countries of Asia cooperating together for that larger ideal. (Nehru 1961: 249–52)

10 The five principles are: (1) Mutual respect for each other's territorial integrity and sovereignty; (2) Mutual nonaggression; (3) Mutual non-interference in each other's internal affairs; (4) Equality and mutual benefit; and (5) Peaceful coexistence (Nehru 1961: 99).

11 A more thorough discussion of the elite–mass relation in the independence movement falls beyond the scope of this chapter. For an excellent discussion see Chatterjee 1986: chapters 4–5.

12 First to the disadvantage of the Muslims, then, towards the end of the colonial era, to the disadvantage of the INC and the Hindus (to an increasing extent synonymous for the British).

13 The following statement by Nehru in 1958 probably derives from such a big-brother complex:

Pakistan, our neighbour country with whom we want to be friendly, is a part of the Baghdad Pact and thereby gets the help and assurance and backing of some of the most powerful nations in the world. As a result, Pakistan itself is prevented from adopting that friendly attitude to us which it otherwise might have adopted. (Nehru 1961: 96)

14 They can even cut across regional security complexes. Curiously, Indian intelligence tried to supply arms to the Indian rebels in Fiji in 1986. They got caught in Perth in Australia.

15 In fact this aspect of security has far wider implications than can be pursued within the confines of this chapter. For a thorough discussion see Krishna 1996.

16 Jammu and Kashmir is separated geographically and ethnically into three major regions: Jammu in the south, Kashmir in the north, and Ladakh in the east.

17 Note that none of the smaller countries in the region border on one another.

18 The example of G–15 illustrates the extent to which the concept of region has become less geographical, at least for Nitish Chakravarthy, reporting from the latest G–15 summit in Harare:

Among the issues likely to engage their attention ... are terrorism, South–South cooperation, networking of the information system and also liberalisation of market access within the *G-15 region*. Relaxation of travel restrictions within the *region* may also come up for discussion. (India News Network, Harare, 4 November, my emphasis)

It is not only that the issues are typical for regional cooperation: Nitish Chakravarthy has actually described this disparate crowd of countries as a region. The 'region' embraces Algeria, Argentina, Brazil, Egypt, India, Indonesia, Jamaica, Malaysia, Mexico, Nigeria, Peru, Senegal, Venezuela, Zimbabwe and Yugoslavia!

19 Indian Ocean Rim contains South Africa, Kenya, Egypt, Tanzania, Oman, Saudi Arabia, United Arab Emirates, Qatar, Bahrain, Mauritius, Maldives, Madagascar, India, Sri Lanka, Pakistan, Singapore, Malaysia, Indonesia, Australia, and New Zealand. The 'chief powers' are South Africa, India, Singapore and Australia.

20 'India Planning to Reach out to Neighbours' (Reuter in *The Globe & Mail*, Toronto, 19 March 1997).

21 Recently there have been attempts to create a 'subregional grouping' including Bangladesh, Nepal, Bhutan and the northeastern states of India (Nitish Chakravarty in India News Network, 13 January 1997).

South East Asia 8
at a Constant Crossroads
An Ambiguous 'New Region'

JOAKIM ÖJENDAL

Some names, like 'rose', acknowledge what exists. Others, like 'unicorn', create what otherwise does not exist. In between lie names that simultaneously describe and invent reality. 'Southeast Asia' is one of these. (Emmerson 1984: 1)

Southeast Asia as a world region is a recent invention. While, of course, people have lived and thrived in the area for thousands of years, it was not commonly known in the English language as Southeast Asia until the Second World War when the British Southeast Asia Command coined the name (Frost 1990: 2). And it was not until the mid-1960s that the Southeast Asian region had a political expression. At the turn of the century this matter of regionalization is a key issue. This chapter will assess various aspects of regional cooperation and regionalization.[1]

Social change is an immanent feature of contemporary Southeast Asia: tradition and modernity, poverty and affluence, economic miracles and underdevelopment, political stability and political turbulence all occur simultaneously and interact in a dynamic and complex pattern within the region (Rigg 1997). Interestingly though, change may lead to development as well as to increased instability. The 'threats' to the status quo – whether they are demands for political democratization, global financial turbulence or Chinese territorial claims in the South China Sea – are currently to an overwhelming degree emanating from outside the region. In a way, it is 'natural' to seek support and cooperation from within the region, although it should not be forgotten that various latent conflicts – over territory, natural resources, the environment, refugees, migrants, ethnic groups – may be reactivated when perceived as having the potential to serve a particular interest. Regional relations are by no means all-over harmonious. Southeast Asia is, moreover, a region in rapid transition towards some kind of modernity (McCloud 1995; Rigg 1997). As such it is subject to tensions, but it is also, perhaps just because of this, eager to reap whatever benefits there may be from regionalization – and judging from its own previous experience, as well as from other contemporary developments in the world, it seems that the benefits may be considerable.

Interestingly, both the external threats and the possible internal turmoil could be counteracted by a continued regionalization. Social change seems to be immanent in Southeast Asia and one way for the ruling elites to control or stabilize change is to enhance regional cooperation. Moreover, from a 'pure' neoclassical perspective – advocating trade and market freedom – enhanced economic liberalization and integration are seen as necessary to defend the region's position in the global economy and thereby maintain high economic growth (Yoshihara 1998; McGee 1997). From the civil society / activist perspective a regional network is also being built in order to increase bargaining strength and its possible impact. This atmosphere of intensifying globalization and regionalization has, moreover, fed into the long-established Association of Southeast Asian Nations (ASEAN) cooperation, which reached fulfilment in April 1999 when Cambodia was accepted as its tenth member.

This chapter will discuss the region and its possible process of regionalization. Does Southeast Asia exist as a meaningful politico-economic subject in its own right, or is it just an invention in the English language reinforced by temporary academic trends? If it 'exists', what is it? How and why has it evolved? Underlying many of the assumptions of future regionalization is whether it is possible to support the rationale of regional cooperation based on politics and economics with cultural and historical arguments defining 'Southeast Asianness'. This chapter will discuss the limits and the content of the region, assess its foundations and consider a number of processes and phenomena that are relevant for a possible continuing regionalization. Finally, it will consider whether Southeast Asia fits the pattern of 'new regionalism'.

The Southeast Asian Region –
Geographical Delimitations and Historical Context

As we have seen in this volume, the concept of 'region' is often hard to catch, incoherent as a subject of analysis, difficult to compare, and tricky to delimit: nevertheless, it seems to exist. Southeast Asia saves us some of these problems. Concretely and in geographic terms, the ten countries widely viewed as 'Southeast Asian'[2] are delimited by the Indian subcontinent, the world's greatest and most persistent political entity, China, the vast Pacific, and the Indian Ocean. Only to the southeast has a controversy of identity arisen: Papua New Guinea (PNG) has met with little success in its endeavours to be regarded as a Southeast Asian country.[3] Burma, because of its political isolation, is sometimes referred to as a buffer between South and Southeast Asia (Buzan 1988), but is now making deliberate efforts to link up with the latter. This geographical delimitation is illustrated by the fact that when Sri Lanka, some 4,000 kilometers away from the nearest 'real' Southeast Asian country, applied for membership in ASEAN, it was denied.

Southeast Asia is an extremely diverse region, and whether we consider history, tradition, religion or cultural belonging, the heterogeneity is striking. Most of the major religions are present, with Buddhism and Islam predominant. Christianity, Confucianism and Hinduism appear, as well as an ever-present undercurrent of animism, ancestor worship and spirit beliefs. Typically, the countries harbour many ethnic groups as well as religions. The Chinese are an economically success-ful minority group in almost all countries of Southeast Asia.

Historically, Southeast Asia was a thriving region (although not as a regional entity) long before the colonial powers appeared. It was situated on the trade route between India and China and benefited greatly from maritime trade, supplied with goods needed for the trade from 'the hinterland'. To assume that commercial activities started with the arrival of the colonial powers is thus grossly misleading: the trade with species to Europe was never large compared to the trade within Southeast Asia; it was not even large compared to the trade with species *within* Southeast Asia. One should remember that historically waterways served to connect people and empires, not to divide – as they may function today. The absence of any early conception of 'regionness' in Southeast Asia is no coincidence. It has emerged in the shadow of the larger, neighbouring, entities of India and China, who, on and off, have intervened and/or dominated the area.

Its colonial history, however, has contributed to its heterogeneity; all major colonial powers were present, and only one state (Thailand) was never colonized.[4] This meant that different law systems, political cultures, first foreign languages, architectures and independence struggles shaped the emerging nationalisms and subsequent independent states, possibly making integration or even cooperation more difficult (Tarling 1998). On the other hand, most countries share a modern history of colonialism, liberation and intense nation-state building.

The decolonization process was a challenge to any vision of regional coopera-tion as well as to overall peace in Southeast Asia. Initially it created regional disorder. Territorial disagreements were, and still are in some cases, manifold and infectious. In the postcolonial era the region was early on regarded as conflict-prone and was marked by real and imagined conflicts – internally and externally. The states were shaky constructions shaped around a core of nationalism, brought into being and cultivated by small elites trying to maintain the relative status quo that decolonization had provided. Initially small, but soon growing, rebellious and radical movements began to challenge recently established right-wing or royal regimes (Tarling 1998).

These initial problems were followed by an intensifying presence of the global Cold War. The Vietnam War turned into a major conflict in the 1960s, and Southeast Asia (seen from the US) was about to become *the* region where the front was held against the alleged communist expansion. In other countries, like Indonesia, the internal struggle between (alleged) communists and the non-communist power elite was fierce and often very violent. Within the capitalist sphere of Southeast Asia, however, several economies generated both high and sustained economic growth, leading to a rapid modernization.

In spite of occasional overtures to the contrary, the regional bipolarity remained in force until 1989 when the communist camp globally started to disintegrate, producing an altered pattern of amity and enmity, as well as changed economic relations in the region. Rapidly the former zero-sum game was transferred into a situation where improved cooperation could serve all major parties' interests. Ten years later the 'ASEAN-10' was achieved. ASEAN became thus the (perceived) panacea for regional unity and institutionalized good neighbourly relations and the regional organization *par preference* – monopolizing formal regional institution building. However, its initial logic of counteracting a common enemy (in the 'communists') is not active anymore, and this may threaten the cohesiveness of ASEAN. Moreover, regionalization in Southeast Asia, as we shall see, goes beyond ASEAN.

The nation-building drive has continued, at least for some Southeast Asian states, into the 1990s. In fact, that struggle still continues, or is being reinvented, although this time it is neither the colonial powers nor revolutionary ideologies which are the 'enemies'. Instead, the challenge comes from the modern globalizing world with its demand for financial foresightedness and political flexibility, in balance with the relief of poverty and social unrest. During the 1990s some prominent leaders and policy makers (notably Mahathir in Malaysia and Lee Kwan Yew in Singapore) have – with arguments inspired from the 'orientalism' debate – developed a political programme around the slogan of 'Asian values', implying that there are certain values held by Asians which require a matching political system.

To sum up, in the 1990s Southeast Asia appears for the first time as an independent (non-colonial) international subsystem without any Cold War overlay. As such, a strong sentiment of (or alternatively a strong will to construct) regional unity based on economic, political and cultural platforms has been cultivated. Coinciding with the region-creating current global political economy, this makes an interesting cocktail. We must not forget, however, that this is challenging a solid nation-state structure – or at least a solid idea that nation-states should be built –

that is fiercely defended by the national elites. Let us look at a number of the processes that possibly challenge the nation-state structure.

Foundations for Regional Cooperation

The driving forces for regionalization are commonly to be found in security and economics, confined within a cultural context, and often in a complex combination. Southeast Asia, too, could be viewed in this light. Rhetoric has emphasized economic cooperation, while praxis tends to hold out security issues as the most fundamental aspect of regional cooperation.

Security and Conflict Resolution[5]

Decolonization appeared in the midst of the rising tensions of the Cold War, adding difficulties to an already complex transition. International security has been a recurrent theme in Southeast Asia since the Second World War. Indeed it was widely perceived as a region with acute security problems, and a widely asked question was, 'Why has Southeast Asia, despite its natural propensity to do so, not become the Balkans of Asia?' (Mabhubani 1992: 110).

The lack of functional security arrangements made the situation worse. There was a time in the mid-1960s when most Southeast Asian countries were involved in either border disputes or civil warfare. Malaysia and Singapore, Malaysia and Indonesia, and Malaysia and the Philippines all had serious conflicts with each other of various sorts. Thailand had latent conflicts with Burma, Cambodia, Laos and Malaysia of a historical nature and as a result of colonization, the Second World War, and the subsequent decolonization. Vietnam and Burma were born into civil wars, and Indonesia was a geographically challenging construction with regional great-power ambitions. Laos and Cambodia were old kingdoms in decline, with little chance of defending their territory faced by internal challenges for power.

The polarization of the region into a capitalist and communist sphere, and the birth of ASEAN in the late 1960s and early 1970s, clarified the conflict lines and stabilized (with violence and authoritarian methods) the domestic situation in most countries. The conflicts within the ASEAN group of countries were also subdued by the more intense Cold War pattern prevailing in the region until the late 1980s.

During the 1990s, however, Southeast Asia has experienced a number of crucial changes in its security environment. The overlay (Buzan 1991) of superpower interest has abruptly disappeared, and a number of lower-level conflicts re-emerged in the early 1990s (Acharya 1993: 15). The 1992 ASEAN summit officially placed the issue of security on the regional agenda for the first time. The communist threat had diminished and turned into a concern to reform the former communist countries and prepare them to join ASEAN and the new global political economy.

Despite its success there is still scepticism about the difference ASEAN will make (Clad 1997). Considering the weak nature of the hard security arrangements, the short history of focused security discussions and the reluctance to enter into binding arrangements, it is quite obvious that it is not in the hard security arrangements that the major significance of ASEAN lies. Rather it is its ability to promote progressive regional relations that is important: the frequent talk of ASEAN 'friendship' is seemingly not just rhetoric. Over the years a lot of initiatives (and resources) have been launched and at least a minimal degree of trust has developed. Enough has been spent to make the states think twice before wasting this trust, and short-term gains will not necessarily be cashed in at the expense of long-term benefits. The non-pursuit of the unresolved Sabah conflict between the Philippines and Malaysia is an example of this. So is the relative calm on the issue of overlapping territorial claims in the Gulf of Thailand and the South China Sea.

The situation fits well into Jervis's theorizing on how regional cooperation can lead to the establishment of a 'security regime' (1982). That is, the countries do not cash in short-term gains, but rest in the conviction that others will reciprocate in due time. This is undeniably a quite distinct sign of progress in regional relations in a relatively short time. In a normative sense the security regime outlined above can develop into a 'security community' (Deutsch 1957), of which there exist very few in the world.[6] To achieve this qualitative leap, continuing contacts, increasing interdependence and, above all, time are required. Integration – which is not a favoured ASEAN path – is not, according to Deutsch, necessary for building security communities. Rather the pluralistic security community, involving independent political units, is the most stable and attainable model. Alagappa has shown that a regional organization such as ASEAN (not involving any superpower) can be effective in dealing with conflicts in a preventive manner, as long as it does not concern actors outside the region (1993). In terms of security, this provides ASEAN with a strong posture and arguments for its future existence as well as for its extension to the whole of Southeast Asia.

It is, moreover, likely that totally different categories of security issues provide a more real threat: environmental degradation, increased marginalization (for certain groups), declining resource bases, rampant labour migration, health dangers (such as HIV/Aids and malaria), urbanization and the uprooting of social values, and spreading poverty are all dangers which threaten the livelihoods of a large number of people. Not all are present now – or likely to be in the future in some places – but it seems reasonable to view these, and other, problems as real threats, thus deserving attention.

Economic Development

Economically, the major economies of capitalist Southeast Asia (Thailand, Malaysia, Indonesia and Singapore) achieved a tremendous growth from the late 1970s onwards, resulting in a hasty modernization and a rather well-spread welfare improvement (World Bank 1993).[7] The high growth figures of these 'miracle' economies have since the early 1990s been repeated by Vietnam and to some extent Laos and Cambodia, although general welfare improvements have been felt only marginally in these countries so far. The Philippines has a different growth pattern, but recently has resembled the high-performing miracle economies. The drawback – foreseen by few – is the Asian Crisis emerging during 1997, unveiling a surprising vulnerability that (temporarily?) has slowed most of the economies down.

Various regional approaches have been taken in order to create and speed up economic cooperation and integration.[8] Since 1976, attempts have been made, with limited success, to generate trade and to promote industrial cooperation. Basically this has been done within two separate, but interrelated, frameworks: industrial cooperation and a Preferential Trading Agreement (PTA). The former was divided into three subcategories: common industrial projects, complementarity schemes and joint venture schemes. The industrial package of projects never took off as planned, but the other two did show some progress. The complementarity schemes aimed at allowing different countries to specialize in the production of certain parts or components (UNIDO 1992: 13). The joint venture scheme was perhaps more successful and even out-competed the complementarity scheme (*ibid.*: 14). The strategy was to lower tariffs on projects involved in this scheme. However, it never reached major proportions because of bureaucratic sluggishness and indecisiveness in lowering tariffs, and possibly also because the idea was not particularly dynamic in the first place.

The other measure for creating economic integration, the PTA, started in 1977. It began slowly with an item-by-item approach, later speeded up to an across-the-board approach (UNIDO 1992). It has not been very efficient for a number of reasons: first, the cuts in the tariffs were generally not very deep; second, the offers within the agreement often did not exceed bilateral agreements already reached; third, 'exclusion lists' were drawn up so that substantial areas were left untouched; and, finally, non-tariff barriers covering quotas and import prohibition were applied. These schemes have been more or less abandoned and replaced with free trade schemes such as the ASEAN Free Trade Area (AFTA) (see below). We can conclude that as an engine of economic growth regional cooperation has not been particularly important so far. In reality these measures have been outscoped by the dynamics of more recent and less politically steered development approaches, such as microregionalism and adaptation to global markets.

Nevertheless, the relative political stability that ASEAN has contributed is of major economic importance; indeed it is sometimes held up as the single most important reason for the Southeast Asian economic miracle (Pomfret 1997: 314). Or it used to be: in the wake of the Asian Crisis and the economic and political turmoil that ensued, 'stability' is not the most accurate word to describe the fortunes of the region. Yet the stabilizing role of ASEAN should not be discounted entirely since, after all, the recent turmoil in Southeast Asia has not caused any major regional conflicts. And regional cooperation, of course, has contributed directly or indirectly to this aspect of stability.

Cultural Aspects of Regionalization

In spite of the heterogeneity described above, a certain 'Southeast Asianity' has been claimed to exist: sometimes on the basis of common cultural traits (Mulder 1992) recently expressed politically in the debate on Asian values (Mahathir and Ishihara 1995), and sometimes building on a perceived political unity (Rajaretnam 1991). 'Unity in diversity' is a catchphrase often heard in discussion with academics and policy makers in Southeast Asia. This approach is also, according to some scholars, gaining ground outside the region.

> With the end of the Second World War the tendency to think of Southeast Asia as a whole gained even greater currency, as there was a sharp increase in the amount of scholarly attention given to the region. Now, more than ever before, the underlying similarities to be found throughout a wide range of the region were stressed by historians, anthropologists, political scientists, and linguists. (Osborne 1990: 5)

As if to prove the validity of Osborne's claim, Tarling writes in his recent historical odyssey:

> [This book] is also responding to a current interest in Southeast Asia as a region. The concept is indeed in some sense itself quite a modern one. In previous centuries, there were words that attempted to describe it despite its diversity by suggesting some common feature, like 'Further India' or the 'Nanyang'. The term 'Southeast Asia' is more recent, and though it originates in the Second World War, it has tended to gain acceptance. (Tarling 1998: vii–viii)

It is the 'Southeast Asianity' implied in these words that has been expressed recently in the Asian values debate mentioned above (and discussed further below). This is, arguably, an attempt to construct an 'imagined community' on a transnational level in East Asia in order to fortify regional independence in a deeper sense. Interestingly, this is attempted on the regional level, choosing 'Asian-ness' as the mobilizing key factor.

Successes and Failures of Regional Cooperation

In the current Southeast Asia a number of processes may be working in the direction of increased regional cooperation, such as: a history of (attempted) regional cooperation; the ambition of a deepened trade regime (through AFTA); a political programme with a certain potential (the Asian values debate); a 'spontaneous' microregionalism ('growth triangles'); the increased importance of environmental issues; and, finally, an international climate that demands increased regional cooperation (or a 'negotiation club'). These processes all deserve further elaboration.

In terms of regional cooperation in the post-Second World War history of Southeast Asia, ASEAN is by far the most important project – but it is also far from being the only one. Several attempts have been made previously. These suffered from what has come to be known as the 'old regionalism' (Palmer 1991); they were not initiated from within and they neither solved regional problems nor addressed regional needs as defined from within. Moreover, they had no deep legitimacy in the region. Instead they corresponded to superpower jockeying in the Cold War, and particularly to the US mission to keep communism at bay in Southeast Asia (and elsewhere). These early organizations (SEATO, ASA, and MaPhilIndo)[9] are good examples of why the old regionalism failed.

Three interesting cases, however, escape the old regionalism's broad pattern of failure. The first is the Southeast Asian League (SEAL), which was an unofficial body containing several revolutionary and/or independence movements. It worked across – what came to be – the iron curtain of Southeast Asia, containing, for instance, both Thailand and (North) Vietnam. Soon, however – with the downfall of the radical Thai Prime Minister Pridi in 1947 – Thailand came to choose an alliance with the West rendering close connections to (North) Vietnam impossible. It had, moreover, little bearing on the wider region. The second and perhaps more significant exception is the Mekong Committee (MC),[10] operational since 1957 and from 1995 reformed into the Mekong River Commission (MRC). The MRC will possibly serve as a platform for regional resource management and as a vehicle for the development ambitions of ASEAN (Öjendal and Torell 1997: 62). The third exception, of course, is ASEAN.[11]

ASEAN exceeded, from its birth in 1967, the early expectations of the organization; at first it was typically regarded as just the latest in the series of failed organizations in Southeast Asia. The reason for the formation of the ASEAN was, analysts agree, to stabilize the participating countries' internal and external environments. The original five states[12] were all, for different reasons, unstable and needed regional support to be able to channel their energy towards nation-state building rather than external and internal conflicts. Concretely there were three overarching objectives: (1) to establish good relations in the 'neighbourhood'; (2) to create a bulwark against the seeming expansion of communism; and, perhaps most important, (3) to counter the internal communist insurgency movements threatening the regimes in all five member countries. ASEAN thus came into being not in spite of internal conflicts, but because of them (Broinowski 1990). It was thus the states and in particular the national elites that were the agents of regional rapprochement. Nowhere in the statutes, nor in statements and debates, is integration or supranationality mentioned as an end goal. Rather, ASEAN became an integral part of the various states' nation-building strategies.[13]

ASEAN came to be the lowest common denominator for the five capitalist countries in Southeast Asia. For each country a certain logic prevailed, and this has been reinforced over time:

> Only when Indonesia, the largest country in the region, saw that regional events had a direct bearing on its own national development did it give strong support to regional cooperation through organizations such as ASEAN. Thailand has always sought a strong regional structure as a counterweight to its US alliance, whereas Malaysia has looked for regional support as Britain has expanded its European relationships at the expense of its Commonwealth. Singapore has sought regional cooperation to stabilize its regional economic role, and the Philippines has used regional linkages to strengthen its Asian self-image. (McCloud 1995: 16)

Contrarily to the other regional organizations – with the exception of the MRC – ASEAN has attained a life of its own, meaning that it is defended and supported entirely from within and that various leaders view ASEAN as a self-evident part and even cornerstone of regional politics. 'These past few years we have been involved in confidence-building, knowing each other's intentions and plans,' the Thai Foreign Minister said recently in an interview regarding possible regional tension in the wake of the East Timor crisis (*Newsweek*, 18 October 1999).

Regional Trade Integration and the Development of AFTA

Traditionally trade has assumed a crucial role in the analysis of regionalization (Balassa 1962). While the new regionalism does not award trade issues that sovereign position, trade is of course still one parameter when assessing the degree of regionalization. The original ASEAN states have been remarkably successful in their export orientation, but they have not been particularly successful in generating economic cooperation of a regional nature. There are several reasons: one is that economic cooperation has not been needed – most of the national economies have done well on their own. Another reason is that trade with extraregional markets has been more profitable and thus regional trade has not been an attractive option. Moreover, the economies are competing rather than complementary, reducing the incentives for regional trade. Finally, strong national industrial groups have lobbied efficiently to keep national tariffs high and to maintain non-tariff barriers (Hussey 1991: 93; Alvstam 1993: 29ff; Parsonage 1997).

None of the state-led attempts to create and increase regional economic integration have been particularly successful so far. Internal trade has only risen from 15 to 17.8 per cent during the period 1968 to 1992 (Alvstam 1993: 30).[14] This looks fairly high in terms of regional trade (compared to other regional trade figures in this volume); disaggregating the figures, however, we conclude that an overwhelming part of this trade consists of regional trade with the outside world, passing through Singapore (Pomfret 1997: 300ff). Different approaches and stronger commitment are thus needed to reach any significant results in terms of trade integration. To speed up regional trade integration AFTA, based on an agreement aiming at a free market (CEPT, the Common External Preferential Tariff) within ASEAN, has been launched. This is a concept that is directly modelled on the EU and created in the light of the bumpy free trade negotiations in the last GATT agreement.

AFTA was agreed upon at the fourth ASEAN summit in Singapore in 1992. It is commonly seen as a major political commitment to increase economic integration or even as a breakthrough into a new phase[15] of ASEAN cooperation. The reduction of tariffs cannot – of course – be forced upon any state because the agreement is not legally binding, but regional relations would be severely hampered by a failure to comply. In the wake of the Asian Crisis, unwillingness to reduce barriers has increased to the degree that the entire formula has been in doubt.

Under any circumstances the question of sovereignty versus national integration would be further highlighted by these developments. With deepened economic integration and the drive for an inner market, states that want to belong to the scheme must in effect accept a loss of national sovereignty: as long as they want to remain members of ASEAN and AFTA, they no longer control their import tariffs. This reduction of the room to manoeuvre has previously been unthinkable in the ASEAN cooperation:

> In fact, Akrasanee and Stifel conclude that the European Community (now Union) model is not suitable for ASEAN since the objective of ASEAN member states has been to cooperate with each other in order to ensure national independence and mutual benefit for all members, and not to integrate within a supranational structure. Moreover, the Bangkok Declaration, which is the basis of ASEAN's existence, guarantees the supremacy of the members states' sovereignty over ASEAN. (Akrasanee and Stifel, discussed in Santiago 1995: 27)

For this and other reasons there are many critics of AFTA's prospects. It needs to be pointed out that the rationale of AFTA is not only important in the sense of increased intraregional trade. A second objective is to attract foreign direct investment. If Southeast Asia becomes a free trade area, the Japanese production network in Southeast Asia would be strengthened considerably. From a Japanese point of view there is an increased incentive to be 'inside' the Southeast Asian region, should trade barriers arise. Another reason for promoting AFTA is to increase the international competitiveness of ASEAN industry (Kettunen 1994).

The situation is changing in many respects with the rapidly changing international situation: the global economy puts progressively more stress on regional coordination and possibly regionalization. A number of states in ASEAN are reaching a more sophisticated level of industrialization and the advantages of specialization and cooperation increase accordingly. With the primary security threat removed, the question of promoting economic development has ascended the list of real priorities for ASEAN with a sudden urgency. Articulation of the Association's interests in the world economy is realizing itself through ASEAN as a global 'negotiation club'. To join the 'flying geese',[16] to compete with the Chinese economy and to get access to the European and US markets are crucial goals for many of the export-oriented economies of Southeast Asia. This articulation and stabilization are all the more important after the currency devaluation in Southeast Asia in the summer of 1997. Even a joint currency mechanism has been seriously discussed (*Far Eastern Economic Review,* 19 March 1998).

Asian Values – a Formula for Political Integration?

When it comes to ideal forms of governance, democracy has maintained a virtual hegemony in the world since the end of the Cold War. This 'end of history' argument, however, has been rebuked in many ways. It is interesting that East and Southeast Asian leaders have evinced a clear resistance to liberal democracy as defined by the Western powers. Emmerson (1995) has claimed that Southeast Asia is the region in the world most resistant to 'democracy'. This resistance is not of the conservative/reactionary, nor the fascist/totalitarian type.[17] Instead, an alternative based on Asian values is forcefully launched as a regime type that is culturally adapted, that better serves the modern political economy and at the same time takes better care of the citizens' needs in a more profound and sustainable way (Commission for a New Asia 1994).

The notion of Asian values that counsel a different kind of governance is appealing in many circles, and even more so when it is backed up by Southeast Asian economic success and a constantly increasing self-confidence. The major supporters of Asian values as a political credo are the former Prime Minister of Singapore, Yew Kwan Lee, and the present Prime Minister of Malaysia, Dr Mohammad Mahathir, and they have rapidly been backed by other Asian countries as well as independent and semi-independent intellectuals.[18] In short, Asian values are interpreted to imply a regime that disregards the sovereign right of the individual and subordinates this to the good of the collective, calling for a righteous leader rather than a democratic system. The well-being of the family is the core value, and hierarchy and social order are not repugnant elements of the society; rather, they are viewed as a necessity to maintain stability and efficient governance. Not much imagination is needed to see how this contradicts the ideals of the political democracy (and possibly even liberal capitalism in the long run) and prioritizes a 'soft authoritarianism', 'enlightened despotism', or 'guided democracy'.

In the seminal work by Deutsch *et al.* (1957) on the necessary conditions for a peaceful integration of societies, a similar political value system is one of the primary preconditions for any successful, long-lasting process of integration. Common political features for many of the states are: general elections which are not really multiparty or competitive; irregularities in connection with elections; freedom of the press and individuals, but only to a limited degree; a certain, but not absolute, respect for human rights; a semi-independent judiciary and authoritarian, but responsible, leadership with a fairly high degree of legitimacy.

With the possible exception of the Philippines, it could be argued that all regimes in Southeast Asia practise one or the other variation of the 'Asian values' package. Thailand (probably) and Indonesia (possibly) are on a trajectory towards increased political democracy, and the regime in Burma is generally regarded as more authoritarian and less responsible than the others outlined above. ASEAN, severely criticized for allowing a regime like the one in Burma to become a member, has claimed that 'constructive engagement' is more efficient for reforming the regime in Burma than isolation would be.[19] Brunei is authoritarian and conservative, but oil-rich and thereby lacking many socio-economic problems. Vietnam and Laos are further away from multiparty democracy than the others, but the regimes are not necessarily lacking in legitimacy. The leaderships in Singapore and Malaysia both enjoy a fairly high degree of legitimacy, but based on economic growth rather than political recognition. Although in practice commonly under authoritarian rule, the Philippines has a much stronger democratic tradition than the others. Cambodia is formally a full-fledged democracy with a democratic framework, but with political practices far from the democratic ideal.[20] Nevertheless, the similarity of the regimes certainly makes it easier to cooperate regionally. When Southeast Asian states are attacked collectively from the West for failing to respect human rights or protect the environment, the collective identity is reinforced.

While the 'similarity of the regimes' thesis might hold water, the core of the 'Asian values' argument has come under devastating fire for simplisticness, incompatibility with the modern project and the overvaluation of culture in politics (Robison 1996; Kim Dae Jung 1994). The Asian Crisis has put a brake on this rhetoric, of course, but not necessarily killed it. See, for example, the defence of 'good Asian values' by Tommy Koh – a semi-official 'ambassador' of Singapore – in the *Strait Times Interactive* (29 June 1999). Although the idea of Asians possessing certain specific values seems so much like a construction to serve certain purposes that it is liable to be dismissed out of hand, it might nevertheless work as a conservative political programme (Öjendal and Antlöv 1998).

Microregionalism – Planned or Spontaneous Regionalization?

Microregionalism – or 'growth triangles' – as experienced in Southeast Asia has, unlike the planned industrialization schemes (see below), been rather successful. It could be perceived as a planned integration strategy, but also as a more spontaneous development (Thambipillai 1991: 303). It has been described in a multitude of ways: as 'an example of regionalism as a response to global political transformation' (Parsonage 1992: 307); as a process paving the way for regionalization in the greater region (Mittelmann 1993); as a complement to macroregional economic integration (Thambipillai 1991: 312); or as a way of achieving regional integration, but avoiding time-consuming full regional grouping procedure (Yuan 1992; Heng and Low 1993).

A number of growth triangles are envisaged in the region: one connects Indonesia, Singapore and Malaysia (the southern triangle) while another covers southern Thailand–northern Sumatra–northern Malaysia. A third, the ASEAN growth triangle, supports the Sarawak–Brunei–Sabah area, and yet a fourth is the Greater Mekong subregion along the Lower Mekong Basin. Furthermore, one can easily envisage arrangements around common natural resources development. What, for example, will be the outcome of joint oil explorations in the South China Sea between Malaysia and Vietnam (Antolik 1992: 147); the proposal for joint management of the exploration of natural resources in the South China Sea; the giant Mekong development plans cultivated by Thailand, Laos, Cambodia and Vietnam (Öjendal 1995); or the peace proposal for a joint management of the Spratley Island resources? The intrinsic logic of these 'triangles' – beside their geometrical make-up useful for international marketing – is to utilize complementary features in proximate geographical areas in spite of their belonging to different states divided by national borders. To put it differently, they are 'natural "economic zones" delineated by economic complementarity rather than formal national borders' (Parsonage 1997: 249).

The southern triangle, for example, is a project comprising the southern province in Malaysia (Johor Bahru), Singapore and Indonesia (Batam Island in Riau Islands, in the archipelago of eastern Sumatra). Historically these areas have shared many interests. In the modern era Johor has delivered fresh water to

Singapore and served as the major entrance port for tourists to Malaysia (Parsonage 1992: 309). Following a Malaysian deregulation, Johor state government announced a strategy of economic 'twinning' with Singapore. Singaporean land and labour constraints and Johor's lower production factor prices, its access to the Generalized System of Preferences and a deregulated market were forces rapidly creating increased capital flows and an economic boom in Johor (*ibid.*: 309ff). The boom has led to further infrastructure investments tying the two even more closely to each other. With this success as an argument, Yew Kwan Lee suggested to Indonesia's President Suharto the opening of Batam Island in the Riau group as a tax-free area. A US$200 million industrial park has since been constructed, as well as a general tourist facility and real estate upgrading (Thambipillai 1991: 305; Parsonage 1997).

In this growth triangle a vertical division of labour is emerging: Batam island (Indonesia) is supplying low-cost labour and land; Johor (Malaysia) semi-skilled labour, industrial sites and competence; and Singapore high technological skills, advanced electronic infrastructure, competent bank and insurance services, a comfortable international entrance port, and international know-how. This can be combined with advantageous establishing rights for foreign investments, which further propels the economic growth in the microregion. Another sector of compatibility is within the tourist sector, where the well-developed Singaporean infrastructure and the natural attractions of Malaysia and Indonesia could be exploited. As a possible additional benefit we also find the compatibility with AFTA.

The idea is not free from complications though: the economic imbalance deriving from an increased flow of capital from Singapore to Riau and Johor has caused inflation and social turbulence. Some worries are noted on the part of Kuala Lumpur and the state government of Johor over its extensive integration with Singapore. The middleman role of Singapore increases as long as Johor and Riau do not have any substantial direct contacts with each other, and both Malaysia and Indonesia suspect that Singapore will cement the existing vertical division of labor (Parsonage 1992: 314). These obstacles – all directly or indirectly connected to the favourable economic position of Singapore – could be counteracted, or at least restricted, by the political advantage Malaysia and Indonesia have over Singapore in terms of size and weight. Thus the microregional approach ideally could extract all its inherent advantages and still remain balanced – or it could turn exploitative.

In terms of natural resource management, the transgression of national borders is 'natural' since the logical management of these resources does not coincide with the politically constructed borders. The Lower Mekong River Basin and its vast water resources are of paramount interest to all the Mekong states, triggering or 'forcing' cooperation across state borders. By the same token, however, conflicts may appear if joint projects fail or turn exploitative. The parallel with the more famous Coal and Steel Union in Europe in the late 1950s is obvious. These projects, partly having their *raison d'être* in adapting to, and drawing benefits from, international forces – such as adapting tax-free export zones for attracting foreign direct investment or subsidizing infrastructure construction for generating hydropower for promoting industrialization – might serve to strengthen regional cooperation and, quite possibly, be instrumental in long-term economic integration.

Interestingly, ASEAN has formally adopted the idea of growth triangles (1992), outlined a legal and economic framework, viewed it as complementary to AFTA and thereby integrated this microregionalism in the more visible, political and status-filled macroregionalism. It has even been claimed that success for the growth triangle strategy will advance Southeast Asian identity and enhance the ASEAN role in the greater East Asian region (Parsonage 1997: 273). This phenomenon is one of the most interesting processes of regional integration in Southeast Asia, arresting the incompatibility between continued nation-state building and regional integration. Indeed, it could be viewed as an intrinsic aspect of the new regionalism, and as a consequence of the new global political economy.

Regional Politics of Ecology

The ecological question is the 'absent friend' of regional cooperation in Southeast Asia. ASEAN established a regional environmental programme as early as 1978 (ASEAN Environmental Programme, or ASEP), which has evolved through a number of five-year phases. In 1987 a 'Jakarta Resolution on Sustainable Development' was adopted and upgraded to senior level in 1989. This body, however, has been given neither high status nor adequate resources. It has not been able to act in a forceful way to safeguard sustainable development. As a contrast to the rising interest in environmental issues worldwide, state-based reactions and attitudes in this field are typically described as 'passive' (Clad and Siy 1996: 63). In fact, rapid economic growth and forced industrialization have been the hallmarks of Southeast Asian development, rendering issues of environmental protection secondary. As a result most, if not all, countries have major ecological problems (Parnwell and Bryant 1996).

The countries that have been successful in their drive for industrialization, such as Malaysia and Singapore, may be less vulnerable to ecological dilemmas, but the mainland Southeast Asian countries, for example, who still largely rely on the agricultural sector, need to rethink their own and the regional approach towards these questions. Ecological stability and environmental soundness are, in fact, indispensable to the economies of these countries. Other phenomena such as extensive and deliberate burning of rainforests, predominantly in Indonesia, have caused marked political tensions within ASEAN as smoke from the fires has shrouded extensive parts of maritime Southeast Asia. Moreover, whether clearances are to provide more land for the large plantation owners, or for hydropower development as in the Bakun project in Malaysia, or simply to sell the logs, the disappearance of the rainforests is continuing, with unforeseeable long-term consequences. By sheer necessity environmental problems are ascending the list of regional priorities; resource exploitation and land use are in some areas reaching a critical stage and spilling over national borders. Water issues on the mainland and forest fires in the archipelago are two examples of how environmental issues in Southeast Asia are transcending political boundaries and demanding international/regional remedies.

Pressure from the North for ecological preservation has been interpreted as domination or even as an attempt to slow down development, and these repudiations are used to justify inadequate environmental improvements. Thus the Indonesian Foreign Minister claimed that such pressure amounts to a 'new colonialism in a green disguise' (Clad and Siy 1996: 69) and Mahathir castigated 'Western' lobbying groups as 'the mastermind[s] behind a series of logging protests in Sarawak' and asserted that they 'condemn them [the Penans living in the aforementioned forest] to a primitive life forever' (*Far Eastern Economic Review*, 27 August 1992: 8).

To some extent the economic success of many Southeast Asian countries is to blame for ecological degradation. Hitchcock and Sian Jay claim – citing ecotourism as an example – that development has proceeded so quickly that adequate safe guards against environmental exploitation could not be established in time (Hitchcock and Sian Jay 1998: 306). In the same mode Zawawi argues that it is neither a North–South contradiction nor cultural perceptions of nature that lie behind exploitation in Southeast Asia, but rather a too one-sided 'power–capital– environment' relation (in both North and South) that has caused the current state of the environment. The focus should change to a 'people–environment' discourse (1998: 344ff). Stott claims that such a change is imminent in that there is an 'indigenization' of environmental thought going on (Stott, quoted in Rigg 1997: 59). Clad and Siy go as far as to say that 'No other issue in Southeast Asian contemporary history has so swiftly assumed prominence in the region's domestic, interregional and international affairs as the emergence of an increasingly politicized ecological awareness' (Clad and Siy 1996: 52).

At universities and in NGO circles the environmental issue has also triggered a certain degree of engagement, although few reach the international/regional level. Interestingly, environmental protection groups are growing quite rapidly, especially in Thailand and possibly also in Malaysia, and they seem to be fairly successful in joining political environmental protection agendas and local interests. In fact, environmental groups might be the most visible outlets of an internationalized civil society in Southeast Asia.

Global Markets: Demands on Regional Organization

The most substantive reason for economic regionalization in current Southeast Asia is likely to be the demands of the global market (Parsonage 1997: 248; McGee 1997: 29). It requires, more than anything else, vast markets and few complicating regulations. As a single subsystem, comparable to markets like South Asia and China, Southeast Asia is attractive; as atomized semi-developed countries the individual states offer limited interest for major engagement by the transnational actors.

Although not necessarily the root of the problem, globalization played a part in the Asian Crisis and reminded Southeast Asian (and other) leaders how vulnerable even seemingly stable economies can be in the current global political economy (Jomo 1998). This has caused a debate both on whether the 'miracles' are real and sustainable or merely facades, and on whether the current global political economy is stable.

In the global arena ASEAN works as a 'negotiation club', gaining access to markets and protecting its members from external critique of, for example, logging practices or (the lack of) democratic policies. As an illustration of its political protection against external influences it can be mentioned that ASEAN tends to side with China against the US's China-bashing on the human rights issue. Another example of negotiation club activities was the EU's first official visit to the ASEAN on a regional level in February 1996. This was a breakthrough in interregional relations. This Asia– Europe Meeting (ASEM) has since been repeated and institutionalized (Simandjuntak 1997).

One Southeast Asia?
Is ASEAN a Regionalist Problem-solving Panacea?[21]

ASEAN did not constitute much of a regional organization for its first eight years of existence, but with the communists coming to power in 1975 in Laos, Cambodia and Vietnam, the organization was alerted. It was at the Bali meeting in 1976 that the first summit was held, the installing of an ASEAN Secretariat was agreed upon, and the decision on having annual ministerial meetings was taken. The cooperation deepened over the years and the Vietnamese occupation of Cambodia, starting in 1978/9, gave it a 'safe' *raison d'être*. ASEAN became the foremost agent in the cause of countering Vietnam (and Laos and Cambodia, or 'the communists'), thereby running its members' own errands as well as those of the West and China. In the period 1979–89 it tried – politically, diplomatically, economically – to force

Vietnam to leave Cambodia. During the first half of the 1980s, relations between ASEAN and the Indochinese bloc were conflictive, but they slowly improved from 1987 onwards, in pace with the progress of the peace process in the Cambodia conflict. With the somewhat surprising Vietnamese military retreat in September 1989, the way was opened for a genuine rapprochement. Indonesia, Vietnam's best friend in ASEAN, with support from Malaysia conducted negotiations towards conflict resolution in the Cambodia conflict (Amer *et. al.* 1996).

In 1992 Vietnam and Laos signed the Bali Agreement, meaning that they recognized the principles of non-interference and territorial *status quo* mentioned therein, and thereby the political reconciliation between ASEAN and Vietnam was formally blessed (Acharya 1993: 48). In the summer of 1995 Vietnam became a full member of ASEAN; in the summer of 1997 Laos and Burma were included; and, finally, in the spring of 1999 Cambodia gained full membership. Thereby ASEAN had done away with the regional division, by now artificial and obsolete, imposed by the Cold War.

Throughout the 1980s the member states developed a certain political style in their internal relations. Consensus is normally the method of decision and the concept of 'regional resilience' is employed, meaning that the country with the most vested interests has the greatest say in any particular conflict. This was applied during the Cambodia conflict, for example, when Thailand, the closest neighbour and most affected country, had a disproportionately great influence in group decisions and regional politics. The 'ASEAN way' is another catchword for describing (and creating) the special relation between the ASEAN countries: based (it is claimed) on friendship rather than power, on common sense rather than fear, and on stability rather than adventurism. It prides itself on quite a number of successes through the years.

The Cambodia conflict served for a decade to harmonize the ASEAN states' foreign policies and created thereby a common security concern. ASEAN has, since its inception, acted as a 'soft security organization' – and, as such, a rather successful one. The member states have deliberately abstained from producing 'hard' security arrangements. Instead bi- or trilateral ties have been formed (for example, between Singapore, Malaysia and Indonesia). As a regional security arrangement, however, this is a rather patchy spider's web. For an organization that was, arguably, born from external threat (or perceptions thereof), a fundamental change in the external environment is by definition crucial for its future. With globalization and the altered regional situation, both regionalization as such and ASEAN are taking on new roles that possibly strengthen the regionalist agenda.

'Southeast Asia' was once a term used by outsiders far more than by those living in the region; but now it is becoming something of an economic and political reality, and its leaders themselves are moving to make ASEAN an organization *of and for* the region, instead of an organization designed to add to the security of some of its states vis-a-vis others. (Tarling 1998: viii, my emphasis)

There is, for good and bad, a tendency that ASEAN, with its more than 250 meetings per year, is swallowing up all other regional initiatives and thus assuming the role of *the* regional organization, ready to respond to *all* upcoming problems and issues (as with the growth triangles reviewed above). This might be too much of a task (Öjendal 1998). One reason for this tendency is that there is no self-evident agenda for ASEAN anymore: it has to find its own role and meaning (Crone 1996). It should then come as no surprise that major changes were and are needed to keep ASEAN together:

ASEAN [was] standing at a watershed between widening its membership (towards Indo-China) and deepening cooperation and/or integration internally.... At the same time, it has to redefine its role as a subregional institution in a wider Asia-Pacific grouping. (Langhammer 1991: 137)

ASEAN chose both to widen its membership towards Indochina and to redefine its regional role. Two of the most important new tasks it has taken on are thus the creation of one Southeast Asia and the cultivation of its external relations.

Extension of ASEAN – One Southeast Asia?

The then Vietnamese premier, Vo Van Kiet, visited Indonesia, Malaysia and Thailand as early as 1991, expressing a wish to become an integral part of Southeast Asia (Buszynski 1992: 833; Frost 1993: 64). This tour inspired a joint Vietnam–Singapore symposium discussing 'Interaction for Progress – Vietnam's New Course and ASEAN Experience' (NCSS, CIEM and IRC 1991). The symposium made it clear – before it was politically 'safe' – that the idea of 'Vietnam joining ASEAN in the future' (Jayanama 1991: 35) was clearly under consideration by official representatives from most ASEAN states. And the idea of 'One Southeast Asia' (Rajaretnam 1991: 9) was also made explicit. This was an echo of earlier statements by, for instance, Ali Atalas, the Indonesian Foreign Minister: 'Now that Cambodia can hopefully be resolved we can go back to our original blueprint: Southeast Asia must become one, not a region of two polarized mini-blocs' (quoted in Frost 1993: 65). Nor, one might add, was a patchwork quilt of allies and enemies what was envisaged; instead, 'unity in diversity' was desired. Vietnam was, after the definite dissolution of the Cold War and the resolution of the Cambodia conflict in 1993, eager to become a member of ASEAN. After a brief preparation phase this previously unthinkable move was accepted. Laos and Burma followed suit in 1997 and Cambodia in 1999.

The extension of ASEAN experienced in the last four years irrevocably changes its balance and interests. It is no longer possible to generate legitimacy from any external threat within the region. Other sources of ASEAN cohesiveness need to be found. Moreover, with a higher number of members it will be more difficult to reach political consensus – which so far has been a hallmark of the ASEAN cooperation. There is a risk that what ASEAN gains in weight, it will lose in acting capacity. Another change coupled with the entrance of the new members is that the point of gravity of ASEAN will be moved northwards, towards mainland Southeast Asia.

So far, however, the extension has proceeded rather smoothly and ASEAN has survived as a meaningful and comprehensive regional organization – indeed, membership has been highly valued by its new members. However, another paradox enters: having succeeded in creating 'Southeast Asia-10', a new vision needs to be found for ASEAN. To put it differently, the pressure to keep up with the changing dynamics of the surrounding world increases, and the slightly changed profile and weight of ASEAN, due to its new members, also pushes for change.

Extraregional Relations – Is ASEAN a Pawn or a Player?

ASEAN has been active as a regionalist catalyst even outside Southeast Asia (Öjendal 1997). Its role in the development of East Asia is interesting. In a way, it is ASEAN that is leading the giants, Japan and China. In East Asia, with an acute lack of politically legitimate regional leadership (see Chapter 9), ASEAN, in spite of its insufficient political and economic weight, plays the role of initiator. In security matters the ASEAN Regional Forum (ARF) is on a regular basis gathering a large number of East and Southeast Asian leaders; it is by far the most inclusive forum dedicated to security discussions in East Asia. The first ARF in 1994 was widely considered a success (*Far Eastern Economic Review*, 11 August 1994: 34). The Secretary-General of ASEAN stated that 'In the long term the forum will generate its own momentum and become the focus of all matters relating to political and security issues' (Datuk Ajit Singh, quoted in Clements 1993: 6).

This forum also fits the Japanese policy approach, which views ASEAN as a forerunner for a potential 'two-track' security arrangement in East Asia; subregional forums could be linked to a region-wide conference of officials (Uren 1992: 122). ARF is in fact one of very few organizations in the Asia-Pacific region which assumes the urgent task of building indigenous security arrangements.

> What is distinctive about [East] Asia is its combination of several industrialized societies with a regional international society so impoverished in its development that it compares poorly with even Africa and the Middle East. Perhaps the most alarming aspect of East Asian security is the virtual absence of effective multilateralism. (Buzan and Segal, 1994: 15)

In line with the vision of Singh quoted above, the ARF seems to be growing in importance. It attracted the US Foreign Secretary to its July 1999 meeting, for instance, where one of the most controversial issues for East Asian security – the 'one China or two' issue – was discussed publicly. In few other fora could such an issue be raised.

The East Asian Economic Caucus (EAEC) is an extraregional initiative by Malaysia. It fishes for pan-Asian sentiments with the aim of creating stronger ties between East and Southeast Asian countries at the expense of 'external' relations. This has been received coolly by the non-Asian states and by Asian states with a special relation to the West, since it carries an explicit exclusion mechanism. Concretely it is aimed at attracting and accelerating Japanese investments, trade and official development assistance (ODA), and at establishing a political commitment to the durability of these links. The EAEC, originally the stronger East Asian Economic Group (EAEG), is for the moment, as a compromise solution, placed within the larger Asia Pacific Economic Cooperation (APEC) grouping.[22] The degree of proactive engagement in creating larger regional structures is, however, a source of tension between the ASEAN countries. Any involvement in larger structures carries the risk that ASEAN becomes superseded and made into an irrelevant actor on that scene, or even diluted as a (or the) regional organization.

Formal interregional contacts or not, there is seemingly a *de facto* economic integration emerging between East and Southeast Asia, especially through the expansion of the Japanese economy to the ASEAN sphere.[23] The Japanese foreign direct investment (FDI) in ASEAN-4 has risen more than fivefold between 1985 and 1990, and in states like Thailand and Singapore it claims close to 70 and 50 per cent respectively of these states' total received FDI. During 1980–90 ODA to the ASEAN states increased more than threefold, even though states like Singapore and Malaysia have become too rich to receive large amounts of aid. Imports and exports from the ASEAN-4 have increased by 74 per cent and 194 per cent respectively during 1986–90. Furthermore, the Japanese manufactured import from ASEAN has risen more than fourfold from 1985 to 1990, indicating that there is an ongoing industrialization process in the ASEAN states. One should observe, however, that it is taking place on Japanese terms; the increased trade is to a large extent executed by Japanese corporations established in ASEAN. Collectively, ASEAN ranks as the third-largest trade partner to Japan after the US and EU. These figures should be related to ASEAN's generally favourable attitude towards the Japanese business community's presence. In Thailand, for instance, it is reported that Japan is given unusual benefits when establishing new investments (Cronin 1992: 32); in Malaysia there is an official 'Look East' campaign; and in Indonesia (before the Asian Crisis) Japan supplied 60–70 per cent of total ODA.

Willing or not, the ASEAN economies have become an integral part of a production structure that is emerging in the Pacific region with Japan at its core. The strong Japanese involvement in the economies of the ASEAN states has also generated resentments, however, throwing suspicion on Japan's *real* intentions in the region. Politically Japan has a long-standing interest in Southeast Asia. The Fukuda Doctrine reinforced it in 1977, stating that Japan would promote closer ties to the ASEAN states, play a constructive role towards the Indochinese states, and not become a military power in the region. This special relationship has been carefully nurtured since then, via the Takeshita speech at the third ASEAN meeting and the policy speech by Prime Minister Miyasawa in Bangkok in 1993. This latter speech stressed economic development, increase in ODA in ecological matters and conflict resolution on a regional basis (with special reference and an invitation to the Indochinese states). Even more important, Miyasawa supported the ongoing formation of an Asia-Pacific political and security dialogue. In all areas, he outlined a significant role for the ASEAN states (Miyasawa 1993).

One question is where China enters this pattern. In a way China could be seen to be somewhat outside owing to a potential hostility between China and Southeast Asia, most obvious in the Spratley Islands issue, which is throwing a dark shadow over large parts of Southeast Asia (but probably strengthening ASEAN coherence). This detachment is contradicted, however, by three substantial arguments. First, the economies in most Southeast Asian states are dominated by nationalized ethnic Chinese, constituting an invisible but most significant network (not necessarily connected to the Chinese state). Second, the southern and eastern part of China is getting increasingly involved in the economics of Southeast Asia. Third, there is an embryo of a 'quasi-alliance' between China and Southeast Asia as regards political values and the 'right' to defend oneself against 'Western domination'.

The idea of 'one Southeast Asia' is of course the simplification of a far more complex reality. It is true that the match between ASEAN, on the one hand, and the states which normally identify themselves as Southeast Asian (on a geographical rationale), on the other, provides for a solid and operational regional organization. However, the paradox is that the point in time at which the regional organization building has overcome the political obstacles and been able to include all ten states coincides with the global process of the loosening of state-centrism. The old, simple conception of the state as the sovereign and only actor of major influence is increasingly untenable. As a result, Southeast Asia is 'complete' in one dimension only; in others it provides for a multitude of pluralisms. For instance, what will the future of microregionalism imply for the wider idea of Southeast Asia, and what will the heavy Japanese and Chinese presences in Southeast Asia, and the ambitious ASEAN involvement in East Asia, imply for any perception of a 'finally determined' region?

New Regionalism in Southeast Asia?

Southeast Asia is entering a new era and ASEAN with it. Whether or not it has been successful in the past, there are new challenges coming up. It is time to sum up some of the regionalization determinants discussed above.

1 There is a fairly high degree of regional interaction in the subsystem we call Southeast Asia. This is, however, largely elite-driven, with popular indifference. Having said that, it should be acknowledged that business, academic and NGO networks are increasingly active on the regional level.

2 There is a history of attempted regional cooperation/organization, although it has always been based on the strengthening of the state, and never on integration or supranational ambitions; rarely has it had any direct economic effects.

3 There is a political will to seek further and deeper cooperation – although, simultaneously, national sovereignty is fiercely defended.

4 There is a certain degree of political and cultural conformity, even if this conformity is to a degree both constructed and complex.

5 Internal trade and investment issues are being dealt with through AFTA but, in spite of rhetorical enthusiasm, implementation of AFTA is not easy – especially not after the Asian Crisis.

6 Depending on which route the region's giant – Indonesia – is taking, major security threats are currently unlikely to emerge between the Southeast Asian countries, but latent conflicts are present.

7 The role of ASEAN as a 'negotiation club' seems to make sense in the contemporary era of globalization.

8 Finally, the will and the resources necessary for regionalization seem to be forthcoming from within, indicating that ASEAN is seen as good value by its member countries.

Will Southeast Asia then prove to be a region that corresponds to the features of new regionalism? Yes and no. Certainly ASEAN is a project well rooted in the region, taking place on the members' conditions, and taking care of the members' problems. No longer does it serve Cold War interests. Instead, it has a proven capability to act as a political subject, and, perhaps more importantly, a rather flexible and pragmatic approach. Some kind of economic, social and political integration is taking place. However, the region is far from being a people's project; it is not the regional cooperation which is driving the economies, and regional conflict resolution, is dealt with slowly, and very cautiously. Nation-state building is still the priority in most Southeast Asian states (Parrenas 1997: 190; Tarling 1998), and to the extent that nation-state building is contrary to regionalization, the latter, for the foreseeable future, will have to remain resigned to a backseat position. Yet there is no reason to think of Southeast Asian regional development in terms of any simple state-versus-region dichotomy, nor in terms of any regionalization-versus-global-ization incompatibility. In fact, at least up to a certain degree of integration, the two processes tend to be mutually supportive and are going forward together.

NOTES

1 'Regional cooperation' is used, in accordance with the usage in other chapters in this book, with the meaning of state-to-state cooperation. 'Regionalization' is regarded as a multidimensional process including many different actors.
2 Brunei, Burma, Cambodia, Indonesia, Laos, Malaysia, the Philippines, Singapore, Thailand, and Vietnam.
3 An interesting turn of events, reversing perceptions of colonialism, is that Australia is seemingly trying to (re-)identify itself as an 'Asian' or 'Southeast Asian' country. Politically and economi-cally it makes sense but the ethnic/cultural factor probably inhibits any easy transformation. This is illustrated by the controversies around the role of Australia's positioning in the peace-keeping forces in the intervention in East Timor. This will be an interesting case to follow, teaching us about the role of culture in high politics.
4 North and South Vietnam (gained independence 1954 and 1975 respectively), Cambodia (1954) and Laos (1954) were all parts of French Indochina. Malaysia (1957), Singapore (1963) and Brunei (1984) were British; so was Burma (1948). Indonesia (1949) was under Dutch colonial rule and the Philippines was under Spanish rule until 1898 and under American rule from then until 1945.
5 This section is largely based on Acharya (1993) and Thayer (1995).
6 A security community is made up of a number of countries that have developed a relationship such that solving intra-community conflicts with violence is unthinkable.
7 This World Bank study is the best-known discussion of the Asian 'miracles'. It has been seriously criticized, however, largely for its 'ideologically adjusted' conclusions and selective use of secondary literature (Rigg 1997: 10).
8 The following section is based on a text originally compiled by Öjendal (1998).
9 The Southeast Asian Treaty Organization (SEATO) was formed in 1954 as part of a worldwide US strategy aimed at containing the communist world. Thailand and the Philippines were its only members in Southeast Asia. The Association of Southeast Asia (ASA, 1961) had few members, little influence and a short lifespan. MaPhilIndo (1963) collapsed in the wake of the Indonesia–Malaysia konfrontasi and the differences between Malaysia and the Philippines over Sabah.
10 Thailand, Laos, Cambodia and (South) Vietnam were the original members of the MC.
11 The basics of ASEAN are reviewed here on a par with other phenomena of interest for regional-ization in general. In recognition of its sovereign position as a regional body in Southeast Asia it will be treated in greater depth below.
12 Thailand, Malaysia, Singapore, Indonesia and the Philippines.
13 For example, the first state visit that Corazon Aquino undertook after the people's revolution in the Philippines in 1986, facing a still unstable internal situation, was to the ASEAN countries as a way of consolidating her regional legitimacy.
14 The figures on ASEAN internal trade are somewhat difficult because data on the Singapore–Indonesia trade are restricted and because of the dubious nature of some trade within the region. See Pomfret (1997) for a slight variation on the figures mentioned above. Another way of viewing this modest increase in intra-ASEAN trade, however, is to note that the intra-ASEAN

trade has not only kept up with the exploding external trade, but actually gained a few per cent.

15 The first phase was 1967–76, in which the states developed relations, followed by the second phase during 1976–92. This phase included active political cooperation, increasing expectations for the period 1992–2008, which may lead to consolidation in building AFTA, as well as other forms of regional cooperation. This is the scenario of Naya and Imada (1992: 513), who are generally sympathetic to ASEAN.

16 The 'flying geese' is a metaphor for how the East Asian economies are following each other, just as geese fly in a V-formation. This metaphor is based on an economic theory but carries with it a political polemic and over-emphasizes, arguably, the harmony between East Asian economies, and particularly the leadership role of Japan.

17 Burma and its military junta, the State Law and Order Restoration Committee (SLORC), is perhaps an exception to this rule.

18 The major published arguments have been presented by Lee (1994), Mabubhani (1995), Quang Co (1994), and Commission for a New Asia (1994). It would be incorrect, however, to detect an East–West incompatibility. There are several voices within the Asian community that speak against the existence of these 'Asian values' (see, for example, Kim Dae Jung 1994), and the socialist tradition in general emphasizes the collective more than the individual. The East–West contradiction is simplistic and political, and serves to blur the issue. Instead, the importance of *culture* and *tradition* in politics is the real issue (Öjendal and Antlöv 1998).

19 This approach, to consolidate a progressive step in political governance by hooking it to a political standard on a regional level, was explicit in the attempts to include Spain, Portugal and Greece in the EC. See Fawcett (1995: 28ff) for a discussion. In the case of Burma, however, few progressive steps have been evident.

20 This is a fragment of a long debate on the role of culture in politics in Asia. See Alagappa (1995) for a fuller treatment. The topic has become increasingly complex in the light of rapid social change and the Asian Crisis.

21 The literature on ASEAN is vast and cannot be treated in this limited space. The Institute of Southeast Asian Studies (ISEAS) in Singapore has published a two-volume *ASEAN Bibliography*. For an early, well-informed publication see Broinowski, ed. (1982). A more recent overview is given in Broinowski (1990). An ambitious summary of essays and monographs is compiled in Sandhu *et al.* (1992). See also the bibliography in this latter volume: pp. 549–82. For an overview of official documents and treaties see Rieger (1991). For a bundle of semi-official early views, see Martin (1987). For two recent pro-ASEAN publications, see Chan Heng Chee (1997) and Chia Siow Yue and Pacini (1997).

22 The Asia Pacific Economic Cooperation (APEC) is another regional cooperation body, largely active in economic issues. It has a wide membership, including East Asia, Australia, New Zealand and a number of American states. See Chapter 9.

23 Figures below are, where nothing else is stated, from the Japanese Ministry of Finance and Ministry of Foreign Affairs, taken from Cronin (1992), *passim*. For a more up-to-date account of similar issues see Chapter 9.

East Asia 9
Regionalization Still Waiting to Happen?

CLAES G. ALVSTAM

The obvious difference between East Asia and other geographical entities described in this book is its superiority in population size. Covering only half the area of Europe, the countries of East Asia – China (People's Republic, Hong Kong, Taiwan and Portuguese Macao), Korea (North and South), Japan and Mongolia – accommodated at the end of 1998 nearly 1,500 million inhabitants, or almost a quarter of the world's population, with a population density three times larger than the world average. In describing regionalist traditions in this part of the world, one has to keep various geographical scales in mind. China may be seen as a continent in its own capacity, although the Chinese region is usually viewed as synonymous with the Chinese state. The mighty, although intangible, overseas Chinese network might also be interpreted as an example of cultural and ethnic regionalization, though geographically dispersed throughout East and Southeast Asia, Australia and Pacific America. Japan, containing more than two-thirds of the total GDP of East Asia, could equally be seen as an economic region in itself, twice as large as the combined economic size of Africa and South America. If, in addition, one incorporates the business interests of Japanese companies in other countries, the Pacific Basin emerges as an archipelago-like region with an economic size excelled only by the United States. On the other hand, East Asia, as seen from a regionalist perspective, is often treated as a compound entity together with Southeast Asia, forming the East Asian Economic Caucus, to use a concept launched by the Prime Minister of Malaysia, Dr Mohammad Mahathir.

This chapter treats East Asia separately from Southeast Asia, although it ends with a discussion of present plans to create deeper cooperation between the states of Southeast Asia, united by their common European colonial heritage, and Northeast Asia, never under non-Asian rule. A further interpretation of regionalization

173

in East Asia would be to include various attempts to create regional cooperation across nation-state boundaries, such as the Tumen river project between North Korea, China and Russia, supported by Japanese and South Korean financial interests. Despite all these possibilities, I will take a more limited view in this chapter, electing to start with various forms of regional cooperation between (Greater) China, Japan and Korea. The chapter thereafter gradually extends its focus to the broader concept of regionalization and ends by trying to assess whether regionalization is on the rise in East Asia, and, if so, what expressions of regionalization are currently the strongest.

There is, indeed, very little by way of a common regionalist tradition in East Asia, and historically the regionalization concept has had an unpleasant ring in this part of the world. Its content and meaning are deeply related to the territorial expansion of the Chinese Middle Kingdom on neighbouring powers during various periods in the past, or, in modern times, to the infamous 'Greater East Asian Co-Prosperity Sphere', an attempt to legitimize the Japanese military and political drive for supreme regional power over all Pacific Asia in the 1930s and the early 1940s.

The dominant tradition of East Asian nation-states has rather been self-contented isolation, autarchy, inward-looking and technological self-reliance, interfoliated by shorter periods of military aggression, confrontation and territorial expansion. The patterns of Chinese continentalism and Japanese insularism have basically had the same roots – the outside world viewed as a constant threat, populated by barbarians, invading 'our' territory from West, East, North or South, depending on incidental events in a remote periphery or in the close neighbourhood. The 'Barbarians from the West' were Arabic and Turkish traders or warlords, penetrating the Middle Kingdom via the Silk Road. From the North came the Mongols, and from the south the colonial invaders from Europe, led by the Portuguese, securing a foothold in Macao as early as 1557. The 'Eastern Barbarians', as seen from the Chinese perspective, were of course the Japanese, reflecting a complex and disputed relationship between China and Japan, lasting ever since earliest history up to our times, and explaining the ambivalence that exists between the two countries. Japan's role as an emergent political power as a result of its fabulous economic growth in the post-war era, is even more delicate, reflecting its exposed geopolitical location between the Chinese mainland and North America across the Pacific – 'between the dragon and the deep blue sea'.

As a logical result of the total collapse of Japanese economic and political power after the Second World War, reinforced by the Chinese and Korean civil wars and the subsequent territorial division of these two nation-states, East Asia became divided along the lines of the bipolar economic and political system that emerged during the Cold War era. The People's Republic of China, Mongolia and North

Korea were incorporated within the socialist realm, while Japan, the Kuomintang regime on the island of Taiwan and South Korea ended up under American political and economic hegemony. If there are emergent trends of regionalization within East Asia during recent decades, these equally reflect a long-term decline of American hegemony and the much more abrupt collapse of the Soviet-style political and economic political order. Admittedly, the so-called Asian economic miracle as well as the more recent Asian Crisis have both in different ways provided a platform for intraregional cooperation that was lacking in the past. Such regionalization aims may be seen as antithetical to national isolation traditions, as well as to colonial subordination. Several scholars have tried to interpret this kind of ambivalent regional cooperation, using various labels such as 'soft regionalism' (Scalapino *et al.* 1988) or 'regional dialogue' (Foot 1995). This chapter places considerable emphasis on investigating the historical roots of the ambivalence East Asian governments express in promoting intraregional cooperation. In this way recent tendencies (described in the second part of this chapter) to stress common Asian values, and to promote cooperation between neighbours are placed in a perspective as manifold, complex, full of nuances, and difficult to survey as any Chinese box ever presented to our Eurocentric gaze.[1] Japan's ambivalence – whether to play to the full its role as a regional power or to emphasize its global ambitions – emerges as a key issue in the analysis.

Ancient Obstacles to Regionalization in East Asia

Despite the apparent priority given to isolation, there is abundant historical evidence of cultural regionalism in East Asia: notable examples are the spread of Buddhism and the adoption of Chinese characters in Japanese written language during the Asuka period in the sixth and seventh centuries. The Heian period (794–1185) represented the first reaction against foreign, mainly Chinese, influence on Japanese culture. This was, however, still a relatively mild manifestation of national self-reliance compared to the extreme cutting off from foreign contacts that commenced with the rise of the Tokugawa shogunate in 1603 and lasted for more than 250 years. This isolation was to a certain extent the natural reaction to overambitious and insensitive attempts to impose European religious and cultural values on Japanese society. That closure from international relations was probably the most effective and long-lasting national isolation project seen anywhere in the world in modern times. No Japanese vessels were permitted to sail to other states after 1635.

At the same time as Japan chose to cut off its territory from any kind of foreign influence, a weak and degenerate Chinese Qing dynasty became subject to accelerating European commercial penetration. Portuguese and Spanish trade and religious missions dominated the East Asian waters throughout the sixteenth century, superseded by the Dutch in the seventeenth century, and the British and, to a lesser degree, French and Germans from the eighteenth century onwards until the Second World War. It is important, though, to stress that the European penetration of China, although brutal and characterized by an unequal pattern of exchange, never reached more than a marginal part of the Chinese society: a few special ports, parts of the coastline, and the larger river estuaries. The inland provinces remained largely unaffected by Western influence. Politically, however, the colonial presence destabilized the entire empire.

A Hundred Years of Evolutionary Transition (1840s–1940s)

A new era in the political and economic history of East Asia's regional identity, as well as its relations with the outside world, began in the early 1840s with the Opium War. This forced the Qing dynasty to open new ports for direct trade with Great Britain and the cession of the island of Hong Kong (the 'barren rock') in the Treaty of Nanjing in 1842. The British victory in the Opium War was followed by a number of new wars with European and Asian intruders, all contributing to the continuous weakening of the Chinese Empire. The Arrow War (1856–60), the expansion of the Crown Colony of Hong Kong to incorporate the Kowloon peninsula in 1867, the Chinese–French War (1883–95), the war with Japan (1894–95), and the British imposition on the Chinese authorities of the 99-year New Territories landlease in 1898 were among the most significant. Russia was extending its territorial claims north of the river Amur (Heilong Jiang) and east of the Ussuri. After the war with France, China lost its authority over Indochina (Annam), while disastrous defeat in the Chinese–Japanese war forced China to give independence to the Korean peninsula under Japanese predominance, as well as the territorial loss of the island of Taiwan and the Pescadores to Japan. Symbolically the Treaty of Shimonoseki in 1895 implied the surrender of the decomposing Qing dynasty to a new, dangerous, regional power rival and neighbour – Japan.

Four decades earlier, in 1853 and 1854, an American Admiral, Matthew Perry, had twice arrived in Japanese waters with an armada of 'black ships', demanding that the Tokugawa shogunate allow its territory to open trade and contacts with the outside world. Inspired by the British success in the Opium War, the external pressure for an end to the 250-year-long Japanese isolation was not the only force driving the society into a new era: a new generation of Japanese provincial leaders was ready to shoulder the leadership of modernization.

When the juvenile Emperor Mutsuhito (later Meiji) was installed in 1867, the new era began to bring fundamental change to Japanese society. Study missions were sent to Europe and North America in order to acquire the latest in science and technology, as well as to seek inspiration for a modern political system. A new constitution was written (1889), with features culled from the American, British, French and German experiences. The introvert society was turned into an outward-looking, assertive political power, eager to pick up selected elements of the Western society in order to increase education and economic welfare, but at the same time taking an aggressive stand against its closest neighbours in the region. The motto of the new regime was *fukoku kyohei* (rich land, strong army).

The Japanese demands on China were made in a period when the latter was deeply preoccupied with its internal affairs. The continuous decline of the Qing dynasty and the repeated humiliations suffered by the authorities at the hands of foreign powers in never-ending wars stirred the roots of the growing internal opposition that led to the Taiping rebellion (1850–64), and the Nian revolt (1853–68). Numerous uprisings involving minority groups also took place during the late nineteenth century. These events gave new indications that the imperial power no longer exercised entire control of its territory. The unrest culminated in the revolution in 1911–12, overthrowing the infant Emperor Pu Yi, and the proclamation of the Republic of China (ROC) under the direction of Dr Sun Yat-sen, later the first leader of the dominant political fraction, the Nationalist Party (Kuomintang, KMT).

Events during the following decades are crucial to an understanding of the lack of true regionalization in present East Asia. The brutal Japanese colonization of the occupied territories of Taiwan and Korea, the military invasion of Manchuria, the penetration of the entire Chinese coastline, including traumatic events like the 'Shanghai incidents' (1932 and 1937) and the Nanjing massacre (1938) revived historical animosity. In the occupation of Manchuria and the creation of the Japanese vassal state of Manchukuo, a symbolic gesture of humiliation towards China was to install the deposed last Chinese Emperor, Pu Yi, as the puppet head of state. In the terrible massacre in Nanjing it is claimed that at least 250,000 persons, and maybe up to 500,000, were killed, a brutal act later whitewashed as a 'minor incident' in Japanese schoolbooks. Japanese leaders have been forced repeatedly to 'apologize' for this and other unresolved episodes. Another example of active Japanese involvement in internal Chinese affairs during the 1930s was its supply of weapons and ammunition to different competing armies during the Chinese civil war, in order to destabilize and divide the government authority. In 1940 Wang Jingwei established a puppet regime under Japanese control in Nanjing. At its largest, the Japanese control of China covered most of the northeastern provinces, including Beijing, the lower Yangtse river valley and the major share of the southeastern coastline, including Hong Kong and Canton.

The Meiji restoration had thus created a kind of East Asian regionalization by the turn of the century. Ceaseless wars with China expanded the territory formally claimed by Japan between 1874 and 1910. During the Taisho era, commencing 1912, the formal power of the Emperor over the military forces was further eroded, and Japan developed steadily into a virtual military dictatorship during the 1920s. The Japanese government maintained a skilful balance in its relationships with the Western powers during the First World War. When it took over the Shandong peninsula in eastern China from Germany in 1914, Japan was supported by the *Entente* powers; but it then challenged Great Britain and North America during the following years by imposing the 'twenty-one demands' on China. This was done in order to acquire further political and military control of Manchuria and parts of the northeastern coastline. The Washington Conference (1921–2) was an attempt by the Western powers to cooperate with Japan in order to control Japanese activities in the Pacific. Previous bilateral security policy arrangements were replaced by a four-power treaty between the USA, Great Britain, France and Japan containing a common agreement to mutual consultations in the event of external threats against the territorial interests of the contracting parties. Between 1885 and 1919 Japan had managed to carry through an industrial revolution and to double its GDP per person in 34 years.[2] Already at the beginning of the Meiji restoration its economic success thus rested on what could be labelled 'forced regionalization', a strategy that was accentuated further during the 1920s and 1930s. It is notable that the famous 'flying geese' metaphor suggesting a Japanese primacy in the region was first aired in the late 1930s, a few years before the summit of Japanese regional domination (Akamatsu 1961).

The idea of a Greater East Asian Co-Prosperity Sphere (*Dai toa kyoei ken*) was launched in early 1941, and signalled Japan's further expansion to the south after the capture of Indochina. Apart from the military and geopolitical aspects of Japanese territorial expansion southwards, the creation of a regional sphere under Japanese supremacy was intimately linked to Japan's growing need for raw materials following the rapid industrialization in the Meiji and Taisho eras. Although traditionally the Japanese economy had been based on self-sufficiency regarding food and mineral resources, the high economic growth rates demanded commodities at volumes that the existing insular production system could not meet. The agriculturally rich potential on the island of Taiwan suited Japan's growing need of rice and sugar very well. The main objective of the Japanese occupation of the Korean peninsula was access to rich mineral supplies, particularly in the northern parts of the country, and the use of Korea as a gateway to the even richer Manchuria. During the 1930s, Korean and Manchurian coal and ore supplies became an essential part of the building up of Japanese steel production.

At its peak in 1942–3, the Greater East Asian Co-Prosperity Sphere reached from Sakhalin and the Kuril Islands in the north, through Korea, eastern China, Indochina, the Malacca peninsula and the entire Indonesian archipelago to northern New Guinea and the Solomon Islands in the south, to Burma in the west, and to the Marshall and Gilbert Islands in the east. It thus comprised the third largest regional economic power in the world after the USA and the German Third Reich. The Sphere may be said to have been the first modern attempt to create regional political and economic integration in East Asia. It is noteworthy that the geographical extension of the Sphere in the early 1940s comprised almost exactly the same region as the Japanese economy came to dominate commercially in the 1980s and 1990s, although then it was able to secure the important addition of Australia, whose raw material deposits and energy-intensive industries certainly serve as a cornerstone of the Japanese production system today.

Revolution, Collapse and Revival – East Asia in the Post-War Economic Boom (1945–74)

The Japanese military disaster in 1944–5 and the final surrender after the two atomic bombs over Hiroshima and Nagasaki changed fundamentally the preconditions for East Asian regionalization. The reconstruction of the Japanese political and economic system that took place during the American occupation under the leadership of General Douglas MacArthur aimed at disarming Japan and making it dependent on the US's economic, military and political dominance. The *zaibatsu* industrial system that had been emerging after the Meiji restoration, and within which strong business conglomerates had been able to develop, was declared illegal, and Japan's relations with its neighbours in East and Southeast Asia were more or less put under American guardianship. Apart from losing its direct access to raw material resources in the region, Japan also faced the loss of all territory that had been gained from its neighbours since 1875. The USSR, which had declared war on Japan shortly after the Hiroshima bomb, had claimed jurisdiction over the island of Sakhalin as well as over the Kuril archipelago, including even the southernmost islands situated close to the larger island of Hokkaido, and thus controlling the northern passage to the Sea of Japan. Even today, more than fifty years after the Japanese surrender, no peace treaty has been agreed between Japan and the territorial successor of the collapsed USSR, the Russian Federation. This unresolved issue still blocks any kind of deeper regional cooperation between the two states.

The Japanese withdrawal of its military presence on the Chinese mainland sharpened the conflict between the Nationalists and the Chinese Communist Party (CCP). Soviet troops had occupied most of Manchuria, and handed it over to the Chinese communists in 1946 after stripping its occupied factories of all valuable machinery and equipment. In 1947–8 the communists captured all of northern China. Meanwhile the Nationalists received substantial assistance from the US in order to regain territories in southern and southeastern China abandoned by

Japan. Despite initial military superiority, the Nationalists lost more and more ground, due to widespread corruption, conservatism and general lack of popular support. After the decisive defeat in the battle of Huai in early 1949, the entire Yangtse river valley was opened to communist troops. The People's Republic of China (PRC) was proclaimed on 1 October 1949, while the leader of the KMT, Generalissimo Chiang Kai-shek, followed by parts of his conquered army, took refuge on the island of Taiwan.

The communist victory on the Chinese mainland strengthened the American conviction that it required a strong military presence in East Asia. The Nationalist regime on Taiwan was declared by most Western countries to be the legal upholder of the Republic of China, and was to represent China in all international organizations and treaties such as the United Nations, the IMF, and the GATT. Another key development was the coming of the Cold War to the Korean peninsula. Two opposing political and economic systems were established on either side of the demarcation line. North Korean military forces crossed this line in June 1950 and captured within one month more than three-quarters of South Korean territory. The united Western military forces recaptured all lost territories during the following autumn, and crossed the demarcation line in the other direction in October, aiming at conquering the whole of North Korea. The entrance of Chinese troops on the Northern side brought a new power balance, and during the following years, the Korean War surged up and down over the peninsula at an immense cost in human lives as well as material damage. As neither side could claim a final victory, armistice talks were finally concluded in July 1953, creating a power vacuum, roughly along the 38th parallel, that has remained until today as one of the last vestiges of the Cold War.

The Korean War brought about a new role for Japan in the American Pacific strategy. It became more important than previously to create a strong Japan, and economic reconstruction was speeded up. The creation of the Ministry of International Trade and Industry (MITI) as a strong government body overlooking both internal and external economic development with far-reaching authority to intervene in the private sector, while at the same time supporting long-term capital investment by favourable loans and subsidies, has been seen as one of the key factors behind the remarkable economic growth of Japan during the 1950s and 1960s. The strength and sustainability of Japanese economic success was generally underrated in America and Europe for a long time, despite growth figures that spoke for themselves.

In investigating the roots of the lack of regionalization in East Asia, it is also important to bear in mind that when Japan lost its sources of raw materials in the regional neighbourhood after the Second World War, it had to turn to far more remote suppliers outside the region. Its iron ore imports, which grew exponentially during the 1950s and the 1960s, had before the war been shipped from Korea and Manchuria, but now had to be delivered from India, Southern Africa and, later, mainly from Brazil and Australia. Its need of coal, which had been supplied domestically from Hokkaido and Kyushu, as well as from occupied territories in Korea and Manchuria, was during the post-war period shipped from North America and, later, also from South Africa and Australia. It had a growing import dependency on grain: originally supplied from Taiwan, it was now purchased in North America and Australia. The soaring import volumes of crude oil were mainly imported from the Middle East and to a lesser extent from Indonesia. Only the imports of forest products and tropical food were still supplied mainly from the East and Southeast Asian region, even though North American and Siberian reserves tended to grow in importance. Thus Japanese trade growth during the first two decades after the Second World War mainly separated the country from its own geographical region, rather than binding it more closely to its neighbours. Australia, once an integral part of the British Empire and during the inter-war years more reliant on America, started during the 1960s and the 1970s to play an entirely new role: it became the main supplier of various raw materials to Japan. North America and Europe were the main markets for the first stumbling efforts of Japanese industry to sell its products abroad rather than to its geographically closer neighbours with limited market potential.

The typical pattern of East Asian non-regionalization in the 1950s and 1960s was thus American economic and military hegemony over most countries, as the main supplier of investment capital and the major market for cheap manufactured consumer goods. During the same period, economies that later were labelled 'newly industrializing economies' (NIEs) were positioned between America and Japan, the latter becoming the most important source of semi-manufactured goods, and the major home country for inward foreign direct investment after the US. Even though Japanese foreign trade grew rapidly after the war, its importance in the national economy has been marginal and roughly the same during the entire post-war period. In 1950 the value of exports amounted to 9 per cent of Japan's GDP, a share that only increased to 14 per cent in 1974. The first wave of outward FDI started in the early 1970s. It was natural for Japanese companies at this stage to relocate labour-intensive production to its neighbours – South Korea, Taiwan and Hong Kong – knitted together with Japan by anti-communist sentiments under the American security policy umbrella.

Thus a kind of a regional specialization and division of labour was created during the 1970s between Japan and the second row of Akamatsu's 'flying geese', the NIEs of South Korea, Taiwan and Hong Kong. These three economies were themselves exponents of highly different political and economic systems. South Korea largely copied the Japanese system of strong administrative guidance of economic life, and created a corresponding system of business conglomerates after the *zaibatsu* blueprint, pronouncing them *chaebol*. These were given an even greater relative strength than their Japanese prototypes, and also went international earlier than Japanese manufacturing companies had done before them. The largest *chaebols* – Daewoo, Hyundai, Samsung, Sangyong and Lucky Goldstar – actually dominated the entire Korean economy even in the early period of industrialization and modernization of the war-torn economy.

The economic policy carried through by the government of the Republic of China on Taiwan was characterized, on the other hand, by the aim of the KMT to return to the mainland at the earliest possible convenience. One obvious outcome of this military aim was that less attention was paid to the development of the island itself. Consequently, a network of small and medium-sized manufacturing companies emerged on the island in the shadow of grandiose but impracticable plans to reform the economic system in remote mainland provinces and cities. It was not until the early 1960s that the KMT initiated large state-owned companies in order to build up an industrial base in certain key sectors such as oil refining, iron and steel, and cement. Due to the intricate diplomatic situation, the internationalization of the Taiwanese economy was held back, despite a rapid increase in foreign trade during these years. Between 1952 and 1974, the share of exports to GDPsoared from 8 per cent to 44 per cent.

The third target for the new wave of Japanese FDI in East Asia, Hong Kong, had a freewheeling market economy with little or no control by the British government. Trade, rather than large-scale manufacturing, had been the major engine in the economic growth of the Crown Colony. Japanese investment spurred a growth of small-scale manufacturing industry in clothing and other light consumer goods. The Cultural Revolution on the Chinese mainland, proclaimed in 1966, brought a new wave of refugees to Hong Kong. During the Cultural Revolution most mainland ports were practically closed to foreign trade, and Hong Kong's role as the entrepot port for goods to and from the People's Republic declined in volume but increased in terms of relative importance. PRC Prime Minister Zhou Enlai came to play an important role in the international political economy at that time, encouraging other Third World states to follow China's example of self-reliance in order to protect their citizens from Western-style imperialism and unequal exchange conditions. During this extreme period in China's modern history a major event took place that changed the foundations of the world political order – the breakthrough in diplomatic relations between the People's Republic and the US. In 1972 President Nixon's key security adviser, Henry Kissinger, came to play a crucial role in formulating a new policy to contain the USSR by making moves to establish closer relations with the People's Republic.

The Japanese economy was solid, but at the same time fragile. For instance, the oil shock of 1973–4 demonstrated brutally the high vulnerability of the Japanese society to foreign raw material supplies. The economic slowdown in Japan during the following years gave rise to a new economic policy, in which further internationalization was promoted in order to balance raw material dependence with an increased presence in foreign markets.

Diplomatic Upheaval, Reforms and Economic Miracles (1975 to late 1990s)

The new diplomatic order gave rise to internal Chinese turbulence as well. The two leading figures, Zhou Enlai and Mao Zedong, both died in 1976, paving the way for a severe internal battle between hardliners, symbolized by the infamous 'Gang of Four', and reformist technocrats. The latter group eventually took the initiative and after the Third Plenum of the Eleventh Central Committee of the CCP, held in December 1978, it was decided to establish full diplomatic relations with the United States, and to adopt a policy of 'Four Modernizations'. This event signalled an entire new era in East Asian regionalization. The sharp turn of mainland China toward participation in the international economy by opening up to inward foreign direct investment, as well as promoting extensive foreign trade, affected more than its political and economic relations with North America and Western Europe. The most important long-term effect of the upheaval was the rise of the People's Republic as a regional power with open relations to its neighbours – Japan, to begin with, but later the Republic of (South) Korea and Vietnam as well. The creation of four Special Economic Zones (SEZs) in the Guangdong and Fujian provinces in 1979 was a symbolic step taken by the new paramount leader of China, Deng Xiaoping. He thus imposed capitalist reform and foreign ownership in limited geographical territories, in order to create a laboratory hothouse for Chinese 'market socialism', for later extension to other parts of the country.

The economic reforms in mainland China also paved the way for a more constructive dialogue with Great Britain on the return of Hong Kong to 'the embrace of the motherland'. The treaty of 1984, establishing a Special Administrative Region (SAR) on 1 July 1997, also signalled the establishment of a strong regional economic zone along the shores of the Pearl River estuary. This zone comprised the booming Guangzhou Metropolitan Area, Shenzhen SEZ, Zhuhai SEZ and the Portuguese colony Macao, which was to be returned to China in December 1999. Mainland China's honeymoon with international opinion ended, however, very abruptly with the suppression of the students' democracy movement on Tiananmen Square in June 1989. Many people outside as well as inside China lost their confidence in China's ability and willingness to complement the economic reforms with political liberalization and increased democracy. The signals sent to neighbouring countries that the CCP was not yet prepared for deeper political cooperation on a regional basis cast doubt on Beijing's willingness to give Hong Kong the necessary degree of autonomy and freedom after the handover.

It should be understood, however, that the spectacular growth of foreign economic relations that started in the wake of the Four Modernizations, and were interrupted only temporarily after the Tiananmen massacre, took off from a very low level indeed. Even in the late 1990s, more than twenty years after entering the new era, the Chinese economy as a whole remains largely autarchic, rural and inward-looking. The immense progress of the modernization process, which can easily be observed in the booming cities along the coast, is thus far mainly concentrated in a limited part of the vast Chinese territory, in the same way as the European and Japanese penetrations of China were geographically limited in historical periods. Despite the fact that up to now the economic transformation has taken place mainly in the larger cities of the coastal provinces, however, these parts of China are large enough to signify a major shift in the economic balance of the region as a whole. More than 500 million of the mainland's total population of 1,250 million inhabitants – and thus more than twice the population of the rest of the East Asian region – live in the coastal provinces directly affected by the transformation. By conventional measures, China is still one of the poorest countries in the world with a *per capita* income of no more than US$800 (1998) and a GDP of US$1,000 billion, compared to Japan's US$4,000 billion for a population ten times smaller. If this measure is modified, though, by adjusting the GDP to the purchasing power parity standard, the Chinese economy can be seen to have surpassed the Japanese in size in 1994.

The economic 'miracles' of Taiwan and South Korea resulted from a complex mix of factors, none of which can be related to institutionalized intraregional cooperation, as in the case of Western Europe. The macroeconomic interpretation of the rapid economic growth in the region has been heavily disputed (World Bank 1993; Krugman 1994). The expansion of foreign trade in both countries was to and from the United States and Japan. Intraregional trade growth, on the other hand, played only a minor role in the total growth of foreign trade volumes until the early 1990s. In particular the trade relations between the NIEs were strikingly weak, because for many decades they have been competitive rather than complementary economies. They owe the competitive strength of their foreign trade to global and regional strategic measures by American and Japanese TNCs, rather than to indigenous companies. It is only during the last five to ten years that Korean and Taiwanese companies have emerged as international actors on a larger scale, and it is thus probable that the large potential of specialization and division of labour between countries in the region will be better utilized in the future (Alvstam and Park 1998). Korea's share in Taiwan's foreign trade has increased from 0.8 per cent to 3.5 per cent between 1985 and 1998, for instance – still a very low level indeed, but rapidly increasing.

After the reunification of Hong Kong and Macao with the Chinese mainland, the logical next step for the Chinese leadership will probably be to intensify pressure on Taiwan to accept the same 'one country – two systems' formula. This time, however, matters will be much more complicated. As long as the old guard within the KMT maintained regaining power on the mainland as the ultimate objective, relations with the 'renegade province' rested on a common objective – reunification. Until the late 1980s, neither the CCP nor the KMT pretended to build a pluralist society or to permit political opposition. Matters changed, however, after the decease of Chiang Ching-kuo in 1989. The new leader of the KMT, and accordingly head of state of the Republic of China (Taiwan), President Lee Teng-hui, an economist of 'pure' Taiwanese origin, who had made an academic career in the US, succeeded in taking the initiative from the older generation within the party. Moreover, he launched far-reaching democratic reforms, permitting the 'independence party' DPP (Democratic Progressive Party) to establish itself as a legal voice of opposition, and to speak of immediate reunification with a calmer voice than its predecessors. The democratization of Taiwan, and the growth of forces that aim at making Taiwan a sovereign state, has been an issue much more difficult to digest in Beijing than the traditional 'return-to-the-mainland' rhetoric. Despite repeated assurances from President Lee that reunification is still at the top of the agenda, popular feelings run in quite the opposite direction. The mainland's upgrading of military exercises in early 1996, closer to Taiwanese waters than for many years and aimed at sending a message to the Taiwanese people at the time of the presidential election, apparently had the opposite effect to that intended. Despite intensified economic contacts over the Taiwan Strait since the opening up in the late 1980s, the tension between the two regimes seems not to have been soothed. Hong Kong's handover has no doubt weakened Taiwan's position, particularly if Beijing were to insist that the new Hong Kong leadership cut its links with Taiwan. The annual turnover of the indirect trade between the mainland and Taiwan amounted in 1996 to around US$28 billion and US$35 billion in direct investment. The lion's share of these transactions runs through Hong Kong. When analysts describe the growing shares of intra-regional trade in East Asia (Grant *et al*. 1993; Drysdale and Garnaut 1993; Chia and Lee 1993; Dobson and Chia 1997) it is striking to see that what is classified as intraregional trade actually consists to a large extent of the growth of trade between mainland China and Taiwan through Hong Kong.

Nevertheless, internal relations between the leadership in Beijing, the new leaders in Hong Kong and the Taiwanese government are indeed crucial for all kinds of regional cooperation in East and Southeast Asia for the next few years. A lasting smooth transition in Hong Kong, and a harmonious slow-paced development in Beijing–Taipei talks will constitute a good platform for improved relations between China and Japan, Korea, and Southeast Asia; the opposite scenario, implying active communist control of Hong Kong's affairs and an aggravated military threat from the mainland towards Taiwan in order to force reunification, will surely lead the other countries in East and Southeast Asia to develop a policy aimed at reducing political and economic relations with China.

Bilateral Relations in the Region

Japan's Declining Importance

In the absence of solid regionalist institutions, the regionalization of East Asia is an aggregate of bilateral relations, as well as relations with the United States. As has been argued, there is no historical precedent for regional cooperation in this area. On the contrary, history gives copious evidence of military tension, occupations, open wars and border conflicts between the states in East Asia. Yet the opening up of bilateral economic and diplomatic contacts since the early 1970s is a logical result of the gradual military withdrawal of the United States from the region, and of the rapid economic transformation that has created entirely new conditions for regional cooperation in the future. The key issue remains the axis between Beijing and Tokyo: the relationship between a major military power, on the brink of becoming an economic superpower, and an economic superpower with ambitions to become a pivotal political state in the region. A notable change in the existing economic imbalances between Japan and other states in East and Southeast Asia is that while Japan's economic dependence on its neighbours has soared since the 1970s, their relative dependence on Japan has declined over the same period. If this amounts to the restoration of the economic balance that existed in the region in the first half of the twentieth century, it may be a good sign that a political and economic balance between Japan and China can be maintained (see tables). There has been a clear tendency in the direction of partner concentration in Japanese foreign economic relations during the last two decades, as is shown in the rapid decline of the 'Rest of world' group in Table 9.1. This residual group consists mainly of states in the Middle East, Africa and Latin America, but also of raw material suppliers in the closer neighbourhood, like Australia. The rapid growth of Japanese intraregional dependence on Asia since the 1970s should be seen in the perspective of the decline of neighbouring Asia in Japanese exports to East Asia since the peak period of regional dominance in the 1930s. In 1935, more than 50 per cent of Japanese exports went to Asia, of which 25 per cent of the total value went to China alone. The comparative figures in 1995 were 46 per cent and 5 per cent respectively (Yagasaki 1997: 40), so the main difference between these years is not a higher share

Table 9.1 Geographical composition of Japanese foreign trade 1975–97 (per cent)

	1975	1980	1985	1990	1995	1997
Japanese exports to:						
- East/Southeast Asia	27	23	25	30	43	41
- Europe	19	20	16	23	17	18
- North America	22	26	40	36	29	30
- Rest of World	32	31	19	11	11	11
	100	100	100	100	100	100
Japanese imports from:						
- East/Southeast Asia	19	24	28	27	36	36
- Europe	8	9	10	20	18	16
- North America	24	21	24	27	26	25
- Rest of World	49	46	38	26	20	23
	100	100	100	100	100	100

Source: IMF: Direction of Trade Statistics (own adaptations)

Table 9.2 Trade with Japan in total foreign trade of East Asian countries 1975–97 (per cent).

	1975	1980	1985	1990	1995	1997
Japan's share in exports from:						
- P.R. China	24	22	22	15	19	17
- Rep. of China (Taiwan)	13	11	11	12	12	10
- Hong Kong	6	5	4	6	6	6
- Rep. of Korea	25	17	15	19	14	11
- Singapore	9	10	9	9	8	7
- Malaysia	14	23	25	15	13	13
- Indonesia	44	45	46	43	28	24
- Philippines	38	27	19	20	16	18
- Thailand	28	15	13	17	17	15
Japan's share in imports to:						
- P.R. China	38	26	36	14	22	20
- Rep. of China (Taiwan)	31	27	28	29	29	25
- Hong Kong	21	23	23	16	15	14
- Rep. of Korea	33	26	24	27	24	19
- Singapore	17	18	17	20	21	18
- Malaysia	20	23	23	24	27	22
- Indonesia	31	32	26	25	24	21
- Philippines	27	20	14	18	22	20
-Thailand	32	21	26	30	29	26

Sources: IMF: Direction of Trade Statistics (various issues); National Taiwanese statistics (own adaptations)

of exports to the neighbouring region as a whole, but a much lower share to China: in other words, the potential for developing bilateral China–Japan trade is huge.

The most rapid decline in Japan's role as the final destination of exports from other countries in East and Southeast Asia during the last two decades is observed in relation to South Korea and Indonesia. Its position as supplier of goods to other East and Southeast Asian countries has decreased most markedly in the cases of South Korea and the People's Republic – just those markets to which Japanese exporters have been giving special attention during the same period. This paradoxical outcome, though, can easily be explained by the rapid transformation of the economic structure among Japan's closest neighbours, reducing the initially unequal bilateral trade relation to a more balanced exchange (Kreft 1996). The mission of Prime Minister Hashimoto to five of the ASEAN member states in early 1997, eagerly proposing intensified political and commercial contacts between Japan and Southeast Asia, should be seen in the context of Japan's lost supremacy in the region.

Below follow some notes on the most important bilateral relations in East Asia – with the focus on Japan, but also with an eye on the second key issue in the region: relations between the People's Republic on the Chinese mainland and the 'rebellious' province of Taiwan. As long as the long-term contacts between these two territories remain in deadlock, uncertainty, mutual suspicion, and even the prospect of increased tension will hamper rapid development in the regionalization process. The section ends with a few comments on East Asia's common external relations with the largest and most powerful actor in the Pacific region, the US.

It should not be forgotten that the role of *states* in managing foreign trade relations in the region is in rapid decline as a consequence of the opening up of China to foreign companies. It may thus be private companies – Japanese, Hong Kong and Taiwan Chinese and Korean – that will take the lead in further regionalization efforts in East Asia, rather than the governments of the countries in which they operate. This issue will be further dealt with in the final part of the chapter.

Japan versus China

The core element in the development of East Asian regionalization remains the bilateral relation between Japan, on the one hand, and Greater China on the other. Mainland China's rapid economic development since the early 1980s, and the even more remarkable success stories of Taiwan and Hong Kong have created an entirely new power balance in the region. Simultaneously, Japan has more or less been forced to take a more active position in regional political affairs than it was used to have under the shelter of the American security umbrella. Three hypothetical scenarios may be formulated. The first is based on the assumption that Japan and China will become two poles apart in a region constrained by political and military tension, rivalry and open conflict. The second scenario implies a *status quo* in which

China and Japan will compete for regional dominance, but at the same time acknowledge their internal differences and ideologies and maintain a certain level of mutual economic and political contact. The third scenario, finally, assumes that China and Japan will cooperate closely on a regional basis, creating a powerful counterweight to Western influence in general and American interests in particular. In all three cases, it is assumed that the Taiwan issue will be settled peacefully and that China's position *vis-à-vis* Japan will not be weakened by internal conflict.

As has been argued earlier in this chapter, most historical factors speak against a scenario in which Japan and China define common objectives and achieve mutual political and economic cooperation. The best example of how historic animosity can be transformed into peaceful cooperation is the German–French axis within the EU. It may be added, though, that three devastating wars within a time period of 75 years were needed to motivate a change in intra-European affairs.

The recent tension between Japan, on the one hand, and the People's Republic and Taiwan on the other regarding a couple of inconspicuous islets in the East China Sea during 1996–7 is a good illustration of how rapidly minor unsolved territorial issues can create large-scale diplomatic activity. Even though the islands had been considered as Japanese in Tokyo, their legal status had not been actively claimed until an ultra-nationalist group, linked to the *yakuza*, challenged the governments of all three regimes by repairing a lighthouse that had been destroyed by a typhoon in July 1996. Even though the Japanese government sought to defuse tensions with its neighbours by withholding official recognition of the action, the Foreign Ministry emphasized that Japan was not giving up ownership of the islands, around which there had also been unresolved discussions over fishing rights with Taiwan. A number of more or less officially sanctioned demonstrations around the islands from the Chinese mainland as well as from Taiwan, and even incorporating a mission from Hong Kong, revealed the sensitivity of unsolved territorial disputes between regimes who only recently, and only partially, have recognized each other's legal existence. The Daioyu incident thus should not be seen as an isolated marginal issue, but in the light of its symbolic geopolitical implications for all states in the region – with far larger problems, like the conflict over the Spratleys, waiting in the wings.

Japan–Korea

There are few bilateral relationships in East Asia that are affected by as many conflicts and differing interpretations of historical events as that between Japan and South Korea. The 1995–6 contention, developing into a war to the knife, between the two states to achieve the hosting of the presumably non-threatening football World Cup in 2002, brought to the surface a wide range of unresolved ancient controversies and disputes, to a degree that startled the outside world. The decision by the international football association, FIFA, to let the two states arrange the Cup jointly, might in the future be regarded as the stroke of genius that illuminates the history of 'sports diplomacy': it may yet create an excuse for the two contenders to cooperate in other matters as well during the years to come. Unresolved conflicts between the two states include the interpretation of the brutal Japanese occupation of Korea (1910–45), Japanese compensation for Korean 'comfort women' during the Second World War, treatment of the Korean minority in Japan, and disputes regarding sovereignty over a couple of tiny islets in the Sea of Japan, as well as the larger issues of demarcating the boundaries between their respective 200-mile economic zones and signing a fisheries agreement. It is notable that there has been no common security structure between South Korea and Japan since 1953, despite the common link with the US and the fact that both countries have hosted large American forces on their territories during the last 45 years. Emperor Hirohito (Showa), who reigned over Japan after 1926, and accordingly also over Korea for almost twenty years, in 1984 issued his first statement on the events during the occupation and the war, using the words 'an unfortunate period in Japan–Korean relations' (Foot 1995: 233). Later, in 1990, Prime Minister Kaifu did raise the level of excuses by using words like 'sincere remorse' and 'honest apologies' (*ibid.*). Apparently, however, Japan retains the advantage, in economic terms. Its GDPis still twelve times larger than South Korea's, despite forty years of quick Korean recovery from the civil war in 1950–3.

One further complication in the bilateral relations between Japan and South Korea has been the Japanese eagerness to open up and maintain a dialogue with the northern side, a policy that had already started in the 1950s. In numerous cases Japan has acted as mediator in attempts to impose a formal conclusion on the war, and Japanese companies have also been actively involved in various business activities in North Korea. The present paradoxical situation is that since the collapse of the USSR in 1991 and the gradual opening up of relations between the arch-enemies South Korea and China, Japan has continued to promote relations with the North. Japan is probably North Korea's largest trade partner and largest source of foreign direct investment during recent years. It has also played a key role in food supply to North Korea during the recent famine. This 'ill-judged' Japanese policy, as seen from the southern side, has sometimes been depicted as Tokyo's way of keeping the peninsula divided, and economically weak, thus delaying its future economic challenge to Japan (Foot 1995: 232). The newly elected President Kim Dae-Jung's eagerness to carry through a 'sunshine policy' *vis-à-vis* the North – despite the absence of encouraging signals of improvement in internal relations, almost daily minor and major provocations, and the impact of the 'missile crisis' between North Korea and Japan during 1998 – may have reduced the differences in North Korean policy between Japan and South Korea.

China–Korea

Sensitivity to all kinds of Chinese influence is still a cornerstone in Korean foreign policy on both sides of the Panmunjon demarcation line. Despite Chinese military and economic support to Kim Il Sung, the North Korean regime managed for decades to maintain a delicate balance between Moscow and Beijing. It was not until the collapse of the Soviet Union that North Korea became more one-sidedly dependent on Chinese support, at the same time as Beijing reoriented its policy towards the Koreas in a more pragmatic and commercially biased direction. This led to the opening up of diplomatic relations with Seoul, and consequently to keeping the Pyongyang at arm's length. After the decease of the 'Great Leader' in 1994, Beijing took an even more lukewarm attitude to his son, the 'Dear Leader' Kim Jong-Il, thus contributing to the economic misery of North Korea which soon stood at the brink of complete disaster and mass famine. The defection in February 1997 of the chief ideologist and main engineer behind the infamous *juche* system of economic self-reliance, Hwang Jang-Yop, to the South Korean embassy in Beijing took China's relations with North Korea to the brink, and caused widespread embarrassment on both sides. Hwang was permitted to proceed from Beijing to Seoul via Manila, which made manifest China's intention to further isolate Kim Jong Il, and to further promote its diplomatic and commercial relations with the South. Particularly notable is the closer cooperation that in recent years has emerged between the northeastern Chinese provinces of Jilin and Liaoning with South Korean companies. In a future scenario where Beijing gradually loses its ultimate central power, and more initiative is taken by the provinces, the clear strategy of Seoul seems to be to strengthen its contacts with those parts of China that were commercially and militarily united with Korea by Japanese force during the 1930s. In addition to the Tumen river project, the so-called BoHai-Yellow Sea cooperation is an example of regional cooperation initiatives. The Beijing–Seoul–Tokyo (BeSeTo) project, aimed at encouraging Japan to play a more active role in recreating the Northeast Asian diplomatic map, and premised on the likely inevitable collapse of the North Korean society, is another. The driving force behind intimate cooperation between former arch-enemies is naturally common concern at the possibility of a violent rather than peaceful dissolution of North Korea, and the common duty to pay the presumably astronomical bill for Korean reunification, however and whenever this will happen.

East Asia–USA

The American occupation of Japan in 1945 under the direction of General Douglas MacArthur changed the entire security policy preconditions in East Asia. Never before, not even at the peak of British colonial empire, had such an essential part of the region come under non-Asian supremacy. The first symbolic measure of the new regime was the rewriting of the 1889 constitution in 1946, stripping Emperor Hirohito of most of his powers and making him simply the 'symbol' of state. Another was the pacifist doctrine, Article 9 among others in the constitution. In addition to declaring a permanent commitment to peace, it renounces war and 'the threat or use of force as a means of settling international disputes'. The hesitant reorientation of Japanese foreign policy, from being completely dependent on the US to becoming an emergent regional superpower, is reflected in the present demands for a rewriting of the constitution to restore Japan's status as a 'normal country' with the rights of belligerency as defined by Article 51 of the UN Charter. The present interpretation of Article 9 prohibits Japan from engaging in 'collective defence'. On the other hand, there has been a continuous process of amendment to the 1946 constitution. An example of this is the creation of a Self-defence Force in 1956, the mutual security pact with the US in 1960, and the law that made it possible for Japan to be deployed on UN peacekeeping operations abroad. The new American 'China policy', launched by Henry Kissinger in the early 1970s, signalled an entirely new view of the role of the Pacific region in a global security policy context. The 'informal strategic alliance' between the US and China lost its meaning after the end of the East–West conflict, however, as the US no longer needed China to contain Soviet expansion in East and Southeast Asia. From its viewpoint, China did not require the protection of the US against the hegemonic ambitions of the USSR. China is increasingly taking the role of a rival player to the US, trying to change the *status quo* through growing power and increased manoeuvrability. This explains why Chinese foreign policy makers are trying to foster US withdrawal from the region at a bilateral level as well as in multilateral institutions (Schilling 1997: 165). However, China's ambitions for regional leadership have led to doubts in other countries in East and Southeast Asia as to whether China is integrable to the necessary extent. In this respect most Asian countries would prefer to see the US support the various multilateral security cooperation forums and not scale down its military presence (Schilling 1997: 164).

The gradual American withdrawal from Asia remains the key issue in the security policy of the region. The decision to return Okinawa to Japan in 1972, and the abandonment of the Subic Bay marine base in the Philippines in 1994, have been the most obvious milestones in this long-term process. On the other hand, the United States still plays the dominant role in the further development of the Pacific Basin. Examples of the continuing high priority paid by the US to the East Asian security balance came when President Clinton, within a single month in the spring of 1996, confirmed the security partnership with Japan and sent naval units to the Formosa Straits at the height of the crisis. A couple of years earlier the US had taken a key role in reacting to North Korea's announcement of its withdrawal from the Non-Proliferation Treaty, and the signing of the Framework Agreement with Pyongyang in October 1994, under which the United States would assist North Korea with light-water reactors (Foot 1995: 231). Another symbolic measure of the changed American attitude towards Pacific Asian security was the normalization of its relations with Vietnam in July 1995.

The bilateral trade relation between East Asia and the US is another important issue in assessing East Asian regionalization as against a scenario of globalization and multilateralism. When the vast American trade surplus with East Asia in general and Japan in particular in the 1950s and 1960s turned into huge bilateral deficits in the 1970s and since, the American attitude to expanding East Asian trade also changed (Encarnation 1992). The typical pattern of the 1990s has been China's accumulated bilateral trade surplus with the US, which has put the US's remaining deficits with Japan a little out of focus in the general debate.

Regional Cooperation – APEC and EAEC

The recent emergence of a large number of more or less unofficial intraregional organizations in East and Southeast Asia may be interpreted as a sign of the common need of East Asian states, as well as the US, to regain a long-term equilibrium disturbed by the gradual decline of the American security hegemony and the end of the East–West conflict. These organizations range from the Pacific Trade and Development Conference (PAFTAD) and the Pacific Basin Economic Council (PBEC) to the Pacific Economic Cooperation Council (PECC), the more official ASEAN Regional Forum (ARF), the Council for Security Cooperation in Asia-Pacific (CSCAP), and Asia-Pacific Economic Cooperation (APEC). Of these new regional organizations, APEC has become by far the most powerful instrument since its creation in 1989.

The creation of this forum for cooperation between the US and Pacific Asia should be seen in the light of American ambition to make APEC an instrument for maintaining its hegemony in East and Southeast Asia through its economic and commercial, rather than its military, presence. It is evident that APEC is higher on the American agenda than on those of its Pacific Asian counterparts, although its role as an annual social occasion and a platform for regional dialogue has been widely acknowledged by Asian political leaders. From a cynical point of view, it may be observed that the readiness to accept new and more remote countries as members could serve the role of keeping the organization at a non-operational level. The broader the cooperation in terms of countries participating, the less the risk of a deeper and more substantial cooperation. This way, APEC does not hamper American ambitions in other parts of the world, while it postpones the need for Asian countries to initiate more sweeping measures to facilitate economic interaction between the member states. Since APEC was established, there have been extraordinarily few concrete results in terms of lower tariffs, control of non-tariff barriers, monetary cooperation or any of the other explicit objectives. Instead, APEC was used as a preparatory forum for parallel multilateral trade negotiations within the framework of the Uruguay Round in the GATT, and for the creation of the WTO in 1995.

Actually, the concessions made by APEC members regarding the reduction of barriers to trade are generally well in line with the commitments made at the ratification of the Uruguay Round. From the viewpoint of non-members of the WTO such as the People's Republic, however, APEC has served as a platform on which to gain neighbourhood support for its ambition to enter the WTO. During the summit meeting in Osaka in November 1995, China gave notice of drastic liberalization measures, such as an average 30 per cent reduction on the import tariffs of 4,000 commodity items and the partial elimination of quotas, licences and other import controls. During the fourth summit in Subic Bay in November 1996, President Jiang Zemin announced a further reduction of the average tariff to roughly 15 per cent by the year 2000 (Haacke 1997: 168). Haacke also points at contrary indications of Chinese efforts to instrumentalize APEC for a mercantilist economic policy, and observes that the creation of an Asia-Pacific free trade area is not one of their priority goals (Zhang and Zhou 1994: 489). In Osaka, President Jiang Zemin emphasized the equal ranking of all the APEC pillars: the liberalization and facilitation of trade and investment, on the one hand, economic and technical cooperation on the other (Haacke 1997: 169).

Another non-WTO member, Taiwan, has also used APEC as a step-up to approach the WTO. The diplomatic deadlock regarding the impossibility of two Chinas being members of APEC at the same time has been provisionally solved by using the label 'Taipei, Taiwan' or 'Taiwan Province' for the Taiwanese delegation, and ensuring that Taiwan is not represented at summit meetings by its elected head of state. The internationalization of the Taiwanese economy through foreign trade during the 1970s and 1980s and through FDI since the late 1980s has, of course, transformed Taiwan into one of the main players in the region. The explicit aim of the present Taiwanese government is to use APEC and, it hopes, forthcoming WTO membership to develop Taiwan into an Asia-Pacific Regional Operations Centre (APROC). The comprehensive APROC plan connotes two main things. From the viewpoint of the business community, it is a strategy for attracting local and foreign enterprises to make Taiwan their operational base for investment and business activities in the entire Asia-Pacific region, including mainland China. From the macroeconomic perspective, it means turning Taiwan into a base for developing economic and trade relations with the neighbourhood (Chiang 1997: 70). Needless to say, the APROC plan contains several provocative elements in terms of Taiwan's relations with the People's Republic. As with most Taiwanese long-term strategies, the financial backing for such a spectacular project is excellent, and the operational content is much more realizable than many APEC plans. The problem, as always, is the diplomatic isolation of Taiwan. Many observers believe, however, that both the People's Republic and Taiwan will be invited to become members of the WTO within the near future, thus making it possible to find an operational formula for their bilateral economic cooperation within a multilateral framework.

The 1998 annual meeting of APEC probably symbolized a step-back in intra-regional cooperation, deeply affected as it was by the economic slowdown in the region caused by the financial crises in Thailand, Korea and Malaysia, the political turmoil in Indonesia, the heavily criticized IMF actions to restore financial balances, and a widespread gloom over the short-term prospects of overcoming the crisis. The 1998 summit in Kuala Lumpur was furthermore hampered by differences in opinion among the neighbours over internal political developments in the host country, which put the non-interventionist policy of ASEAN in question.

The proposal to create an East Asian Economic Caucus (EAEC) was initially a challenge to the stability of APEC, as it was originally suggested by the Malaysian Prime Minister Dr Mahathir in 1990, explicitly excluding North America, Australia and New Zealand from Asian cooperation. So far, the EAEC seems to symbolize a step too far in the direction of opposing the existing world economic order to be accepted by pragmatic and cautious leaders in East and Southeast Asia. The Japanese reaction is particularly delicate, as Japan would be the main economic power within an EAEC. The Japanese policy has been to see the EAEC as an 'inner core' of APEC, not contradicting the aims and objectives of the larger institution. The Chinese position on the EAEC project should be seen in the context of its unwillingness to transform APEC from a forum of regional dialogue into a more results-orientated negotiating regime. As countries which do not directly 'belong' to the region, such as New Zealand, Australia and the US, are represented in APEC, the EAEC is a suitable institutional instrument, from the Chinese viewpoint, for situations in which prior coordination between the Asian summiteers only seems expedient. In other words, the EAEC should merely be a consultative institution, which does not duplicate APEC activities (Haacke 1997: 170).

Prospects for a Future Regionalization in East Asia

The situation as it has developed during the second half of the 1990s is in many respects different from previous scenarios. After the death of Deng Xiaoping in February 1997, the first generation of Communist leaders brought up after the Long March, the Civil War and the proclamation of the People's Republic had the task of guiding the country towards continued economic reforms without taking the risk of falling into the 'Soviet trap' of losing the political and military initiative. The increasing divergence between the sprawling urban coastal regions and the stagnating inland countryside challenges the overall legacy of the one-party system, and imposes an insecurity and lability on the nearest neighbours of the People's Republic. With the Taiwan issue still unresolved, the political system in North Korea on the brink of collapse, and numerous minor territorial conflicts in the South China Sea, there is no lack of arguments against a future harmonious development of regional cooperation in East Asia. Japan, experiencing its longest period of economic stagnation in the post-war era, has been forced to reconsider its hitherto successful financial policies, and faces a simultaneous need to reassess its relations with the US, and to accept the political consequences of its economic position in the region (Katz 1998).

The financial crises that had hit the majority of East Asian countries by the second half of 1997 caused sharp devaluations of all currencies except the non-convertible Chinese Yuan Renminbi and the severely controlled Hong Kong dollar. The turbulence can be said to have hampered as well as boosted further intra-regional cooperation. On the one hand, it can be argued, further regionalization is dependent on a harmonious economic development. In a situation of turmoil, caused by internal as well as external forces, states may become more inward-looking, and give priority to easing domestic tensions at the cost of promoting relations with their neighbours. On the other hand, financial crisis has also indicated the need for deep economic and political reforms that in the long run may be a necessary precondition for fostering regionalization. The dubious role played by the IMF in the early phases of the crisis has activated persistent anti-American feelings, and stimulated discussion on how to reduce dependence on the US dollar as a benchmark currency. Creating a basket of Asian currencies is an alternative to dollar pegging, and an Asian Monetary Fund would be a counter-weight to the IMF.

The key issue in terms of East Asian regionalization, as we have seen, is the bilateral political and economic relationship between China and Japan, a balance that could be compared to that between Germany and France. An intimate and mutually respectful Chinese–Japanese cooperation would serve as the pivotal force in East Asian regionalization, unleashing an enormous potential, while another scenario could be a 'balance of terror' between two powers in stiff competition for regional political, military and economic hegemony. A third scenario might see a less significant future role for the central state and the emergence of strong sub-national and transnational entities: provinces in southern and eastern China taking off from the Chinese state, creating a more loosely connected pattern of islands of economic welfare in close contact with the overseas Chinese network.

All these scenarios are in turn closely related to which route China's future inter-nationalization of its economy will take. Although Akamatsu's 'flying geese' metaphor may be criticized and modified in many different ways (Korhonen 1994; Hart-Landsberg and Burkett 1998), its empirical content has been surprisingly valid, especially when it comes to the export pattern of the textile and clothing industries in different East Asian countries (Yang and Zhong 1998).

A neglected group of actors in the emergent East Asian regionalization are the private companies operating across borders, thus implementing regional coopera-tion and interdependence irrespective of political and ideological differences. The Japanese large manufacturing companies within closely connected *keiretsu* networks, the Korean *chaebol* as well as the *sogo shosha* were pioneers in investing in other East and Southeast Asian countries, and up to now have totally domi-nated the scene. During the last ten years, however, Japanese and Korean trans-national companies have been challenged by competitors originating from Taiwan, Hong Kong, Singapore, Malaysia and Thailand (Chen and Drysdale 1995; Dobson and Chia 1997). In a region well known for its strong centralized economic planning and active, or even authoritarian state apparatuses, these dispersed companies may bring about a true regional cooperation that the governments, despite extensive rhetoric about regionalization, have failed to achieve.

NOTES

1 There are a number of excellent recently published textbooks that explore these issues in depth, using various angles. Particularly recommended are Embree and Gluck (eds) 1997; Chuang 1997 (on China), Rubinstein (ed.) 1998 (on Taiwan); Lu 1996, Beasley 1995; Perez 1998, and Morris-Suzuki 1997 (on Japan); Suh 1998 (on modern Korea). The historical section rests to a large extent on these sources.
2 The same process had taken 58 years in Britain (1780–1838), and 47 years in the United States (1839–86) (Maddison 1991).

10 North American Regionalisms and Regionalization in the 1990s[1]

MARIANNE H. MARCHAND

The onset of globalization and the end of the Cold War have engendered signifi-cant changes in existing world order structures, ranging from the undermining of state sovereignty and the Westphalian state system to the disappearance of bipolar geopolitics. As a result we have witnessed some dramatic changes in international political practices and theorizing. At least since the mid-1980s a multitude of actors and issues, aided in particular by new information technologies such as the fax and e-mail/Internet, have manifested themselves forcefully in the international arena. These developments make it difficult nowadays to think about a state-centred international politics. Similarly, the emergence of new actors and issues has rendered the explanations provided by the traditionally state-centred realist paradigm virtually obsolete. In an attempt to capture these aforementioned changes, scholars have introduced a range of new concepts, including neo-medievalism (Kobrin 1999), transnational processes (Cox 1994), regionalism (Gamble and Payne 1996; Mansfield and Milner 1997), new regionalism (Hettne and Inotai 1994; Hettne and Söderbaum 1998; Hettne, Inotai and Sunkel 1999; see also introduction to this volume) or, alternatively, new regionalisms (Bøås, Marchand and Shaw 1999).[2]

Three questions will guide my inquiry into the recent push for regionalization in North America. First, who are the major actors behind it? Second, what kind of opposition has the creation of the North American Free Trade Agreement (NAFTA) stimulated? Third, what are some of the implications of North American regionalization? Together, the answers to these questions will illustrate that the process of regionalization is a complex, multidimensional phenomenon. On the basis of the answers, it will be argued that it is better to conceptualize in terms of multiple processes and forms of regionalization which may occur simultaneously and at similar speeds, but which can also (partially) overlap, reinforce – or be contradictory. Whereas regionalization is defined here as the process of increased political, social and economic integration, regionalism is understood both as an ideology and as a political project which is pursued by a range of more and less influential actors, including the state (for details, see Marchand, Bøås and Shaw 1999).

Historical Processes

When studying regionalization processes in North America, one of the first things that should be recognized is that there has always been regionalization in various degrees. One can go as far back as pre-Columbian times, with the Inca and Mayan empires, or the era of Spanish colonization, with its highly centralized and regionally organized long-distance trade, to find instances of regionalization. Since Latin America's independence during the first half of the nineteenth century, these earlier forms of regionalization have been replaced by yet another form, the basic parameters of which are still with us today. This so-called Inter-American system started with the Monroe Doctrine through which the United States claimed the sole right to intervene in Latin America. Throughout the nineteenth century the US was increasingly successful in keeping competing European states out and establishing its influence in Latin America, in particular in Central America and Mexico. With the US ascendance to global hegemony after the Second World War, its unquestioned hegemony in the region was also clearly established. During the 1930s and 1940s this US-created Inter-American system was being institutionalized through such arrangements as the Organization of American States (OAS) and the Rio Treaty.[3]

However, the Inter-American system was not the only expression of regionalization in the Americas. From the outset, the Monroe Doctrine has been countered by notions of pan-Americanism, espoused by the South American independence fighter Simon Bolívar and his followers. The ideas about and practices of alternative regional arrangements, including pan-Americanism, have continued to surface ever since. One can argue that this has resulted in contending forms of regionalization (challenging the US-centred Inter-American system) and an intricate layeredness and overlap of regional arrangements, such as the Central American Common Market (CACM), the Latin American Free Trade Association (LAFTA) and the Sistema Economico Latinoamericano (SELA) which emerged as part of Latin America's quest for a New International Economic Order. Moreover, Canada as well as the French- and English-speaking Caribbean have until recently been left out of the Inter-American system. And if we take a closer look at North

America, encompassing Canada, Mexico and the US, there has been relatively little formal regionalization. For instance, neither Canada nor Mexico joined the Rio Treaty, while the US was not formally involved in LAFTA. However, the lack of North American institutionalization changed dramatically during the late 1980s and early 1990s with the Canada–US Free Trade Agreement (CUFTA) and NAFTA. It is precisely this institutionalization which can be considered an important turning point in the regionalization of the North American political economy.

Although it goes beyond the scope of this chapter to discuss in detail the historical background of the process, it is clear that US hegemonic designs – globally, in the Americas and within the North American region itself – have been the decisive element in the direction, form and degree of North American regionalization and regionalisms. As will be clear from the remainder of this chapter, the ongoing regionalization of the North American political economy is mostly an elite-driven process. While elite-led, this process of regionalization has engendered considerable opposition from other sectors of society in the three respective countries. Groups opposed to NAFTA have attempted to counter this and related (elite-driven) projects, such as the Multilateral Agreement on Investments (MAI), by formulating alternative North American regionalism projects.

There are three major explanations for the sudden interest among the region's political and economic elites in constructing a regional free trade bloc. The first explanation focuses on the changes in the organization of production. Since the mid-1970s, large (American) transnational companies (TNCs) have embarked upon a major transformation of the organization of their production processes. This transformation was in part due to the perceived profit squeeze during the 1970s as well as to the advent of new means of communication and the increasing competition by Japanese and European firms during the 1980s (Cox 1987; Dicken 1992; Gereffi 1996). As a result, it is now common to speak of the 'global factory' which encompasses an integrated production process or global commodity chain (Gereffi 1996). Moreover, many TNCs are now considered 'post-Fordist' because they are producing according to the new exigencies of flexibilization, including 'just-in-time' delivery, keeping small inventories and using CAD/CAT technology to create an integrated (production) network (Dicken 1992; Schwartz 1994; Castells 1998). Although it may be too early to come to a definite conclusion, it appears that these changes in the organization of production have pushed firms to pursue simultaneously regional and global strategies (Gereffi 1996). According to Gary Gereffi, the emergence of global commodity chains leads to

> ... the emergence and transformation of regional divisions of labor that vary by industry. The linkages between countries within a region are the flows of investment capital, technology, goods, services, and people that make up commodity chains. Regional divisions of labor tend to be internally structured in similar ways: core

countries supply much of the technology, capital and high-end services (communications, transportation, and banking); semiperipheral nations do relatively advanced manufacturing and low-end services (e.g., quality control, component sourcing); and the periphery carries out low-wage, routinized production. (Gereffi 1996: 66)

In Gereffi's view there is such a regional division of labour in North America on the basis of existing global commodity chains:

An analogous [i.e. to East Asia] regional division of labor exists in North America, with the United States as the core, Canada and parts of northern Mexico as a semi-periphery (making a range of capital-intensive and high technology products like automobiles and their engines, computers, and electrical machinery), and the rest of Mexico plus a number of Central American and Caribbean nations forming the periphery. (Gereffi 1996: 66)

The spatial organization of the North American division of labour is further elaborated by Isidro Morales Moreno (1999), who distinguishes in Mexico alone five subregions which are hierarchically organized, while other parts of the country find themselves outside this regional division of labour.

In other words, TNCs operate increasingly on the assumption that their home market is not just restricted to a single state, but now encompasses an entire region. Managers and chief executive officers often perceive a strong regional base as imperative if their firm is to remain or become a global player and be able to face competition from other global firms. Hence, they not only benefit from existing *de facto* or *de jure* regional integration schemes, but are also likely to actively lobby for such schemes to be put in place.

A second explanation for increased regionalization in North America derives from the concerns of Mexican political elites in the Salinas de Gortari administration to ensure the continuation of its neoliberal policies in the future. Since the 1980s, Mexico has undergone profound economic (and some political) transformations. In part, these were the result of neoliberal economic policies which were introduced and implemented in response to the debt crisis and the conditionalities imposed by the International Monetary Fund (IMF) and several US administrations. Although his predecessor, Miguel de la Madrid, had already embarked on the introduction of neoliberal policies such as trade liberalization, deregulation and privatization, President Salinas took these much further. However, Salinas's major concern (and that of his advisers) was that his policies might be reversed by his successor as soon as he left office. Holding a power base among industrialists from northern Mexico, who had benefited considerably from his neoliberal policies, Salinas sought a way to ensure the continuation of his policies. He found this in the creation of NAFTA, which committed the Mexican state to neoliberal policies by treaty.

The third explanation focuses primarily on the perceived threat from the EU and East Asia. On the one hand, American companies were increasingly wary of competition from European, Japanese and South Korean companies. This was one of the reasons why they started to introduce Japanese management styles during the 1980s. On the other hand, the relaunching of the EU's integration process from 1985 on was seen as the creation of a 'Fortress Europe' by the US administration and the business community. In response, American economic and political elites started to search for an appropriate answer.

These three explanations should be seen as complementary accounts of the creation of NAFTA. Key economic and political actors in the US, Canada and Mexico found each other in this common project of 'neoliberal open regionalism' and ensured its adoption. Rather than the common perception that NAFTA mostly benefited US transnational firms, it should be stressed that Mexican political (and economic) elites as well as Canadian conservative elites also favoured the creation of NAFTA. How far this has resulted in the actual creation of a more permanent regionally based transnational network of elites is as yet unclear. What is clear, however, is that regional business elites pushed their political counterparts to establish an institutional framework for the regionalization of North America. As such, NAFTA can be seen as part of a larger politico-economic restructuring of the region.

NAFTA: Drawing the Battle Lines

For many analysts the decision to provide an institutional framework, facilitating the regionalization (or, as it is also called, continentalization) of the North American political economy, is in various respects a watershed (Mayer 1998). Not only did Salinas's overture to the Bush administration mark a significant shift in Mexico–US relations, but very few observers expected the Mulroney government to join the trade negotiations so soon after the tough opposition it faced over CUFTA (Mayer 1998).

In addition, the NAFTA negotiations have stimulated much opposition from various sectors within civil society, especially from environmental, labour, women's, consumer, human rights and pro-democracy groups. As a result, regional transnational activist networks, as well as coalition-building activities among a wide range of groups, have now emerged and continue to be mobilized around a broad agenda of trade and investment issues.

Finally, the actual outcome of the negotiations, the NAFTA treaty, is being exported by the US authorities who are using it, in particular, as a blueprint for their negotiations in multilateral contexts like MAI and the WTO, as well as in their bilateral dealings with countries in the hemisphere. The impact of NAFTA thus goes much further than the North American region. It has been turned into a tool for exporting a trade and investment agenda predicated upon the interests of the US business community.

As a result, participants, opponents and observers alike have paid much attention to the negotiation process and the ensuing implementation of NAFTA. Not surprisingly, the opposition to the treaty, and the way in which the negotiations were conducted, have significantly structured the outcome. As most of these negotiations were concentrated on Capitol Hill in Washington, the Canadian and Mexican actors were at a disadvantage (Marchand 1996b). As a rule they received less press coverage for their views and were structurally inhibited from taking an extreme nationalist position in the negotiations as this would have marginalized them immediately.

In identifying the major actors involved in the negotiations and decisions around NAFTA, it is important to realize that these simultaneously involved inter-state or intergovernmental negotiations and discussions within respective domestic political arenas. Many of the actors were, therefore, active in both processes, the boundaries of which would often get blurred. One example of such 'blurring' is that the Mexican government actually set up a NAFTA office in Washington, DC, in order to lobby key politicians on the Hill (Mayer 1998: 236).

Roughly one can distinguish the following key actors who have been involved in the negotiations around NAFTA and have supported its adoption and implementation:

- Transnationally oriented business elites (from all three countries) and their representative organizations, including: the North American Association of Manufacturers; the Business Roundtable, which consists of a select group of US chief executives; the US–Mexican Businessmen's Association; the Coordinadora de Organismos Empresariales de Comercio Exterior (COECE), a Mexican business lobby; and the Alliance of Manufacturers and Exporters (Canada). These groups represent firms which are often directing or are part of regionally integrated production networks or global commodity chains. Therefore, they tend to favour a limited regulatory framework which would facilitate the trade and investment activities of the firms which make up their membership.

- Political elites in the three countries who have been supportive of a neoliberal agenda. In the US and Canada these political elites have been advocating free trade to enhance the competitive position of North American firms. Despite the Mulroney government's early hesitation, Canadian conservatives, in particular, were supportive of NAFTA because it clearly fitted into their overall agenda for restructuring the Canadian political economy. In Mexico the young, techno-cratic, US-educated political elite connected to Salinas's clientelistic network[4] was also interested in ensuring a continued neoliberal restructuring of the Mexican political economy. Moreover, the Salinas administration's close ties with industrial and financial capital in the north of the country, the so-called Monterrey Group, provided an added incentive to turn its gaze northwards and start negotiating a trade and investment agreement.

Although less is known about the lobbying activities and involvement of Canadian and Mexican economic elites, it is clear that in the US the transnational sector of the business community has been involved from the beginning in defining the direction and strategies of the US administration during the NAFTA negotiations (Mayer 1998). From the sketchy information available, it seems that their Canadian and Mexican counterparts have also had an important input into the negotiations. It appears, then, that there was a clear 'coincidence of interests' between political and economic elites, both within the region as a whole as well as within the respective countries. It is mostly because of the combined efforts of these elites that the NAFTA treaty was ultimately ratified in all three countries, despite vehement opposition, particularly in the US (for details, see Mayer 1998).

As mentioned before, NAFTA can be seen as a watershed in terms of mobilizing civil society around trade and investment issues. Whereas opposition to NAFTA has existed and continues to exist in all three countries, the specific legislative requirements in the US concerning trade agreements provided ample opportunity for groups opposed to NAFTA to get organized. According to US law, the President has to get Congress approval for fast-track authority in order to be able to negotiate trade agreements effectively. Fast-track authority means that Congress cannot make any amendments to the proposed trade agreement, but only vote to either accept or reject it.

When the Bush administration first announced that it wanted to negotiate a free trade agreement with Mexico, US labour and, shortly afterwards, sectors of the environmental movement organized to oppose fast-track authority. Because of this early mobilization, which took the administration and business community by surprise, key figures within the anti-NAFTA campaign gained considerable experience. And although the opposition ultimately lost the fast-track fight, it was able to start building coalitions among very diverse groups very early in the process. As Frederick Mayer indicates, the experiences from the early fast-track fights informed the strategies of the opposition when the time came to vote on the NAFTA agreement:

> Opposition strategists recognized the challenge that faced them. If the contest over NAFTA turned out to be trade politics as usual they stood little chance. Their strength did not lie in the inside game of trade lobbyists and trade experts. To win, they would need to change the rules of the trade policy making game. They would

need to mount an outside campaign, mobilizing members of unions, environmental organizations, citizens groups, Ross Perot's followers, conservative and religious groups, and others in the general public to pressure Washington from the grassroots. (Mayer 1998: 224)

As a result of this, by the Spring of 1993 a wide range of opposition groups with a variety of motives and objectives had gathered steam for the anti-NAFTA fight. This broad opposition consisted of the following major groups, organizations and networks (for details, see Mayer 1998: 224–33):

- The American Federation of Labour and Congress of Industrial Organizations (AFL–CIO), the largest labour union in the US, found itself facing a major dilemma because it did not want to undermine Bill Clinton, the first democratic president in 12 years. As a result, the AFL–CIO launched a moderate campaign called 'Not This NAFTA' and spent relatively little on it.

- The Citizens' Trade Campaign (CTC), which is a broad coalition consisting of environmental, consumer, religious, civic and family farm organizations as well as unionists disappointed with the AFL–CIO's position. According to CTC's own information, the coalition is primarily interested in promoting 'environmental and social justice in trade policy' (Mayer 1998: 226).

- The Alliance for Responsible Trade (ART), a successor to the coalition originally organised by Pharis Harvey from the International Labor Rights Education and Research Fund. The CTC and ART worked together quite closely in the anti-NAFTA campaign.

- Ross Perot's 'United We Stand America' campaign consisted of a populist appeal to his supporters during the presidential election campaign. It was his now famous soundbite that NAFTA would create a 'giant sucking sound' of jobs leaving the country that was repeated *ad infinitum* by opponents. For Perot and his followers NAFTA had become symbolic of everything that was wrong with America and therefore it needed to be fought tooth and nail by using such diverse strategies as informercials and town meetings.

- Pat Buchanan and his 'America First' platform reflected an unprecedented right-wing opposition to free trade. Buchanan and his rather poorly organized group of likeminded supporters on the Republican right saw NAFTA as a threat to American society, because it would undermine US sovereignty and force the country to play a subservient role in the New International Economic Order brought about by globalization. Through his presence on the talkshow circuit Buchanan also managed to introduce a racist agenda focused on the threat of Mexican immigration.

Glancing at the broad range of opposition groups listed above, it should be clear that they did not all get along. Obviously, there was a clear divide between the groups situated on the left of the political spectrum and those on the right. While none of the activist groups were willing to speak to Buchanan and his supporters, there was some (middle-level) coordination between the CTC and the United We Stand America campaign of Ross Perot.

One of the main differences between the CTC, ART and to a certain extent the AFL–CIO, on the one hand, and the Perot and Buchanan campaigns, on the other, arose on the issue of how to deal with Canadian and Mexican counterparts. Whereas Perot and Buchanan were campaigning on nationalistic platforms (and, it should be added, so was part of the labour movement) some groups participating in the broad CTC and ART coalitions were interested in forming coalitions and networks with partners in Mexico and Canada. Since then, ART has continued to follow this line, while the CTC has been more focused on lobbying members of Congress. Yet, overall, the bulk of the attention of US opposition groups was directed at the domestic legislative process. In contrast, Canadian and Mexican opposition groups joined hands early on and coordinated their campaigns by sharing information and providing mutual support. Interestingly, while in the US the women's movement was not really involved in the activities around NAFTA, in Canada and Mexico various women's groups played key roles in both domestic campaigns and in the strengthening of transnational activist networks (Gabriel and Macdonald 1994; Marchand 1996b).

After Clinton came to power, the Democratic administration was faced with a dilemma. On the one hand, it could not really go back on the already concluded negotiations with the Canadians and Mexicans. On the other hand, it owed something to both labour and the environmental movement for their support during the elections. The decision by the Clinton administration to negotiate the NAFTA side agreements on labour and the environment can be seen as an important accomplishment of the US opposition to NAFTA. However, as these side agreements can be read as a compromise between more free-market-oriented Democrats (and Republicans) and the more progressive wing of the Democratic Party (tied to moderate labour and environmental interests), it did not satisfy the more outspoken opponents of NAFTA. As a result, these groups have not given up their opposition. They have merely changed their tactics, through using the complaints and dispute settlement procedures to challenge NAFTA, and by continuing to organize around trade and investment issues, such as MAI, the Free Trade Area of the Americas (FTAA) and the WTO. Recently, the opposition was able to convince the Congress not to extend fast-track authority to the Clinton administration to expand NAFTA by engaging in free trade negotiations with Chile. In pursuing these strategies and their objectives for a more socially and environmentally just regional development agenda, these coalitions have strengthened their connections and networks (often by making use of e-mail and the World Wide Web), and are actively involved in creating a regionalized transnational civil society.

Some Implications of North American Regionalization

The regionalization or continentalization of the North American political economy, in conjunction with the institutional framework of CUFTA and NAFTA, is leading to a deepening of the regional division of labour along neoliberal lines. Various metaphors have been employed to describe this, including the hub-and-spoke model or core–periphery model. While supporters of NAFTA have interpreted this regional division of labour as something positive, opponents have focused, in particular, on the social and economic costs of this neoliberal restructuring for ordinary people. For Mexico, in particular, the impact of a further deepening of the regional division of labour has been enormous. After the implementation of NAFTA its exports to the US market have improved considerably, although this has been somewhat offset by increased levels of imports (*Mexico and NAFTA Report,* 12 January 1999).

Yet, this supposedly positive picture alters when it appears that the exports have largely been a consequence of the exponential growth of the *maquiladora* or export-processing industry. As critics have argued, the *maquiladora* industry, now present not only at the border but throughout much of Mexico, does not provide for balanced long-term development as it locks Mexico into a primarily low-productivity, low-tech and labour-intensive strategy. Although conditions seem to be improving somewhat, much of the attention from anti-NAFTA groups has been directed at the *maquiladoras* for their bad labour conditions, sexual discrimination and unsound environmental practices. As a result, various complaints have been filed under the labour side agreement.[5]

Another problem with the Mexican economy is that, despite its export growth to the US and the growth rates of its economy as a whole, wages have been falling in real terms since 1993 (in addition to their steady decline in the 1980s). The unequal growth, both in terms of wages and in terms of the increased differentiation among subregions in Mexico, has even prompted the World Bank to caution against too much optimism. Apparently, the Mexican public is also not very optimistic, as a poll in January 1999 revealed: two-thirds believed that NAFTA had not brought anything positive to the country (*Mexico and NAFTA Report,* 12 January 1999).

Likewise, the restructuring brought about by the deepening of the regional division of labour has also affected communities, industries (in particular, forestry and fishing) and regional economies in Canada as well as parts of the manufacturing sector in the US (Public Citizens' Global Trade Watch 1998; Canadian Labour Congress 1999). It can be argued, then, that the continentalization or regionalization of the North American political economy is creating new social, political, and economic spaces as well as new forms of exclusion and inclusion along the lines of class, race, gender and ethnicity (Marchand 1999). The creation of such (social) spaces is discussed by M. Delal Baer:

> Ultimately, the three economies may blend into an integrated production network and share a universal, science-based culture that traces its roots to Francis Bacon. The modern denizens of urban Mexico will have more in common with their counterparts in Toronto and Chicago than with the campesinos in rural Oaxaca. (Baer 1991: 149)

As this comment by Delal Baer suggests, the deepening of the North American regional division of labour may also bring about an emerging regional identity associated with the 'modern denizens' of all three states. Although it may be too early to speak of the articulation of a North American regional identity, it is possible to see some initial signs of competing notions of a partial or emerging regional identity. The articulations of such identity are clearly not replacing existing identities, but rather complementary to them. Although still rudimentary, it is possible to discern at least two competing emerging identities. The first one is close to Delal Baer's notion of 'modern denizens' and can be defined as a regional cosmopolitan identity which is associated with such notions as individualism, mobility, networking and being a 'player' in the transnational sectors of the regional economy (Marchand 1999).

In contrast with this cosmopolitan regional identity, a second emerging regional identity is being articulated by various opposition groups. In their attempt to counter a neoliberal regional division of labour, they are formulating an alternative ethics-based regional identity around such notions as: corporate responsibility and accountability, social justice, democratic values, basic human rights and environmental/social sustainability. This alternative regional identity is based on the conceptualization of, in particular, the US–Mexican border as a connector rather than a separator, across which an ethics-based cross-border community can and should be built. Moreover, this ethics-based regional identity seeks to be inclusive. Expressions of such an ethics-based regional identity can be found in the documents and practices of the Hemispheric Social Alliance, which includes many of the coalitions and groups already mentioned but which actually extends beyond North America and addresses hemisphere-wide regional integration.[6]

Some Conclusions

The continentalization of the North American political economy, in combination with the institutional framework provided by CUFTA and NAFTA, shows that the present wave of regionalization and regionalism involves a complex set of political and economic factors. As the analysis above shows, it is too simple to understand regionalization as primarily a state-led or political phenomenon. Rather, one of the lessons to be drawn from North American regionalization is that it involves economic as well as political actors and that it results from a continuing interplay between political and economic processes. One of the questions which emerges as a result of this analysis is to what extent regionalization processes are emerging articulations of competing forms of capitalism – Japanese/East Asian, Rhineland/Continental European, and Anglo-American?

Another lesson which can be drawn from the North American experience is that within one geo-economic and one political space, different regionalism projects pursued by different actors may coexist. These different projects can lead to different expressions of regional identity. For instance, the North American elite-led regionalism project based on neoliberal principles is connected to an emerging regional identity based on notions of cosmopolitanism. On the other hand, opposition groups have formulated an alternative ethics-based regional identity around notions of social and environmental sustainability and social justice. These different projects and associated partial identities are also tied to different positions and policies toward those who may be excluded from the overall process of global/regional restructuring. The elite-driven neoliberal regionalism project is primarily focused on a minimalist institutional framework for trade and investment. The broad coalition of opposition forces is clearly supportive of a much more inclusive, socially driven regionalism project.

Finally, the negotiations around and implementation of NAFTA can be seen as a watershed. Not only did it provide, together with the CUFTA, the institutionalization of a new regional trade and investment regime, but it is now also used by the US authorities as a blueprint for multilateral and bilateral trade and investment negotiations. In other words, there is an attempt to export a trade and investment agenda, primarily informed by US business interests. By the same token, however, the negotiations around NAFTA have triggered an unprecedented mobilization of civil society around trade and investment issues. As a result, new coalitions and new forms of organizing have emerged. One example is the emergence of transnational activist networks, for instance surrounding the conditions in the *maquilado - ras*, which involves a coalition of labour, environmental and women's groups, and development, religious and human rights organizations. Another example is the rebellion by the Zapatistas. This rebellion is unique in various respects, because it has not only distanced itself from old-style guerrilla movements, but has triggered the emergence of a much more confident and self-conscious civil society in Mexico. In addition, the Zapatistas have included in their platform an explicitly indigenous and feminist agenda and have been rather innovative in their use of new media and means of communication (Castells 1997). In sum, North American regionalization reflects both the worst and the best of new regionalism.

NOTES

1 The final version of this chapter was written during my visit to SUM (the Centre for Development and Environment) at the University of Oslo. I wish to thank Morten Bøås and Helge Hveem for their hospitality and for allowing me to present some of my ideas during my stay. Their inputs, as well as those of other researchers at SUM, have helped me to further develop my thoughts on the questions of regionalization and regionalisms.

2 From this list of new concepts capturing world order phenomena I have deliberately excluded globalization, not only because it is a much debated term (so that no agreement exists on what it exactly entails), but also because most if not all of the concepts listed can be understood as highlighting specific dimensions of globalization. For a critique of the term globalization see Marchand (1996a) and Marchand and Runyan (2000).

3 For a classic overview and analysis of the Inter-American system, see Gordon Connell-Smith, *The Inter-American System*, Oxford: Oxford University Press, 1966.

4 In Mexican politics much attention has been paid to the transfer of power from so-called *politicos* to *técnicos*, i.e. foreign educated economists and business administration graduates who have not held any elected political positions until they reach the highest echelons of the political system. Generally, these technocrats or *técnicos* are not really in touch with what preoccupies the majority of the population as they tend to favour a neoliberal economic agenda.

5 For detailed information see the publications and/or web sites of such organizations as: American Friends Services Committee, Canadian Labour Council, Committee for Justice in the Maquiladoras, Common Frontiers (Canada), Human Rights Watch, Labornet, Public Citizen, Red Mexicana de Accion Frente al Libre Comercio (RMALC).

6 During 1–5 November 1999, the Hemispheric Social Alliance (HSA) organized an Americas Civil Society Forum in Toronto, which was held in conjunction with the FTAA ministerial meeting. As part of its activities the HSAhas produced a document (reflecting an ongoing collaborative process) entitled *Alternatives for the Americas: Building a People's Hemispheric Agreement*.

The Caribbean
Legacy and Change

ÅKE WIDFELDT

Only two general truths emerge from the study of history. One is that things tend to change much more, and more quickly, than one might think. The other is that they tend to change much less, and much more slowly, than one might think. The past hangs around longer and is more difficult to keep peacefully buried, even by strenuous efforts, than we believe. (Roberts 1993: 922)

The number of very small states in the world has increased considerably in the last few decades. Many of them are islands of very limited size and population. These tiny countries are sometimes referred to as *microstates* – a term which will be used in this chapter.[1] Today there are 18 independent microstates in the world.[2] Of them, six are situated in the Eastern Caribbean, together with several other small territories which still have not gained full independence but are to a great extent acting as nation-states. The dominance of small states and territories makes the Caribbean a unique region of the world and has greatly influenced the way regional cooperation has developed in the area (Thomas 1988: 302). This chapter will first present a short historical background and then look at the present international situation from a Caribbean point of view. The effects of globalization and US dominance in the region are particularly mentioned.

What actually is the Caribbean, and how can it be defined?[3] These questions, which will be discussed below, contain analyses of the organizational structure of the Caribbean region. This analysis starts with the fairly large Caribbean Basin – a term often used by the US government in the 1980s – and then narrows the focus to what one might call 'miniregions' within the Basin: the Organization of Eastern Caribbean States (OECS) and the (potential) Union of the Windward Islands.

In the Caribbean regionalization process several types of actors can be discerned.

There has been a mixture of initiatives, from the more officially political ones launched by colonial powers and independent governments to cultural and psychological factors operating within the realms of civil society, and to the many non-governmental organizations acting on regional levels. These various actors will be analysed in their different contexts.

Also, the causal perspective is borne in mind: why is there an urge to regionalize and – perhaps more relevant in the Caribbean case – why has the process been so problematic and complicated? This chapter looks for answers not only to these questions but also to the final one about future prospects for Caribbean regionalism, where the importance of popular participation is stressed.

As already indicated, the eastern Caribbean has the biggest concentration of small states and territories in the world. Therefore, the specific problems facing such small states are particularly pressing in this area, and they probably make the issue of regionalization more intricate and complicated than in other parts of the world. This is one reason why I have chosen to concentrate the analysis on these very small states when discussing Caribbean regionalization.

Historical Background

A small Caribbean island[4] was the first piece of land Columbus and his crew saw when they 'discovered' America. Their discovery led to the conquering and plundering of a whole continent and, what is more, the wiping out of a great proportion of the islands' indigenous population. This certainly meant 'the end of history' for these island cultures, and a new era started almost from scratch. Soon the infamous slave trade gradually created a society impressed with hierarchic structures and built on imported labour.

Even if the emancipation of slaves came in the nineteenth century, it is only the present generation of former slaves that has fully tasted the fruits of freedom and independence in the small Caribbean states. Most of the territories were released from their colonial ties after 1960. This means that centuries of slave and indentured labour experiences still have a great impact on a vast majority of the Caribbean population. To gain independence in this case is much more than just turning a switch and starting on your own. The many years of patron–client indoctrination have left their marks on the inhabitants, and dependence lingers on, even if the formal bonds are broken. This is actually a common experience in the study of history: 'The past hangs around longer and is more difficult to keep peacefully buried, even by strenuous efforts, than we believe' (Roberts 1993).

One such legacy from colonial times is the extreme fragmentation that characterizes the Caribbean. The colonial powers have left behind them a patchwork of mostly small states and territories. These were originally created to serve distant core centres in Europe. Economically, politically and culturally, the vertical connections are deeply rooted and are as difficult to break as the psychological ties mentioned above:

> [T]he closed circles of imperial political and trading systems induced the islanders to see each island as a world. As a result Fort de France was nearer to Paris than to Barbados, Havana nearer to Madrid than to Kingston, Kingston nearer to London than to Port-au-Prince. Although aeroplanes and wireless waves now span the distance, the isolation still exists in West Indian consciousness and will continue to do so until national history is set in the context of Caribbean history. (Parry, Sherlock and Maingot 1987: 150)

The bonds with Spain were broken fairly early, and two of its former colonies (the Dominican Republic and Cuba) became independent states in the nineteenth century. Linguistically the Spanish influence is still of great importance, however: together with Puerto Rico (a 'commonwealth' associated with the US) the two Spanish-speaking states have about 23 million inhabitants and demographically dominate the region. Another example of the early severing of ties with colonial powers is Haiti. It won independence from France as early as 1804 (the first black republic in the world) after a slave revolt, but has for long periods suffered from civil disorder, political instability and chaotic economic conditions. Like Cuba and the Dominican Republic it has been the subject of frequent US interventions. Not until now has the issue of regional cooperation come markedly to the fore: the Caribbean Community (CARICOM) is taking serious steps to accept Haiti and the Dominican Republic as members. This will signify a historic bridging of old linguistic gaps in the Caribbean.

The French *Départements d'Outre-Mer* (DOM) of Martinique and Guadeloupe are special cases. They were occupied by France in 1635 and got DOM status in 1946. People born there are French citizens and vote in French elections. Consequently, the two DOM are not members of any regional interstate organization although historically they are linked to their neighbours. Many people also speak almost the same French Creole as is used in St Lucia and Dominica, but French policy has belittled 'everything indigenous' (Sunshine 1988: 186). Economically, Martinique and Guadeloupe are closely linked to France, and the French ambition is to facilitate their economic assimilation into the EU. This has other effects: politically the DOM are becoming more isolated from the other parts of the region (Sutton 1995).

Economic ties with the former colonial powers are exemplified by the so-called Lomé Conventions, a system of trade agreements by which the European Community (now European Union) granted former colonies in Africa, the Caribbean and the Pacific (the ACP countries) preferential trade rights. The last convention

(Lomé IV) came into effect in 1990, to run to the turn of the century. The Windward Islands especially have derived benefit from the Lomé banana protocol that maintains a price over that of the 'dollar' bananas and provides a protected market for Windward bananas in the UK.[5] Direct financial aid is also provided under Lomé.

Although the Lomé system has been of considerable value to the ACP states, it has also been criticized by many. Some assert that the Lomé agreements are not genuinely bilateral but have the character of 'a concession by rich nations to poor ones' (Calvert 1994: 119). Others have called them 'a direct descendant of the mercantilist arrangement of empire', built on the belief that poverty and underdevelopment can be cured by 'incentive packages of trade, aid and investment' (Thomas 1988: 339–40). Behind these critiques there is a changing attitude to the issue of development aid. This change was expressed in 1993 by the then EC's acting Director-General for Development, Peter Pooley, who spoke about 'kleptomaniac ACP states'. He questioned 'whether systems of North–South relations based on the postcolonial and Cold War eras should be maintained after the expiry of Lomé IV in 2000' (*Caribbean Insight*, August 1993: 2).

Acting through the WTO, the US has also joined the critics of Caribbean preferential banana exports to the European Union. In April 1997, a WTO Dispute Panel ruling criticized the EU banana import regime as an act of discrimination and protectionism. The panel's findings were based on the claims of the US, Ecuador, Guatemala, Honduras and Mexico and will, when implemented, deal a severe blow to Windward banana exports in the near future (WTO 1997).

Lobbying by powerful banana TNCs – particularly Chiquita – was one of the reasons for strong US action in this case (*Banana Trade News Bulletin*, July 1997: 3). As early as 1995 the European Commission was aware of the activities of this lobby: 'the main preoccupation seems to be with expanding the EU market share of certain US firms rather than with ensuring Caribbean bananas a market outlet' (Delegation of the European Commission in Barbados and the Eastern Caribbean, 1995).

For the Caribbean microstates, dependency on foreign aid is still a dominant feature of their development efforts, but they are also fully aware that something should be done about this predicament. A cornerstone of a new, more independent development strategy is what is often referred to as 'popular participation': 'the majority must be the subject and not the object of their own history' (Xavier Gorostiaga, quoted in Thomas 1988: 361). Everybody agrees that increased regional co-operation is a must, but in this context initiatives must have strong support among the people. And often people have actually shown the way:

> The West Indian people have not waited on Governments; they have integrated – in their own informal but highly effective way. Indeed, through culture and sport and

non-governmental activity of every kind, they have been steadily building structures of unity of their own. (West Indian Commission 1992: 173–4)

Before returning to these issues, I would like to emphasize that even the building of such 'structures of unity' takes place in an increasingly complicated international environment, with effects on regionalization that must be taken into account. To this international situation and its relation to the Caribbean I now turn.

The Present International Context

For centuries the Caribbean has been very much involved in and affected by the development of international relations. Even during the Cold War between the superpowers the frontiers between the combatants were moved to the region: Cuba in the early 1960s and Grenada twenty years later. Now, on the threshold of the twenty-first century, when traditional military security issues no longer predominate, the effects of globalization on the Caribbean are increasingly being discussed.

Among the many aspects of globalization that Caribbean analysts concern themselves with, the ever-faster exchange of resources, technology and information is perhaps the most conspicuous (Honychurch 1997: 13; Giddens 1994: 42, 80). Another is the increasing environmental awareness of 'only one earth', and that the effects of pollution of the environment – particularly critical for small island states – cannot be stopped by fortifying national borders or investing in traditional security measures (Honychurch 1997; Kennedy 1994: 336). As a matter of fact, there seems to be agreement among many scholars that globalization means that the concept of nation-state is called in question and that views on its size, governance and independence are being changed (Giddens 1994: 140, 191). Relatively small political communities will be forming a network of regional, continental and economic associations. This is a vision of an increasingly fragmented world where the nation-state has lost its 'privileged position' (Horsman and Marshall 1995: 264) and 'a rethinking of the nation-state concept is ... necessary' (Hettne and Inotai 1994: 36).

What is actually taking place might be seen as a kind of 'double movement': a dissolution of weak nation-states, accompanied by the strengthening of ethnic groups and the awakening of indigenous peoples, coincides with the forging and evolution of regional blocs in many parts of the world. This regionalization is creating both opportunities and risks for areas like the Caribbean with its concentration of small states. The risk has to do with the smallness of the region itself and its dependence in part on 'uncompetitive' agricultural products. The opportunity lies in the above-mentioned development towards small political units in a globalized world.

Of special importance to the Caribbean is the development of NAFTA and the

EU. This is seen as a threat as long as the Caribbean is left out, and its access to traditional markets reduced (Payne and Sutton 1993). In 1989 A. N. R. Robinson, at that time Prime Minister in Trinidad and Tobago, expressed this problem at a CARICOM meeting when he said that the Caribbean could run the risk 'of becoming a backwater, separated from the main current of human advance into the twenty-first century' (Payne and Sutton 1993: 26). These feelings have often created a sense of desperation in the Caribbean states and sometimes made them intensify their efforts to improve regional cooperation.

As already indicated, the process of globalization offers the Caribbean region a unique chance of evading the isolated 'backwater'. A prerequisite would be the strengthening of regional networks and integration efforts. The rapid extension of Internet resources is supposed to be of great help. The Caribbean is coming 'on-line' at an increasing pace: in 1994 there was a growth of about 50 per cent in Internet connectivity, and new World Wide Web sites multiply continuously. Unlike the industrial revolution, which did not have a great direct effect on the Caribbean (which continued to be dependent on agriculture), the information revolution is supposed to be of great and immediate importance for the region (Roundtable Ec. InfoNet 1996).

Yet the information and communication technologies are no panacea. As Gillian Marcelle puts it, 'they will not in themselves solve the fundamental problems of economic malfunctioning ... nor the even more serious problems of political ... leaderlessness' facing the Caribbean (Marcelle 1997: 2). It must also be emphasized that the information age has increased the dominance of the US in the region. Many Internet connections and an overwhelming proportion of the media channels are of US origin, and locally or regionally produced programmes and websites are still fairly few.[6]

On the other hand, current US economic and political engagement in the Caribbean is half-hearted. The exceptions are – besides the issue of drug trafficking, which will be dealt with further on – Cuba and, possibly, Haiti. Although the Clinton administration has tried to normalize US–Cuban relations, incidents before the US elections in 1996 increased tensions and stirred up Cold War sentiments.[7] The global political situation is now quite different, however, and the new Cuban 'crisis' has already faded away. The engagement in Haiti has been part of a United Nations mission and, as in Somalia, the US reluctantly had to execute its role as the only remaining superpower. Today there is evidently a decline in the US Haitian engagement: in April 1996 the Republican-dominated Congress froze an amount of aid money earlier allotted to Haiti and in the same month the last US troops of the UN mission left the country (*Caribbean Insight*, 1996: 9).

In the long run, however, US interests in the Caribbean will prevail, and US ambitions to have full control of its backyard will grow stronger during periods of increased security threats. Ever since 1823 the US has maintained that the Western Hemisphere shall remain 'American', that is, in practice controlled by the US. President James Monroe's statement that year – later to be called the 'Monroe Doctrine' – meant among other things that every attempt by European powers to intrude into the Western Hemisphere would be regarded as 'dangerous to [the] peace and safety' of the US (Williams 1970: 411). A later corollary of the Doctrine authorized the US to intervene in the same area whenever it found it necessary and to act as an international policeman (Williams 1970: 422).

The right to intervene in the Caribbean to protect its vital interests has thus been deeply rooted in US foreign policy (Calvert 1994: 18–19). As modern Caribbean history shows, such interventions have often been made against the will of the majority of the world's people and international organizations.[8] The weak regional formations in the area have also been ignored or manipulated. The US prefers to deal with each country separately. Unless new, more significant groupings (like a fully developed Association of Caribbean States) are formed, such bilateral approaches will continue to dominate US Caribbean policies (Sutton 1993: 291).

There are, however, exceptions to the bilateral approach. One was the so-called Caribbean Basin Initiative (CBI) proposed to the US Congress in 1982 and signed into law the next year. It was a 'trade and aid package' designed by the Reagan regime. The US-friendly states in the region were favoured while other countries got little or – as happened to Cuba, Nicaragua and Grenada – were completely excluded (Payne 1997). Notwithstanding its name, the CBI has been criticized for actually encouraging bilateral arrangements with the US (Ramsaran 1989: 142).

The other exception is of a different character. As already mentioned, the US cultural invasion via media is covering the whole region – increasingly even Cuba (*Caribbean Insight*, 1998: 5). The 'Yankeefication' of Caribbean states has been taking place continuously (Sunshine 1988: 115, 168). Lennox Honychurch talks about 'changes in patterns of consumerism' (Honychurch 1997: 11). These changes are 'to a great extent caused by television advertising and glitzy programmes … fed into local television systems' (*ibid.*), creating expectations that cannot be fulfilled in a 'harsh' economic environment. The consequence is widespread frustration.

Therefore, the issue of a common Caribbean culture supporting the existence of 'Caribbeanness' is of great importance when it comes to creating a viable regional organization. The West Indian Commission was certainly aware of this when it made recommendations on how to bring about 'a distinctive cultural expression' as a part of a strengthened region (West Indian Commission 1992: 156).

Whether such 'cultural' expressions have permeated the more official attempts at building regional interstate bodies is questionable. Nevertheless, these organizations are important building blocks of the Caribbean post-war regionalization edifice: they are scrutinized below.

Interstate Organizations in the Caribbean Region

The Caribbean is an area which could be described by using Ibsen's metaphor of an onion consisting of a number of layers covering each other, where (in this case) each layer represents a regional interstate organization or formation. Geographically, the uniting factor is the Caribbean Sea, and consequently the Caribbean should constitute all the islands in this sea. Politically and historically, it is a more complex area, however, with the remnants of colonial fragmentation being first devoured by a US overlay and after that left in a state of bewilderment. Let us enumerate four layers, starting from the outside.

1. The Caribbean Basin

This consists of 'all countries washed by the Caribbean Sea'. Even if these states have many things in common, they are linguistically diverse, and some still have colonial ties separating them from the rest. Formalized cooperation has earlier taken place within the OAS, but has been dominated by the US.

A new Caribbean Basin body was set up in 1994 when the Association of Caribbean States (ACS) was formed in Cartagena, Colombia.[9] Its first summit meeting was held in Port of Spain, Trinidad, in August 1995. The ACS has 25 members so far, comprising Cuba, the Dominican Republic, Haiti, Costa Rica, El Salvador, Guatemala, Honduras, Nicaragua, Panama, Colombia, Mexico and Venezuela and the 13 independent CARICOM countries (see below). It is focusing on trade, tourism and transport, stressing trade liberalization and preparing a regional tourism strategy. Intraregional air and shipping services will be improved and travel formalities for citizens of member states simplified. There is hope that the US will eventually join the ACS through Puerto Rico and the US Virgin Islands. The ACS summit also issued a declaration of principles saying that the process of integration should take place

> in a climate of respect for the sovereignty and territorial integrity of [the member] states, the right of [their] peoples to self-determination, the rule of law, the adherence to democratic principles, the observance of human rights and the peaceful resolution of disputes. (Quoted in *Caribbean Insight*, 1995: 12)

Anthony Payne has presented a different regional analysis. He describes what he calls a form of 'hub and spoke' governance in North America where Washington DC is the hub and a number of US states (such as Florida and Texas) act as 'entry-points to the spokes' (from Mexico or the Caribbean states, for example). Payne asserts that these latter states have realized that it is easier to penetrate the US *'within* the US political system' than to try and influence the President or his ministers directly. He introduces what he calls 'Caribbean America', a region comprising the northern part of the Caribbean and the southeastern states of the US (Payne and Gamble 1996). Payne's model implies a new design of Caribbean regionalization where older constellations of a more colonial mould will probably be broken up. One of these is dominated by English-speaking remnants of the British Empire.

The Anglophone Caribbean, most of which consists of former British colonies and is therefore often referred to as the Commonwealth Caribbean, has been the arena of several attempts at regionalization in the last half-century. In colonial times a Federation of the West Indies was founded (1958), but it disintegrated after only four years when the two major member territories, Trinidad and Jamaica, gained independence. Six years later, the Caribbean Free Trade Agreement (CARIFTA) was formed to lower trade barriers between its four members. It gradually expanded and had 13 members by 1971.

2. The Caribbean Community (CARICOM)

We have now reached the second layer of the onion. The Caribbean Community (CARICOM) was established in 1973 as a follow-up of CARIFTA. It was designed to promote 'functional cooperation' in tourism, regional transport, health care and scientific research. Furthermore, the ambition was to coordinate foreign policies within the community.

Today CARICOM comprises 14 states, most of them former British colonies.[10] Geographically, they are widely spread, from Belize in the west to Suriname in the east. In addition to this geographical diffusion, there are several other obstacles to the forming of CARICOM as a viable regional organization:

- With one exception, it is, so far, exclusively Anglophone, leaving important parts of the Caribbean out.

- Its total population is small (8.6 million). Consequently, its internal market suffers from restricted economies of scale.

- The big differences in the size of national markets have made the smaller states very dependent on the leading economies, particularly Trinidad and Tobago. This imbalance has caused problems for CARICOM.[11]

- Notwithstanding its acknowledged agricultural capacity, CARICOM as a whole is still extremely dependent on food imports. As Ramesh Ramsaran puts it: 'the region continues to produce what it does not consume, and consume what it does not produce' (Ramsaran 1989: 175).

- Bilateral approaches still seem to be preferred in contacts with countries outside CARICOM. Thus, Jamaica and Trinidad and Tobago have considered applying separately for membership in NAFTA (*Caribbean Insight*, August 1994: 2).

Although there have been periods of low activity and disunity among the CARICOM countries, the situation today to some extent gives rise to greater optimism. Lately, several small steps towards economic integration have been realized, among them the final removal of all licensing requirements for intra-regional trade in 1995. In the same year several CARICOM currencies (including the Eastern Caribbean dollar) were made convertible to facilitate intraregional trade (*Caribbean Insight*, August 1995: 4). Furthermore, the issue of implementing a common external tariff has recently made progress and efforts to expand the organization have eventually been successful.

An important step was taken in 1995 when Dutch-speaking Suriname was accepted as a member. Language barriers have been strong in the Caribbean, and they must be overcome if regionalization is to be implemented. The Dominican Republic and Haiti are also interested in joining CARICOM. Although they have earlier been considered too big and 'would be "disruptive" to its operation', according to CARICOM officials (*Caribbean Insight*, March 1995: 1), a remarkable change of opinion has evidently now taken place. In July 1997 a CARICOM summit decided to admit Haiti as its fifteenth member (*Caribbean Insight*, August 1997: 3). A final agreement will probably be signed soon.

As already mentioned, even an expanded CARICOM is in itself too small to play a substantial role in the possible regionalization of the political economy of the Western Hemisphere. Therefore, the new move towards the ACS is of great importance for the Caribbean states. This problem of size has inconvenienced the Caribbean economies ever since they gained independence. The many microstates in the area are in a particularly difficult situation when and if it comes to building a bigger regional bloc like the ACS. Needless to say, their bargaining power in potential negotiations is very weak. A way out of this dilemma would be more pooling of resources between the microstates. To some extent, this is actually taking place in the inner layers of the Caribbean onion, to which we now turn.

3. The Organization of Eastern Caribbean States (OECS)

The OECS comprises seven microstates, all of them also members of CARICOM: Antigua, Dominica, Grenada, Montserrat, St Kitts/Nevis, St Lucia, and St Vincent and the Grenadines. (The British Virgin Islands is an associated member.) In May 1998, the OECS heads of government decided that preparations should be speeded up to accept Barbados as a member. A joint task force is working on the matter (*Caribbean Insight*, July 1998: 11).

The OECS is 16 years old and active in many fields, particularly economic affairs where a common currency (the Eastern Caribbean dollar), an Eastern Caribbean Central Bank and an Economic Affairs Secretariat serving the member states are manifest examples of well-functioning cooperation. It is evident that the more homogeneous set-up of the OECS compared with CARICOM makes it easier to handle. Intensified cooperation can be noticed in several areas such as the judiciary, natural resources, fisheries and agricultural diversification. The forming of an OECS union is also on the agenda and a Regional Constituent Assembly has had several meetings, but unification does not seem to be feasible in the near future.

Among the OECS member states, the four Windward Islands (Grenada, St Vincent and the Grenadines, St Lucia and Dominica) have seriously been discussing forming a union. This brings us to the lowest level of Caribbean regionalization efforts, the innermost layer of the onion.

4. A Windward Islands Union

A Windward Islands Union would entail the creation of a four-island state with about 450,000 inhabitants. Geographically the four parts are adjacent to each other, forming the lower part of the long arc of the Lesser Antilles.[12] In the early 1990s, a series of meetings of a Windward Islands Regional Constituent Assembly (RCA) were held (*Exploring the Parts* 1991), and a proposal for a president-led Windward Union was adopted in 1992. Since then, very little has happened, however. Although all political parties and many interest groups were represented in the RCA, evidently the realization of the project has run into difficulties.

This is a common experience among the Caribbean microstates, where the difference between rhetoric and political action seems to be considerable, particularly concerning issues of integration. Why is it so? Explanations might be found among what Ramesh Ramsaran calls 'internal factors':

> The desire in some cases to guard too jealously the newly won political sovereignty … may have been too strong to accommodate the economic arrangements which integration dictated. Perhaps these ambitions came too early after independence when countries were still formulating and consolidating domestic arrangements. The legal framework too, may have been too imitative of that adopted by the developed countries, and, therefore, almost ignored the historical experience and the social, economic and political situations in the regions. (Ramsaran 1989: 169)

Again, the effects of the colonial legacy are to blame.[13] It is a legacy which has marked not only the Caribbean societies but also the minds of many of their leaders:

> Often it stops there, remaining just words. The eloquent rhetoric is … an example of the colonial heritage, an imitation of the old European masters speaking in Parliament

or at banquets in Lancaster House. The 'poor and powerless' are far away, busy working for survival, not very interested in development strategies served from above. (Widfeldt 1992: 153)

As colonial political domination was gradually reduced, the international relations of the Caribbean island territories changed. Situated in the 'backyard' of the US and near vital shipping lanes they have at times been drawn into the maelstrom of superpower policies but have at other times – just now, for example! – also run the risk of being forgotten and ignored in the global political economy.

In summary, the Caribbean regional actors are trying to realize integration at different levels. The ACS, so far at its formative stage, still has a very long way to go but will become of global importance if it can be a functioning unit. Payne's 'Caribbean America' is an example of a new system of governance within the political economy of globalization (Payne and Gamble 1996). CARICOM is the oldest regional organization in the area but until recently has consisted of Anglophone states and has met with substantial difficulties in the implementation of economic decisions such as the introduction of a common external tariff (CET). At the micro level, the OECS, although it is fairly young, has achieved quite impressive results, noticeable in everyday life in the member states. This form of cooperation is of great interest for the study of microstates as it is the biggest regional grouping of such states in the world. It is still a tiny constellation, however, heavily dependent on its more powerful neighbours and distant postcolonial power centres. Even if Barbados joins the OECS this will not mean a big change – definitely not from a global point of view.

After this overview of the more 'official' interstate approaches to regionalization in the Caribbean I now return to the 'informal' ways of 'building structures of unity' through different cultural links and via non-governmental organizations.

Cultural Links

[T]he region comprises one culture area in which common factors have forged a more-or-less common way of looking at life, the world, and their place in the scheme of things. All the societies of the Caribbean share an identifiable *Weltanschauung*, despite the superficial divisions that are apparent ... the Caribbean peoples, with their distinctive artificial societies, common history, and common problems, seem to have more in common than the Texan and the New Yorker, or the Mayan Indian and the cosmopolite of Mexico City. (Knight 1990: xv)

In most Caribbean states there is an ambiguity when it comes to national or regional identification. A majority of them are relatively young as independent states, and this means that national feelings are not deeply rooted in the minds of their citizens. At the same time, however, the 'independence euphoria' is still very strong, and, particularly among many politicians, there is – quite understandably – a reluctance to give up something that one has recently gained.

The 'common way of looking at life' in the Caribbean societies mentioned above should not be forgotten, however. There are many examples of this. When you travel from island to island it is easily discerned among the many features of social life. A ride on the local mini-bus, filled with strong calypso or reggae music, is a similar experience whether you are in Dominica or Barbados. In Kingstown or St George's you are equally impressed by the many well-dressed school children in uniforms reflecting their parents' commitment to the education of their children. Since the period of emancipation, schooling for the children has been a fundamental thing in Caribbean society, because everybody knows that education is essential in the struggle towards real independence.[14]

There are also strong cultural links between the Caribbean countries in such fields as sports and music. In cricket, for instance, there is certainly a manifest West Indian identity in the Anglophone states. Several other areas of culture and civil society demonstrate a pronounced 'regionness'. Since colonial times, education has been a regional issue in the Commonwealth Caribbean, with the University of the West Indies (UWI) as the leading organization.[15] It now has campuses in Jamaica, Barbados and Trinidad & Tobago, and several smaller branches in other islands run by a Department of Continuing Studies (Dyde 1992).

Caribbean religious organizations as a rule cooperate on a regional basis. The Caribbean Conference of Churches (CCC), with its headquarters in Barbados, is an ecumenical organization with a particular commitment to the social and economic improvement of poor people in the region. It encourages participatory development approaches and self-help community initiatives. CCC is also engaged in social research into Caribbean society and publishes reports in various fields. It maintains a wide coverage of the region, including Cuba, Haiti and the Dominican Republic, for example. *Caribbean Contact*, CCC's monthly paper, was published for 21 years until 1994 when publication was discontinued. It was a unique voice in the Caribbean media chorus, where its role was that of a pioneer 'seeking to foster a spirit of regionalism in a part of the world where insularity abounds in the midst of a noticeable strong anti-integration climate' (*Caribbean Contact*, August 1994: 14).

Other cultural elements supporting the 'spirit of regionalism' in the Caribbean are reggae and calypso music and the celebration of carnivals, especially the one in Trinidad which draws big contingents from other parts of the region (Sunshine 1988: 239–43). Inter-island migration also contributes to breaking the insular bonds inherited from the fragmented colonial society and to increasing the feeling of togetherness (Sunshine 1988: 238).

When it comes to possibilities for civil society to influence the creation of viable regional structures the issue of popular participation is essential. In the Caribbean case, formal democracy has not been very successful in engaging the majority of the people in projects such as regionalization efforts. The broad commitment is missing and people's needs and ideas have not been consulted. But there are other ways to bring about increased popular activity in this field by listening to the 'voice of the people'.

The 'Voice of the People'

> If we are to have democracy in the Caribbean, then the voice of the people must be heard. The practising of formal democracy every five years is not enough. It will never create the conditions necessary for sustained socio-economic change. The working class, the peasantry and others who are in effect disenfranchised must find a way to participate fully in the affairs of the state. Instead of having policy imposed from above, the people must be given an opportunity to participate in the making of policy. (Young 1991: 18–19)

Within development theory applicable to the Caribbean the concept of 'participatory development' is of great interest. During the last 20 years it has become one of the catchwords of the international 'development language'. As Anthony Hall puts it: '"participation" has become an article of faith, a fundamental prerequisite for any successful project or programme' (Hall 1988: 91).

As participation builds on the empowerment of local community members it can be seen as a challenge or threat to the state. State responses to the participatory development approach have therefore often been suspicious and reluctant. According to James Midgley, 'community participation is deeply ideological', because it has its roots in theories about the ideal society. It is usually anti-state, criticizing the state as a rigid and bureaucratic institution. Participation means the real and direct involvement of people in development activities (Midgley *et al.* 1986: 4–9).

From a participatory developmentalist's view a new and different type of state attitude is needed, where people at all levels of society are encouraged to take part in decision making and where special efforts are made to empower the poorest sections of society (*ibid.*: 43–4). As already indicated, this is a rare phenomenon, and in the Anglophone Caribbean the political system does not seem to encourage initiatives from below:

> The mechanisms for popular participation … all remain … under the control of the local state. Within the political arena, no more than two political parties predominate, parties that long ago reached an accommodation with the state. (Young 1991: 8)

It is in situations like these that an interest in the role of non-governmental organizations comes to the fore. There are a lot of NGOs active in the Caribbean states and many of them work on a regional basis. Some have actually grown out of the needs and problems of common people:

> hard-pressed farmers, indigenous people losing access to their lands, immigrants to urban areas who lack housing and jobs, exploited factory workers, and women who suffer most from structural adjustment. (McAfee 1991: 215)

In the Caribbean microstates there are many examples of NGOs committed to participatory development and the empowerment of the people concerned. Some – like the Small Projects Assistance Team (SPAT) in Dominica – work directly among the poor and the powerless, others are strongly linked to them. In many NGOs women are key actors. Government-initiated programmes need to be complemented by NGO initiatives. This seems to be of special importance when it comes to regionalization activities and is shown by the various regional NGOs that have been working for quite a long time in the area.[16]

There are many indications that such NGOs have unique chances of playing important roles in a microstate environment, where distances are short and people are better acquainted with each other. At the same time, their well-documented experience of regional cooperation on different levels is of great help when it comes to creating a stronger Caribbean region. If a vitalization of the political system could take place and a more participatory approach could be applied, it would be possible for the NGOs to work as catalysts for an increased popular commitment to solving development problems both within the states and on a regional basis. Among these problems, the question of sustainability has become monumentally significant in recent years.

The adjective *sustainable* has found its way into most aspects of modern life, from the designing of technical gadgets to the growing of crops and social engineering. Since the Brundtland Commission (or World Commission on Environment and Development, WCED) published its report *Our Common Future* in 1987, the term has spread over the globe and is now commonly used not only by state authorities and international organizations but also by ordinary people in their daily lives (Smith 1996: 304). The Rio Summit in 1992 (UNCED) was a clear manifestation of this trend, and as a result Agenda 21 – its action programme – is now being discussed even in local communities worldwide. And market forces have learnt quickly, as usual: sustainable things are becoming increasingly easy to sell. Sustainability is a winning trademark.

For small island states the issue of sustainability is very important (Smith 1996: 307–8; Honychurch 1997: 4–5). There are many reasons for this:

- The ecological consequences of climate change will be severe – such hazards as sea-level rise and an increased number of hurricanes.

- The pressure of population, particularly on forests and coastal areas, causes more damage in microstates with their limited resources.

- Waste management becomes more hazardous and expensive. This problem is aggravated by extensive tourism.

- Rich biodiversity is threatened in these often-isolated islands with many endemic species.

Within CARICOM, the establishment of a Caribbean Environmental Health Institute (CEHI) was initiated about 20 years ago, and in 1988 it became a legal entity with CARICOM's ministers responsible for health as its governing body. Among the objectives of CEHI are the provision of technical and advisory services to member states in all areas of environmental management and the promotion of 'applied research relevant to the environmental problems of the Caribbean Region'. For the regional NGOs active in this field – like the Caribbean Natural Resources Institute (CANARI, see below) – the establishment of CEHI has entailed increased support, for example through information about their activities via CEHI's homepage on the Internet (http://www.cehi.org.lc/).

After the Rio Summit there has been an upsurge of environmental initiatives in the Caribbean, and in 1994 a follow-up of UNCED was held in Barbados, the UN Global Conference on Sustainable Development in Small Island Developing States. The conference was of great importance for the strengthening of cooperation between the islands involved, but it also showed that the Northern donor states are not sufficiently committed to achieving sustainable development on a global scale (Smith 1996: 314). For the Caribbean microstates this was another indication that they must try to improve their bargaining position in an increasingly competitive world where they are powerless as individual actors.

At the Barbados conference there was also a parallel NGO meeting called the Global Village. It presented an extensive Action Plan to the delegates at the official conference, a plan that again demonstrated the strong NGO commitment to the issue of sustainability in small island states (*ibid.*).

In their fight for survival, the Caribbean microstates are caught in a 'competitive export production cycle' with detrimental effects on the environment:

> increased cultivation of watershed areas, erosion-prone slopes and other marginal lands... has led to ... the use of damaging pesticides, and to quick-result farming methods that depend on high-cost chemical fertilizers and deplete soil fertility. (McAfee 1991: 189)

This is particularly the case in the banana industry that is so vital for the Windward Islands. Again, an important initiative has been taken by a regional NGO: the Windward Island Farmers Association (WINFA). The combined threats of increased competition from 'dollar bananas' and environmental degradation have made WINFA look for alternative modes of production. At a seminar in August 1997 it launched the idea of producing 'fair trade' bananas in the Windward Islands and applying for the inscribing of WINFA members in the Fair Trade Banana Register. WINFA is also working for 'a more diversified, less banana dependent economy' (WINFA 1997: 11). Fair trade bananas are now sold in several European countries, including Sweden. Fair Trade Marketing wants to remove unfair trading structures and improve the producers' social, environmental and economic conditions. Producers and workers are given direct access to markets and encouraged to use 'environmentally friendly production methods' (*ibid.*).

Representatives of Caribbean NGOs recommend a 'trisectoral' approach to sustainable human development where governments, NGOs and the private sector cooperate. It is important that the NGOs become integral parts in the process (French 1994: 28). This makes the grassroots more active and engaged in development projects:

> Placing people as a central element in this issue permits a more insightful appreciation of the problem of environmental protection and promotion *vis-à-vis* sustainable development. This consequently enhances our capacity to arrive at and implement more appropriate solutions and programmes for development. (Gill 1994: 12)

As mentioned before, Caribbean NGOs are already working on a regional basis, often in the forefront when it comes to vital issues of development. One such NGO is the Caribbean Natural Resource Institute (CANARI), active all over the insular Caribbean to promote the development and adoption of policies that support increased participation and collaboration in natural resource management. Another is the Caribbean Conservation Association (CCA) which has conservation and the 'wise use of the region's natural and cultural resources' on its agenda (CCA homepage).

One of the regional industries that is particularly dependent on natural resource management is tourism – a branch of business that is often considered a threat to sustainable development.

Tourism – a Key Development Strategy

With all the problems facing agriculture and manufacturing industry, tourism is now seen by many Caribbean states as the panacea for development in the region. A regional agency working in this field is the Caribbean Tourism Organization (CTO), with its headquarters in Barbados. It is trying to combine many different objectives in its policy statement. Sometimes the objectives seem incompatible, however: the CTO both want to 'increase the value and volume of tourism flows' to the region and to 'ensure a harmonious interaction between tourism and the social and natural environment'. The concept of sustainability is not mentioned, neither are the limits to tourism exploitation that are so obvious in small island states (www.caribtourism.com/).

As Klaus de Albuquerque has pointed out, the only viable tourism option for the Caribbean is a model (applied in Bermuda) 'with ... stringent controls on numbers and ... tough environmental regulations' (www.access.digex.net/ ~warlock/ecin/ecinfp.htm). Unfortunately, the present development in the region – with continuous growth of tourist (stay-over) arrivals (average annual rate of 4.9 per cent during 1980–96) and cruise passenger visits (6.6 per cent) (www.cep.unep. org/cast/tourism/htm), and with Cuba's concentration on mass tourism – does not take sustainability into account.

There are examples of an increased awareness of the need for sustainable tourism in the Caribbean, however. The Environmental and Coastal Resources Project (ENCORE) has been working both regionally (OECS) and locally in co-operation with regional authorities, USAID and various NGOs in such fields as environmental public awareness and education and environmental monitoring. Tourism is on ENCORE's agenda and, while working within tourism, it asserts that 'cooperation between public, private and community interests conserves the natural resource base and enhances biodiversity'; it wants to mobilize the 'vastly under utilized energies and expertise of community-based organizations and NGOs' (Widfeldt 1996: 153). As mentioned above, CANARI is also running pro-grammes on tourism on a regional basis. One is about the designing of 'Heritage Tourism Projects for Rural Development' (CCAhomepage).[17]

The Caribbean Hotel Association (CHA), which has created a subsidiary orga-nization called Caribbean Action for Sustainable Tourism (CAST), has taken another initiative. CAST is designed to assist the regional hotel owners in their management of environmental resources and to enable them to approach the goals of Agenda 21. It also cooperates with Green Globe, a worldwide environmental management and awareness programme for the travel and tourism industry (CAST homepage).

The considerable growth of the cruise industry in the area creates special problems for regional cooperation between island states. Thus efforts to introduce a common landing fee for all CARICOM countries have not been successful. Instead of cooperation there has been competition, as the cruise line companies often prefer visiting the islands with the lowest fees. Furthermore, cruise tourists pay very short visits to their Caribbean destinations and spend comparatively small amounts of money there. Because of this, Caribbean tourism organizations and authorities want to attract more stay-over visitors.

As indicated above, all kinds of tourism have negative impacts on the physical environment of the host countries. Such effects are particularly obvious in small island states whose weak economies have problems financing the extra costs caused by these impacts. Again, regional cooperation can be of help. The OECS has shown the way by introducing an environmental levy of US$1.50 *per capita* on all visitors entering its member countries (*Caribbean Insight*, December 1997: 11).

To sum up, tourism is a vital and expanding industry in the Caribbean. At the same time, this development is creating a dilemma, particularly for the many small island states whose fragile natural environment sets limits to the growth of tourism. Regional agencies – like CTO – have so far done little to acknowledge these limits and to adjust their policies to them, but a change is now taking place. Among others, Caribbean NGOs have contributed to the nascent ecological awareness within the tourism industry.

Caribbean tourism is particularly sensitive to disturbances of different kinds. Political upheaval and outbreaks of violence in Jamaica and Grenada, for example, caused declines in tourist arrivals in the 1970s and 1990s. The hurricane season has a similar effect but has also induced common action to cope with the problem – another indication of the pressing need for regional cooperation.

Common Threats and Security

Feelings of togetherness are strengthened when Caribbean people experience threats to their security. Practically every year hurricanes wreak havoc in different parts of the region. These recurrent attacks by a 'common enemy' have provoked the Caribbean societies to increase their combined efforts to defend themselves against disaster. Both in terms of early warning systems and solidarity action to assist islands and territories hit by hurricanes, regional cooperation plays an important role. Again, churches and other NGOs, particularly community-based groups, have been very active and have received full endorsement from regional disaster organizations. Examples are the CARICOM Disaster Relief Unit (CDRU) and the Barbados-based Caribbean Disaster Emergency Response Agency (CDERA), which coordinates assistance from the region and from other parts of the world to the worst-affected areas. But much more could be done. In its last issue, *Caribbean Contact* proposed a comprehensive disaster management policy with substantial support from regional governments and also suggested that the University of the West Indies 'should be required to establish a policy on disaster management, training and research' (*Caribbean Contact*, August 1994: 17).

Drug trafficking is another problem experienced as a common threat by the Caribbean states, located as they are between Latin American producers and the huge US market (it is perhaps perceived as an even greater threat by the US). Combined efforts to stop the drug trade are made, and the United States has recently decided to expand its Drug Enforcement Administration (DEA) both in Puerto Rico ('the "lynchpin" of drug trafficking in the Caribbean') and in other parts of the region (*Caribbean Insight*, October 1998: 11). In the Eastern Caribbean, regional security forces belonging to a Regional Security System (RSS) are involved in such activities. In December 1998 US marine helicopters flew Caribbean security forces to *ganja* (marijuana) fields in northern St Vincent. Satellite surveillance had disclosed the activities and the Prime Minister, Sir James Mitchell, had asked the US to intervene (*The Economist*, 12 December 1998: 65).

The security forces were formed a few years after the Grenada revolution in 1979 and have later received substantial support from Britain and the US.[18] RSS has its origin in the OECS Treaty, Article 8 of which describes the 'composition and functions' of a special 'Defence and Security Committee' which is responsible for the coordination of 'collective defence and the preservation of peace and security against external aggression' (Treaty establishing the OECS, 1981).

In 1982, regional concern about developments in revolutionary Grenada caused a split in the OECS when all independent members except Grenada signed a 'Memorandum of Understanding' together with a non-member, Barbados. It was this memorandum (together with Article 8) 'which provided the framework for the cosmetic involvement of 350 paramilitary personnel' from six Caribbean states in the US-led invasion of Grenada in October 1983 (Ferguson 1990: 121–2; Lewis 1990: 291). By 1985, practically all foreign troops and police forces had left Grenada, and regional security matters were gradually taken over by the RSS, whose main concern became the escalating drug problem.

After declaring in 1986 that drugs were a national security threat, President Reagan started comprehensive actions to 'reduce the supply from the Third World' (Sutton 1993: 289) and invested in military operations to intervene in the drug transit trade in the Caribbean. Joint military training exercises, run by US and Caribbean military and paramilitary units, were started and continued in the 1990s. The Caribbean Basin is still a 'priority area in [US] counter narcotics operations' (*ibid.*). Drugs as the incarnation of malice are now replacing the 'evil power' of communism, and the Caribbean is again the stage for a regional security drama.

The maritime cooperation between US and Caribbean forces has had its problems, however, especially in Jamaican waters, where US personnel have been active without the permission of Jamaican authorities. This 'shiprider' issue was raised and resolved at the time of Clinton's visit to Barbados in May 1997 (*Caribbean Insight*, June 1997: 1, 12). But even if common threats can be considered a unifying factor, such phenomena are occasional in nature and cannot be of fundamental importance when it comes to building more substantial forms of regional cooperation. If these are to be viable they should be created by procedures where a vast majority of the population are permanently involved.

Concluding Remarks

The Caribbean is a region where the power of the past is still very strong. External influences have dominated its history and created a fragmented patchwork of societies separated not only by their colonial legacies but also by the geographical structure of the area with its abundance of small islands. When now, at the start of the twenty-first century, the winds of change have started blowing more intensely and the majority of the Caribbean territories have become independent states, the past is still 'hanging around' creating problems for those who want to work for regional cooperation. Just now there is this fight going on: between legacy and change, between lingering insularity and growing Caribbeanness.

As the influence of the European colonial powers gradually declined, the US became more and more involved in the Caribbean, a vital strategic area on its southern flank. Its engagement is still obvious, but with the Cold War over, US security concerns in the Caribbean are reduced to the area of drug trafficking. At the same time, the US cultural influence in the region has become even stronger.

After the creation of NAFTA, with the Caribbean left outside, the feeling of desperation has increased in the region. The economic situation is extremely difficult and the urge to form bigger and more competitive bodies is strong. Among the many regional interstate organizations forming what I have compared to an onion, the ACS is the biggest, but it is still at its formative stage and it is uncertain if it will develop into a strong player in the international arena. At the microstate level, the OECS has been quite successful, however.

The most important factor in the forming of a Caribbean region is what Alma Young has called 'the voice of the people' (Young 1991). In the Caribbean a great many NGOs, often working at the grassroots level, are engaged in regional issues of different kinds. One is the protection of the environment, a matter of decisive importance for small island states. The many regional cobwebs spun by NGOs over language and state barriers contribute to overcoming feelings of insularity and isolation. So also do the many cultural links, like sports, calypso music and ecumenical church organizations, that can be found in many parts of the region.

One regional activity in which both competition and cooperation are taking place is tourism, now the most important industry in the Caribbean. In order to co-ordinate and facilitate regional tourism, organizations like the CTO have been established. Their problem is that the promotion of unrestricted tourism is at odds with the concept of sustainable development, widely accepted as an important guideline for Caribbean societies. This dilemma was evident when Jean S. Holder, general secretary of the CTO, spoke in 1997 at a meeting on Tourism Sustainability – a term not even mentioned in the objectives of the CTO (www.caribtourism.com/)! He emphasized two important features of the development of Caribbean tourism:

- Protecting the environment ('if for no other reason than that, as the world's most tourism-dependent region, we seem to have the most to lose by not doing so').

- Regional cooperation ('the only means by which we can harness the human and financial resources needed in these small states to effect change and undertake the momentous task we face') (Holder 1997).

Here he summarized the two dichotomies that characterize current development problems in the Caribbean region: regionalization versus insularity, and unfettered economic growth (mainly through tourism) versus sustainability. The choices between these alternatives are crucial for the survival of a region so dominated by small island states. And the choices must be made soon. There is very little time left. The Caribbean microstates, particularly, are already facing a situation where the introduction or increase of mass tourism could be devastating for the environment. This problem is too complex to be handled by single microstates. The 'insular option' is out:

> Maybe the time has finally arrived to seek out bold local solutions for local problems. The survival of individual Caribbean sovereignty rests not in the continued pursuit of insular options but in regional cooperation on a scale never before attempted. In cooperation lies future possibilities. (Knight 1990: 330)

Many voluntary organizations working for the empowerment of the people have great experience of regional cooperation, and they can and must play a more important role in the development of 'regionness' and the realization of development strategies. The key to progress in these efforts is to be found in the strong potential of the Caribbean people. If they can participate more actively in forming their own future, the results will be remarkable.

NOTES

1 A microstate according to my definition has less than 200,000 inhabitants and its area is no greater than 1,000 square kilometres.
2 They are: Andorra, Antigua and Barbuda, Dominica, Grenada, Kiribati, Liechtenstein, Micronesia, Monaco, Nauru, St Kitts/Nevis, St Lucia, St Vincent and the Grenadines, San Marino, São Tomé and Principe, Seychelles, Tonga, Tuvalu, and the Vatican City. The average size is 392 square kilometres and the average population about 66,500 (*The World Guide* 1997/8).
3 To define the Caribbean reality is 'tantalizingly difficult': 'The region is like a prism with light passing through – whatever enters is transformed. This leads to enormous imprecision in self-definition.... Things tend to be placed along a fluid spectrum, and the local speech richly reflects this graduated variety. Even the term "Caribbean" can be subject to various political and geographical definitions' (Knight, 1990: 308–9).
4 Samana Cay in the Bahamas (*National Geographic* 1986: 585)
5 When the Single European Market was established in 1993, Britain was put under pressure to change these preferential arrangements, but, as mentioned above, they continued to apply to

the year 2000. Germany and the Benelux countries are still very much against them, though (Jackson 1994: 63).

6 In February 1997 the US Federal Communications Commission (FCC) made a unilateral move to change the telecom settlement rates for traffic from the USA to other countries. This plan meant that Caribbean telephone companies could lose up to 70 per cent of foreign exchange earnings (*Caribbean Insight*, 1997: 12). The threat was temporarily removed, however. When President Clinton visited Barbados in May 1997 the US 'agreed to delay for an unspecified time the unilateral changes' (*Caribbean Insight*, 1997: 1)

7 It is interesting to note that, at a meeting on 5 March 1996, the 14 CARICOM members together with Canada strongly condemned the so-called Helms-Burton bill and advised President Clinton not to sign it. This bill 'would penalize overseas-based subsidiaries of US firms, as well as foreign companies, that trade with Cuba'. According to the Caribbean leaders and Prime Minister Jean Chretien the bill was 'inconsistent with the principles of international law and undetermined the trend towards the liberalization of trade'. President Clinton finally signed the bill (then named the Cuban Liberty and Solidarity Act) into law on 12 March 1996 (*Caribbean Week* Website, 1996, *Caribbean Insight*, 1996).

8 After a history of invasions in the Caribbean Basin – the latest in Panama in 1989 – the US evidently sees no current need for that type of military action in the region.

9 The ACS was one of the many recommendations suggested by the West Indian Commission in 1992 (West Indian Commission 1992: 59–62).

10 Member countries: Antigua, Bahamas, Barbados, Belize, Dominica, Grenada, Guyana, Jamaica, Montserrat (still a British colony), St Kitts/Nevis, St Lucia, St Vincent and the Grenadines, Suriname, Trinidad and Tobago.

11 An example: after the rapid economic decline in the early 1980s, Trinidad introduced strong measures to defend its economy. This seriously affected the other member states (Ramsaran 1989: 173–4).

12 There is one exception: between St Lucia and Dominica is Martinique, a French DOM.

13 Referring to the title of this chapter, one of my basic points is that the concept of colonial legacy has affected and is still affecting so many strands of Caribbean society and political life that it keeps appearing in various contexts. And so does the dialectical relationship between legacy and change, a process that is slowly building new regional identities and relations.

14 This is based on interviews with different people, among them a teacher in Grenada in 1989.

15 UWI was 'one of the few federal organizations that survived the collapse of the Federation of the West Indies in 1962' (Dyde 1992: 172).

16 Among them are
   • ACE (Association of Caribbean Economists)
   • CAFRA(Caribbean Association for Feminist Research and Action)
   • CARIPEDA(Caribbean People's Development Agency)
   • CARNEID (Caribbean Network of Educational Innovation for Development)
   • CCC (Caribbean Conference of Churches)
   • CNIRD (Caribbean Network for Integrated Rural Development)
   • CPDC (Caribbean Policy Development Centre)
   • WAND (Women and Development)
   • WINFA (Windward Islands Farmers' Association)

17 For more examples of alternative tourism strategies in the Caribbean, see Widfeldt 1996.

18 An example: direct military assistance to the eastern Caribbean reached more than US$5.6 million a year in 1985–7 (Sutton 1993: 285).

12 The New Regionalism in South America

CYRO BANEGA, BJÖRN HETTNE
AND FREDRIK SÖDERBAUM

The Americas, as a single large region, has been grouped, usually and conveniently, into North America, on the one hand, and Latin America and the Caribbean on the other hand. There has been a rather sharp dividing line between the two: while the latter has lain within the US sphere of interest, merely constituting the US 'backyard', it has been distanced, too, by individual or collective efforts to escape US hegemonism. With the end of the Cold War and the southward expansion of North America in the form of NAFTA, this division is in the process of being transformed. Mexico as well as Central America and the Caribbean are quickly becoming 'North Americanized' due to geopolitical and economic realities, while the countries in the southern cone – Argentina, Brazil, Paraguay and Uruguay – have began to develop their own regional grouping through the Mercosur (or Southern Common Market; Mercosul in Portuguese). Here one may expect the various Latin cultures to be more resilient, particularly given the emphatic cultural distinctiveness of Brazil. In spite of this, there is an overall trend of regionalization and increasing 'regionness' as the southern region leaves behind it a legacy of civil war, violence and terror (Koonings and Kruijt 1999). In fact Latin America can be described as an emergent security community (Hurrell 1998). Peace has now become a Latin American comparative advantage. And the concept of 'the Americas' makes more sense than ever before.

This chapter concentrates on the processes of regionalisms and regionalizations in South America, and particularly in its core region, the southern cone, with regard to four key issues: (1) What marks the change from the old to the new regionalism in South America? (2) How to account for the remarkable shift from rivalry to cooperation among the two main powers, Argentina and Brazil? (3) What characterizes the emergence and consolidation of institutionalized cooperation in the form of Mercosur? (4) How to understand the boundaries and identities of the southern cone in relation to the rest of South America, as well as the Americas more generally?

From Old to New Regionalism

The idea of Latin American unity by way of regional economic integration has been on the agenda ever since the end of the Second World War, as indicated by various resounding declarations and the establishment of a number of regional organizations. The old regionalism in Latin America was firmly grounded in the structuralist school of thought. The structuralist position may have been forgotten by the younger generation of economists but it is undoubtedly (together with dependency theory, discussed later) basic to the evolution of Latin American economic thought. The keyword was industrialization, which took the form of import substitution, reflecting both the historical background and the external context of the early post-war period. A state-promoted industrial structure was meant to respond to an already existing domestic demand, thus creating at least some industrial basis in countries that were essentially exporters of primary goods. The structuralist vision was to change this historical legacy, to transform the structure of comparative advantages towards a higher level of productivity and competitiveness.

Despite some rapid economic growth in the early phases, the limitations of import substitution industrialization on the national level soon became evident. Very much encouraged by the United Nations Economic Commission for Latin America (ECLA) and its dynamic executive secretary, Raul Prebisch, the reformulated vision was to create an enlarged economic space in Latin America in order to enhance import substitution regionally when it became exhausted on the national level. Liberalized intraregional trade in combination with regional protectionism seemed to offer large economies of scale and wider markets, which could serve as a stimulus to industrialization, economic growth and investment.

This resulted in the creation of the Latin American Free Trade Association (LAFTA) in Montevideo in 1960. LAFTA was a genuinely continental project, and included all countries on the South American continent (plus Mexico). However, in spite of some early progress and the lively theoretical discussions that became part of the history of economic thought, the old regionalism in Latin America made little economic impact and was never implemented on a larger scale.

The dismal record of regional integration is due to internal conflicts, a general failure to cooperate, and the whole structure of dependence. The member countries of the various partly overlapping regional schemes were politically and/or economically unstable and neither willing nor capable when it came to pursuing cooperation. The objective of a free trade area never materialized, partly defeated by extremely cumbersome and unfruitful tariff reduction negotiations. Demands for exceptions in combination with continued protectionism against third countries led only to economic stagnation. The smaller member countries claimed that LAFTA mainly benefited the 'Big Three' – Mexico, Argentina and Brazil – and opted for a more radical and ambitious strategy focused on a jointly planned industrialization strategy. This was the basic foundation for the establishment of the Andean Pact in 1969, but its high-flying ambitions were never implemented. The military dictatorships established throughout the continent during the 1970s were poor partners in regional cooperation schemes.

External factors and dependence were also important, especially the relationship to the US. As long as the US was a global superpower, there was little room for manoeuvre for the Latin American states. On the other hand, there was very little positive interest in Latin America on the part of the US. Radical development models were unacceptable as they were interpreted as advancing the interests of 'the other side' in the Cold War. The only regionalism that was accepted was thus 'hegemonic regionalism'. The Organization of American States (OAS), for instance, has been perceived more as an instrument of US policies than as a genuinely regional body (Frohmann 2000). Only recently, particularly after the Cold War, has there been genuine interest from the US, as manifested in the Enterprise for the Americas Initiative (EAI) taken by President Bush in 1990. And today the OAS seems less an instrument for US imperialism and more a genuine expression of the interests of most countries in the Americas. Recently, it presented the first hemispheric regional convention (in April 1996, signed by 21 member states) dealing with corruption and bribery. This trend towards hemispheric regionalism started with the 1994 Summit of the Americas in Miami. The so-called Contadora process, although lacking in concrete results, can also be said to demonstrate this new regional spirit. According to Alicia Frohmann (2000), the establishment of the Rio Group in 1986 resulted from the Contadora experience, and the main concern now became democratization, the delicate *concertacion*.

The return to democracy in the mid-1980s was a big boost for regional cooperation in at least two ways. First of all, the new democracies were still very fragile, and the fresh generation of democratic leaders were therefore inclined to involve themselves in regionalist schemes in order to back each other up. Second, to the extent that the democracies were consolidated, which so far has happened in most cases, there was a transformation of the political landscape in the direction of more openness and towards a genuine political culture, indicating a political homogenization of South America, and of the southern cone in particular. The beginnings of a regional civil society, matching the inherent cultural community, slowly replaced the suspicion and geopolitical paranoia that had surrounded previous military regimes. Since the mid-1980s the Latin American countries have also been restructuring economies now opened to greater international competition. The convergence of liberal economic policies and the resultant economic homogenization throughout the continent creates unprecedented possibilities for regional integration.

This consolidation of democracy in a context of cooperation and growing interdependence started when Argentina and Brazil decided to put an end to decades of rivalry and suspicion, and engage in a process of bilateral cooperation. Even if the hostilities between Argentina and Brazil did not lead to large-scale war, the rivalry had created a very gloomy, unstable and even explosive situation in South America, which for a long time prevented genuine and deep cooperation from taking place. The process of cooperation between Argentina and Brazil was conceived as a new incentive to Latin American integration and to the consolidation of peace, democracy and development in the region. The cooperation progressed gradually during the late 1980s until finally a free trade area between the two countries was created. In August 1990 Paraguay and Uruguay joined the process and, as a result of this, on 26 March 1991 the Mercosur was created through the Asunción Treaty (Mercosur 1991; 1994). The implementation process was successful and on 1 January 1995 Mercosur began to operate 'somewhere halfway' between a free trade zone and a customs union (Williams 1996).

The Mercosur agreement, in its present configuration, represents both continuity and change with regard to the previous integrationist efforts in South America. On the one hand, it seeks to build on the tradition of regionalism that has been such an important school of thought on the continent. As Economic Complementation Agreement No. 18 of the Latin American Integration Association (LAIA, the successor of LAFTA), Mercosur constitutes a subregional grouping within the larger association. On the other hand, and arguably more importantly, the Mercosur agreement represents a radical shift in the integration model in South America. Given the exhaustion of the import substitution model, and the restructuring and opening of local economies since the mid-1980s, the new regionalism in South America spells open regionalism.

Typically, the new regionalism is characterized by its openness, most clearly in East and Southeast Asia but also in this South American case, where it is called *regionalismo abierto* in a recent ECLAC document:

> What differentiates open regionalism from trade liberalization and non-discriminatory export promotion is that it includes a preferential element which is reflected in integration agreements and reinforced by the geographical closeness and cultural affinity of the countries in the region. A complementary objective is to make integration a building block of a more open transparent international economy. (ECLAC 1994: 12)

The concept may sound like a contradiction in terms: to have the cake and eat it. To some extent open regionalism is a way of reviving interest in an issue that in South America has been dead for a decade and which, in a neoliberal political context, smacks of protectionism and state interventionism. It is also, of course, a recognition of the fact that the global economy of today is different from that of the 1960s. Finally, it is a precautionary strategy in a situation where there is great uncertainty about the future development of the world economy. It is believed that, even if a less optimistic international scenario develops, open regionalism is still justifiable as the second-best alternative. It is better than a return to economic nationalism in dealing with the external environment, since it at least helps to preserve the expanded regional market (Santiago 1995: 13; Rosenthal 1994; Ciccolella 1993).

As will become evident in this chapter, the process of regionalization in South America is potentially more comprehensive than is suggested by the label 'open regionalism', although the latter concept has become part of the official rhetoric.

From Rivalry to Cooperation

A central characteristic of South America is the economic and political dominance of Argentina and Brazil, the latter in particular. In geopolitical terms, there is a power subsystem composed of two elements: one of these is the long historical tradition of competition for regional leadership between Argentina and Brazil; the other is the role of Bolivia, Paraguay and Uruguay, all serving as a geopolitical buffer between the two larger countries (Tulchin 1986; Biles 1988).

The rivalry has a long historical tradition. Throughout the colonial era, the River Plate was a colonial frontier between two rival European empires, Spain and Portugal. In order to contain Portugal's pretensions in the southern part of South America, Spain created the Viceroyalty of La Plata in 1776, with its seat in Buenos Aires. After achieving independence from Spain the Viceroyalty was divided into three countries, Argentina, Paraguay and Uruguay. Competition for control of the River Plate Basin – which in geographical terms includes the tributaries of the River Plate, the great inland rivers, Paraná, Paraguay, Iguazú and Uruguay, along the southern border of Uruguay – lies at the heart of the configuration of the region.

The rivalry between Argentina and Brazil is the oldest of all Latin American conflicts and has clearly had an influence on the shaping of South America for the past two hundred years. It is even crucial for understanding the formation of Paraguay and Uruguay. The strong formation of political axes: one between Brazil and Chile, the other between Argentina and Peru, played an important role in the balancing of power which subsequently occurred. The balance of power was also affected by the outside world, particularly the US (Quagliotti 1976; Biles 1988). Furthermore, 'although military conflict was avoided, high levels of mutual threat perception continued through the twentieth century – the possibility of war and the importance of military preparedness were constant themes in strategic and diplomatic discussion' (Hurrell 1998: 230).

Moving on to more recent times, Andrew Hurrell (1998: 232–3) points out that there were three main areas of conflict in the 1970s: (1) the quest for influence in the buffer states; (2) conflict over the hydroelectric resources of the Paraná river; and (3) the nuclear rivalry. These conflicts received such strong attention due to historical rivalry between Brazil and Argentina, as well as the change in the balance of power due to Brazil's rapidly growing economy.

The first signs of rapprochement between Brazil and its Spanish-speaking neighbours, especially Argentina, are evident from the late 1970s (Hurrell 1998: 235). The policy makers realized that they had little to gain from conflict-ridden relations with their neighbours. Instead of open rivalry the parties sought coexistence and desecuritization. In sharp contrast to the previous extreme geopolitical doctrines, Argentina and Brazil found themselves in a new situation where they understood that they could gain from strategic cooperation, and this in turn transformed the buffer system in the River Plate Basin.

Relations cooled somewhat again in the early 1980s, but from the mid-1980s onwards the process of cooperation between Argentina and Brazil gained momentum and subsequently was consolidated. The improved relations started in November 1985 under the Iguazú Declaration, which formally put an end to the rivalry between the two countries and emphasized bilateral cooperation on energy issues, nuclear issues, arms control agreements, declining levels of military spending, confidence-building measures, and the necessity of advancing economic integration under the LAIAsystem.

The Iguazú Declaration led to the setting up of a high-level Joint Committee presided over by governmental representatives and businessmen from the two countries (Rodríguez 1995; Williams 1996). The work of the Joint Committee resulted in an Argentine–Brazilian Integration Act, signed in July 1986 in Buenos Aires. This Act contained a Programme for Economic Integration and Cooperation (PICE), under which 24 bilateral protocols were signed during the next three years. The strategy of integration searched for a selective opening of the respective markets based on the principles of gradualness, flexibility and stability, in order to allow the progressive adjustment of the two country's business sectors to the new situation. Next, two bilateral treaties on integration, cooperation and development were signed in 1988 and 1989 respectively, with the purpose of consolidating the integration process, and by which the two countries expressed their willingness to build a common economic area. In July 1990 the Buenos Aires Act converted this framework, including Paraguay and Uruguay into the renovated integration project that was Mercosur.

One should note that this process of increased cooperation coincides with the democratization process in the region. In fact, democratization and regionalization have been mutually reinforcing processes in the reconfiguration of South America. The transition from authoritarianism to democratic government began with the collapse of the Argentine dictatorship in 1983 and ended with the palace revolution that toppled Paraguayan dictator Stroessner in 1989. In 1985, Argentina, Brazil and Uruguay all had, for the first time in history, democratic political regimes at the same time, and closer relationships developed between the three countries. According to Dávila-Villers (1992), the civilian governments in Argentina, Brazil and Uruguay saw a close relationship between mutual cooperation and the consolidation of the democratization process. Regular consultations between the three countries took place at both the presidential and foreign affairs levels. In essence, the historic return to civilian rule in the whole region imparted new confidence to the regional plans, while increased transparency later created opportunities for confidence-building measures. Regionalism and regionalization, which by then had become institutionalized in Mercosur, may be said to provide a guarantee against undemocratic tendencies. The very strong discontent expressed by the other three Mercosur partners probably prevented a threatening *coup d'état* in Paraguay in April 1996.

The Dynamics of Mercosur

This section analyses the dynamics of institutionalized regionalization within the framework of Mercosur during two periods: first, the making of the agreement and the so-called transition period, and then at the contemporary halfway point, looking forward from free trade zone to customs union and onwards.

The Making of Mercosur and the Transition Period

By the signing of the Treaty of Asunción in March 1991, Paraguay and Uruguay joined the process of renewed South American integration initiated by Brazil and Argentina. In the preamble to the treaty the signatories declare that 'the expansion of their domestic markets, through integration, is a vital requirement for accelerating the process of economic development with social justice'. It is also emphasized that the individual states cannot generate economic growth on their own, separate from one another, and that regional economic integration and the competitive insertion of the region into the global economy are preconditions for increased development and economic growth. The treaty also suggest that there is a close relationship between the rapid changes on the international level and the restructuring of national economies. In essence, the Treaty of Asunción stresses the importance of regional integration, since as separate units the four countries cannot respond effectively to the challenges of the world economy.

The treaty is a framework agreement with four principal objectives: (1) the free circulation of goods, services and factors of production; (2) a common external tariff and common trade policy in relation to third countries; (3) the coordination of macroeconomic polices, to be carried out gradually and in a manner consistent with the tariff reduction programme; and (4) the harmonization of legislation in key areas such as trade, agriculture, industry, services, fiscal and monetary affairs, transport and communication. The treaty is open to other Latin American countries as they restructure their economies to fit into the Mercosur framework.

Various intergovernmental institutions have been created to enforce implementation; their decisions are to be made by consensus in regular meetings. The treaty establishes a flexible structure responsible for shaping the agreements. The Council of the Common Market, composed of the presidents of the four countries, constitutes the supreme body of Mercosur. The Common Market Group is the executive body and oversees the work of eleven subgroups which are authorized to issue recommendations. In contrast to the EU's structure, the formal institutions of Mercosur are directly dependent on national administrations, which are responsible for the coordination and preparation of negotiations between the member governments. Mercosur's institutional structure has therefore been labelled a 'negotiating structure' (Perez del Castillo 1993).

The treaty regulates only the first phase of the integration process, the so-called 'transition period' up to 31 December 1994. During this period, the treaty also stipulates the constitution of a General Rule of Origins, a system for the solution of controversies and safeguard clauses. The 'System for the settlement of controversies', signed in Brasilia in 1991 (the Brasilia Protocol), is a landmark decision on institutional issues in the transition period. The Brasilia Protocol was the first juridical instrument for the solution of conflicts in Mercosur. The new system applies to any dispute which arises between the member countries within the framework of Mercosur, and its quick creation reveals that the member states overcame one difficulty inherent in previous regional integration efforts. However, the failure of the parties to establish a set of supranational political–juridical institutions and rules, or a Court of Justice, is a major institutional weakness of Mercosur according to a common line of thinking (Economía and Mercado 1997: 4–5).

The implementation of the treaty has followed a rocky road (Williams 1996; Instituto Artigas 1994). Two main processes were characteristic of the transition period: vigorous commercial trade liberalization combined with efforts to move towards the customs union; and a difficult struggle to coordinate macroeconomic policies. The Commercial Liberalization Programme constitutes the backbone of

Mercosur. Significant progress was made in the process towards free trade between the Mercosur countries during the first half of the 1990s. In fact, between 1991 and 1994 tariff reduction came to be applied to about 85 per cent of the goods. Most tariffs were thus eliminated, even if there are lists of exceptions to the programme of trade liberalization, especially for Paraguay and Uruguay.[1] The two smaller countries have also been given special treatment in the adoption of the Common External Tariff (CET). Here it should be mentioned that the integration project does not contain any compensation clauses or development funds to support the small countries or weak subnational regions. The CET entered into force on 1 January 1995. It applied to 85 per cent of the products imported from countries outside the bloc and contains 11 different levels, from a minimum of zero to a maximum of 20 per cent. Trade between the Mercosur countries is the most dynamic in Latin America, and intraregional trade as a proportion of total trade grew from 28 per cent in 1985 to 43 per cent in 1994. By value it reached around US$12 billion in 1994, compared to US$3.6 billion in 1990 (Ferrer 1995).

The process of coordination of macroeconomic policies wrestled with two main problems (Antia 1993; Ferrer 1995). One was the marked differences in the opening of the economy and the implementation of macroeconomic policies. Traditionally, Brazil is more industrialized than Argentina, but also more protectionist and more gradualist in the implementation of macroeconomic policies. Brazil chose a slower opening of its economy, while Argentina, on the other hand, initiated a very rapid opening and shock therapy to come to grips with hyper-inflation. Argentina's policy proved successful and the country soon had the lowest inflation in the region (3.6 per cent in 1994), while Brazil had the highest inflation (930.5 per cent in the same year) (*Gazeta Mercantil*, 13 April 1997).

This is closely related to the fact that Argentina and Brazil have adopted different economic reform strategies because of their different views about how to meet the challenges of globalization in the national context. This also had important consequences for how they viewed the relevance of the regionalist project. In Argentina the idea of *peripheral realism* prevailed, according to which there only remained a small space to adapt to exogenous forces, which are unmanageable. A quite extreme example of this is the argument that some put forward for the scrapping of the Argentinian currency in favour of adopting the US dollar. For Argentina regionalization is principally an instrument to integrate itself into the global economy, whereas for the Brazilian government, regional integration is of a more political and defensive nature, which can enhance national development (de la Balze 1995).

Regardless of these differences, it should be underlined that, at the end of the transition period, South America was a markedly different region compared to what was conceivable only a decade before. The drastic change in relationship between Argentina and Brazil was institutionalized not only within the frame-work of Mercosur, but also through a wide range of other agreements and confidence-building measures, particularly in the security field:

> By the mid-1990s it was clear that a major break had taken place in the historic rivalry between Brazil and Argentina in the sense that previous disputes had been settled; that diplomatic, military and economic resources were no longer committed to opposing the other side; and that the two countries were enmeshed in an increas-ingly dense process of institutionalized cooperation across a range of issues. (Hurrell 1998: 249)

Thus the reconfiguration and regionalization process in South America is poten-tially broader and deeper than the Mercosur process as such. However, Mercosur remains probably the most important hub of the essentially state-directed region-alization process. This is a good example of the dynamics of reduced hostility between two leading regional rivals, a lesson that perhaps should be studied in South Asia.

Integration and Challenges at Halfway

Remarkable progress has been made in the implementation of Mercosur objec-tives, especially compared to the speed of operation of many other regionalist projects worldwide, especially in the South. Nevertheless, difficulties exist and became more evident after the transition period. At the end of 1994, the four partic-ipant countries redefined the ambitions, sequencing and timeframe of the region-alization process (Rodriguez 1995; Mercosur 1995a, 1995b). The timespan for the full implemetation of the free trade area, the creation of a customs union and the coordination of macroeconomic policies proved too short. The member countries agreed on a new transitional phase for the implemention of the customs union ending in 2001, and 2006 for Paraguay. The timeframe for the final liberalization of the several hundred 'sensitive products' was extended as well.

As already noted, trade matters have defined much of the Mercosur agenda: the measures to guarantee and promote both intraregional and external trade, and the terms for the economic restructuring of member countries' domestic markets. During the transition period, trade matters received most attention and the trading agenda was rather one-dimensional. There are now signs that this might be changing. The Mercosur Programme of Action until 2000 (Mercosur 1995a) called not only for the consolidation of the customs union (through more flexibility and increased timespan), but, in line with the treaty, also for the adoption of new dimensions of regional integration – such as environment, labour relations, social security, health care, education and culture.

The process of increased regionalization in South America has been a strongly statist project. As Andrew Hurrell points out:

> The development of transnational social networks has not been a significant factor in either the ending of rivalry or the moves towards cooperation. If we look for evidence of interaction and internationalization, then this is mostly to do with changes within the buraucracies and the growth of institutionalized interaction, among an ever broader range of bureaucratic actors. There is, however, evidence that the success of integration is leading to an expansion in the range of actors involved – for example the greater organization of business interests and the creation of formalized involvement of those regions and provinces most closely affected by integration. (Hurrell 1998: 252)

As a small step to accommodate this weakness, the new programme of action recommends widespread consultation with relevant representational institutions of capital and labour, employers' associations and trade unions. Furthermore, the Ouro Preto Protocol established a Joint Parliamentary Commission for Mercosur, with the aim of facilitating the implementation of the common market and the coordination of several elements, such as the harmonization of legislation. However, this Commission has no formal power of initiative or control. The participation of the private sector is established in the permanent institutions of Mercosur through the Economic and Social Consultative Forum (although there is no evidence that this has worked properly). It is interesting to note that the trade unions in the four countries have accepted the idea of a social charter of rights, although the states and the Mercosur institutions have responded hesitantly to these attempts.[2]

The Mercosur institutionalization process is a central object of dispute between member states. The distinctive feature of Mercosur institutions is still their intergovernmental nature: they lack a supranational or at least autonomous dimension and a capacity to make laws that can push the regionalization process. On the other hand, the creation of specialized regional organs and the rules of competition give legal reality to Mercosur. This means that the intergovernmental institutions exist side by side with an embryonic legal doctrine in two areas: common trade regulations and the system for the resolution of disputes. Each of the member countries is obliged to implement the decisions adopted by community authorities. Furthermore, the number of issues that inevitably require community-level regulation has grown and increased the workload of the subgroups: this has resulted in the recent establishment of *ad hoc* commissions for the monitoring of some topics that go beyond the scope of national competence. These are decision-making bodies under the Common Market Council and the Common Market Group. The best-known example is probably the Mercosur Trade Commission, with responsibility for monitoring the implementation of the common rules governing trade policy.

Notwithstanding these institutional changes, the key member states appear to prefer the political solution of disputes that otherwise might be settled by a supranational court of justice. The weakness of central institutions diminishes the importance of regulation and joint decisions in the process of integration, and tends to strengthen the position of the strongest partners. Indicative of this, for instance, is Brazil's insistence that Mercosur should be an intergovernmental institution, in which decisions are taken by consensus: in this way it can maintain the autonomy to pursue whatever strategy is in its own interests. Meanwhile the smaller countries – Paraguay and Uruguay, but also Argentina – argue that a permanent court of justice with supranational powers is a necessary instrument to sustain regionalization and address the existing imbalances. Hence, the two contradictory future scenarios for Mercosur differ with regard to the character of the institutions and the deepening of the regional integration process. Brazil's individualistic strategy implies weak central institutions and trade integration only. The other scenario emphasizes strengthened regional institutions, including supranationality, and deepened economic regionalization going beyond simple trade integration and intergovernmentalism. These divergences continue to affect and shape the functioning of Mercosur.

More recently, South America was hard hit by the financial crises in 1998, and 1999 was also a rough year for Mercosur. The economic slump and the devaluation of the Brazilian currency, which has given Brazilian firms a big boost in the region, have constrained regionalization and also given rise to a number of trade disputes, especially over goods such as cars and car parts, steel, paper and shoes.

Finally, at the Mercosur summit in December 1999 the members agreed on the foundation of what Brazil's President Cardoso called a 'mini-Maastricht' (*The Economist*, 11 December 1999: 37). This local version of the EU Treaty includes: (1) harmonization of national statistics in order to facilitate comparisons; (2) establishment of common standards for 'fiscal responsibility' (legally mandated limits on public spending); and (3) stipulation that in the future each country will have to report on its efforts to achieve economic stability. It was stated that a set of common economic targets, such as those in Maastricht, would emerge naturally from this mini-Maastricht, which in turn would help each country to push through domestic reforms.

South America and the Future of the Americas

This chapter has described the emergence of a new regionalism in South America, following the profound post-Cold War transformations of the global political economy and the change of attitude of the US, in conjunction with the dramatic changes in the buffer system of the River Plate Basin and the shift from rivalry to cooperation between Argentina and Brazil. The process started out with rapprochement between Argentina and Brazil, the two largest, most populous and most influential South American countries. Bilateral cooperation was both political and economic in nature and it should be underlined that it coincided with the democratization process in these two countries. Subsequently the cooperation process was institutionalized in the form of Mercosur, with the entry of Paraguay and Uruguay.

In spite of the remarkable progress already made, tensions will continue to arise and challenge the regional arrangement due to the unequal size of the countries, their different development strategies and the different impulses generated from the world system. The greatest problem is the relationship between Argentina and Brazil and their different attitudes towards the speed and nature of the integration process and the institution building of Mercosur. To some extent the outcome of these contradictory forces is manifested as 'trade war' and 'investment war' between Argentina and Brazil. On the other hand, it is the commitment among the dominant elites in these key countries to overcome their historic rivalry and these divergent patterns that gives rise to a hegemonic bloc and in turn sustains the new regionalism in South America.

The future of the new regionalism in South America is ambiguous. Although Mercosur is likely to continue to exist, at least as a customs union, its future progress beyond this stage is somewhat uncertain. The economic slump after the financial crises at the turn of the century has caused problems and has already led to heated trade disputes among the key countries. Integration and disintegration go hand in hand and future progress depends on the ability to overcome challenges along the way. Institutional strengthening seems important for the consolidation of the integration process as well as broader participation by non-state actors, beyond the current state-centrism.

The Mercosur project contains a drive to expand international links. Since 1995 Mercosur has had a Group for Foreign Affairs shaping policy towards third countries and organizations. The strengthened cooperation between the EU and Mercosur has emerged as a most interesting example of interregional relations. The process began formally with the signature of the Agreement of Inter-Institutional Cooperation in 1992, whose major objective was developing technical cooperation projects. The Interregional Framework Agreement on Trade and Economic Cooperation (December 1995) has put forward the objective of a political and economic interregional association by the year 2000.

What is of greater interest here, however, is the future of South America and the Americas. Will regionalization expand beyond the loosely knit security and economic community in the southern cone? Is Mercosur part of a broader hemispheric regionalization process, reducing its distinct features? Since there currently exist several paths towards a new world order, it is difficult to provide a firm answer to these questions. What we can say at this point, however, is that at present there are strong convergences both within Latin America and between Latin America and North America. The democratization process in conjunction with the convergence of liberal economic policies throughout Latin America creates unprecedented possibilities for both regional and hemispheric integration. The US proposal of an American Free Trade Area from Alaska to Tierra del Fuego is based on two approaches: the EAI and NAFTA. In the EAI context, the Mercosur member countries have signed framework agreements with the US. In May 1997, at an American Free Trade Area summit meeting, Mercosur defended the idea of gradual hemispheric integration through the strengthening and convergence of subregional initiatives, the so-called 'building block process'. NAFTA in the north and Mercosur in the south have thus emerged as the two poles of attraction in the American hemisphere. However, no formal agreement between Mercosur and NAFTA has been made. Their future relationship is crucial but hard to foresee. Mercosur, for its part, is at the centre of the negotiation process to establish a South American Free Trade Area, and discussions have already been initiated with the associate members Chile and Bolivia, as well as with the Andean Pact member countries (Colombia, Ecuador, Peru and Venezuela).

In spite of these trends towards hemispheric regionalism and convergence, there is little to suggest that a genuine regional identity is emerging among the traditionally not very closely related subregions: North America, Mexico and Central America, the Caribbean Basin and South America (with its northern part, dominated by the Andeans, and its southern cone). On the other hand, these subregions are themselves internally heterogeneous, in a way that reiterates the Americas at large. This feature is somewhat similar to South Asia, but presents a contrast with the more homogeneous and consolidated nation-states of Western Europe.

The new situation is above all determined by the fact that the US is acting more like a regional power, and that meanwhile, as a nation-state, it is becoming increasingly 'Latinized'. The cultural border (between 'Anglo' and 'Latino') is now being drawn within the US itself, as the *reconquista* of Texas and California makes at least the southwestern microregion of the US Hispanic area.

In Mexico the tradition of nationalism, protectionism, and 'anti-gringoism' is still alive (as it has been ever since the early war with the US). However, the country's economic reforms have accelerated its integration into the North American economy, previously so much feared by the Mexican left, and the search for self-reliance (financed by oil) has now lost credibility. Mexico, which earlier had some potential and ambition to become a regional power, is the first Latin American country to draw the conclusion that joining North America – in the form of NAFTA – is the only possible way out of stagnation. Mexico, traditionally an introvert and protectionist state, joined GATT in 1986, primarily as a precautionary measure to protect its bilateral economic relations with the US. The further integration implied in the NAFTA agreement is the first case of North– South integration and therefore offers interesting experiences for other regions to draw on.

Mexico has consequently abandoned the Third World concept, so important for the image of some of the previous Mexican presidents. This has also tilted the small states of Central America and the Caribbbean towards the north, and the same economic and geopolitical changes have put a certain pressure on South America. The magnetism or bandwagon effect of NAFTA may repeat the EU pattern in Europe, with rival organizations gradually losing relevance. It may be that South America is organizing itself for inclusion in NAFTA or at any rate in a US-centred reorientation of the Americas.

The northern part of South America, the Andean subregion, has thus also begun to feel the pull both from the north and the south. For instance, Bolivia and Chile (at present vacillating between north and south) are invited to join Mercosur. The case of Chile is particularly interesting in this regard and deserves further elaboration.

Chile has had a unique development path in Latin America – first of all as the first elected Marxist government (under Allende, 1970–3), then as a neoliberal laboratory guarded by a ruthless military dictatorship (under Pinochet, 1973-90) with a modified economic policy after 1986, then under a transition government (Alwyn, 1990–4) and, finally, in 1994 and 1999, a return to free elections. The road to the current dynamic economic situation has been long and winding but it is undeniable that Chile's economy is in comparatively good shape. This is a result of an extreme openness, linking Chile to many parts of the world. Consequently, Chile does not want to be locked into any particular agreement. In Chile liberalization has gone so far as to make the regionalization option smack of protectionism and inwardness, and a fear that any regionalist scheme may reduce the number of potential trading partners. Chile is therefore sceptical towards Mercosur (with an eye on Brazil's protectionist record) but was nevertheless welcomed by it, and in March 1996 became an associate member. There was also discussion on whether Chile would become part of NAFTA but it would prefer to do that through bilateral agreements. It wants closer links with Europe (making use of the many Chileans in asylum, according to *La Nacion*, 23 March 1994). The President, Eduardo Frei, wanted open regionalism, *apertura* as well as *integracion regional* (*ibid*.).

Chile is one of those 'multitracking' countries that would like to have its cake and eat it. The world is becoming regionalized, but Chile wants to stay open by joining all blocs. This is not an unusual situation. Iceland and perhaps also Norway want to be European *and* Atlantic, Sri Lanka wants to be South Asian *and* South East Asian, Botswana can do better on its own than by pushing the SADC initiative. To the extent that regional integration is on the agenda, the option for Chile is *regionalismo abierto* (van Klaveren 2000). One may therefore ask what is the difference between generalized open regionalism and a global free trade regime. Regionalism and globalism are fully compatible as long as the other regionalisms also remain of the open type. In case the free trade regime should collapse, regionalism is a better defence strategy than falling back on economic nationalism.

For a host of various reasons, external as well as internal, the new regionalism in South America, open or not, is likely to be more persistent than the old regionalism. With the exception of a few peripheral pockets, the prospects for a Latin American regional peace order are comparatively good; in fact the peacefulness of the continent has become its major relative advantage, and the cost of breaking this trend would be very high indeed. The other comparative strength of regionalization within the main regionalist project, Mercosur, is that it will only contain members committed to the integration project. It is thus to a large extent a case of 'regionalism from within'. However, its main purpose is to establish sustainable relations with emerging trading blocs, particularly NAFTA (but also the EU). In its current form, the Third Worldist posture of Mercosur therefore lacks credibility. The coherence of the highly elitist and hierachical societies in South America is fragile. More likely is an expansion of NAFTA to cover the whole of the Americas in line with George Bush's EAI. The Latin American regionalist schemes seem to be a preparation for this, a continental opting out of the Third World, a move from an intermediate to a core position in the world order of regions.

NOTES

1 Article 6 of the Treaty stipulates that Paraguay and Uruguay may implement the Trade Liberalization Programme at a slower speed than Argentina and Brazil. The numbers of exceptions are: 950 items for Uruguay; 427 for Paraguay; 221 for Argentina and 29 for Brazil.
2 Interview, Montevideo, April 1997.

13 Conclusion

MICHAEL SCHULZ, FREDRIK SÖDERBAUM
AND JOAKIM ÖJENDAL

Working with regions means working with elusive entities, undefined boundaries, and newly invented concepts in the midst of a thoroughgoing structural change in our world order. The development is complex and sometimes contradictory. However, with the issues raised in the introduction in mind, we are now able to draw some conclusions from the empirical case studies on the state of the art of global regionalization. How is a region constituted in the emerging world order? What differences can be found in terms of the causes of regionalization? Who are the main actors pushing regionalization processes forward, and what is their relative strength?

Below follows a discussion of the main findings from the empirical cases in relation to the various forms of regionalism. We do not attempt an exhaustive synthesis of all aspects but rather select some of the most relevant issues found in our case studies. The forms of regionalism that can be identified in various parts of the world differ widely, but can be grouped into some overarching types.

Definition(s) of a World Region

The authors have used various criteria for defining/describing their respective regions. The geographical delimitation of a region has commonly been seen as a concrete but at the same time imprecise instrument to apply. For instance, from a geographical viewpoint what constitutes South Asia may at first sight be regarded as self-evident; culturally, it is not. Since regions do not exist within fixed boundaries, employing other criteria such as cultural affinity means that other patterns emerge. For instance, from a well-organized and distant core in Western Europe, Hettne opens up a Europe possibly including both Eastern Europe and parts of the present Russian state, allowing the border zone to be far larger than the core of the region. Although contradictory, Hettne is right: Europe both 'exists' and at the same time escapes the definition. The Urals might be the limit of Europe, but geography as such does not define that; it provides only a starting point, and must always be related to other, continuously changing criteria.

It is important to notice that historical and cultural variables have to be included, even though the cultural aspect, particularly, may prove difficult to pin down. For instance, geographically, politically and economically it makes sense to view Australia as part of Asia. However, strong cultural opposition exists – both in Australia and in Asia – to the 'Asianization' of Australia. Moreover, the cultural aspects that motivate a particular delineation in a particular region may be found in other world regions as well, blurring any self-evident belongings. 'Asian values' have been asserted as a springboard for regional unity. A closer scrutiny reveals, however, that those cultural traits both resemble the rhetoric of Hindu nationalism and draw inspiration from the 'Orientalism' debate originated by Edward Said (1978). Thus, at the same time as the cultural label is inclusive (of aspects from outside the regional unit), it serves as a mechanism of exclusion within the region itself. For instance, Islam cannot be used as a criterion for defining Central Asia or the Middle East. Islam existing outside these regions and areas containing other religions would then be excluded. Moreover, 'culture' operates on different levels: in South Asia the entire regional complex of independent states is a response to demands for religious separation, but nevertheless, as Jørgensen points out, a deeper cosmology is by and large shared by most people in the region.

Furthermore, in the regions discussed in this book there is a span from 'old' regions with historical, cultural and political articulations to new constructs seemingly invented for fitting in, or adapting, to a new world order. The delimitation of Southern Africa as SADC, for instance, must be seen as a modern construct since, as Odén notes, 'this definition is of recent origin'. The same goes for Southeast Asia and, and to some extent, West Africa. By contrast Europe, South Asia and possibly South America have long traces of inherent regionness.

Finally, it is also obvious that some regions defy any straightforward, simple definition. The Middle East, for instance, causes extravagant confusion since neither geographical nor historical labels, neither political nor economic processes, provide a satisfactory definition, leaving the question 'What is the Middle East?' open-ended. The term as such was imposed from outside. Central Asia and Caucasia provide similar difficulties and neither of these thus provides a 'typical' NRA region. The reason for this might be that the internal conflicts simultaneously inhibit a close relation *and* prevent the states in such a complex from distancing themselves from one another beyond a certain limit. Apart from the two regions mentioned, East Asia falls into this category of regions with strong power rivalry, and – simultaneously – embryonic regionalization, thereby constituting yet another troublesome paradox.

This might however not be an analytical problem, because the less regionalized a 'region' (or geographical area) actually is, the more difficult it is to define it. That is, the processes of regionalization ultimately define the region. The common denominator for the authors is that regionalization, in the end, is manifested by the patterns of interaction. These may be economic exchange, intra-regional trade relations, migration, cultural exchange, common historical experiences or shared beliefs; but they may also be common security issues. Hence, depending on the contextual situation, the patterns of interaction vary from one region to another. For instance, Southern Africa, Southeast Asia, East Asia and the Middle East all have a history of relations of enmity between the main state actors. Before the fall of apartheid in South Africa, Southern Africa could be understood in terms of the patterns of amity between the Front Line States and South Africa; before the fall of the Berlin wall ASEAN was defined according to conflict patterns determined by the Cold War; the fortune of East Asian regionalization is still defined by the historical rivalry between Japan and China. And the Middle East, we have learnt, is determined in its regionalization efforts by future conflict resolution.

It is not only conflicts that define a region: other more 'positive' processes might be instrumental too. The South American cone seems to be formed around a common wave of democratization (as southern Europe was in the late 1970s), as well as by a common need, shared by the elites, to create an open economic market in the region (Europe in the late 1980s). The reduced conflict between the regional powers Brazil and Argentina also played a crucial role.

In conclusion, it is not useful to search for *one* universal criterion that defines regions, nor to define a once-for-all specific mix. In contrast to the neorealist approach, which would use a specific understanding of state interest as a criterion for region, we emphasize that geographical, historical, cultural and economic variables – as well as patterns of conflict/security and other criteria – all create patterns of interaction and produce conceptions of 'regionness'. A world region, thus, is not a fixed entity; it may dissolve, and it may incorporate new 'members'; and it may change its internal relations in various fields, ranging from the political and economic to the cultural. A region is socially constructed and is analytically identifiable *post factum*; in other words, it defines itself. Regions, therefore, can also be deconstructed. Clearly, an empirical test, that forces the researcher to determine the key variables, is usually beyond the possible (Cantori and Spiegel 1973). Simultaneously, there are often 'regions within regions', further complicating the attempt at any one-dimensional and static definition of regions. This ambiguity indicates the need for a more flexible definition of a region. We therefore suggest maintaining eclectic and flexible definitions of regions as the most viable approach.

State, Market, and Civil Society Regionalization

Given the flexibility of the concept of region the next step in the analysis is to identify the major actors in the regionalization processes. These actors could be associated loosely with state, market, and civil society regionalization. Naturally, states are important actors in regionalization processes as well as in decision-making arenas. However, too much emphasis on the behaviour of the states risks neglecting the actors in the economic sphere. Civil society must be brought in as well.

State-led regionalization is common, and important, in nearly all the examined regions, although it differs in content and form from case to case. The three spheres of regionalization are often intimately related, however, and differ only in mixture and content from region to region. For instance, the process of European regionalization is seen as both state- and market-led. The distinction between state-driven and market-driven regionalization in the economically stronger world regions can best be described when comparing East Asia with Europe: both are dynamic regions, but Europe has entered into a highly ambitious bureaucratic institutionalization of its regionalization project, while East Asia goes ahead with economic integration without the institutional superstructure. On the other hand, the difficulty in finding 'pure' state or market approaches can be seen when comparing North America and East Asia: East Asian regionalization (to the extent it exists) is caused by a common need among the states to maintain 'business as usual', while North American regionalization in the form of NAFTA has undertaken an aggressive process of deepening economic integration among the North American states. Both processes are market-driven, but with very different features.

Southeast Asia, with a relatively high degree of intraregional trade and investment, could nevertheless be defined as a state-driven form of regionalization. While state interests and security concerns may have started the process, however, we now see a change taking place that is bringing the economic rationale into clearer focus. This is evident in the region's adaptation to the world market, in its response to the formation of a common market in Europe, and most recently in its attempted creation of a common market of its own. Regionalization in Southern Africa could likewise be described as largely state-driven (and state-resisted), but here too the process has been responsive to the global market.

Civil society plays an ambiguous role in relation to regionalization, not least in the case of North America. Here, paradoxically, (some of) the opposition to NAFTA among NGOs has itself become regionalized. Thus, *formal* regionalization has been counteracted, but a more *broad-based* regionalization – pertinent to the idea of the new regionalism – has been strengthened. Moreover, the resistance has served to 'improve' regionalization policies to the extent that the pro-regionalist actors have had to consider the opposition, reformulate policies, build public opinion, and so forth, in order to gain broader popular and political support. Thereby the process of regionalization may have been slowed down but simultaneously, possibly, the result has 'improved'. Different NGOs (and some political parties) in Europe have positioned themselves against Economic and Monetary Union (EMU), providing an example of a similar process. In Europe the anti-EU and anti-EMU forces are often keen to cultivate, and to show that they are cultivating, European contacts of another sort in order not to be accused of supporting narrow chauvinistic nationalism. A further example of regionalization 'from below', seen more or less in all regions but particularly in Europe, is the spectrum of influences stemming from regional migrant workers, tourism, student exchanges and so forth, that all contribute to foster important social networks, as well as a sense of regional belonging. Regional identity can be strengthened thereby as a parallel identity to national identity.

As noticed above, the three aspects cannot be separated from each other but should rather be seen as three corners of the same triangle. For instance, in the Middle East it is obviously the states which lead the process towards a possible regionalization, in so far as they first have to solve historical intraregional conflicts. Neither liberal economic demands, stemming from the market, nor civil society can expand their influence in the region unless a certain political stability exists. Many regionalization processes, however – whether they are driven by state, market or civil society – tend to be elite projects.

Regional Organizations and Institutions

When emphasis is placed on the institutionalization of regionalization in different world regions we find that each has, at least, one dominant regional organization. The European regionalization serves as the most advanced case of regionalization in terms of institutionalization. The European Union is on its way to becoming a political and economic unit, suggesting a forthcoming federal structure of Europe – although its future outcome, character and shape are far from final.

East Asia does not have an exclusively Asian regional organization, and it is a question whether the region has entered any stage of regional institutionalization. The future of East Asia is very dependent on the relations between China and Japan. A long history of enmity still disturbs the creation of large-scale common policies and regional organization. APEC serves as 'the' regional organization but is 'diluted' with many countries that cannot be considered East Asian.

NAFTA is by its very foundation an organization that aims at the removal of restrictions on the free trade of goods. Asymmetrical relations within the region, most notably between Mexico and the US, but also domestic asymmetries in each country, suggest that NAFTA could become yet another neoliberal elite project, proving a dangerous instrument for further deepening already existing social cleavages. As a general pattern the record of regional organizations is disappointing: they have not implemented the original intentions in the economic and/or political areas, and have a low degree of institutionalization. Mercosur, ECOWAS/ UEMOA, ASEAN and SADC are all examples of organizations that are dominated by state interests; and all, so far, have had great difficulty in coordinating and implementing economic integrative strategies. This is hardly a coincidence: one must conclude that one-dimensional implementation of such strategies is of limited value for the national elites.

After the European Union, South America is perhaps the region which has reached furthest in the institutionalization of functioning economic sectors. Yet even Mercosur has not yet established a set of supranational political-juridical institutions.

West Africa serves as an interesting case among the more peripheral regions in terms of having a multitude of regional organizations aimed at the deepening of economic integration. One of the main organizations, ECOWAS, is experiencing a revitalization due to its broadening to security.

Southern Africa and Southeast Asia also demonstrate a broader vision of regional integration. While the initial objective of SADCC was to reduce its dependence on apartheid South Africa, it began to transform as the 'new' South Africa was established in 1992. South Africa's entry into the organization two years later marked the beginning of new relations that may foster integration and cooperation in various sectors such as hydropower, transport and communication, higher education and research. The new SADC vision also includes security and foreign policy. SADC is in a stage of rather weak institutionalization, because of a unique strategy with decentralized institutions. This is further complicated because some of its members are also members of COMESAand involved in East African regionalization as well. The overlap between members' participation in several regional organizations again underlines the plurality of contemporary regionalization. Despite these interesting features, both West Africa and Southern Africa fit the historical pattern of harbouring a multitude of never-implemented regional schemes and organizations.

In contrast to the African cases, Southeast Asia is dominated by one regional organization that is fairly stable and well established. Although it is strong in one sense, it has been entirely dependent on the consensus principle and its unquestioning support for various national interests. To put it differently, ASEAN has so far not amounted to much more than the collective political will of the member states. However, with a less clear-cut political situation, more ambitious programmes, and extended membership, political pluralism is bound to enter the equation, putting pressure on previous working methods and possibly forcing through a streamlined decision-making structure.

South Asia is similar to Southern Africa and Southeast Asia in the sense that security interests originally formed its major regional organization. SAARC was first initiated in order to balance the power of India. Today, it is a regional organization with a new vision of broader economic regionalization, which has been advocated by the two regional archrivals India and Pakistan. How a deepening of regional institutionalization will be realized depends on the current challenges from outside (adaptation to the global political economy) and inside (the capability of each state to maintain stability and political initiative in the face of ethnic challenges). In South Asia indications of a deepened regionalization can be seen; simultaneously, however, strong national(istic) sentiments can be detected.

The four least institutionalized regions on a broader regional scale are East Asia, the Caribbean, Caucasia and Central Asia, and the Middle East. However, numerous weak organizations exist in these regions. In the Middle East, the Arab League constitutes the main regional organization. Although pan-Arabism and the Arab League never implied true integration, regional institutions were certainly formed. As with earlier examples, security was the main motivation for the foundation of the Arab League, aimed at counteracting Israel and mobilizing on the question of Palestine. In the 1970s, however, state interests and state nationalism somewhat displaced the symbolic appeal of pan-Arabism, although Arabism continued to play an ideological role. The degree of regional institutionalization in the Palestinian–Israeli security complex is still very marginal and embryonic. Regional cooperation has been initiated as an elite project based on common interests between states and market forces, and the outcome is far from clear.

In some respects, Central Asia–Caucasia and the Caribbean are facing situations comparable to that of the Middle East. Several regional organizations exist, but it is uncertain in which direction the regionalization process will move and which actors it will include. For instance, the future role of the most important regional organization in Central Asia and Caucasia, the Economic Cooperation Organization, is very much dependent on the future courses of member states such as Turkey (EU?), Iran (Middle East?), Pakistan (South Asia?) and Afghanistan (collapse and total disintegration?) In the Caribbean CARICOM and OECS serve as examples of two regional organizations which may yet play a crucial role in future regionalization, but so much depends on external actors, not least the US.

As for East Asia, the contrast between the generally high intensity of trade, investments and financial flows, and the extremely slow development of formal regional institutions is spectacular; the same goes for the high conflict potential in relation to the non-existent regional security organizations. Interestingly, the most vigorous attempts that have been made to fill this void have both originated in Southeast Asia (EAEC and ARF); the former is 'buried' in APEC, but the latter is thriving.

CONCLUSION
Power and Regionalization

It is important to notice that 'regionalization' is part of a 'game' in which a new world order is being constructed. Or, as Mittelman claims, '[r]egionalism today is emerging as a potent force in the global restructuring of power and production' (Mittelman 1999: 25). The outcome of this restructuring is highly dependent on the intraregional power relations.

When comparing the various regions, one notices that there are basically two main patterns of distribution/balance of power among actors: rivalry between two states under the umbrella of regional cooperation, or one dominant actor in the region. A third, less common pattern is when there is neither a rivalry between two states nor a single dominant state.

For instance, in East Asia, South Asia and South America (and historically in Europe) we have a strong rivalry between two states. In East Asia, the two main powers are China and Japan, which historically have always been in conflict with each other. In South Asia, the India–Pakistan rivalry is in itself the very foundation of the current complex and serves as an overlay inhibiting the deepening of regionalization, at least in terms of state-led regionalization. In South America the two giants Brazil and Argentina have a long tradition of competition for regional leadership. These rivalries are always likely to create deadlock in the attempts of other states to overcome developmental and security problems. In Europe, the EU emerged from a formula for accommodating the rival powers Germany and France

When these competing powers realize that cooperation could become a strategic asset, however, regionalization may be fostered. In South America and even more in Europe the nature of the historical pattern of intraregional relations has changed, fostering cooperation and thereby making regionalization possible. In East Asia, it is still hard to judge where the China–Japan rivalry is leading. So far, their complicated relationship has fostered low expectations in terms of regionalization. In South Asia, recent changes have generated hopes among the weaker states, since increasingly India has accepted a deepening of SAARC.[1] Also, India and Pakistan have both agreed to form SAFTA by the year 2000, possibly enabling a deepening of economic and political integration in South Asia.

When two rival states find a common path, regionalization may gain strong momentum. Having said that, it should be noted that below the great-power rivalry there is often a second layer of amity and enmity. In East Asia, for instance, countries like Korea and Taiwan have very special relationships to the greater powers. In the Middle East region it may be argued that there exists a rivalry between Israel and the Arab world – but there also exists a multi-layered rivalry between Egypt, Saudi Arabia, Iraq and Syria.

The regions which are dominated by one strong state actor are North America (the US), Southern Africa (South Africa), West Africa (Nigeria), and to a certain extent Southeast Asia (Indonesia). In North America the US is, of course, a dominant power through its political and economic weight, but also because geographically it occupies the central position. Canada has a similar income level and a certain room to manoeuvre. Mexico, however, is locked into dependency on the US. This fact has been one of the most controversial aspects of the NAFTA agreement.

In Southern Africa, 'old regionalism' directly expressed the will of the Front Line States to resist South African dominance. Today the main issue at stake is what role South Africa will play as a regional partner well aware of the potential benefits of cooperation. Indeed, the former Front Line States fear that South Africa might become a regional bully in terms of economic and political influence and dominance. Chapter 5 alerted us to a potentially devastating historical irony: that what the apartheid state failed to achieve through its political and military designs from 1974 to 1990 may be accomplished economically through the structural power of South Africa's finance, industrial and merchant capital in the post-apartheid era. In West Africa, Nigeria's position is similar to that of South Africa in Southern Africa: it is larger, politically and economically dominant, and has a history of military engagement *vis-à-vis* its neighbours. In terms of security regionalism Nigeria has played a major role in finding 'solutions' (by sending troops) to internal conflicts such as that in Liberia and Sierra Leone. Regionalization in West Africa clearly necessitates a benign attitude on Nigeria's part.

In Southeast Asia, regionalization did not happen until Indonesia wanted it; in size and population Indonesia – the 'first among equals' – is the regional giant. It is not the most economically developed country, however – far from it – nor is it as militarily and politically impressive as it looked just a few years ago. The recent extension of ASEAN, moreover, has served to dilute Indonesian dominance. Perhaps Southeast Asia should be grouped instead with regions based on a number of fairly equal states.

In the case of Europe, one could argue that historically the French–German rivalry constitutes a dominant axis. The rapprochement between Germany and France, enforced by Adenauer and de Gaulle during the Cold War, was a necessary step for any future European integration. European dreams of integration were very much the result of the tragic experiences of the Second World War, which paved the way for new security thinking. Germany's reunification in 1990 has caused some concern among European states, however, reviving the spectre of a single dominant power in Europe. Moreover, as always in European history, Russia plays an interesting role: weakened for the moment, but still there. Culturally, politically and geographically, part of it 'naturally' belongs to Europe; but, then again, part of it does not.

Central Asia–Caucasia and the Middle East are examples of power rivalry between many actors without a single dominant power. Neither are there two dominant powers constituting an overlay. In the Middle East, several subregions can be identified, with their own power constellations. In the Maghreb Union, Morocco and Tunisia are two of the major players. However, both of them are marginal in the broader Middle Eastern context. In the GCC, Saudi Arabia is, on the one hand, a giant in relation to the smaller Gulf States. On the other hand, Saudi Arabia has never achieved a dominant position in the entire region, although it has always been a major power in terms of its capacity as a financier of various security-related activities. Israel is usually seen as a great power, particularly in the Palestinian–Israeli security complex. Other influential powers are Egypt, part of the same security complex, and Iraq. Iran and Turkey are non-Arabic states with strong regional influence.

Regionalization agendas in these regions appear to be the result of state interests rather than a real sense of regionness. European states may have abandoned conventional sovereignty thinking in a post-Westphalian era and moved from security complex to security community, but Central Asia and (even more so) the Middle East are still caught in power politics.

In the Caribbean, power struggles are mainly related to the dominant role of the US. Since the establishment of NAFTA in 1993, however, even the French and Anglo-Saxon cultural differences are overshadowed by a shared feeling of being 'left alone' which has fostered a regional Caribbean awareness favourable to integrationist policies.

What is unmistakable is that in regions where conflict resolution has taken place, and/or where power is distributed fairly equally, regionalization has advanced the most (Europe, but also North and South America, and Southeast Asia). There may be a three-polar process encompassing regionalization, internal conflict resolution, and improvement of relative position in the world system. It is equally clear that in areas plagued by manifest conflicts, and where the division of power is contested, regionalization is only embryonic (Central Asia, the Middle East, East Asia) and the areas in question constitute regions largely through their tense security relations. This is no surprise. What is interesting, however, is to view the regions where a dominant power has the structural position and capacity to foster regionalization and conflict resolution, and thereby initiate a benign regional development (Southern and West Africa, South Asia).

Three Layers of Regions

It should be obvious from the discussion above that certain regions come out stronger than others in this process of change in the world system. This is likely to result in super- and subordination among regions, and in a three-layered global division of labour. Hettne uses the concepts of 'core', 'intermediate' and 'peripheral' regions (Hettne 1997a). This is a simplification, but the distinction is useful when understanding motives for regionalization. The current trend towards regionalization is the result of many forces at different levels. As has often emerged in this book, regionalization is simultaneously the result of global-scale transformations since the end of the Cold War, and one of the forces driving these transformations.

The core regions are politically stable and economically dynamic, and they organize mainly for the sake of gaining better access to the global economy by improving their competitive strength, both internally and externally. Intermediate regions are linked to the core regions and are in the process of being incorporated as soon as they conform to the criteria of 'coreness', that is, economic development based on a liberal agenda and political stability. Peripheral regions are politically turbulent and economically stagnant; they must organize in order to arrest a process of marginalization, despite their fragile and inefficient present regional arrangements. Yet in these peripheral regions important changes have occurred recently, opening up the possibility of a take-off towards regionalization. Their only other power resource lies in their capacity to create problems for the core regions ('chaos power'), thereby inviting some sort of external engagement.

Thus it could be argued that Europe, North America and East Asia need to, and possibly are forming – in different degrees, at different paces and with different organizational outcomes – regional units for achieving better positions in the world market and a higher capacity to affect the formation of the world system. Their role as policy makers in the global economy corresponds to their degree of success in region building. There are, however, great differences in performance between the regions. For instance, Europe is the most advanced regional arrangement in the world, and it may (and already does) serve as a paradigm for the new regionalism. North American interests in integration, with NAFTA as its main organization, emerged out of member states' (or at least their elites') need to create a large free trade zone. In the face of global protectionist pressure (the new regionalism itself, for instance, is in some quarters perceived as such), the liberal elites pushed for a North American free trade order, safeguarding at least some of the most important markets and investment areas. NAFTA is hardly a paradigmatic case for the NRA, although its narrow efficiency is a response to the spur of increased competitiveness currently felt by many regions.

In East Asia, competition between the states has provided an obstacle to regionalization. The formation of APEC and other regional organizations at first seems to signal the coordination of common interests. However, these organizations have been formed as a result of the power vacuum that was the result of the decline of the Cold War. Arguably, they are also an American attempt, through APEC, (1) to maintain its hegemonic position in East and Southeast Asia from the economic and commercial point of view, and (2) to safeguard the extension of free trade areas. In contrast, the formation of EAEC is an attempt – although seemingly one that is failing – to counter American influence in East Asia. The fact that the US is able to exert such influence is in itself to be interpreted as evidence of the East Asian failure to protect its regional interests. State interests are still important in East Asian regionalization attempts, and differ in content and form in comparison with North America, and even more so in comparison with Europe. The so far largely unsuccessful regionalist agenda in East Asia impacts negatively on its capacity to influence world order issues.

The common denominator of the so-called core regions is that they are able to choose, given the limitations of the international structure, strategies for gaining benefits from the global economy. Neoliberal strategies are argued although mercantilist undercurrents are detectable. Whether the presence of these neoliberal free trade zones in the core is the first stage of a wider process of opening up is certainly questionable – in particular because, within the core, internal peripheral zones are created (southern Mexico in NAFTA, certain southern parts of Mediterranean Europe, and parts of China and North Korea in East Asia).

When one examines the degrees of autonomy exercised by intermediate and peripheral regions, one can further identify differences in relative power. The intermediate regions differ greatly from peripheral regions because their neo liberal approach is similar to that of the core regions. The core regions encourage intermediate regionalization in order to line up the next step in terms of global integration. President Clinton's visit to South America in October 1997 can be seen as an attempt to open up closer trade relations between NAFTA and Mercosur, thereby enlarging the current free trade zone. Of our eleven regions, South America and Southeast Asia should be labelled 'intermediate'. Although it could be argued that core regions have a certain interest in the regionalization of South America and Southeast Asia, it can also be said that the latter constitute a threat to the core regions, in terms both of winning new markets and of offering increasing competition in high-tech sectors.

The more peripheral regions in this study are Southern Africa, West Africa, South Asia, the Middle East, Central Asia and Caucasia. The paradigmatic case, the Balkans, is unfortunately missing. Regionalism has often been put forward as an instrument for enhancing development and/or peace/security. A case in point is the Caribbean: although peripheral enough in a general political-economic sense, through its regionalism it has been able to counter some of the negative aspects of that peripheral status. Common to most peripheral regions, however, are conflictual internal relations, often with a long history, that have prevented the fostering of a deeper process of regionalization.

Prospects for Future Regionalization

Europe is often seen as a paradigm and model for stimulating (even forcing) other regions to enhance regional cooperation and integration. So far, European regionalization has been a long and slow process. It has overcome slowdowns and it often seems that different logics create spillover effects that make it more difficult to reverse the process. Maybe reversal can occur, but as long as regionalization goes hand in hand with national interests (which are really the interests of the predominant national elites), the process is likely to continue. But new challenges to the process are likely to emerge.

In North America political integration is still lagging behind, and it is uncertain whether NAFTA's continued interest in expanding the free trade zone towards South America will be followed by moves towards political regionalization. Mercosur, meanwhile, must overcome disputes between member states on the future role of political institutionalization. Like NAFTA, Mercosur is a trade-based regional organization; and, like NAFTA, it still lacks the ambition to formalize political integration. Thus the political outcome is still unclear in both narrow and broad regional perspectives.

In East Asia, it is far from clear what type of regionalization process we can identify, and how strong it will prove to be. Bilateral relations are still the rule, and the future depends on the outcome of the intricate China–Japan relationship. Bilateral political and economic relations between these countries can either serve as the central force in East Asian regionalism, or construct a balance of power between two states in competition for regional political, military and economic hegemony. Despite state-level limitations, however, the activities of the private sector may bring about regional cooperation.

Future regionalization in both Southeast and South Asia is dependent on whether old state security conceptions can be overcome by new visions of cooperation. In Southeast Asia some kind of economic, social and political integration is taking place, but it is still a very slow process with a low degree of popular legitimacy, despite solid long-term regional institutionalization.

The old rivalry between Pakistan and India has long placed the South Asian region on the periphery of the world economy. While changes are slowly taking place in the region, we can expect this regionalism to be an attempt to find new solutions to the national question in countries like Pakistan and India; in terms of multiregionalization, South Asia is still in an embryonic stage. Change is being led by a growing internationalized elite, attached to the larger international community and living on opportunities provided by the world market, but it is still difficult to judge if the foundation is being laid for a new regionalism.

In Southern Africa, the scenario features South African dominance, but options for a more balanced intraregional exchange are being discussed. The key questions are (1) whether the member states will see the advantages of a regional formation *vis-à-vis* the world market; and (2) whether these advantages can be taken without South African domination and exploitation.

West African regionalization is pluralistic and turbulent and may not develop evenly. Much depends on the process of democratization in Nigeria. The rapid and unpredictable changes occurring in the region are well demonstrated by the dynamics of peace enforcement, peacekeeping and peace making in Liberia and Sierra Leone. Like Southern Africa, West Africa plays a marginal role in the global economy – but deepened regionalization may be one way to gain benefit from the international structure.

In the Middle East and Central Asia we can identify at most an embryonic regionalization process. The regional integration of the Maghreb and the Gulf is likely to continue, suggest ing the formation of subregional entities as well as the deepening of the existing interaction on a subregional basis, but the pace of sub-regionalization is very much dependent on the uncertain Israeli–Palestinian peace process.

Finally the future of the Caribbean microregion will depend on the outcome of its relationships with the US and NAFTA. However vigorous local regionalization efforts may be, it is hard to avoid the conclusion that the prospects for successful regionalization are all too dependent on the external factors.

Overall, our perception is that the pressure globalization puts on the various regions of the world is compelling, and that they will all attempt a process of deepened regional cooperation/regionalization. Not to do so is to risk increasing marginalization.

Types of Regionalization

We can now construct a typology of regionalization processes in the globalizing world. Depending on the relative importance of state, market and civil society impacts, the integrative level of the regional organizations, and the distribution of power in the regional and global contexts, various types of regionalization emerge. We can identify four ideal types of regionalization trends (see Figure 13.1), based on relative degrees of *nationalism* and *regionalism* (horizontal axis) and *core* and *periphery* (vertical axis). Along the horizontal axis we try, eclectically, to assess to what degree the Westphalian logic has given way to regionalist thinking; on the vertical axis we try to assess where in the world system various regions are. In the same figure we thus achieve a graphical illustration of the processes within the regions as well as between them.

Regions that, first, combine a relatively high degree of formal and informal institutionalization of various regionalization efforts with a developed regional identity, and, second, constitute strong core regions, characterize the *first type*. They have the greatest space for manoeuvre in decision making. Further characteristics are that the importance of the logic of regionalism is increasing in relation to the logic of nationalism, and that the importance of the state is gradually decreasing. Europe and, to a lesser degree, North America represent the first type.

State interests and the protection of national sovereignty dominate the *second type*, although with relatively high decision-making capacity in the international structure, and with strong national economies. Here a relatively low interest in regionalization prevails. The logic of nation-state building dominates regionalism. Bilateral cooperation rather than a more integrative approach is the preferred strategy. East Asia represents this type best.

The *third type* is distinguished by regions that have little space for manoeuvre in decision making, and are still caught in internal or regional conflicts; they often have relatively weak and/or dependent economies. Nationalism as well as sovereignty issues are still powerful. Regionalization may be seen as an option but is at best still an embryonic future. This type is best represented by the Middle East, Central Asia and Caucasia, the Balkans and South Asia.

The *fourth type* is characterized as a peripheral region, but with existing and functional regional arrangements. Ambitions for further regionalization exist as well, since relevant actors realize the instrumental value of regionalism for development as well as security management. Furthermore, despite strong state interests, an awareness of the need for regionalization is high: the logic of regionalism rules. Southern Africa, West Africa and Southeast Asia could be placed between the third and fourth types. South America and the Caribbean could be positioned under the fourth type.

Thus at least four main types of regionalization processes are in the making. The regions in types one and three confirm the underlying hypothesis of this volume: regionalization and a favourable position in the world system are mutually reinforcing, and increasingly so, in the forming of a new world order. Interestingly, however, we find East Asia in type two, and the Caribbean in type four. These are anomalies according to the logic of the hypothesis above: a 'failed' regionalization (East Asia) goes together with a favourable position in the world system; and a 'successful' one (the Caribbean) occupies a peripheral position in the world system. The Caribbean anomaly is, however, quite easily dismissed: first, it is only partly

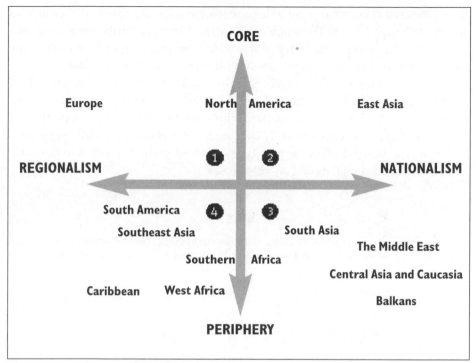

Figure 13.1 • Types of regionalization according to forms of vertical zones (core–periphery) and terms of logic (nationalism–regionalism)

successful; and, second, its tiny size turns it into a very atypical region. East Asia is more intriguing. If we stick to our hypothesis, two options are possible: first, it is falsely coded; and, second, it will move away from its current position.

First, to some extent East Asia *is* falsely coded here. That is, East Asia proper deserves its positioning in Figure 13.1; however, its relatively close institutional, political and economic relation to Southeast Asia provides for a proxy regionalization. Thus regionalization in 'Greater Asia' is more thorough than one might be led to believe. Second, in due course East Asia may be forced to assume a position more resembling type one; or else fail and end up in type three. The former, we believe, is more likely than the latter. With these adjustments, the positioning of the regions in Figure 13.1 tends to confirm the hypothesis above. As we have stressed on numerous occasions, however, at this stage theorizing is tentative, and intended to suggest new research questions.

Regionalization is a global phenomenon, but certainly neither a deterministic nor a homogeneous one. It must be seen as a social project with no given outcomes. Projects may be reformulated, they may succeed or they may fail. Much is also dependent on what popular legitimacy these social projects will be able to attract. Although beyond the scope of the current study, a further analytical and empirical elaboration of these types should be conducted in order to refine the types, as well as investigate more closely their viability and future prospects.

If regionalization should become increasingly sustainable as a global development strategy, as well as becoming a mechanism for enforcement of peace and development, it also has to go beyond elites, mobilizing broader support and activating a wider range of actors. Finally, regionalization asks a challenging new empirical question: which of the four types can best promote peace and development in the various regions and on a global scale?

NOTE

1 The outbreak of violence between India and Pakistan in the summer of 1999 did not improve the outlook for this. However, in a structural sense the clashes as such do not necessarily have a determining impact.

Bibliography

Documents

Agreement on the Gaza Strip and the Jericho Area, Cairo, 4 May 1994, Ministry of Foreign Affairs, Government of Israel.

Casablanca Declaration, Casablanca, Morocco, 1 November 1994, *Journal of Palestine Studies*, Vol. XXIV (94), No. 2, Winter, 1995, pp. 144–6.

Declaration of Principles Between Israel and the PLO, Washington, 13 September 1993, *Journal of Palestine Studies*, Vol. 23, No. 1, Autumn 1993, pp. 115–21.

Israeli–Palestinian Interim Agreement on the West Bank and the Gaza Strip, Washington, 28 September 1995, Israel Information Service Gopher, Israel Foreign Ministry, Jerusalem.

Protocol on Economic Relations, Paris, 29 April 1994, in Agreement on the Gaza Strip and the Jericho Area, Cairo, 4 May 1994, Ministry of Foreign Affairs, Government of Israel.

Treaty establishing the Organization of Eastern Caribbean States (1981).

Magazines & Newspapers

Al-Ahram Weekly
Banana Trade News Bulletin
Caribbean Contact
Caribbean Insight
Far Eastern Economic Review (FEER)
Gazeta Mercantil
Globe & Mail
India Today
Middle East Economic Digest
La Nacion
National Geographic

Newsweek
OMRI Daily Digest
Strait Times
The Economist
The Hindu
West Africa

Internet Addresses

Caribbean Week // www.cweek.com/mainpage.htm
CAST homepage // www.cep.unep.org/cast/cast.htm
CCAhomepage // www.uwimona.edu.jm/cesd/cca/cca.html
CEHI homepage // www.cehi.org/c/
CTO homepage // www.caribtourism.com/
EC.InfoNet // www.access.digex.net/~warlock/ecin/ecinfp.htm
India News Network // listserve.indnet.org/cgi/wa.cgi
Roundtable Ec.InfoNet // www.access.digex.net/~warlock/ecin/rnd/index.htm
WTO, 1997 // www.wto.org

Books & Articles

Aarts, Paul, 1997, *The Middle East: ARegion without Regionalism or the End of Exceptional - ism?*, Draft text for workshop on 'The Political Economy of Regionalization', University of Amsterdam, 18–19 December 1997.

Abdel-Fadil, Mahmoud, 1997, 'Macroeconomic Tendencies and Policy Options in the Arab Region', in Guazzone (ed.), pp. 119–34.

Acharya, Amitav, 1993, *A New Regional Order in South-East Asia: ASEAN in the Post-Cold War Era*, Adelphi Paper, August 1993.

Adibe, Clement E., 1997, 'The Liberian Conflict and the ECOWAS-UN Partnership', *Third World Quarterly*, Vol. 18, No. 3, pp. 471–88.

Adler, E. and M. Barnett, 1998, 'Security Communities in Theoretical Perspective', in Adler, Emmanuel and Michael Barnett (eds), *Security Communities*, Cambridge: Cambridge University Press.

Adotevi, S., 1997, 'Cultural Dimensions of Economic and Political Integration in Africa', in Lavergne, R. (ed.), *Regional Integration and Cooperation in West Africa: AMultidimen - sional Perspective*, Trenton, NJ: Africa World Press.

Ahwireng-Obeng, F. and P. McGowan, 1998, 'Partner or Hegemon? South Africa in Africa. Part One', *Journal of Contemporary African Studies*, Vol. 16, No. 1, pp. 1–34.

Akamatsu, K., 1961, 'A Theory of Unbalanced Growth in the World Economy', *Weltwirtschaftliches Archiv*, Vol. 86, No. 1, pp. 198–209 (originally published in 1937 in Japanese: 'Shinkoku Kogyokoku no Sangyo Hatten', *Ueda Tejiro Hakushi Kinen Ronbunshu*, No. 4 (July)).

Alagappa, Muthiah, 1993, 'Regionalism and the Quest for Security: ASEAN and the Cambodian Conflict', in *Journal of International Affairs*, Vol. 46, No. 2, 1993.

—— (ed.), 1995, *Political Legitimacy in Southeast Asia – The Quest for Moral Authority*, Stanford: Stanford University Press.

Aliboni, Roberto, 1997, 'Change and Continuity in Western Policies Towards the Middle East', in Guazzone (ed.), 1997, pp. 216–36.

BIBLIOGRAPHY

Alvstam, Claes G., 1993, 'Östasiatiskt frihandelssamarbete?' ('East Asian Free Trade Cooperation?'), in *Internationella Studier*, No. 3, Stockholm, pp. 21–36.

—— and S. C. Park, 1998, 'Intra-regional Division of Labour and Industrial Change in East Asia: The Case of the Emerging High-Technology Interaction Between Korea and Taiwan', in van Grunsven (ed.), *Regional Change in Industrializing Asia*, Aldershot: Ashgate, pp. 54–76.

Amer, Ramses, Johan Saravannamuttu and Peter Wallensteen, 1996, *The Cambodian Conflict 1979–1991 – From Intervention to Resolution*, Penang: REPUSM and Uppsala: Dept. of Peace and Conflict Research.

Amin, S., Chitala, D. and Mandaza, I., 1987, *SADCC: Prospects for Disengagement and Development in Southern Africa*, London and New Jersey: United Nations University/Zed Books.

Anderson K. and R. Blackhurst (eds), 1993, *Regional Integration and the Global Trading System*, Sussex:Harvester Wheatsheaf.

Antia, F., 1993, 'El Mercosur dos años después', in *Cuadernos del CLAHE*, No. 65–6.

Antolik, M., 1992, 'ASEAN's Singapore Rendezvous: Just Another Summit?', in *Contemporary Southeast Asia*, Vol. 14, No. 2, pp. 142–53.

Aruri, Nasseer, 1999, 'The Wye Memorandum: Netanyahu's Reciprocity', *Journal of Palestine Studies*, Vol. 28, No. 2, Winter, pp. 17–28.

Asante, S. K. B., 1985, 'CEAO-ECOWAS: Conflict and Cooperation in West Africa' in Onwuka, R. I. and A. Seseay (eds).

—— 1997, *Regionalism and Africa's Development: Expectations, Reality and Challenges*, London: Macmillan.

Awartani, Hisham and Ephraim Kleiman, 1997, 'Economic Participants in the Middle East Peace Process', *Middle East Journal*, Vol. 51, No. 2, Spring.

Axline, W. Andrew, 1984, 'Underdevelopment, Dependence, and Integration: The Politics of Regionalism in the Third World', in Gosh, Pradip K. (ed.), *Economic Integration and Third World Development*, Westport, Conn.: Greenwood Press.

—— (ed.), 1994, *The Political Economy of Regional Cooperation: Comparative Case Studies*, London: Pinter Publisher.

Ayoob, M., 1989, 'India in South Asia: The Quest for Regional Predominance', *World Policy Journal*, Winter 1989/90.

Ayubi, Nazih N. (ed.), 1995, *Distant Neighbours: The Political Economy of Relations between Europe and the Middle East/North Africa*, London and New York: Routledge.

Azad, M. A. K., 1989, *India Wins Freedom*, New Delhi: Orient Longman.

Bach, D., 1997, 'Institutional Crisis and the Search for New Models', in Lavergne, R. (ed.), *Regional Integration and Cooperation in West Africa. A Multidimensional Perspective*. Trenton, NJ: Africa World Press.

—— (ed.), 1999, *Regionalisation in Africa: Integration and Disintegration*, London: James Currey.

—— and H. Hveem, 1998, 'Regionalism, Regionalization and Globalization', paper presented at the ECPR/ISAConference in Vienna, 16–20 September 1998.

Balassa, Bela, 1962, *The Theory of Economic Integration*, London: Allen & Unwin.

Baral, Lok Raj, 1988, *The Politics of Balanced Interdependence: Nepal and SAARC*, New Delhi: Sterling Publishers Private Ltd.

Bartlett, Robert, 1993, *The Making of Europe: Conquest, Colonization and Cultural Change 950–1350*, London: Penguin Books.

Beasley, W. G., 1995, *The Rise of Modern Japan: Political, Economic and Social Change since 1850*, 2nd edn, New York: St Martin's Press.

Bergsten, C. F., 1994, 'APEC and World Trade: A Force for Worldwide Liberalization', *Foreign Affairs*, Vol. 73, No. 3.

—— and M. Noland (eds), 1993, *Pacific Dynamism and the International Economic System*. Washington, DC: Institute for International Economics.

Bernard, M. and J. Ravenhill, 1995, 'Beyond Product Cycles and Flying Geese: Regionalisation, Hierarchy and the Industrialisation of East Asia', in *World Politics*, Vol. 47, No. 1, pp. 171–209.

Beruff, J. R., Figueroa, J. P. and Greene, J. E. (eds), 1991, *Conflict, Peace and Development in the Caribbean*, Houndmills and London: Macmillan.

Bhargava, Moti Lal, 1986, *Indian National Congress – Its Affiliates in South and East Asia*, New Delhi: Reliance Publishing House.

Biles, R. (ed.), 1988, *Inter-American Relations*, Boulder and London: Lynne Rienner Publishers.

Blinkenberg, L., 1972, *India–Pakistan: The History of Unsolved Conflicts*, Copenhagen: Danish Institute of International Studies.

Broinowski, Alison. (ed.), 1982, *Understanding ASEAN*, London: Macmillan.

—— (ed.), 1990, *ASEAN into the 1990s*, London: Macmillan.

Brugiglio, L. *et al.* (eds), 1996, *Sustainable Tourism in Islands and Small States: Case Studies*, London: Pinter.

Bryan, A.T., Greene, J. E. and Shaw, T. M. (eds), 1990, *Peace, Development and Security in the Caribbean*, London: Macmillan.

Bull, H., and Adam Watson (eds), 1985, *The Expansion of International Society*, Oxford: Clarendon Press.

Burgess, Adam, 1997, *Divided Europe: The New Domination of the East*, London: Pluto Press.

Buszynski, Leszek, 1992, 'Southeast Asia in the Post-Cold War Era – Regionalism and Security', in *Asian Survey*, Vol. 32, No. 9, September, pp. 830–47.

Buzan, B., 1986, 'AFramework for Regional Security Analysis' in Buzan and Rizvi, 1986, pp. 3–33.

—— 1988, 'The Southeast Asian Security Complex', *Contemporary Southeast Asia*, Vol. 10, No. 1, pp. 1–16.

—— 1989, 'A Framework for Regional Security Analysis', in Ohlsson, L. (ed.), *Case Studies of Regional Conflicts and Conflict Resolution*, Göteberg: Padrigu Papers.

—— 1991 (1983), *People, States and Fear: An Agenda for International Security Studies in the Post-Cold War Era*, Sussex:Harvester Wheatsheaf.

—— and G. Rizvi (eds), 1986, *South Asian Insecurity and the Great Powers*, London: Macmillan.

—— and Gerald Segal, 1994, 'Rethinking East Asian Security', in *Survival*, Vol. 36, No. 2, Summer, pp. 3–21.

—— Waever, Ole and Jaap de Wilde, 1998, *Security: A New Framework for Analysis*, London: Lynne Rienner.

Bøås, M., 1997, 'Liberia – the Hellbound Heart? Regime Breakdown and the Deconstruction of Society', *Alternatives*, Vol. 22, No. 3.

—— 2000, 'Nigeria and West Africa: from a Regional Security Complex to a Regional Security Community?' in Einar Braathen, Morten Bøås and Gjermund Sæther (eds), *Ethnicity Kills? The Politics of Peace, War and Ethnicity in Sub-Saharan Africa*, London: Macmillan.

—— Marchand, M. and T. Shaw (eds), 1999, *New Regionalisms in the New Millennium*, Special Issue: *Third World Quarterly*, Vol. 20, No. 5, October.

BIBLIOGRAPHY

—— and Helge Hveem, 2001, 'Regionalisms Compared: the African and Southeast Asian experience' in Hettne, Björn, Inotai, Andras and Osvaldo Sunkel, (eds), *Comparing Regionalisms: Implications for Global Development*. London: Macmillan (forthcoming).

Cable, V. and D. Henderson (eds), 1994, *Trade Blocs? The Future of Regional Integration*, London: Royal Institute of International Affairs.

Calvert, P., 1994, *The International Politics of Latin America*, Manchester and New York: Manchester University Press.

Canadian Labour Congress, 1999, *The Morning NAFTA: Labour's Voice on Economic Integration*, May, 14: 1–10 (an electronic version can be downloaded via the website of the CLC: http://www.clc-ctc.ca/publications/index.html).

Cantori, L. J. and S. L. Spiegel, 1970, *The International Politics of Regions: A Comparative Approach*, Englewood Cliffs: Prentice-Hall.

Çarkoglu, Ali, Mine Eder and Kemal Kirisci, 1998, *The Political Economy of Regional Cooperation in the Middle East*, London and New York: Routledge.

Carlsson, J. and Widfeldt, Å. (eds), 1992, *The Caribbean: A Case of Micro Regionalism*, Göteborg: Padrigu.

Castells, M., 1997, *The Information Age: Economy, Society and Culture, Vol. 2: The Power of Identity*, Oxford: Blackwell Publishers.

Cawthra, G., 1997, 'Sub-Regional Security Co-operation: The Southern African Development Community in Comparative Perspective', *Southern African Perspectives*, No. 63. Bellville: Centre for Southern African Studies, University of Western Cape.

Chacholiades, Miltiades, 1990, *International Economics*, New York: McGraw-Hill.

Chan Heng Chee, (ed.), 1997, *The New Asia Pacific Order*, Singapore, ISEAS.

Chatterjee, Partha, 1986, *Nationalist Thought and the Colonial World: A Derivative Discourse*, London: Zed Books

Chen, E. K. Y. and P. Drysdale (eds), 1995, *Corporate Links and Foreign Direct Investment in Asia and the Pacific: Trade and Development*, Canberra: Harper Educational Publishers.

Chia S. Y and T. Y. Lee, 1993, 'Subregional Economic Zones: A New Motive Force in Asia-Pacific Development', in Bergsten and Noland (eds), 1993, pp. 225–69.

Chia Sow Yue and Pacini, Marcello, (eds), 1997, *ASEAN in the New Asia*, Singapore: ISEAS.

Chiang, P. K., 1997, 'Internationalization and Liberalization: Challenges for the ROC and Opportunities for the USA', in *Industry of Free China*, Vol. 87, No. 6, pp. 67–76.

Choucri, Nasli, 1997, 'Demography, Migration and Security in the Middle East', in Guazzone (ed.), pp. 95–118.

Chronologies, *Maghreb Machrek, Monde Arabe*, No. 130, 1990: No. 131, 1991; No. 162, 1998; Paris: La documentation Française.

Chronology, *Middle East Journal*, Vol. 51, No. 2, 1997.

Chuang, R., 1997, *China: A Macro History* (revised edn), London: M.E. Sharpe Publishers.

Ciccolella, P. *et al.*, 1993, *Modelos de Integración en América Latina*, Buenos Aires: Centro Editor de América Latina.

Clad, James, 1997, 'Regionalism in Southeast Asia: A Bridge Too Far?', in *Southeast Asian Affairs, 1997*, ISEAS, Singapore, pp. 3–14.

—— and Aurora Medina Siy, 1996, 'The Emergence of Ecological Issues in Southeast Asia', in Wurfel, David and Bruce Burton (eds), pp. 52–73.

Clapham, Christopher, 1996, *Africa and the International System: the Politics of State Survival*, Cambridge: Cambridge University Press.

Clements, Kevin., (ed), 1993, *Peace and Security in the Asia Pacific Region*, Tokyo: United

Nations University Press.

Coleman, William D. and Geoffrey R. D. Underhill (eds), 1998, *Regionalism and Global Economic Integration: Europe, Asia and the Americas*. London: Routledge.

Commission for a New Asia, 1994, *Towards a New Asia*, A Report of the Commission for a New Asia, Kuala Lumpur.

Conflict Prevention Newsletter, October 1999/3: 8

Cox, R. W., 1987, *Production, Power and World Order: Social Forces in the Making of History*, New York, NY: Columbia University Press.

—— 1994, 'Global Restructuring: Making Sense of the Changing International Political Economy', in Stubbs, R. and G. R. D. Underhill (eds), *Political Economy and the Changing Global Order*, London: Macmillan.

—— 1996, *Approaches to World Order*, Cambridge: Cambridge University Press.

—— (ed.), 1997, *The New Realism: Perspectives on Multilateralism and World Order*, Macmillan and United Nations University Press.

Crone, Donald, 1996, 'New Political Roles for ASEAN', in Wurfel, David and Bruce Burton, (eds), 1996, pp. 36–51.

Cronin, R. P., 1992, *Japan, the United States, and Prospects for the Asia-Pacific Century – Three Scenarios for the Future*, Singapore: ISEAS.

Dávila-Villers, D. R., 1992, 'Competition and Co-operation in the River Plate: The Democratic Transition and Mercosur', *Bulletin of Latin American Research*, Vol. 11, No. 3.

de Albuquerque, K., 1996, *Review of Last Resorts: 'The Cost of Tourism in the Caribbean' by Polly Pattullo, 1996*, London: Cassell.

de Cordier, Bruno, 1996, 'The Economic Co-operation Organization: Towards a New Silk Road on the Ruins of the Cold War?', in *Central Asian Survey*, Vol. 15, No. 1, 47–57.

de la Balze, F. A. M., 1995, 'Argentina & Brasil: Enfrentando el siglo XXI', *Revista Militar*, No. 733, July–September.

de Melo, J. and A. Panagariya (eds), 1993, *New Dimensions in Regional Integration*, Cambridge: Cambridge University Press for Centre for Economic Policy Research.

de Melo, J., Panagariya A. and D. Rodrick, 1993, 'The New Regionalism: A Country Perspective' in de Melo, J. and A. Panagariya (eds), *New Dimensions in Regional Integration*, Cambridge: Cambridge University Press for Centre for Economic Policy Research.

Delal Baer, M., 1991, 'North American Free Trade', *Foreign Affairs*, 70, 4: 132–49.

Delanty, G., 1995, *Inventing Europe – Idea, Identity, Reality*, London: Macmillan.

Delegation of the European Commission in Barbados and the Eastern Caribbean, Press release, 31 October 1995.

Deutsch, Karl W. *et al.*, 1957; *Political Community and the North Atlantic Area*, Princeton: Princeton University Press.

Devarajan, S. and J. de Melo, 1987, 'Evaluating Participation in African Monetary Unions: A Statistical Analysis of the CFA Zones', *World Development*, Vol. 15, No. 4.

Dicken, P., 1992, *Global Shift: The Internationalisation of Economic Activity* (2nd edn), London: Paul Chapman.

Diwan, Ishac and Michael Walton, 1994, 'Palestine Between Israel and Jordan: The Economics of an Uneasy Triangle', *Beirut Review*, Fall, 1994, pp. 21–44.

Dobson, W. and S. Y. Chia (eds), 1997, *Multinationals in East Asian Integration*, Ottawa: International Development Research Centre.

Drysdale, P. and R. Garnaut, 1993, 'The Pacific: An Application of a General Theory of Economic Integration', in Bergsten and Noland (eds),1993, pp. 183–223.

Dyde, B., 1992, *Caribbean Companion*, London: Macmillan.

ECLAC, 1994, *Open Regionalism in Latin America and the Caribbean: Economic Integration as a Contribution to Changing Production Patterns with Social Equity*, Santiago: ECLAC.

Economía and Mercado, 1997, 'La integración está a mitad de camino y el riesgo de estancamiento – y aun de retroceso – es grande', 14 April.

Economist Intelligence Unit (EIU), 1995, Quarterly Report, Armenia, Azerbaijan and Georgia.

—— 1998, Various Quarterly Reports for SADC countries.

Einar Braathen, Morten Bøås and Gjermund Sæther (eds) 2000, *Ethnicity Kills? The Politics of Peace, War and Ethnicity in Sub-Saharan Africa*, London: Macmillan (forthcoming).

El-Agraa, A. M. (ed.), 1997, *Economic Integration Worldwide*, London: Macmillan.

Ellis, S. 1998, 'Liberia – The Heart of a West African Struggle', *News from Nordiska Afrikainstitutet*, No. 1, pp. 2–4.

Elmusa, Sharif and Mahmud El -Jaafari, 1995, 'Power and Trade: The Israeli–Palestinian Economic Protocol', *Journal of Palestine Studies*, Vol. 24, No. 2, Winter, pp. 14–32.

El-Naggar, Said and Mohamed El-Erian, 1993, 'The Economic Implications of a Comprehensive Peace in the Middle East', in Stanley Fischer, D. Rodrik, and E. Tuma (eds), *The Economics of Middle East Peace*, London: MIT Press, pp. 205–25.

Embree, A. T. and C. Gluck (eds), 1997, *Asia in Western and World History*, London: M. E. Sharpe Publishers.

Emmerson, Donald K., 1984, 'Southeast Asia: What's in a Name?' in *Journal of Southeast Asian Studies*, Vol. 15, March.

—— 1995, 'Region and Recalcitrance: Rethinking Democracy through Southeast Asia', in *Pacific Review*, Vol. 8, No. 2, pp. 223–48.

Encarnation, D., 1992, *Rivals Beyond Trade: America versus Japan in Global Competition*, Ithaca: Cornell University Press.

Enzensberger, Hans Magnus, 1994, *Civil War*, London: Granta Books.

Eriksen, Thomas Hylland, 1993, *Ethnicity and Nationalism: Anthropological Perspectives*, London: Pluto Press.

Exploring the Parts, 1991, Extracts from the Report of the First Meeting of the Regional Constituent Assembly of the Windward Islands.

Fawcett, Louis and Andrew Hurrell, (eds), 1995, *Regionalism in World Politics: Regional Organization and International Order*, Oxford: Oxford University Press.

Ferguson, J., 1990, *Grenada – Revolution in Reverse*, London: Latin America Bureau.

Ferrer, A., 1995, 'Mercosur: trayectoria, situación actual y perspectivas', *Comercio Exterior*, November.

Fischer, Stanley, 1993, 'Prospects for Regional Integration in the Middle East' in de Melo and Panagariya (eds), pp. 423–48.

—— Rodrik, D. and Tuma, E. (eds), 1993, *The Economics of Middle East Peace*, London: MIT Press.

Foot, R., 1995, 'Regionalism in Pacific Asia', in Fawcett, L. and A. Hurrell (eds), *Regionalism in World Politics*, Oxford: Oxford University Press, pp. 228–49.

Fossato, Floriana, 1997, 'Customs Union' Meets Ahead of CIS Summit', 22 October 1997, RFE/RL, http://www.rferl.org.

French, J., 1994, 'NGOs – Meeting Our Needs', *Caribbean Contact*, May 1994, p. 28.

Frohman, A., 2000, 'The New Regionalism and Collective Diplomacy in Latin America', in Hettne, B., Inotai, A. and O. Sunkel (eds), *The New Regionalism and the Future of Security and Development*, London: Macmillan.

Frost, Frank, 1990, 'Introduction: ASEAN since 1967 – Origins, Evolution and Recent Developments', in Broinowski, (ed.), 1990, pp. 1–31.
—— 1993, *Vietnam's Foreign Relations – Dynamics of Change*, Singapore: ISEAS.
Gabriel, C. and L. Macdonald, 1994, 'NAFTA, Women and Organising in Canada and Mexico: Forging a "Feminist Internationality"', *Millennium*, Vol. 23, No. 3: 535–62.
Gamble, A. and A. Payne (eds), 1996, *Regionalism and World Order*, London: Macmillan.
Gereffi, G., 1996, 'The Elusive Last Lap in the Quest for Developed-Country Status', in Mittelman, J. (ed.), *Globalization: Critical Reflections*, Boulder, CO: Lynne Rienner.
Gershoni, Israel and James Jankowski (eds), 1997, *Rethinking Nationalism in the Arab Middle East*, New York: Columbia University Press.
Gharabaghi, K., 1994, 'New Regionalisms in Central Asia in the 1990s', in Swatuk, L. A. and Shaw, T. M. (eds), *The South at the End of the Twentieth Century*, St Martin's Press.
Giddens, A., 1994, *Beyond Left and Right – The Future of Radical Politics*, Cambridge: Polity Press.
Gill, M. D., 1994, 'People: The Key to Sustainable Development', in *Caribbean Contact*, May 1994, p. 12.
Gordon Connell-Smith, 1966, *The Inter-American System*, Oxford: Oxford University Press.
Grant, R. J., M. C. Papadakis and J. D. Richardson, 1993, 'Global Trade Flows: Old Structures, New Issues, Empirical Evidence', in Bergsten and Noland (eds), 1993, pp. 17–63.
Grinspun, R. and M. Cameron (eds), 1993, *The Political Economy of North American Free Trade*, New York: St Martin's Press.
Grugel, T. and Hout, W. 1999, *Regionalism Across the North-South Divide: State Strategies and Globalization*, London: Routledge.
Guazzone, Laura, 1997, 'A Map and Some Hypotheses for the Future of the Middle East', in Guazzone (ed.), 1997, pp. 237–59.
—— (ed.), 1997, *The Middle East in Global Change: The Politics and Economics of Interdependence versus Fragmentation*, London: Macmillan, New York: St Martin's Press.
Guillamont, P. Guillamont, S. and P. Plane (1988) 'Participating in African Monetary Unions: An Alternative Evaluation', *World Development*, Vol.16, No. 5.
Haacke, J., 1997, 'China's Participation in Multilateral Pacific Co-operation Forums', in *Aussenpolitik*, Vol. 48, No. 2, pp. 166–76.
Haarløv, Jens, 1988, *Regional Cooperation in Southern Africa. Central Elements of the SADCC Venture*. CDR Research Report No. 14, Copenhagen: Centre for Development Research.
—— 1997, *Regional Cooperation and Integration within Industry and Trade in Southern Africa*. Aldershot: Avebury.
Haas, Ernst B., 1958, *The Uniting of Europe: Political, Social and Economic Forces 1950–57*, Stanford: Stanford University Press.
—— 1964, *Beyond the Nation-State*, Stanford: Stanford University Press.
—— 1976, *The Obsolescence of Regional Integration Theory*. Berkeley: Institute of International Studies. University of California.
Halevi, N., 1993, 'Economic Implications of Peace: The Israeli Perspective', in Fischer, Rodrik and Tuma (eds), 1993.
Hall, Anthony, 1988, 'Community Participation and Development Policy: a Sociological Perspective' in Hall and Midgley (eds), 1988, pp.91–107.
—— and Midgley, James, (eds), 1988, *Development Policies: Sociological Perspectives*, Manchester: Manchester University Press.

BIBLIOGRAPHY

Hall, D. G. E., 1958 (1993), *A History of South-East Asia*, London: Macmillan.

Harik, Ilya and Denis Sullivan (eds), 1992, *Privatization and Liberalization in the Middle East*, Bloomington: Indiana University Press.

Harrison, P. and A. Todes, 1996, 'The Development Corridor Route: New Highways or Old By-ways.' *Indicator SA*, Vol. 13, No. 3, Winter.

Heng, Toh Mun and Low L., 1993, *Regional Cooperation and Growth Triangles in AESAN*, Singapore: Times Academic Press.

Hettne, Björn, 1989, *The Globalization of Development Theory and the Future of Development Strategies*, Gothenburg: Padrigu Papers

—— 1990, *Etniska konflikter och internationella relationer* (Eng.: Ethnic Conflict and International Relations), Gothenburg: Padrigu Papers.

—— 1993, 'Neo-Mercantilism: The Pursuit of Regionness', *Cooperation and Conflict*, 28 (3): 211–32.

—— 1995a, *Development Theory and the Three Worlds: Towards an International Political Economy of Development*, London: Longman (1990).

—— (ed.), 1995b, *International Political Economy: Understanding Global Disorder*, London: Zed Books.

—— 1997a, 'Development, Security and World Order: A Regionalist Approach', *European Journal of Development Research*, Vol. 9, No. 1, June, pp. 83–106.

—— 1997b, *Den Europeiska Paradoxen*, Stockholm: Nerenius och Santérus.

—— 1999, 'Globalization and the New Regionalism: The Second Great Transformation' in Hettne, Björn, Inotai, Andras and Osvaldo Sunkel (eds), *Globalism and the New Regionalism*, London: Macmillan.

—— and Inotai, A., 1994, *The New Regionalism – Implications for Global Development and International Security*, Helsinki: UNU/WIDER.

—— Inotai, Andras and Osvaldo Sunkel (eds) 1999a, *Globalism and the New Regionalism*, London: Macmillan.

—— Inotai, Andras and Osvaldo Sunkel (eds) 2000a, *National Perspectives on the New Regionalism in the North*, London: Macmillan.

—— Inotai, Andras and Osvaldo Sunkel (eds) 2000b, *National Perspectives on the New Regionalism in the South*, London: Macmillan.

—— Inotai, Andras and Osvaldo Sunkel (eds), 2000c, *The New Regionalism and the Future of Security and Development*, London: Macmillan.

—— Inotai, Andras and Osvaldo Sunkel (eds), 2000d, *Comparing Regionalisms: Implica - tions for Global Development*, London: Macmillan.

—— and Söderbaum, Fredrik, 1998, 'The New Regionalism Approach', *Politeia*, Vol. 17, No. 3.

Hitchcock, Michael and Sian Jay, 1998, 'Eco-tourism and Environmental Change in Indonesia, Malaysia and Thailand', in King (ed.), pp. 317–41.

Holder, J. S., 1997, 'Regional Cooperation: The Key to Caribbean Tourism Sustainability Problems'. Speech at an Earth Council, WTTC and WTO conference on Sustainable Tourism in London on 6 February 1997 (manuscript).

Hollis, Rosemary, 1995, 'Whatever Happened to the Damascus Declaration?: Evolving Security Structures in the Gulf', in M. Jane Davis (ed.), *Politics and International Relations in the Middle East, Continuity and Change*, Aldershot, UK: Edward Elgar, pp. 37–60.

Honychurch, L., 1997, 'The Challenge of Communicating Ideas on Environmental Concerns in Relation to Small Island States', paper for Communication and Sustainable Development in the Caribbean. A NorFa Workshop, Padrigu, Göteborg, 21–22

March 1997.

Hook, G. and Kearns I., 1999, *Subregionalism and World Order*, London: Macmillan.

Hopkins, A. G., 1973, *An Economic History of West Africa*. Longman: London.

Horsman, M. and Marshall, A., 1995, *After the Nation-State – Citizens, Tribalism and the New World Disorder*, London: HarperCollins.

Hurrell, Andrew, 1995, 'Regionalism in Theoretical Perspective' in Fawcett, Louise and Andrew Hurrell (eds), *Regionalism in World Politics: Regional Organization and Interna - tional Order*, Oxford: Oxford University Press.

—— 1998, 'An Emerging Security Community in South America?', in Adler, E. and M. Barnett (ed.), *Security Communities*, Cambridge: Cambridge University Press.

Hussey, A., 1991, 'Regional Development and Cooperation through ASEAN', in *Geo - graphical Review*, Vol, 81, Issue 1, 1991, pp. 87–98.

International Monetary Fund, *Direction of Trade Statistics*, various issues, Washington DC.

Jackson, B., 1994, *Poverty and the Planet – A Question of Survival*, Harmondsworth: Penguin.

Jackson, R. H. 1990, *Quasi-states: Sovereignty, International Relations and the Third World*, Cambridge: Cambridge University Press.

Jarbawi, Ali, 1995, 'The Triangle of Conflict', *Foreign Policy*, No. 1100, Fall 1995, pp. 92–108.

Jayanama, A., 1991, 'One Southeast Asia: The Issues at Stake', in NCSS, CIEM and IRC, Introduction.

Jervis, Robert, 1982, 'Security Regimes', *International Organization*, Vol. 36, No. 2, pp. 357–78.

Joffé, George, 1992, 'The Development of the UMAand Integration in the Western Arab World', in Nonneman, 1992a, pp. 203–18.

—— 1998, 'Relations between the Middle East and the West: The View from the South', in Roberson (ed.), 1998, pp. 45–73.

Jomo, K. S., (ed.), 1998, *Tigers in Trouble – Financial Governance, Liberalisation and Crises in East Asia*, London: Zed Books.

Jotun, Patrik, 1997, 'Azerbajdzjan inför 2000-talet: Etniska konflikter, olja och politisk instabilitet', in *Nordisk Östforum*, 11(3), 5–20.

Kaldor, Mary, 1999, *New and Old Wars: Organized Violence in a Global Era*, Cambridge: Polity Press.

Kangas, Roger, 1996, 'Central Asian States Sort Out Unions, Treaties, and Indepen- dence', OMRI Analytical Brief No. 53, 1996.

Katz, R., 1998, *Japan: The System That Soured: The Rise and Fall of the Japanese Economic Miracle*, London: M.E. Sharpe.

Katzenstein, P., 1996, 'Regionalism in Comparative Perspective', *Cooperation and Conflict*, Vol. 31, No. 2, pp. 123–59.

—— (ed.), 1996, *The Culture of National Security: Norms and Identity in World Politics*, New York: Columbia University Press.

Kearns, Ian, 1996, 'Eastern Europe in Transition into the New Europe', in Gamble, Andrew and Anthony Payne, *Regionalism and World Order*, London: Macmillan.

Keating, Michael and John Loughlin (eds), 1997, *The Political Economy of Regionalism*, London: Frank Cass.

Keller, E. J. and D. Rothchild (eds), 1996, *Africa in the New International Order: Rethinking State Sovereignty and Regional Security*. Lynne Rienner Publishers: Boulder.

Kennedy, P., 1994, *Preparing for the Twenty-first Century*, London: Fontana Press.

BIBLIOGRAPHY

Keohane, Robert O., 1984, *After Hegemony: Cooperation and Discord in the World Political Economy*. Princeton, NJ: Princeton University Press.

Kerr, Malcolm, 1967, *The Arab Cold War*, 2nd edn, London.

Kettunen, Erja, 1994, 'AFTA: From Protection Towards Freedom in Intra-ASEAN Trade', in Winter (ed.), 1994, pp. 202–14.

Kim Dae Jung, 1994, 'Is Culture Destiny? The Myth of Asia's Anti-Democratic Values', in *Foreign Affairs*, Vol. 73, No. 4, pp. 189–94.

King, Victor T., 1998, (ed.), *Environmental Challenges in South-East Asia*, London: Curzon Press.

Knight, F. W., 1990, *The Caribbean – The Genesis of a Fragmented Nationalism*, New York: Oxford University Press.

Kobrin, S. J., 1999, 'Back to the Future: Neomedievalism and the Postmodern Digital World Economy', in A. Prakash and J.A. Hart (eds), *Globalization and Governance*, London: Routledge.

Kofman, E. and G. Youngs (eds), 1996, *Globalisation: Theory and Practice*, London: Pinter.

Koonings, K. and D. Kruijt (eds), 1999, *Societies of Fear: The Legacy of Civil War, Violence and Terror in Latin America*, London: Zed Books.

Korany, Bahgat, 1997, 'The Old/New Middle East', in Guazzone (ed.), 1997, pp. 135–50.

Korhonen, P., 1994, 'The Theory of the Flying Geese Pattern of Development and Its Interpretations', in *Journal of Peace Research*, Vol. 31, No. 1, pp. 93–108.

Kothari, Rajni, 1970, *Politics of India*, New Delhi: Orient Longman.

—— 1988, *Rethinking Development: In Search of Humane Alternatives*, Delhi: Ajanta Publications.

Kreft, H., 1996, 'Japan's Links with East and Southeast Asia', in *Aussenpolitik*, Vol. 47, No. 1, pp. 71–81.

Krishna, 1996, 'Cartographic Anxiety: Mapping the Body Politics in India', in Shipero and Alker (eds), 1996, pp. 193–214.

Krugman, P., 1994, 'The Myth of Asia's Miracle', in *Foreign Affairs*, Vol. 73, No. 6, pp. 62–78.

Langhammer, R., 1991, 'ASEAN Economic Cooperation: A Stock-Taking from a Political Economy Point of View', in *ASEAN Economic Bulletin*, Vol. 8, No. 2 (November), pp. 137–50.

Laqueur, Walter, 1992, *Europe in Our Time: A History 1945–1992*, London: Penguin Books.

Latin American Mexico and NAFTA Report, 1999, January, RM-99-01

Lavergne, R., 1997, 'Introduction: Reflexions on an Agenda for Regional Integration and Cooperation in West Africa', in Lavergne (ed.), 1997.

Lavergne, R. (ed.), 1997, *Regional Integration and Cooperation in West Africa: A Multidimensional Perspective*, Trenton, NJ: Africa World Press.

LeClair, M. S. (1997) *Regional Integration and Global Free Trade: Assessing the Fundamental Conflicts*. Aldershot: Avebury.

Lee, Yew Kwan, 1994, 'Interview with Yew Kwan Lee', in *Foreign Affairs*, Vol. 73, No. 2, March/April.

Lesch, Ann Mosley, 1992, *Transition to Palestinian Self-government*, Report of a Study Group of the Middle East Program, Committee on International Security Studies, American Academy of Arts and Sciences, Cambridge, Massachusetts. Published in collaboration with Indiana University Press, Bloomington and Indianapolis.

Lewis, V. A., 1990, 'International, National and Regional Security Arrangements in the Caribbean' in Bryan *et al.* (eds), 1990, pp. 281–98.

Lu, D.J., 1996, *Japan: A Documentary History*, London: M. E. Sharpe.

Luciani, G. and Ghassan Salamé, 1988, *The Politics of Arab Integration*, London: Routledge.

Luciani, Giacomo (ed.), 1990, *The Arab State*, London: Routledge.

Mabhubani, K., 1992, 'Measures for Regional Security and Arms Control in the South-East Asian Area', in *Disarmament and Security Issues in the Asia-Pacific Region*, New York: United Nations.

—— 1995, 'The Pacific Way', in *Foreign Affairs*, Vol. 74, No. 1, January / February, pp. 100–11.

Maddison, A., 1991, *Dynamic Forces in Capitalist Development: A Long-Run Comparative View*, Oxford: Oxford University Press.

Madood, Tariq and Pnina Werbner (eds), 1997, *The Politics of Multiculturalism in the New Europe: Racism, Identity and Community*, London: Zed Books.

Magyar, K. P. and E. Conteh-Morgan (eds), 1998, *Peacekeeping in Africa: ECOMOG in Liberia*, London: Macmillan.

Mahathir Mohamad and Shintaro Ishihara, 1995, *The Voice of Asia: Two Leaders Discuss the Coming Century*, Tokyo: Kodansha International.

Malan, M. and J. Cilliers, 1997, *SADC Organ on Politics, Defence and Security: Future Development*. Paper No 19, Halfway House: Institute for Security Studies.

Mansfield, E. A. and H. V. Milner (eds), 1997, *The Political Economy of Regionalism*, New York: Columbia University Press.

Marcelle, G., 1997, 'Can Communication Technologies be Put in Service of Caribbean Women's Sustainable Development Objectives?', paper for Communication and Sustainable Development in the Caribbean, A NorFa Workshop, Padrigu, Göteborg, 21–22 March 1997.

Marchand, Marianne H., 1994, 'Gender and New Regionalism in Latin America: Inclusion/ Exclusion', *Third World Quarterly* 15, 1: 63–76.

—— 1996a, 'Reconceptualising "Gender and Development" in an Era of Globalization', *Millennium*, 25, 3: 577–603.

—— 1996b, 'Selling NAFTA: Gendered Metaphors and Silenced Gender Implications', in E. Kofman and G. Youngs (eds), *Globalisation: Theory and Practice*. London: Pinter Publishers, 395–429.

—— 1999, 'Informal Regionalism in the Context of NAFTA: From Cross-Border Alliances to Cross-Border Identities?', paper presented at the 4th International Congress of the Americas, Universidad de las Americas Puebla, Puebla, 29 September–2 October.

—— and A. S. Runyan (eds), 2000, *Gender and Global Restructuring: Sightings, Sites and Resistances*, London: Routledge, 1999.

—— M. Bøås and T. M. Shaw, 1999, 'The Political Economy of New Regionalisms', *Third World Quarterly*, Special Issue: 'New Regionalisms', 20, 5: 897–910.

Marr, Phebe, 1998, 'The United States, Europe and the Middle East: Cooperation, Co-optation or Confrontation', in Roberson (ed.), 1998, pp. 74–103.

Martin, Linda (ed.), 1987, *The ASEAN Success Story – Social, Economic and Political Dimen-sions*, Honolulu, East-West Center.

Mathias, P., 1969, *The First Industrial Nation: An Economic History of Britain*, London: Methuen.

Mayer, F. W., 1998, *Interpreting NAFTA: The Science and Art of Political Science*, New York, NY: Columbia University Press.

McAfee, K., 1991, *Storm Signals – Structural Adjustment and Development Alternatives in the Caribbean*, London: Zed Books.

McCloud, Donald., 1995, *System and Process in Southeast Asia: The Evolution of a Region*,

Boulder, Colorado, Westview Press.

McGee, T. G., 1997, 'Globalization, Urbanisation and the Emergence of Sub-Global Regions: A Case Study of the Asia-Pacific Region', in Watters and McGee, (eds), 1997, pp. 29–45.

Meagher, K., 1997, 'Informal Integration of Economic Subversion? Parallel Trade in West Africa', in R. Lavergne (ed.), *Regional Integration and Cooperation in West Africa: A Multidimensional Perspective*, Trenton, NJ: Africa World Press.

Médard, J.-F., 1982, 'The Underdeveloped State in Tropical Africa: Political Clientelism or Neopatrimonialism?', in Christopher Clapham (ed.), *Private Patronage and Public Power: Political Clientelism in the Modern State*, Frances Pinter: London.

Mercosur, 1991, 'Tratado para la Constitución de un Mercado Común'.

—— 1995a, 'Programa de Acción del Mercosur Hasta el año 2000'. CMC/DEC. No. 9/95.

—— 1995b, 'Suplemento. Red de Diarios Económicos', No. 2.

Mexico and NAFTA Report, 12 January 1999.

Michalski, Anna and Helen Wallace, 1992, *The European Community: The Challenge of Enlargement*, London: Royal Institute of International Affairs.

Midgley, James, *et al.*, 1986, *Community Participation, Social Development and the State*, London and New York: Methuen.

Mitrany, David, 1966, *A Working Peace System.* Chicago: Quardrangle Books (1946).

Mittelman, James H., 1993, 'Restructuring the Global Division of Labour: Old Theories and New Realities', paper presented at the International Symposium on Global Political Economy and a New Multilateralism in Oslo, 15–17 August 1993.

—— 1999, 'Rethinking the New Regionalism in the Context of Globalization', in Hettne, Björn, Inotai, Andras and Osvaldo Sunkel (eds), *Globalism and the New Regionalism*, London: Macmillan.

—— 2001, 'Subregional Responses to Globalization: A Comparative Analysis' in Hettne, Björn, Inotai, Andras and Osvaldo Sunkel (eds), *Comparing Regionalisms: Implications for Global Development.* London: Macmillan.

Miyasawa, 1993, 'The New Era of the Asia-Pacific and Japan-ASEAN Cooperation', Policy Speech printed in *ASEAN Economic Bulletin*, Vol. 9, No. 3, March 1993, pp. 375–80, ISEAS, Singapore.

Morales Moreno, I., 1999, 'NAFTA: The Institutionalisation of Economic Openness and the Configuration of Mexican Geo-Economic Spaces', in M. Bøås, M. H. Marchand and T. M. Shaw (eds), 1999, *Third World Quarterly*, special issue: 'New Regionalisms', 20, 5: 971–999.

Morris-Suzuki, T., 1997, *Re-Inventing Japan – Time, Space, Nation*, London: M. E. Sharpe Publishers.

Mortimer, R. A., 1996, 'ECOMOG, Liberia, and Regional Security in West Africa' in E. J. Keller and D. Rothchild (eds), *Africa in the New International Order: Rethinking State Sovereignty and Regional Security.* Boulder, CO: Lynne Rienner Publishers.

Mulder, Niels, 1992, *Inside Southeast Asia*, Bangkok, DK Book House.

Muni, S. D, 1993, *Pangs of Proximity: India and Sri Lanka's Ethnic Crisis*, Oslo: PRIO; New Delhi: Sage.

—— 2000, 'India in SAARC: A Reluctant Policy Maker', in Hettne, Inotai and Sunkel (eds), *National Perspectives on the New Regionalism in the South*, London: Macmillan.

—— and Baral, Lok Raj, 1996, *Refugees and Regional Security in South Asia* (Regional Centre for Strategic Studies, Colombo), New Delhi: Konark Publishers Pvt. Ltd.

Murphy, Craig N. and Roger Tooze (eds), 1991, *The New International Political Economy*,

Boulder: Lynne Rienner.

Naya, S. and P. Imada, 1992, 'Implementing AFTA, 1992–2007', in Sandhu *et al.* (eds), 1992, pp. 513–15.

NCSS (National Center for Social Sciences, Vietnam), CIEM (Central Institute for Economic Management) and IRC (Information and Resource Center, Singapore), 1991, 'Interaction for Progress – Vietnam's Course and ASEAN Experiences', Hanoi, 20–23 August 1991.

Nehru, Jawaharlal, 1961, *India's Foreign Policy: Selected Speeches*, September 1946–April 1961, New Delhi: The Publication Division.

Nonneman, Gerd (ed.), 1992a, *The Middle East and Europe: The Search for Stability and Inte - gration*, London: Federal Trust for Education and Research.

—— 1992b, 'Problems Facing Cooperation and Integration Attempts in the Middle East', in Nonneman, 1993a, pp. 35–45.

—— 1992c, 'The Gulf: Background Assessment', in Nonneman, Gerd (ed.), 1992a, pp. 55–62.

Nye, Joseph, 1965, *Pan-Africanism and the East African Integration*. Cambridge, Mass.: Cambridge University Press.

—— 1987, *Peace in Parts: Integration and Conflict in Regional Organization*, Boston: Little, Brown and Company. (1971).

Nyong'o, A. (ed.), 1990, *Regional Integration in Africa: Unfinished Agenda*. African Academy of Sciences: Nairobi.

Odén, B., 1996, *Regionalisation in Southern Africa*. World Development Studies 10. Helsinki: UN University / World Institute for Development Economics Research.

—— 1998, 'Södra Afrikas ekonomi. Regionalisering och polarisering' *Afrikafakta 6.* Uppsala: Nordiska Afrikainstitutet.

Ohlson, T. and S. Stedman, 1994. *The New Is Not Yet Born: Conflict and Conflict Resolution in Southern Africa*. Washington DC: The Brookings Institution.

Ohlsson, Leif, (ed.), 1989, *Case Studies of Regional Conflicts and Conflict Resolution*, Padrigu Papers, Göteborg.

—— (ed.), 1995, *Hydropolitics: Conflicts over Water as a Development Constraint*, London, Zed Books.

Ohmae, Kenichi, 1995. *TheEnd of the Nation State: The Rise of Regional Economies*, London: HarperCollins.

Okolo, J. E. and S. Wright (eds), 1990, *West African Regional Cooperation and Development*, Boulder, CO: Westview Press.

Olukoshi, A., 1995, 'The FCFA Devaluation Revisited', *SAPEM* 8 (7).

Oman, C., 1994, *Globalisation and Regionalisation: The Challenge for Developing Countries*, Development Centre of the Organisation for Economic Co-operation and Development, Paris.

Onwuka, R. I. and A. Seseay (eds), 1985, *The Future of Regionalism in Africa*, St Martin's Press: New York.

Orr, Michael, 1996, 'The Russian Army and the War in Tajikistan', Conflict Studies Research Centre: London.

Osborne, Milton, 1998 (1990), *Southeast Asia: An Introductory History*, New York: Allen and Unwin.

Owen, Roger, 1992, *State, Power and Politics in the Making of the Modern Middle East*, London and New York: Routledge.

—— 1994, 'Establishing a Viable Palestinian Economy', *Beirut Review*, Fall 1994, pp. 45–58.

Padoan, P., 1997, 'The Political Economy of Regional Integration in the Middle East', in Guazzone (ed.), 1997, pp. 174–200.

Palmer, Donald, 1991, *The New Regionalism in Asia and the Pacific*, Massachusetts: Lexington.

Parnwell, Michael J. G. and Raymond L. Bryant, (eds), 1996, *Environmental Change in Southeast Asia: People Politics and Sustainable Development,* London: Routledge.

Parrenas, Julius Caesar, 1997, 'The Future of ASEAN', in Chan Heng Chee (ed.), 1997, pp. 186–219.

Parry, J. H., Sherlock, P. M. and Maingot, A. P., 1987, *A Short History of the West Indies,* London: Macmillan.

Parsonage, James, 1992, 'Southeast Asia's "Growth Triangle": A Subregional Response to Global Transformation', in *International Journal of Urban and Regional Research*, Vol. 16, No. 2, 1992.

—— 1997, 'Trans-state Developments in South-East Asia – Subregional Growth Zones', in Rodan, Hewison and Robison, (eds), 1997, pp. 248–83.

Payne, A., 1997, 'The Association of Caribbean States', Paper delivered to the Regionalism Symposium, Kobe Institute, 13–14 March 1997.

—— 1998, 'The New Political Economy of Area Studies', *Millennium*, Vol. 27, No. 2, September, pp. 253–73.

—— and A. Gamble, 1996, 'Introduction: The Political Economy of Regionalism and World Order', in A. Gamble and A. Payne (eds), *Regionalism and World Order,* Basingstoke: Macmillan, pp. 1–21.

—— and Sutton, P. (eds), 1993, *Modern Caribbean Politics*, Baltimore and London: Johns Hopkins University Press.

Peres, Shimon, 1993, *The New Middle East,* New York: Henry Holt and Company.

Perez del Castillo, S., 1993, 'Mercosur: History and Aims', *International Labour Review*, Vol. 132, No. 5–6.

Perez, L. G., 1998, *The History of Japan*, London: Greenwood Press.

Peters, Joel, 1996, *Pathways to Peace: The Multilateral Arab-Israeli Peace Talks*, London: Royal Institute of International Affairs.

Petersson, Bo and Svanberg, Ingvar (eds), 1996, *Det Nya Centralasien*, Studentlitteratur, Lund.

Pettman, R. 1999, 'Globalism and Regionalism: The Costs of Dichotomy', in Hettne, Björn, Inotai, Andras and Osvaldo Sunkel, (eds), *Globalism and the New Regionalism*, London: Macmillan.

Phadnis, U., 1989, *Ethnicity and Nation-building in South Asia*, New Delhi: Sage Publications.

Polanyi, Karl, 1957, *The Great Transformation*, Boston: Beacon Press (1971).

Pomfret, Richard, 1997, 'The Association of South-East Asian Nations', in El-Agraa (ed.), 1997, pp. 297–319.

—— 1997, 'The Economic Cooperation Organization: Current Status and Future Prospects', *Europe-Asia Studies*, Vol. 49, No. 4, 657–67.

Public Citizen's Global Trade Watch, 1998, 'NAFTA at Five: School of Real-Life Results Report Card', http://www.citizen.org/pctrade/nafta/reports/5years.htm, December: 1–26.

Puri, Balraj, 1989, 'Rajiv–Farooq Accord: What Went Wrong?', *Economic and Political Weekly*, 29 July 1989, New Delhi.

Quagliotti de Bellis, B. 1976, *Uruguay en el cono sur*, Tierra Nueva, Buenos Aires.

Quang Co (tran.), 1994, 'Rights and Values', in *Far Eastern Economic Review*, 4 August

1994, p. 17.

Rajaretnam, M., 1991, 'Introductory Remarks', in NCSS, CIEM and IRC, 1991, pp. 8–9.

Ramsaran, R., 1989, *The Commonwealth Caribbean in the World Economy*, London and Basingstoke: Macmillan.

Richards, Alan and John Waterbury, 1996, *A Political Economy of the Middle East*, 2nd edn, Oxford: Westview Press.

Rieger, H. C., 1991, *ASEAN Economic Cooperation*, Singapore: ISEAS.

Rigg, Jonathan, 1997, *Southeast Asia – The Human Landscape of Modernization and Develop - ment*, London: Routledge.

Riley, S, 1999, 'West African Subregionalism: The Case of the Economic Community of West African States (ECOWAS)' in Hook G. and I. Kearns (eds), *Subregionalism and World Order*, London: Macmillan.

Rizvi, G., 1986, 'Pakistan: The Domestic Dimensions of Security', in Buzan, 1986, pp. 60–87.

Roberson, B. A. (ed.), 1998, *The Middle East and Europe: The Power Deficit*, London and New York: Routledge.

Roberts, J. M., 1993, *History of the World*, London: BCA.

—— 1996, *Caspian Pipelines*, Former Soviet South Project, London: Royal Institute of International Affairs.

Robison, Richard, 1996, 'The Politics of Asian Values', *Pacific Review*, Vol. 9, No. 3.

Robson, P., 1983, *Integration, Development and Equity: Economic Integration in West Africa*, George Allen & Unwin: London.

—— 1993. 'The New Regionalism and Developing Countries', *Journal of Common Market Studies*, Vol. 31, No. 3, pp. 329–48.

—— 1998. *The Economics of International Integration*, London: Routledge. 4th edn.

Rodan, Garry, Kevin Hewison and Richard Robinson, (eds), 1997, *The Political Economy of South-East Asia – An Introduction*, Oxford: Oxford University Press.

Rodríguez, J. M., 1995, *El Mercosur después de Buenos Aires*, Montevideo: FCU – CUI.

Rosenthal, G., 1994, 'El regionalismo abierto de la CEPAL', *Pensamiento Iberoamericano*, No. 26, pp. 47–65.

Ross, George, 1998, 'European Integration and Globalization', in Axtmann, Roland (ed.) *Globalization and Europe: Theoretical and Empirical Investigations*, London and Washington: Pinter.

Roy, S., 1994, 'Development or Dependency? The Gaza Strip Economy Under Limited Self-Rule', *Beirut Review*, Fall 1994, pp. 59–80.

—— 1995, *The Gaza Strip: The Political Economy of De-development*, Washington, DC: Institute of Palestine Studies.

—— 1999, 'Palestinian Economy and Society since Oslo', *Journal of Palestine Studies*, Vol. XXVIII, No. 3, pp. 64–82.

Rubin, Barnett R. and Jack Snyder (eds), 1998, *Post-Soviet Political Order: Conflict and State Building*, London and New York: Routledge.

Rubinstein, M. A. (ed.), 1998, *Taiwan: A New History*, London: M. E. Sharpe.

Ruggie, John G., 1998, *Constructing the World Polity*. London: Routledge.

Rwegasira, D. G., 1997, 'Economic Cooperation and Integration in Africa: Experiences, Challenges and Opportunities', paper presented at the Seminar on Towards a New Partnership for African Development, 20–21 January, African Development: Abidjan.

Sachar, Howard, M., 1996, *A History of Israel from the Rise of Zionism to Our Time*, second edition, revised and updated, New York: Alfred A. Knopf, Inc.

Said, E. W., 1978, *Orientalism*, New York: Pantheon Books.

BIBLIOGRAPHY

Salamé, Ghassan, 1988, 'Integration in the Arab World', in Gicaomo Luciani and Ghassan Salamé, 1988, *The Politics of Arab Integration*, London: Routledge, pp. 256–79.

—— 1998, 'Torn between the Atlantic and the Mediterranean: Europe and the Middle East in the Post-Cold War Era' in Roberson (ed.), pp. 20–44.

Sandhu *et al.* (eds), 1992, *The ASEAN Reader*, Singapore: ISEAS.

Santiago, J. S. S., 1995. 'Postscript to AFTA's False Start: The Loss of Sovereignty Issue', in *ASEAN Economic Bulletin*, Vol. 12, No. 1, July, pp. 18–28.

Sayigh, Yusif, 1982, *The Arab Economy: Past Performance and Future Prospects*, New York: Oxford University Press.

Scalapino, R. A. and S. Sato *et al.* (eds), 1988, *Asian Security Issues: Regional and Global*, Berkeley: Institute of East Asian Studies, University of California.

Schilling, W., 1997, 'Changing Power Structures in the Asia-Pacific Region', in *Aussen - politik*, Vol. 48, No. 2, pp. 158–65.

Schofield, Richard, 1993, 'Border Disputes in the Gulf Region', in Nonneman (ed.), 1992a, pp. 99–109.

Scholte, Jan Aart, 1993, *International Relations and Social Change*, Buckingham: Open University Press.

Schwartz, H.M., 1994, *States versus Markets: History, Geography and the Development of the International Political Economy*, Basingstoke: Macmillan.

Sharipzhan, Merhat, 1997, 'Customs Agreement Runs Into Rough Patches', 19 August 1997, RFE/RL, http://www.rferl.org.

Shaw, T. M. and J. E. Okolo (eds), 1994, *The Political Economy of Foreign Policy in ECOWAS*, London: Macmillan.

Shipero, Michale J. and Hayward R. Alker (eds), 1996, *Challenging Boundaries. Global Flows, Territorial Identities*, Minneapolis: University of Minnesota Press.

Shtayyeh, Mohammad, 1998, *Israel in the Region: Conflict, Hegemony or Cooperation?*, Jerusalem: Palestinian Economic Council for Development and Reconstruction.

Simandjuntak, Djisman S., 1997, 'EU-ASEAN Relationship: Trends and Issues', in Chia Sow Yue and Pacini (eds), 1997, pp. 92–117.

Smith, R., 1996, 'Prospects for Sustainable Development: Experiences of Small Island Development States', in Kofman and Youngs (eds), pp. 304–17.

Smith, Steve, 1997, 'New Approaches to International Theory', in Baylis, John and Steve Smith (eds), *The Globalization of World Politics: An Introduction to International Relations*, Oxford: Oxford University Press.

—— Booth, Ken and Marysia Zalewski (eds), 1996, *International Theory: Positivism and Beyond*, Cambridge: Cambridge University Press.

Söderbaum, F., 1996, *Handbook of Regional Organizations in Africa*, Nordiska Afrika-institutet: Uppsala.

—— 2000, 'The Role of the Regional Factor in West Africa', in Hettne, B, Inoati, A. and O. Sunkel (eds), *The New Regionalism and the Future of Security and Development*, London, Macmillan.

Srinivas, M. N., 1989, *The Cohesive Role of Sanskritization and Other Essays*, Delhi: Oxford University Press.

Stallings, Barbara (ed.), 1995, *Global Change, Regional Response: The New International Context of Development*, Cambridge: Cambridge University Press.

Suh, Moon-Gi, 1998, *Developmental Transformation in South Korea*, New York: Praeger Publishers.

Sum, Ngai-Ling and Markus Perkmann (eds), 2000, *Globalization, Regionalization and the Building of Cross-border Regions*, London: Macmillan, forthcoming.

Sunshine, C.A., 1988, *The Caribbean – Survival, Struggle and Sovereignty*, Washington, DC: EPICA.

Sutton, P., 1993, 'US Intervention, Regional Security, and Militarization in the Caribbean', in Payne, A. and Sutton, P. (eds), *Modern Caribbean Politics*, Baltimore and London: Johns Hopkins University Press.

—— 1995, 'The "New Europe" and the Caribbean', *European Review of Latin American and Caribbean Studies*, No. 59, December, pp. 37–57.

Tarling, Nicholas, 1998, *Nations and States in Southeast Asia*, Cambridge, Cambridge University Press.

Thambipillai, Pushpa, 1991, 'The ASEAN Growth Triangle: The Convergence of National and Sub-national Interests', in *Contemporary Southeast Asia*, Vol. 13, No. 3, pp. 297–314.

Thayer, Carlyle, A., 1995, *Beyond Indochina*, Oxford: Adelphi Paper.

Thomas, Clive Y., 1988, *The Poor and the Powerless – Economic Policy and Change in the Caribbean*, London: Latin America Bureau.

Tibi, Bassam, 1990 (1971), *Arab Nationalism: A Critical Enquiry*, 2nd edition, New York: St Martin's Press.

Tilly, C., 1975, *The Formation of National States in Western Europe*, Princeton: Princeton University Press.

—— 1985, 'War Making and State Making as Organized Crime', in Evans, Peter B., Rueschemeyer, Dietrich and Theda Skocpol (eds), *Bringing the State Back In*, Cambridge: Cambridge University Press.

Tulchin, J. S., 1986, 'Uruguay: the Quintessential Buffer State', in J. Chay and T. E. Ross (eds), *Buffer States in World Politics*, Boulder, CO: Westview Press.

Tuma, Elias H., 1994, 'The Peace Negotiations, Economic Cooperation, and Stability in the Middle East', *Beirut Review*, Fall, pp. 3–20.

UNIDO, 1992, *Towards New Forms and Mechanisms of ASEAN Industrial Cooperation*, UN, New York.

UNESCO Quarterly Report, 30 April 1999.

Uren, Roger T., 1992, 'Measures for Regional Security and Arms Control in the South-East Asian Area', *Disarmament and Security Issues in the Asia-Pacific Region*, New York: United Nations.

van Klaveren A., 2000, 'Chile: The Search for Open Regionalism' in Hettne, B., Inotai, A. and O. Sunkel (eds), *National Perspectives on the Regionalism in the South*, London: Macmillan.

Vandewalle, Dirk, 1994–95, 'The Middle East Peace Process and Regional Economic Integration', *Survival*, Vol. 36, No. 4, Winter 1994–95, pp. 21–34.

Vogt, M. A. (ed.), 1992, *The Liberian Crisis and Ecomog: A Bold Attempt at Regional Peace Keeping*. Lagos: Gabumo Publishers.

—— 1996, 'The Involvement of ECOWAS in Liberia's Peacekeeping', in Keller, E. J. and D. Rothchild (eds), *Africa in the New International Order: Rethinking State Sovereignty and Regional Security*, Boulder: Lynne Rienner Publishers.

Watson, Adam, 1992, *The Evolution of International Society*, London: Routledge.

—— 1997, *The Limits of Independence: Relations Between States in the Modern World*, London: Routledge.

Watters, R. F. and T. G. McGee (eds), 1997, *Asia-Pacific: New Geographies of the Pacific Rim*, London: Hurst.

Wendt, Alexander, 1992, 'Anarchy is What States Make of It: The Social Construction of Power Politics', *International Organization*, Vol. 46, No. 2, Spring.

BIBLIOGRAPHY

West Indian Commission, 1992, 'Time for Action – Overview of the Report of the West Indian Commission', St Michael, Barbados: The West Indian Commission.

Widfeldt, Å., 1992, 'Micro-states in the Caribbean: Approaches to Development', in Carlsson, J. and Widfeldt, Å. (eds), *The Caribbean: A Case of Micro Regionalism*, Göteborg: Padrigu.

—— 1996, 'Alternative Development Strategies and Tourism in Caribbean Microstates', in Brugiglio, L. *et al*. (eds), 1996, *Sustainable Tourism in Islands and Small States: Case Studies*, London: Pinter, pp. 147–61.

Williams, Eric, 1970, *From Columbus to Castro: The History of the Caribbean 1492–1969*, New York: Random House (1984).

Williams, S. M., 1996, 'Integration in South America: The Mercosur Experience', in *International Relations*, Vol. 12, No. 2.

WINFA, 1997, *The World of Bananas*. Background Document – WINFA seminar on fair trade 12 - 13 August 1997.

Winter, Nils H., (ed.), 1994, *How Free are the Southeast Asian Markets?*, Aabo: Centre for Southeast Asian Studies, pp. 202–14.

World Bank, 1989, *Sub-Saharan Africa: From Crisis to Sustainable Growth*, Washington, DC: World Bank.

—— 1993, *The East Asian Miracle - Economic Growth and Public Policy*, New York: Oxford University Press.

—— 1995, *Global Economic Prospects and Developing Countries 1995*, Washington, DC: World Bank.

World Guide, 1997/98, Oxford: New Internationalist Publications Ltd.

Wurfel, David and Bruce Burton, (eds), 1996, *Southeast Asia in the New World Order – The Political Economy of a Dynamic Region*, London, Macmillan.

Wyatt-Walter, A., 1995, 'Regionalism, Globalization, and World Economic Order' in Fawcett and Hurrell (eds), 1995.

Yagasaki, N. (ed.), 1997, *Japan: Geographical Perspective on an Island Nation*, (3rd edn), Tokyo: Teikoku-Shoin.

Yang, Y. and C. Zhong, 1998, 'China's Textile and Clothing Exports in a Changing World Economy', in *The Developing Economies* (Tokyo), Vol. 36, No. 1, pp. 3–23.

Yoshihara, Kunio, 1998, *Building a Prosperous Southeast Asia: Moving from Ersatz to Echt Capitalism*, London: Curzon.

Young, Alma H., 1991, 'Peace, Democracy and Security in the Caribbean' in Beruff *et al.* (eds), 1991, pp. 3–21.

Yuan, L. T., 1992, 'Growth Triangles in ASEAN', in *PITO (Private Investment and Trade Opportunities) – Economic Brief,* No. 10, Honolulu, East West Center.

Zarrouk, Jamal, 1998, 'Arab Free Trade Area: Potentialities and Effects', a paper presented to the Mediterranean Development Forum, Marrakesh, Morocco, 3–6 September 1998.

Zartman, I. W. (ed.), 1994, *Collapsed States: The Disintegration and Restoration of Legitimate Authority*. Lynne Rienner Publishers: Boulder.

Zartman, William, 1997, 'The International Politics of Democracy in North Africa' in John Entelis (ed.), *Islam, Democracy and the State in North Africa*, Bloomington: Indiana University Press.

Zawawi Ibrahim, 1998, 'Epilogue: A South-East Asian Perspective on Environment', in King (ed.), 1998, pp. 342–49.

Zeleza, T., 1993, *A Modern Economic History of Africa. Volume I: The Nineteenth Century*, Dakar: Codesria.

Zhang, Z. and J. M. Zhou, 1994, 'Asia-Pacific Economic Co-operation and China', *Journal of Asian Economics*, No. 4.

Öjendal, Joakim, 1995, 'River Management Cooperation or Water Conflict – Mainland Southeast Asia at a Crossroads', in Ohlsson, Leif (ed.), 1995, pp. 149–77.

—— 1997, *Regionalization in East Asia Pacific – An Elusive Process*, Helsinki, WIDER/UNU.

—— 1998, 'Regionalization in Southeast Asia – The Role of ASEAN in a New Context', in *Politeia*, Vol. 17, No. 3, 1998, pp. 112–29.

—— and Hans Antlöv, 1998, 'Asian Values and Its Political Consequences: is Cambodia the First Domino?', in *Pacific Review*, Vol. 11, No. 4, pp. 525–40.

—— and Elin Torell, 1997, *The Mighty Mekong Mystery*, Stockholm, Sida.

Østergaard, T., 1993, 'Classical Models of Regional Integration – What Relevance for Southern Africa?' in Odén, B. (ed.) *Southern Africa After Apartheid. Regional Integration and External Resources*. Seminar Proceedings No 28, Uppsala: The Scandinavian Institute of African Studies.

Index